CONTENTS

Foreword

This revision is dedicated to firefighters from the past, the present, and the future.

Everyone has a dream and mine started about twenty five years into my life. I didn't always want to be a firefighter, but the opportunity arose with a volunteer fire department and the need for firefighters in our new community. I answered the call along with several other new "probies" wanting to help our village. We trained several days and nights a week to learn this new and exciting vocation. We all worked full time jobs and never thought about being hired as professional firefighters. We didn't have a fire station in our village, but one was going to be built, one day. If there was a fire or emergency call we had to wait for the neighboring town to send an engine or ambulance. On several occasions we fought fires with garden hoses until the engine arrived.

Finally the big day came when we actually had a fire station, an engine, and a 1960 Pontiac hearse, this was our ambulance. Over the next several years we grew in numbers to about 30 volunteer firefighters. We hired a full time Chief and then started testing for full time firefighters. Testing at that time was pretty lenient, usually a one mile run, 10 pushups, 20 sit ups, and being able to walk, talk, and chew gum at the same time. We were able to hire many of the volunteer firefighters and make them full time firefighters because we were a new department just starting out. I happened to be one of the first twelve hired in our village. I had a good job with a utility company, but becoming a firefighter was the best move of my life. The hiring process has changed a lot since those early years. There are too many organizations watching every hiring move a village or fire department makes. Now there is a standard ability test called the Candidate Physical Ability Testing or CPAT along with other processes put in place to get the best potential candidate for the job.

I have many people that I could thank individually, but that would take too much time and there is not enough room in this book for that. I want to thank my family for putting up with me leaving in the middle of the night to answer emergency calls while I was a volunteer, and then being hired full time, gone every third day for my duty shift. This went on for over 30 years. Thanks to all the fire departments from the Chief down to the newest recruits for letting me stop by and exchange ideas and let me know what training would be beneficial to all firefighters. I worked as an instructor and coordinator of fire science for two community colleges and have them to thank for letting me develop so many new programs and get all of them certified with the Fire Marshal's Office in the State of Illinois. We had one of the largest fire science programs in the mid-west.

I was very fortunate to have a great staff of instructors and friends at the colleges as we had many programs to offer and without this group, none of this would have come to be. Many of these instructors were hired by me after 1 became the Fire Science Coordinator and worked for me until I retired. I retired from the Fire Service after 33 years in 1998, but kept working at the College of DuPage until August 2011.

I am thankful that I had such a great opportunity to work with so many young people assisting with their academic achievements, encouraging them to take test after test until they were hired, share my expertise with them, and watch them grow into firefighters and officers with some of the greatest fire departments in the country. They all touched my life as well and I thank them for that. They kept me young and the reason for keeping long hours, so we could have the best programs around.

Thank you and never give up because one day you will fulfill that dream just like I did.

Remember once you are a firefighter you will always be a firefighter.

Darryl J. Haefner (retired)
Bolingbrook Fire Department
College of DuPage

Introduction

WELCOME TO THE FIRE SERVICE

You have taken a most important first step—from thinking to acting, from planning to doing. You've decided to study, to prepare, and to be ready. The fire service is an action-oriented organization, with the actions determined by previous training, study, and other preparation. Your actions in preparing for your upcoming examination demonstrate that you have the qualities necessary to be a successful candidate.

This test preparation guide has your success as its goal. It requires, as will the fire service, study, training, and commitment. It contains not only information about the role of the fire service and the career of the firefighter but also sample examinations with clear explanations of all answers, analysis of the various types of questions and helpful review material, practice exercises to determine your weaknesses, tips for improvement; and hints on preparing for the examination. The physical ability portion of your examination is explained in detail with suggestions as well as tips and techniques.

The techniques and strategies you will learn as you answer these questions are those that have proved to be consistently successful.

Material contained in *Barron's Firefighter Candidates Exams* is not all inclusive. It is used primarily to assist the candidate with reading comprehension, mechanical reasoning, math, physical ability, and written examinations.

To make yourself more marketable as a firefighter candidate, you may consider enrolling at a community college in fire science or a related program. Obtaining an Associate of Applied Science (AAS) degree in fire science or working toward one may let you add preference points to your final scores on the candidate eligibility list.

Contact your local fire department for possible employment as a part-time, paid on call, or volunteer firefighter. You typically need little or no experience to join a fire department in one of these capacities. In addition, you will get on the job training for firefighting.

Fire departments may require certifications as an Emergency Medical Technician (EMT) and/or a paramedic. These programs are available almost everywhere and are open to anyone interested in pursuing these certifications. Colleges, hospitals, and the Department of Public Health offer these programs. Some colleges even give credits toward a degree. If no college in your area offers these programs, contact your state health department for course locations. Many fire departments require these certifications to apply. Having the certification may give you preference points on the candidate eligibility list. Many of these courses have national certifications, but each system may have its own requirements for licensure. If you already have these certifications and want to apply for a firefighter position, check with the fire department or the Department of Public Health for the licensure requirements.

Fire departments have established minimum requirements to select the best credentialed, the most experienced, and most competent candidate for the position. The more education you receive, the more credentials you attain, and the more experience you have, the better your chances are of passing the entrance exams and of becoming a firefighter.

Using this book and the practices described should give you the knowledge and skills to attain your dream.

Good luck and keep testing.

BECOMING A FIREFIGHTER

Overview

1

JOB AND ROLE OF THE FIREFIGHTER

Firefighting has traditionally been a team-based occupation, saving lives and conserving property with an emphasis on preventing fires, reducing the loss of life and property, confining the fire to its place of origin, and controlling and extinguishing fires.

Although these four activities are still prominent for the role of firefighter, the occupation of firefighting has expanded and become a multidimensional occupation. The Fire Service is now our nation's first responder to natural and man-made disasters and medical emergencies.

Firefighters are routinely called for earthquakes, plane crashes, hurricanes, tornadoes, collapses, terrorist attacks, gas leaks, downed wires, water leaks, people trapped, hazardous-material spills, train wrecks, bus wrecks, cave-ins, mountain rescues, wild-land firefighting, bridge collapses, underwater rescue, above-grade and below-grade incidents, and extrication.

Firefighters are taught, tested, and evaluated during the probation period, which can be 1 or more years. During the first year they are on probation, they are evaluated closely to determine if they satisfactorily meet the standards and requirements of the position of firefighter. After approximately 16 weeks of training, which includes firefighting and emergency medical procedures, the recruit firefighters are assigned to a firefighting unit, where they work with experienced firefighters under the direction and control of a fire officer. During duty hours, they must maintain a state of preparedness that will allow them to respond quickly to fires, emergency medical calls, or other emergencies.

At a fire, they connect hose lines to hydrants, carry hose lines to the fire, and operate hose lines to protect the occupants of the building and extinguish fires. Firefighters position and use portable and aerial ladder equipment to make rescues and to gain entrance to buildings to search and ventilate smoke-filled areas. Other firefighting activities include salvage (the protection of property from water and fire damage), and the operation of specialized emergency equipment such as rescue tools, fire pumps, fire boats, and communication equipment. Firefighters may be required to drive vehicles to the scene of a fire and to set up and operate the equipment during firefighting operations. Firefighters must know basic life support practices and patient assessment techniques, how to take vital signs and perform pulmonary and cardiopulmonary resuscitation, and how to treat shock and wounds, control bleeding, and be able to transport the sick and injured from their location to a hospital. When not responding to calls for help, firefighters are involved in many other activities such as fire prevention inspections and enforcement, fire education and fire investigation classes, and the promotion of good community relations.

Although firefighting is the most visible aspect of a firefighter's role, and continues to be a primary function of their duties, emergency medical response and care have become a large part of the firefighters' daily activities. Emergency medical care, fire prevention, fire education, and community relations occupy a major part of the time on the job. Firefighters are trained to inspect buildings for hazardous conditions that may result in a fire. Armed with their knowledge of fire hazards and local fire and building laws, they check exit routes, the storage and use of flammable and combustible materials, overcrowding of public places, and improper use of equipment or materials in all kinds of buildings. Firefighters are also trained to administer emergency first aid. There are several levels of training: Emergency Medical Technician (EMT) and Paramedic. Some states may have other designations. These are the major Emergency Medical Services Systems classifications. The training and skill requirements are standardized and are based on the National Emergency Medical Services Education Standards.

Another important task of a firefighter is public education—the chance to meet with people and discuss the hazards of fire, and the opportunity to interact with a class of schoolchildren, to teach them the dangers of fire, and to show them the correct reaction to such an emergency.

Firefighting is a diversified job with many minorities and female firefighters making it their career. The Fire Service recognizes diversity and includes sensitivity and sexual harassment awareness training as an integral part of their training programs. Being a member of the Fire Service requires a commitment to learn and to put into operation what has been learned. It requires that large amounts of time be spent in drilling and in practicing firefighting operations. It also requires that time be spent in learning fire safety practices and laws. Finally, it requires an active interest in learning about people.

Interacting with People

As a firefighter, you will have to interact with many people: firefighters, superior officers, school children, business owners, and the public. Keep in mind the following:

- Firefighters are expected to do their job with a high degree of professionalism.
- Firefighters are expected to show concern for the public, their peers, and their superiors.
- Firefighters are expected to treat all people with courtesy and respect

At a fire, a firefighter has to prioritize his or her responsibilities. The most important responsibility is protecting life. Next, the firefighter works to prevent property damage. Then the firefighter works to extinguish the fire.

One effective technique is to put yourself in other peoples' shoes.

- How would they expect to be treated?
- What do they know about the fire department's actions?
- What do they expect from the firefighter?
- What are their fears?
- From what point of view are they seeing your problems?

Interacting with Firefighters and Officers

The occupation of firefighting requires a very close working relationship with other firefighters and superior officers. It calls for teamwork and an ability to count on the group for support. It requires a commitment to give support to the group and to be part of the team. When a superior gives an order, you will be expected to carry it out. When another firefighter needs help, you will be expected to give it. When you have a problem, you will be expected to act responsibly and seek help through the chain of command.

Interacting with the Public

When interacting with the public, a firefighter must bear in mind that most people have limited knowledge of how and why fires start, how and why fires spread, and how fires are extinguished. Many in the public do not understand why it takes time to control and extinguish fires. They also do not understand why firefighters sometimes cause property damage.

The firefighter should keep in mind the emotions caused by the civilian's personal involvement and the psychological pressure brought on by the fire. People may be excited, defensive, or in shock. They may not listen to what firefighters are saying.

EMPLOYMENT OPPORTUNITIES AND CONDITIONS

The job of a firefighter is extremely dangerous and demands knowledge, physical strength, agility, stamina, and courage, as well as compassion, understanding, and adaptability. It requires working in hostile environments, being a member of a team, and interacting with fellow firefighters and the public.

Fire departments are equal opportunity employers and strive to have a diverse work force. Many minorities and women have successfully competed for these positions and are now firefighters, fire officers, and chief officers. Fire departments encourage women, minorities, veterans, and people with disabilities to apply and compete for these positions. Some fire departments and community colleges offer test preparation programs to help aspiring candidates successfully pass the examinations to become firefighters. You are encouraged to look into these programs while you use this book.

Some fire departments, working with local high schools and colleges, have established fire cadet programs. These programs prepare the cadet to be a firefighter and to meet the requirements for entry into the fire department. This training may be accepted as experience for those departments that have an experience requirement, or may qualify for some preference credit. Some fire departments require fire cadets to take the firefighters test as a promotional examination from fire cadet to firefighter. The candidates on the eligibility list may be given preference when hiring is done. Firefighting experience can be gained by active participation in other fire departments (volunteer or paid) and fire cadet programs. EMT experience can be obtained by working or volunteering in ambulance service organizations or hospitals.

Fire departments must comply with the Americans with Disabilities Act (ADA) *www.ada.gov* and with the Equal Employment Opportunity Commission (EEOC) *www.eeoc.gov*. This means they must make a conditional offer of employment before any testing relating to physical or medical conditions occurs. This conditional offer of employment can be withdrawn by the fire department if, after a reasonable accommodation, the candidate cannot perform the essential tasks firefighters must perform.

Firefighting is a 24-hour-a-day, 365-day-a-year occupation. To meet this demand, firefighters work in shifts. Each fire department establishes its own shift schedule and manning requirements. Although there are no absolute rules governing how shifts are worked, the two most prevalent shifts are 24-hour tours and the split shift. The first requires that firefighters work 24 hours of duty followed by either 48 or 72 hours off duty. The second has two different schedules. One requires that firefighters work 9-hour-day and 15-hour-night tours, or 10-hour-day and 14-hour-night tours. After each set of day tours, the firefighter is given approximately 48 hours off, and after each set of night tours 48 to 72 hours off. The other breaks the day into three 8-hour shifts, with systematic rotation through each of the 8-hour tours over a period ranging from 1 to 3 months. The work week can vary from 40 to 56 hours, depending on local conditions.

While on duty, firefighters live in a close relationship, doing routine cleaning of and maintenance on apparatus, equipment, and the fire station; performing at drills and training sessions; preparing and eating meals together; and sleeping in dormitories. When called to a fire or emergency, they are expected to respond immediately and to put into operation all that they have learned with an almost zealous sense of commitment. Firefighters are the guardians of safety for society and must be devoted to that end.

Salaries and Benefits

The salaries of most firefighters are determined by labor and management negotiations. Salaries vary from region to region and often reflect the local cost of living and the size of the community being serviced.

As a rule, the larger cities offer higher salaries and greater benefits. It must be kept in mind, however, that these urban centers often represent greater fire and emergency activity and greater exposure to danger. To determine the salary scale of a local fire department, read the notice of examination or consult the department's personnel office. If you wish information about salaries and benefits of other fire departments, you may refer to *The Municipal Year Book*, published by the International City Management Association. This should be available at a local library. You may also write to the International Association of Fire Fighters, 1750 New York Avenue NW, Washington, D.C. 20006, *www.iaff.org*, or to the International Association of Fire Chiefs, 4025 Fair Ridge Drive, Fairfax, Virginia 22033-2868, *www.iafc.org*.

Most fire departments provide medical and health care coverage, paid sick days, and pension and retirement benefits, which include disability or service retirement. Retirement benefits are paid according to years of full-time employment with a fire department/s. If you are employed by a fire department for 20 years, you could receive 50 percent of your salary, and after 30 years or more 75 percent of your salary. For particular states' pension information, contact that state. Many states now let firefighters take their pension with them when they leave one department and go to another. To inquire about benefits, for various fire departments, use the Internet and type in "Fire Department," click on "United States Fire Departments," and select the state of your choice. If you are looking for a particular fire department, you can type in the name of the fire department. Vacation periods and personal days are provided, and almost all fire departments furnish appropriate uniforms and safety equipment.

Career Outlook

Firefighter recruits will be trained for approximately 16 weeks at their local fire academy. Generally these recruits will serve a one-year probation during which time their abilities, demeanor, and character will be evaluated. Traditionally, promotion in the fire service has been from firefighter to lieutenant or captain, to battalion chief, to assistant chief or deputy chief, and, finally, to chief of department. These promotions may come from within the department. At the present time, however, some lateral entry into high-level positions is possible.

Some departments have multiple career tracks specializing in areas such as fire investigation, fire inspector, or emergency medical service. The National Fire Protection Association Standard, NFPA 1001, Firefighting Professional Qualifications, is accepted as the standard for entry-level training. There are other NFPA standards, such as Fire Officer Professional Qualifications, Fire Inspector Professional Qualifications, Fire Investigator Professional Qualifications, Fire Service Instructor Qualifications, Airport Fire Fighter Qualifications, Aircraft Rescue and firefighting Qualifications, and Fire Department Safety Officer. These national standards are not mandatory but are generally accepted as guides to what is expected of a person in the position. For information about the NFPA, go to *www.nfpa.org,* your local library, or your community college library.

In most fire departments, candidates for promotion are selected from a promotional service list, developed in a manner similar to that used for the Fire Fighter Examinations. This list, however, reflects eligibility requirements as well as the specific knowledge, skills, and abilities required of a particular rank. As might be expected, the higher the rank, the more difficult and challenging the examination process will be. The successful candidate can also expect a higher salary, more diversified assignments, and greater self-satisfaction.

GENERAL REQUIREMENTS FOR APPLICANTS

Although no absolute requirements can be given, the following are examples of typical requirements to be a firefighter. For application requirements, contact the local human resources office or fire department. Although basic requirements are due at the time of application, some others may be due at other times. Your application will indicate dates, times, deadlines, and when all portions of your application are due. Read the application packet completely. If you have questions, contact the application agency before you fill it out. Always keep copies of any correspondence concerning your application.

- **AGE:** If you are between the ages of 18 and 21, you may be able to apply to a fire department. For full-time employment most states require the candidate to be between the ages of 21 and 35 and meet certain requirements of the fire department. If you are over 35 and meet state statutes, you may still be eligible to apply, but you must prove you are currently employed with a fire department on a full-time, part-time, volunteer, or paid-on-call basis. Check the statutes for the particular state where you wish to apply and ask for their requirements.
- **CITIZENSHIP:** Most fire departments require the candidate to be a citizen to take the entrance examination. You may need proof of citizenship, birth certificate, naturalization papers, passport or other appropriate documentation.

- **RESIDENCE:** Many departments require the candidate to be a resident of the community at the time of the examination and to maintain such residence thereafter. Some fire departments give additional credit to candidates who reside in the community. If you are not a resident of the community, you may be required to become a resident as a condition of employment after you are hired. You may be required to submit proof that you live in the community.
- **DRIVER'S LICENSE:** This is normally a requirement to submit an application in most states. You may need to send in a copy of your driver's license with your application. The driver's license may be used as a means of identification for the orientation, testing, and oral interviews. Having received a ticket may disqualify you from testing because a valid driver's license is normally required.
- **EDUCATION:** All fire departments require a high school diploma or its equivalent. Some fire departments require college education equal to 30 college credits or more; some will accept two years of military service as an alternate for the 30 college credits; other may require a degree.
- **CERTIFICATION:** Certification as a firefighter, an Emergency Medical Technician (EMT), or a paramedic may or may not be a prerequisite to apply. Many fire departments may require these certifications sometime during the probationary period. The requirements for firefighter can be found in the National Fire Protection Association publication (NFPA) 1001, Standard for Firefighter Professional Qualifications. EMT and paramedic standards or requirements may be found from the state Department of Public Health.
- **EXPERIENCE:** Although this is not always required, some departments do require it and others give additional credit, or allow it to be substituted for other requirements such as education. Experience can be obtained by working full time, part time, or as paid-on-call with a fire department. Most cadet programs are for people between the ages of 16 and 21. If you are a high school student or a college student, meet with a counselor or adviser for information about cadet programs or fire science programs at a community college.
- **GROOMING:** This is generally not a consideration initially for applying. However, many fire departments do have strict hair length and facial hair standards, which may be a condition of employment. Many departments may have strict regulations about tattoos and body piercings.
- **VETERAN PREFERENCE:** Qualified armed forces veterans can request that veterans' preference points be added to their final score. A qualified veteran could receive 5 to 10 additional points on the final eligibility list score. Points are normally added after the preliminary list of qualified candidates is posted. The fire department will send letters to all of the candidates asking if they have preference points that can be added to the preliminary list. Once the preference points have been added, the final list is posted. When the final list is posted, it is too late to add preference points. You should inquire about preference points during the oral interview.
- **NONSMOKING REQUIREMENT:** A number of fire departments require that the candidate be a nonsmoker. Upon appointment, firefighters are required to sign a pledge that they will not smoke during their employment; otherwise, they face dismissal. This is to ensure that heart and lung disability claims are in fact job-related.
- **CHARACTER INVESTIGATION:** After an eligibility list has been established, an investigation may be conducted to secure additional evidence of the candidate's qualifications and fitness with particular reference to integrity that may include legal impediments,

felony convictions, domestic violence, sexual assault, child abuse, illegal drug activity, misdemeanor convictions, harassment, driving while intoxicated, soft drug use, your work and attendance records, and your quality or state of being acceptable for the work requirements, demands, and conditions.

GETTING INFORMATION AND APPLYING FOR EXAMS

Firefighting positions are often very competitive. It may be in your best interest to apply for and take several examinations in communities other than your own. To apply for the test, begin by finding out when the examination will be held and then obtain an appropriate application. Information about the examination and application process can usually be obtained from your city's department of personnel and from your local fire department. Sometimes applications and information can be obtained from your school guidance office or your local library. Information on fire department examinations can also be found on the Internet.

The most effective method of locating these agencies is to look them up in your local telephone directory. If you cannot find them, call the operator and ask for assistance. When you telephone the agency, have a pencil and paper ready to jot down instructions and directions. Explain clearly and politely that you need:

1. Information about the Firefighter Examination.
2. The necessary application.
3. The correct procedure for filling out the application.

If there is a test in the near future, the agency will give you the necessary information. However, if no examination is currently scheduled, you must ask the agency how the examination notice is made public: when it will be made available, and how it may be published (newspaper, Internet, fire department, or city website).

Most jurisdictions require applicants to file for the examination by filling out and submitting an application by a certain date. If you mail your application, it should be postmarked by midnight on the closing date indicated in the job announcement. After you file, you will be notified by mail as to where and when you should appear for the examination. In some communities, "walk-in exams" are given that do not require prior filing. Know what is required in your community. If there is a filing date cutoff, make sure you file before that date.

Accommodations for People with Disabilities or Certain Religious Beliefs

Many cities make special testing accommodations available if the applicant indicates this need exists and properly documents the reasons for the request. If information about the accommodation request process is not found on the application or instructions sheet, the candidate should contact the testing agency and determine the appropriate way to make this request.

Candidates must submit documentation from a professional qualified to assess and diagnose the specific disability. The documentation must include a comprehensive evaluation with objective evidence demonstrating the existence of a disability that substantially limits one or more major life activities. The name, title, and professional credentials of the qualified professional must be clearly stated in the documentation. Documentation must be submitted on official letterhead, typed, dated, and signed. At a minimum, all requests for accommodations must be received by the testing company no less than three (3) weeks before the scheduled test date.

The professional diagnosis must include the following:

(a) A current, valid, professionally recognized diagnosis of the candidate's disability by an appropriately qualified expert with copies of and reported scores from professionally recognized diagnostic tests, where applicable.
(b) Documentation that clearly identifies the nature and extent of the functional limitations that exist as a result of the diagnosed disability.
(c) Sufficient evidence to demonstrate that the functional limitation substantially limits the individual in performing one or more major life activities.
(d) Specific information about the significance of the impact the disability has on the candidate in the testing environment.
(e) Specific recommendations for accommodations.
(f) An explanation of why each accommodation is recommended and why it is necessary to alleviate the impact of the disability in taking the examination.

Keeping in Contact with the Agency

Several months may elapse from the date of the examination to the posting of the preliminary list. When the list is posted, you will be notified by mail. The time period until the first appointment may be even longer.

It is your responsibility to keep abreast of what is going on during these waiting periods and to notify the examining agency of any change of address or status that may affect its ability to get in touch with you.

Getting Appointed

Once the list is established, the agency will begin to process the candidates in numerical order beginning with the highest number. The agency will ask for background employment information while setting up appointments for medical and psychological examinations. It is important that you complete and return all forms as soon as possible. Follow instructions carefully, and ask questions when you don't know what to do.

LOOKING FOR FIREFIGHTER OPPORTUNITIES ON THE INTERNET

The Internet is a valuable source of information about upcoming firefighter examinations and fire service positions. There are many ISPs, and you should do a little research to determine which one fits your needs.

While you are sitting at your desk, you could be reading about the company picnic at a local firehouse on the West Coast or a review and critique of a recent fire on the East Coast, or you could be downloading information about upcoming entrance exams from cities around the world.

The information that follows assumes that you have at least a basic understanding of computers and are able to access the Internet. If you are not familiar with computers, you may be able to get help from a friend, relative, local library, or school. If these options are not available, then consider visiting a good bookstore and asking them to show you some of the most popular books for beginners on the Internet.

World Wide Web

The Web combines graphics and text to provide the user with a content-rich and visually exciting trip into just about any topic known to man. Firefighting is no exception. Hundreds of websites are fire-related and deal with nearly every aspect of the job from entrance examinations to new firefighting techniques. Remember that the Internet is dynamic, and websites are continually appearing and disappearing. This is not an endorsement of the following sites; they are provided solely as examples of places on the Web where you can get information about firefighter positions and to provide a starting point for your journey:

http://www.firecareers.com
http://www.firejobs.com
http://www.publicsafetyrecruitment.com
http://www.firehire.net
http://www.fpsi.com
http://www.fire-fighter-exam.com
http://www.fireprep.com
http://www.stats.bls.gov/oco/ocos158.html
http://www.sonnet.com/usr/wildfire/jobs.html
http://texasfire.com/
http://nps.gov/
http://www.fs.fed.us/fsjobs/fire-hire.html
http://www. firerecruit.com
http://www.firejobs.doi.gov
www.fdcareers.com
www.firecareerassist.com
www.911hotjobs.com
www.firefighter-jobs.com
www.fireserviceinfo.com/glossary.html
www.fire-fighter-exam.com
www.fireserviceinfo/emsglossary.html
www.iosolutions.org
www.esec.org

To start your search, use the following terms: Firefighter Jobs, Firefighter Examinations, Firefighter Employment, Firefighter Opportunities, Firefighter Career, or Fire Department.

A good site to visit is *www.onelist.com,* where you can sign up for news groups of your choice. Join several mailing lists; they are free and they provide you with an opportunity to read about issues that other firefighters and prospective candidates are concerned about.

Most Web sites are sincere in their dealings with the public, but be careful how much information you put out over the Web. If you are unsure of the security of the site, don't give out any personal information.

Educational Sites

Many colleges offer programs to assist students with written examination anxiety. If you are one of those students, contact your local college for their assistance well in advance of your scheduled examination. Many state and local organizations specialize in preparing students for taking examinations. Here is a partial list of educational resources.

www.barronseduc.com
www.ems.gov
http://wwww.jblearning.com/catalog
www.firefighter.jbpub.com
www.jblearning.com
www.kaplansolutions.com
www.firehouse.com
www.fireengineeringbooks.com
www.cdc.gov/niosh/fire
www.nfpa.org
www.nremt.org
www.ifsta.org
www.gcu,edu/enroll
www.nfa.org
www.bradybooks.com
www.actiontraining.com
www.pennwell.com
www.firefighterexamprep.com

PUBLIC SAFETY DEPARTMENTS/CONSOLIDATION

You may find some villages advertising to hire public safety officers. What does this mean for the candidate? The words "public safety" and "consolidation" are usually part of the description in the ad.

Consolidation is defined as the elimination of the fire and police chief in favor of a public safety director serving over both police and fire. Consolidation combines the jobs of career fire and police employees into public safety officers who perform both police and fire functions. The duties are not performed at the same time but could overlap.

In different cities, consolidation can take many different forms. One city may merge only a few specific fire and police functions, such as arson investigations. More changes occur when a city has operational consolidation. In that case, a city eliminates police and firefighter positions altogether and replaces them with public safety officers who are trained in both fire and police work. It is in your best interest to inquire about this before testing. If you want to perform only fire functions, being a public safety officer may not be the job for you.

WHAT MAY BE ON AN APPLICATION

Before filling out any application, read it over thoroughly and completely. As you read it over, note the dates for filing, what forms and documents are being requested, if you know where your documents are, if you need to contact someone to get the documents, if you will need to get diplomas or other papers mailed to you, and why they need all of this information. As you read the application packet, you will be supplied with information as to why all of this paperwork in needed. If in doubt, contact the testing agency or the fire department. After applying, you may be requested for additional forms and documents or be required to take other tests. Applications may be 30 to 40 pages in length or only 2 or 3 pages long.

If you download an application from a website, be sure you print all of the pages. If you complete it online, make sure to fill out all pages. If you don't complete a page, you may not be able to continue until you fill in everything. If the ad tells you to go to the village hall, human resources, or the fire department, ask for the complete application packet and whether you will need any other forms. You may be asked to visit other locations for additional forms or applications. Always ask if you should pick up any more forms.

SAMPLE APPLICATION

The following is part of what may be on an actual application from a fictional village fire department. Any resemblance to a real application is purely coincidental and was not done on purpose.

Village of Somewhere Fire Department

Thank you for your interest in the Village of Somewhere Fire Department. Please read this document carefully, paying particular attention to deadlines and required documents.

MINIMUM REQUIREMENTS

- $30.00 nonrefundable application fee
- U. S. citizenship
- High school diploma or equivalent
- Valid driver's license
- There may be a minimum and maximum age required
- Proof of Candidate Physical Ability Test (CPAT)
- May have a residency requirement
- Complete an application

APPLICATION REQUIREMENTS

1. Fill out an application. This may be online or a hard copy. Submit it by the deadline.
2. Return signed release forms and required documents by deadline.
3. Must submit proof of passing the CPAT.
4. Attend an orientation and written exam on date specified in application packet.

Disclaimer: All portions of the testing process are mandatory. Failure to meet and complete all requirements could result in elimination of further testing.

Checklist of Forms

A checklist for forms will be included in the application packet. As you fill out the forms or documents and sign them, put a check in the corresponding box so you know you've completed each one. When you send the forms and documents to the testing agency or fire department, use the checklist again. Make sure you have included everything! Always, always make copies of all documents, and file them for future reference.

Release or consent forms and documents could include:

- Drug screening
- Credit history
- Criminal history
- Driving record
- Employment
- High school diploma
- Medical records
- Personal information
- Written examination
- Copy of driver's license
- Birth certificate
- Passport
- Naturalization papers
- References
- Copy of a physical agility test

Fill in all of the information requested. If the question does not apply, put in "n/a." However, make sure you fill in every blank. You will be asked to sign a consent and release of information form. This may be requested by the testing agency and/or the fire department so information can be shared. Some of the forms may require a notary public to witness your signature. Be sure you send the forms to the proper agency or your notification for testing may be delayed.

BE SURE YOU READ THE APPLICATION COMPLETELY AND FILL IN EVERYTHING.

Exams, Knowledge, and Abilities

2

Firefighter examinations across the nation have been challenged in the courts and as a result have been improved substantially. Numerous court decisions have resulted in examinations designed to measure skills not related to the occupation of firefighting. Today's examiners strive to ensure that the examinations they prepare are nondiscriminatory, correspond to the firefighting position in question, and measure the physical and mental ability required of a candidate. Questions that require the candidate to have prior knowledge of firefighting, fire prevention laws, or rules and regulations of fire departments should not be asked. You will not be tested on actual job knowledge, unless some clearly stated prerequisite is required. You will be tested for the kinds of knowledge, skills, and aptitudes needed to become a successful candidate.

This guide has been designed to identify your weaknesses, sharpen your test-taking skills, and reduce the stress and anxiety of the examination process—in short, to help you become a member of the fire service.

PURPOSE OF THE EXAMS

The central purpose of Firefighter Examinations is to develop a list of qualified candidates who have expressed a desire to become firefighters. This list is used as a guide by agencies in hiring new firefighter recruits. Candidates who score the highest are usually offered positions first; therefore, it's in your best interest to place as high on the list as you can. Careful, diligent work with this guide will lead to the achievement of this goal.

WRITTEN EXAMINATION

Exam Formats

Analysis of testing practices for the position of firefighter throughout the nation indicate that the typical 3½-hour firefighter exam may contain the following types of questions:

1. **RECALLING, VISUALIZING, AND SPATIAL ORIENTATION QUESTIONS.**
   A. Recall Questions. The candidate is given written and/or pictorial material and is permitted a period of time, usually 20 minutes, to commit to memory as much about the contents as possible. The booklet containing the material is then taken away, and the candidate is asked a series of questions, usually 10 to 20, based on the contents.
   B. Visualization. The visualization portion of the exam is used to test the candidate's ability to mentally rotate and change the perspective of an object. The candidate is shown a test image in one perspective and is then asked to choose, from a group of objects depicting other viewpoints, the object that is most closely associated with the original image.
   C. Spatial Orientation. The candidate is given a map or floor plan and is asked to locate objects, or to navigate a path from one point to another following whatever rules might be indicated on the drawing.

2. **READING AND VERBAL/LISTENING COMPREHENSION QUESTIONS.** These test the candidate's ability to understand written or verbal material that reflects the kind of written or oral instruction that firefighters must be able to understand. This material may be entitled "Understanding Job Task Information."

3. **QUESTIONS ON UNDERSTANDING AND APPLYING BASIC MATHEMATICS AND SCIENCE.** The candidate is given a series of basic math and science questions and is tested on the ability to understand them and to apply the information to typical firefighter situations.

4. **QUESTIONS RELATING TO TOOLS AND EQUIPMENT.** These are designed to evaluate the candidate's knowledge and understanding of tools and their proper use.

5. **QUESTIONS ABOUT DEALING WITH PEOPLE.** This type of question tests the candidate's ability to interact with peers, supervisors, and the general public. Both emergency and nonemergency situations are considered.

6. **QUESTIONS RELATING TO MECHANICAL DEVICES.** The candidate is asked to demonstrate knowledge and understanding of general mechanical devices. Pictures are shown, and questions are asked about the mechanical devices shown.

7. **QUESTIONS THAT TEST JUDGMENT AND REASONING.** This type of question tests the candidate's ability to interpret and handle situations that a firefighter may encounter on the job.

Don't be concerned if the description of the test format given above seems difficult. Each of the areas is thoroughly explained in this book. For each area, helpful hints and strategies are offered. Finally, you will be given many sample questions in each area, as well as fully explained answers to each question.

ORAL INTERVIEW/ASSESSMENT CENTERS/VIDEO SCENARIOS

Oral Interview

The oral examination or oral interview is, as its name implies, a nonwritten examination; it has been used in the fire service for many years. There are two types of oral interviews: the unstructured and the structured interview. The unstructured interview makes use of open-ended questions, that is, questions that do not require specific answers. In the structured interview a set of predetermined questions and appropriate responses to them are developed by the testing agency before the interview. The questions are normally hypothetical and job related and require solutions that measure the ability to think clearly and creatively while demonstrating knowledge of the subject area.

The city of Los Angeles has prepared material on the oral interview as an aid to firefighter candidates. For your benefit it is reprinted here by permission. Although all oral examinations will not be exactly as outlined on the following pages, you will do well to follow the directions and recommendations given.

ABOUT THE INTERVIEW

There are three parts to every job interview. Each part is important.

1. **The Job:** the duties and responsibilities that need to be done.
2. **The Interview Board:** the men and women who make a judgment on how well your qualifications match the requirements of the job.
3. **Your Qualifications:** your education, experience, knowledge, abilities and/or personal qualities. You must show the interview board how well your qualifications fit the job.

work history	attitudes
knowledge	abilities
education	interests

The interview board compares you with the job.

The interview board that conducts your firefighter interview will probably be composed of three or four members. They could include Fire Personnel, Personnel Department staff, and men and women from business, government and community organizations. They are chosen because of their familiarity with the firefighter program and are experienced in hiring employees for their own organizations.

All interviews conducted may be recorded in some way.

Before the interview, the interviewers will be briefed by the Personnel Department and the Fire Department. They will describe the department's operation and the qualifications that this department believes are necessary to do the job.

Their job is to make the interview board aware of the duties of the job which the applicants who, are eventually hired, will be doing. They are not permitted to discuss individual candidates.

The Personnel Department will provide the interviewers with rating sheets that describe the qualifications to be evaluated in the interviews and the standards to be applied in these evaluations.

They make the interview board aware of areas they should not consider in the interview—areas that are not related to job performance—such as race, religious creed, color, national origin, sex, age, political affiliations, or sexual orientation.

The Personnel Department tries to avoid using interviewers who are likely to know some of the candidates. This is to avoid any bias, favorable or otherwise, toward any candidate. Interviewers are instructed to disqualify themselves from interviewing any candidates whom they believe they cannot rate objectively because of prior knowledge about the candidates.

If an interviewer does not disqualify himself or herself from examining a candidate whom the interview knows, it is the candidate's right, if he or she wishes, to have the interviewer remove himself or herself from the board or to have an interview with another board if one is available.

The names, titles, and affiliations of interviewers on interview boards may be posted in the waiting room area. Check the list to see who your interviewers are. If you recognize an interviewer and believe that you could not receive a fair interview from him or her, tell the receptionist so that the interviewer can be taken off the board for your interview.

Before the Interview

The job interview is one of the most important events in the average person's experience since the relatively short time spent in the interview may determine his or her future career. Yet it is amazing how many applicants come to job interviews without any preparation.

Often applicants study for hours for a written test, but don't spend a fraction of that time preparing for the interview. Since the interview will determine your final grade, as much time should be spent preparing for the interview.

Some applicants assume they will qualify for a job because they meet "The Requirements" described in the examination announcement. This is not true. By meeting these requirements, you are qualified only to compete in the examination, which measures other important qualifications for the job. If you are successful in passing all parts of the examination, including the interview, you may then be considered for a job.

Getting Ready

Be aware of the exact date, time, and place of your interview. This may sound almost too basic to mention, but it's an unfortunate candidate who assumes that the interview is to be held in a certain place, and then discovers two minutes before the interview that the appointment is somewhere else. Equally unfortunate is the candidate who arrives at the right place and time, only to find that the appointment is tomorrow or, worse, yesterday. Keep the interview notice with you. Don't rely on your memory.

Plan to arrive for your interview at least 30 minutes early. A few extra minutes will help to take care of unexpected emergencies. It is frequently difficult to find a parking place quickly. . . . Late arrival for an interview is seldom excusable.

You should present a neat, businesslike appearance for your job interview. It is usually appropriate for you to dress as you would for an office job.

Do not wear gaudy clothes, oversize jewelry, overpowering perfumes or deodorants, shorts, sweats, or T-shirts. Practice your body language. Your answers may be correct, but your body language may keep you from attaining your dream. Practice sitting and standing in front of a mirror. Ask your friends if they would hire you. What you wear can make a strong statement or keep you out of the running.

Men should wear a suit or sport coat and slacks, with a matching tie, and polished shoes. Keep your outfit simple to make the impression that you want this position. A beard or mustache may not be appropriate. If you have concerns, shave.

Ladies wearing a business suit with a skirt is not out of the question. You can also wear a skirt with a jacket. Do not wear short skirts or slacks. Wear moderately high heels or dress flats.

DURING THE INTERVIEW

Just as you are about to enter the interview room, the receptionist will tell you the name of the chairperson, who is selected randomly. The chairperson will introduce you to the other board members and ask you to sit down.

Your Conduct

Much of the impression you make upon the interview board will be determined by your conduct.

Your courtesy, alertness, and self-confidence are important, so you should try to speak in a self-assured tone of voice, smile occasionally, look the interviewers in the eye as you listen and talk. Sit erect, but be relaxed, and be prepared to answer the questions that are likely to be asked of you.

The board members realize that it is normal for people to feel nervous in this situation. Experienced interviewers will discount a certain amount of nervousness. But you should try to avoid doing obvious things such as drumming your fingers or twisting a handkerchief. If you are prepared to answer the questions that will be asked of you, you will probably find that you will not be as nervous as when you are unprepared. Do not smoke or chew gum.

The Questions

Remember that the interview board will be trying to measure your qualifications based on the information about job requirements given to them by the departmental briefer and the Personnel Department briefer.

The interview board will be exploring and evaluating those qualifications that have not been measured by prior parts of the examination. These qualifications include such things as personal qualities, oral communication, attitudes, goals, and interests. This does **not** mean, however, that material covered on the prior tests you have taken will not be explored further.

The interview board will be given your application to review before you enter the room. **Be ready for at least one question at the start, such as the following:**

1. Tell us something about yourself.
2. Why are you applying for a firefighter position?
3. Why do you want to work for the city?
4. What are your strengths?
5. What are your weaknesses?
6. Why should we hire you?

These are not easy questions to answer without some previous thought. Try them before deciding for yourself. You should be able to answer these kinds of questions without hesitation. Your preparation will help get you off to a good start.

You should also be prepared to answer questions about your abilities, training, and experience, such as these:

1. Tell us how your previous work experience or training has prepared you for this job.
2. What are your major assets in regard to this job?
3. In what areas related to the job you are applying for do you need to improve yourself the most? How have you compensated for this weakness or deficiency?

Each of these questions will be answered differently by each person. There is no specific right or wrong answer, but there is an opportunity for you to make an impression on the members of the oral board.

An effective technique that can help you prepare for this portion of the test is to write out responses to the questions, then have someone playing the role of an oral board member ask you each question and critique your answers. By reciting your answers aloud, you get comfortable with formulating your response, the words begin to flow, and your confidence builds. Don't memorize your answers word for word.

Use the comments of the person you are working with to improve your delivery. Remember, he is trying to help you; try very hard not to get offended by something negative he might tell you. If you don't agree with his comments, ask him to explain why he feels the way he does, and then try to openly and honestly reevaluate your delivery. The oral board won't give you a chance to redo your presentation, but your friend or relative will.

By practicing your delivery several times, you may find issues that you want to add or omit. If you are unable to get a friend or relative to help you, then use a tape or digital recorder to practice your response. The important part of this exercise is that you MUST practice. Being confident and smooth in your delivery shows the board that you have prepared for the questions and are ready to become a firefighter.

The specific areas to be measured in the interview for firefighter fall in five general areas. All candidates should expect to be asked questions relating to the subjects listed below:

A. **WORK HISTORY**—This area will include your present job, jobs you have held in the past, and your experience in the military, if any.
B. **EDUCATIONAL HISTORY**—This area of questioning may deal with your experiences in high school as well as any schooling or training you have undertaken since your graduation.
C. **INTERPERSONAL RELATIONS HISTORY**—This area will include questions about how you deal or have dealt with the people around you in everyday life.
D. **INTERVIEW BEHAVIOR AND COMMUNICATION SKILLS**—This area of measurement refers to the way in which you handle yourself in the interview. Raters will be looking at your behavior and manner as well as your communication skills.
E. **REASONING AND PROBLEM-SOLVING IN ANSWERING SITUATION QUESTIONS**—Questions in this area will be geared to find out about your ability to think out reasonable solutions to everyday problems that can arise in a firefighter's work. Answering them calls for good practical judgment, not special knowledge of firefighting.

You are **not** expected to have had previous training or experience in firefighting. The interviewers will be concerned mainly with how you have responded to whatever jobs and educational opportunities you have had. The Fire Department expects to train you in firefighting, so the interviewers will not be looking for any direct connection between the kinds of work you have done and firefighting.

By discussing the areas listed above, your interview board will be able to measure **your** suitability for firefighter work. Keep in mind that you will be rated competitively with all other candidates on these factors.

A review of a copy of your application and the examination announcement should help you to answer these and other questions related to the job you are applying for. You should review them immediately before the interview to make sure they are fresh in your mind.

Your Answers

Most interviews follow a simple question-and-answer formula. Your ability to answer quickly and accurately is very important, but don't rush yourself if it will hurt your ability to answer questions well. If your answers are confused and contradictory, you will not do well.

The greatest preventive against contradictory answers is the plain truth. A frank answer, even if it seems a little unfavorable to you, is better than an exaggeration that may confuse you in the next question. Being friendly, honest, and sincere is always the best policy.

Don't answer just "yes" or "no" to any question. Expand on your answer at least a little. Volunteering information is often helpful in showing how you qualify for the position, but be completely honest, because you will almost always be asked more about your answer. It is also important to know when to stop answering a question. You should try to avoid repeating yourself, giving information that is unrelated to the question, or talking too much on any one point.

Ask the interviewers to repeat or explain any questions you do not understand. This may be embarrassing, but it is better than answering the wrong question.

Be certain your employment application is complete and accurate in all respects before presentation to the interview board. False or incomplete statements made during the selection process may be cause for disqualification or dismissal at a later date.

If something went wrong on a previous job, explain the circumstances and accept the blame if it was your fault. If you have been fired and you are asked about it, admit it, and explain what you have learned from this experience. Negative experiences can be turned into an asset for you, if you can show how you have changed or improved yourself after recognizing your mistakes.

Make sure that your good points get across to the interviewers, but try to be factual and sincere, not conceited. If you are describing your best qualities, be concrete. Give examples of how these qualities have helped you and your previous employers. This is where your preparation will pay off.

Remember that you have known yourself all of your life. The interviewers, however, have only a short period of time to try to get to know you and to recognize your capabilities. Be sure to help them all you can by giving them the information they need to properly evaluate you.

The End of the Interview

Toward the end of the interview, you will be asked if you would like to add anything. If you believe that there is something in your background the interviewers should know that hasn't been mentioned, this is your chance. This is also a good time to briefly sum up what you believe makes you a good candidate for the job. You need to prepare for this opportunity. Write out in advance key items about yourself, and include why you are the candidate the board should select. You might begin your answer with "Thank you for giving me this opportunity. As I mentioned earlier, *repeat something about yourself that is positive and that will help the board members focus in on your strengths...,*" then list your key points. Include any items that were not previously mentioned that would enhance your chance of being selected. Keep your statement concise, and deliver it with confidence and sincerity.

Sometimes candidates protest their interviews after receiving their scores, with the claim that the interview board did not ask them about experience, training, or other background that the candidate believes is important. Interviewers don't have time to ask enough questions to bring out all the qualifications a candidate may possess. Interview boards may ask candidates if they have anything they would like to add. Protests as the one mentioned above are not valid if you do not take advantage of the opportunity to answer the last question fully.

Try, however, to make your final statements or your answer to the above question concise, because the interview board has a schedule to keep and there are other candidates waiting.

The chairperson will indicate the end of the interview by thanking you for coming in. Thank the interviewers for their time and consideration.

After the Interview

The results of your examination should be mailed to you within two weeks after your interview.

The Personnel Department makes every effort to assure that all candidates receive a fair interview and that the people who serve on interview boards are competent.

The score that a candidate receives in an interview depends to a large extent on the presentation of his or her qualifications to the interview board. Candidates who receive low scores frequently disagree with the judgment of the interview board. The board does not consider a difference of opinion between the candidate and the interviewers regarding the candidate's qualifications as a valid grounds for protest.

Interview Appeals

If you believe that any of the people on your interview board were prejudiced, or that there was fraud involved, or that the interview was not properly conducted, you should file a written protest within two working days after you complete your interview. The reasons for your protest and the facts supporting your charges must be submitted in writing.

All too frequently when we fail, we blame someone else for our failure. The wise thing is to try to determine why we failed so that the next time we can succeed.

CHECKLIST FOR PREPARING FOR THE INTERVIEW

- ☐ Read this section carefully.
- ☐ Make a list of your good points and think of concrete examples that demonstrate them.
- ☐ Practice answering the questions on the previous pages.
- ☐ Review a copy of your application and the examination announcement.
- ☐ Make sure you know the exact date, time, and place of your interview.
- ☐ Dress neatly.
- ☐ Bring the interview notice with you.
- ☐ Have enough money for parking.
- ☐ Leave in time to arrive at least 30 minutes before the appointed time.

Assessment Centers

The use of the assessment center is relatively new. It is seen as an effective alternative to the oral examination and can be expected to find greater use in the future. The assessment center is an interactive process allowing a group of firefighter candidates to participate in simulations of job-related functions and processes under controlled conditions. The candidates are rated on how well they respond to the activities and how they handle each assignment. As the candidates go through the simulations, they are systematically observed and rated by a panel of assessors.

The concept of the assessment center derives its strength from the fact that tasks can be identified and that these tasks have certain underlying qualities that can be measured. The assessment exercise is developed to measure specific behaviors in an atmosphere that approximates the real thing.

The assessment center (assessment exercise) is much more comprehensive than the traditional examination. It generally takes a full day or more to complete the tasks. The exercise consists of five to eight separate components, each designed to evaluate a different set of skills, abilities, and knowledge. Each assessment center is developed specifically for a particular community and its candidate exam.

The assessors will measure your ability to perform; they will do this both as individuals and as a group. Their composite score will be your score. In other words, your overall score will not be determined by just one assessor.

The assessment exercise is made up of several job-related tasks. Each component is scored individually. Here are examples of typical exercise components that have been used:

1. Triad—candidates are divided into groups of three and allowed two minutes to get acquainted with each other as much as possible. The candidates are then regrouped until all participants get to meet each other.
2. In Basket—candidates are allowed up to an hour to complete a series of administrative tasks that would be required of a firefighter. These include reports, memorandums, notifications, complaints, and decision-making tasks.
3. Manipulative Tasks—a job-sampling procedure in which participants connect hoses, fittings, and hydrants so they are operational.
4. P.T.A. Presentation—participants are allowed five minutes to devise a solution to fire prevention problems, using materials provided. They then present their solution to a panel, simulating a P.T.A. audience.
5. Written Reports—given the description of a fire, the participants must transfer the information to a standardized reporting format.
6. Dilemma Sources—an individual selected as the leader is allowed to study a Tinker Toy model and then must direct his/her "team" in the construction of a duplicate structure.
7. Firehouse—an individual must react to a hypothetical problem he/she may face as a firefighter when not actually fighting fires, such as establishing and coordinating a cooking schedule.

*See pages 25 and 26 for an explantion of these exercises.

There are eight dimensions that are typically used in assessment centers:

- Work standards
- Mechanical/manipulative aptitude and skill
- Oral communication skill
- Written communication skill
- Interpersonal relations
- Problem analysis
- Learning ability
- Leadership

ASSESSMENT CENTER DIMENSIONS

WORK STANDARDS

Does a good job in a safe manner and stays with a task until it is completed; displays initiative by taking action beyond what is required and by modifying behavior appropriately to maintain effectiveness in changing situations; meets organizational norms of punctuality and reliability and maintains effectiveness in pressure situations.

MECHANICAL/MANIPULATIVE APTITUDE AND SKILL

Correlates common tool usage with mechanical/manipulative task performance; discerns pipe and hose dimensions and matches related thread types; "makes things work" with or without the aid of tools or other equipment; understands interrelationship of moving parts in mechanical apparatus.

ORAL COMMUNICATION SKILL

Listens effectively and comprehends verbal instructions; makes a clear, effective, and persuasive presentation of ideas or facts in individual or group situation; speaks in clear, distinct, and understandable manner; uses appropriate tone, grammar, and vocabulary; exhibits effective nonverbal communication skills, such as eye contact, gestures, and listening practices.

WRITTEN COMMUNICATION SKILL

Reads with good comprehension and clearly expresses ideas in writing using correct spelling, vocabulary, grammatical form, and legible penmanship.

INTERPERSONAL RELATIONS

Identifies and reacts to the needs of others and analyzes the impact of yourself on others; displays empathy as appropriate and deals with others nondefensively; uses tact, diplomacy, and discretion as appropriate.

PROBLEM ANALYSIS

Perceives relations between various items, gathers relevant information, and takes appropriate action based on the information at hand.

LEARNING ABILITY

Comprehends and assimilates, retains, and recalls large amounts of factual information required for fire protection and emergency medical task performance.

LEADERSHIP

Guides individuals and/or a group toward successful task completion or goal attainment by soliciting participation from all members; gets effective ideas accepted without being domineering; motivates others to action; and mediates in troublesome situations.

HOW TO PREPARE FOR THE ASSESSMENT CENTER

Is Preparation Possible?

It has been said by a number of prominent examiners that a candidate cannot prepare for an assessment center. This statement is both correct and incorrect.

It is correct in the sense that there is no text to study, nor are there sample test questions that can be practiced or rehearsed. The assessment center is an interactive exercise derived from the work of the firefighters in a particular community. There is no way to predict what specific activities the examiners will choose for the exercise.

The statement is incorrect, on the other hand, because prior knowledge of what kinds of questions or tasks will be encountered and how they will be scored is significantly helpful.

Knowing What to Expect

Knowing what to expect reduces anxiety and stress while eliminating the chance of being caught totally unprepared. The following description of each of the typical components listed will give you an idea of what to expect.

- *Triad.* You will be required to interact with several strangers, not just once but several times. The purpose is to see how you fit into a group and how comfortable you are with strangers. This component relates to the dimension of *interpersonal relations.* You should make an effort to put others at ease, say "please" and "thank you," display concern and fairness, and be sensitive to the needs of others. You can improve your interpersonal relations skills by trying to be more outgoing, for example, by starting a conversation with another person while waiting in lines. The more relaxed and familiar you are with this exercise component, the better you will do.
- *In Basket.* This is a paper and pencil test of your administrative abilities. You will be required to fill out forms, write short memos, record a telephone message, and/or take a complaint from a citizen. This component relates to the *written communication skill* dimension. You must write legibly, clearly, and concisely. Use appropriate vocabulary, grammar, punctuation, spelling, and sentence structure. You can improve your penmanship by practice, and you can gain confidence in other skills by developing the habit of writing down some of your telephone conversations and by paying attention to directions when filling out forms such as credit card, bank loan, and driver's license applications.
- *Manipulative Skills.* Here you are required to do a job-related task, and your performance is assessed either as to how well you did the process or as to how well it turned out. This component relates to the *mechanical/manipulative aptitude* and *skill,* the *learning*

ability, and the *work standards* dimensions. Follow all directions to the best of your ability. Ensure that only safe practices are used, and do not become rattled or upset if things do not go the way you expected. Keep trying and stay calm. Since this exercise requires a familiarity with basic tools and mechanical devices, a review of Chapters 10 and 11 will be helpful.

- *P.T.A. Presentation.* In this exercise you will be given time to prepare or rehearse a short presentation to a group. Some public speaking ability is required. This component relates to the *leadership* and the *oral communication skill* dimensions. Your challenge is to organize quickly and then deliver a reasonably realistic presentation. To organize quickly, get the known facts and put them in order. Discuss them quickly with the other members of your group; take notes as the discussion proceeds. Prepare a short outline that addresses the questions *who, what, when, where, why,* and *how.* Your talk will be informal. You will not be expected to make a speech, but you should be able to express yourself audibly, clearly, and concisely, maintain eye contact, and utilize proper body and hand gestures, while stating the problem, offering some solutions, and answering questions. To prepare for this section, study the materials in this guide, discuss them in a group setting, and keep in mind that nervous tension is both natural and good for you. Above all, don't allow yourself to be intimidated at the idea of "making a speech."
- *Written Reports.* See *In Basket.*
- *Dilemma Sources.* This is also known as decision making. In this section you will be given a problem for you and the rest of the group to solve. It may be a Tinker Toy model, a game problem, or a written problem. This component relates to the *problem analysis* dimension. Be prepared to express your opinions, making specific recommendations, deriving a possible course of action, discarding irrelevant factors, and finally making a decision. You must decide what information is necessary to solve the problem. You can prepare for this section by reviewing Chapter 9. Keep in mind that the ability to size up a problem, develop possible alternatives, put a solution into operation, adapt to setbacks, and then revise your plan is the key element to this exercise.
- *Firehouse.* This component requires you to be a self-starter, to be an organizer, and to act as an informal group leader. It can measure many dimensions: *leadership, interpersonal relations, work standards,* and *problem analysis.* To be prepared, you must do what has been outlined in the sections you have just read, and you must practice and follow the instructions detailed in this guide.

Because of the vast number of individual problems and the great variations in what can be expected in the exercise components, it is impossible to define each component specifically.

We have attempted to show you how an assessment center may be set up and conducted. Remember that it will be testing for general knowledge and abilities. Knowing what to expect and doing some thinking beforehand about the topic areas are the best ways to prepare.

Video Scenario

The video test is designed to predict how candidates for the position of firefighter will respond when facing the real-life challenges encountered by a firefighter. It is generally a test designed to show how well the candidate can be expected to fit into the emergency service community and if he or she will be able to work with other firefighters. This format can be used to evaluate human relation skills relevant to the tasks of firefighters, your ability to work in a firehouse environment, your problem-solving abilities, your ability to anticipate and predict what will or could occur in complex fires or emergencies, and your ability to improvise and adapt to these situations.

The candidates may be required to answer questions verbally as if they were actually at the scene, or to select possible answers to a series of questions (yes or no; best or worst; appropriate or inappropriate; fill in the blank). There may also be multiple-choice questions that relate directly to the information a candidate observed while watching a scripted video production of firefighters in action.

Unlike paper and pencil tests where candidates have the opportunity to reflect on an answer and then change their minds at some point later in the examination, the video test requires candidates to answer the question within a short time frame without the luxury of taking back their response. The video will depict a scene from a typical situation that firefighters encounter and require candidates to observe what is occurring, analyze the events and actions, and then make a quick judgment about how to respond. Candidates are expected to pretend they are actually part of the video. It requires them to make a decision and then "do" something. Candidates are told not to say what they "would do" in this situation but instead to actually play the role and "do" something such as "I'll help the child," "hold the door open," or whatever is appropriate for the situation at that point in the video. Candidates can expect to be exposed to multiple short scenarios designed to measure their interpersonal abilities, competencies, and skills.

Preparing for this type of examination is similar to preparing for the assessment center examination. There is no text to study, and there are no sample test questions. Each scenario is different, and the questions that can be asked will vary. However, it is possible to improve your chance of doing well. You can improve your decision-making and observation skills by practicing in real-life situations. These mock rehearsals will increase your base of knowledge and build confidence. Discussing how to handle difficult and controversial situations with people who have experience in these areas can help you improve your understanding of the decision-making process and its ramifications, and show you different views that you may not have considered. You can improve your interpersonal skills by gaining an awareness of your own feelings and the feelings of others. The real key to learning is self-determination and a desire to succeed; the stronger the desire, the greater the self-determination, and the greater the chance for success.

Physical Ability, Medical Examination, and Related Testing

3

PHYSICAL ABILITY TEST

The physical ability test is a major part of the examination for the position of firefighter. The test is a job-related assessment of tasks that model the work of firefighters. The tasks do not exactly mimic the work but help to show if you have the range of physical skills and abilities to be trained as a firefighter. There are three distinct areas to be aware of to prepare for the physical examination process.

- Knowing the activities you will be asked to perform.
- Knowing how to perform the activities and having some experience performing each of the activities.
- Doing personal physical training—the process of getting your body and mind ready to do your best. Your size, large or small, should not be considered an advantage or disadvantage. Firefighters come in all sizes; it is how well you prepare that ultimately determines how well you do.

Firefighting is extremely demanding on your physical and mental powers. It requires you to coordinate your mental skills of problem identification, recognition, and solving with your strength, stamina, and agility to accomplish dangerous work. The firefighting environment is normally hazardous and in a constant state of change and challenge. Firefighting calls for the wearing of special protective clothing, self-contained breathing equipment, and the use of tools that are often heavy. Because of the extremes encountered in the firefighting environment—hot and cold, wet and dry, night and day, clean and contaminated air—the protective clothing and equipment must be durable and effective. The need for these qualities has led to the development of equipment that is often heavy and cumbersome.

Given the demands of the occupation—saving life and property, the challenges of the environment, and the weight and constraint of the protective equipment—the need to ensure that firefighter recruits are physically capable of learning and performing the tasks required is obvious.

The physical ability examination is designed to evaluate the candidate's ability to perform firefighting activities. In the past the courts have held that the physical ability examination must be related to the tasks that are actually performed by firefighters. Studies reveal that the firefighter must have a high level of aerobic energy and strength, and a significant ability to resist fatigue.

The tasks that firefighters perform require a person who can run, jump, and bend while lifting, pulling, or carrying heavy weights. The physical test will be designed to challenge your aerobic ability, overall body strength, and endurance. Some communities have used the events in the "Combat Challenge" as their physical testing process; however, this does not appear to be widespread. There is a national standard for the physical examination. This model examination, Candidates Physical Abilities Test (CPAT), is made available by the International Association of Firefighters and the International Association of Fire Chiefs (IAFC), United States Department of Justice (DOJ), in cooperation with the members of The Fire Service Joint Labor Management Wellness/Fitness Initiative. Many fire departments and states have adopted the CPAT as their standard Entrance Physical Ability Test. However, there are still communities that choose to develop a physical examination that is appropriate for their specific community and their fire service delivery system. The activity explanations and recommendations that follow in this chapter are consistent with the standard and other events that have been used by other cities. The description of the event, recommended questions you should have answered before you begin the event, and the tips/techniques associated with each event are also included in this chapter. This chapter will help you to understand what is required, how to perform the various tasks, and how to improve your ability to score high on each of the events.

What to Expect

There is a great deal of similarity in firefighting from community to community. The physical portion of the examination is designed to measure your ability to perform typical firefighting tasks wearing typical firefighter clothing or equipment of similar weight (50–75 pounds). Proper exercise and a familiarity with the typical events will help boost your score significantly. Because of the importance and difficulty of the Physical Abilities Test you are urged to get as much information about the activities and requirements for your examination as you can. You must also find out if the testing agency will (1) be providing a training program for this test, and (2) permit you to use or practice with the actual equipment that will be used on the test. If you are permitted to do this, you are very strongly urged to make a concerted effort to get to the training site and experience the test events. Do this very early in your test preparation process; this is one of those times in life when experience pays off. Many cities and states that are using the CPAT provide candidates an opportunity to view a film on how the exam is structured and how to effectively perform the events. If your community or state will use the CPAT, you should make arrangements to view the film and be prepared to take notes about proper techniques and the actions that could lead to disqualification.

Before you begin each event, it is extremely important to find out from the testing agency, Fire Department, or Personnel Department what restrictions may be imposed for each event. Some questions you should try to get answered are:

- How will the test be graded?
  - Is it a PASS/FAIL test?
  - Is there a set time limit for completion? The test can be timed in either a total time to complete all events or a specific amount of time for each event. For example, the CPAT is a total time for all events, 10 minutes 20 seconds, whereas many fire departments have a specific time interval for each of the eight events.
  - If it is a speed test, what is the time to get the highest score? What is the longest time to get a passing score?
- What kinds of personal protective equipment are required or excluded from being used during the testing process?
- What constitutes the completion of each test event? You must know and understand what constitutes the beginning and the end of each event.
- Is there a rest period between events? If so, how long is it?

Each event can have a different criteria that signifies the completion of the exercise. You may be required to cross a designated finish line, place a hose, a tool, or a ladder in a specified area, ring a bell, hit a completion button, or tell the monitor you have completed the exercise. You do not want to lose time or points by having to backtrack to execute the "event completion component."

When practicing these events, make sure the event completion component is part of your practice routine. If it becomes a routine part of your style, there is less chance that you will forget or skip it on the day of the test.

CANDIDATE PHYSICAL ABILITIES TEST (CPAT) ORIENTATION GUIDE

Fire Service Joint Labor Management Wellness/Fitness Initiative

CANDIDATE PHYSICAL ABILITY TEST ORIENTATION GUIDE

This candidate physical ability test (CPAT) consists of eight separate events. The CPAT is a sequence of events requiring you to progress along a predetermined path from event to event in a continuous manner. This test was developed to allow fire departments to obtain pools of trainable candidates who are physically able to perform essential job tasks at fire scenes.

This is a pass/fail test based on a validated maximum total time of 10 minutes and 20 seconds.

In these events, you wear a 50-pound (22.68 kg) vest to simulate the weight of a self-contained breathing apparatus (SCBA) and firefighter protective clothing. An additional 25 pounds (11.34 kg) using two 12.5-pound (5.67 kg) weights that simulate a high-rise pack (hose bundle), is added to your shoulders for the stair-climbing event.

Throughout all events, you must wear long pants, a hard hat with chin strap, work gloves, and footwear with no open heel or toe. Watches and loose or restrictive jewelry are not permitted.

All props were designed to obtain the necessary information about your physical ability. The tools and equipment were chosen to provide the highest level of consistency, safety, and validity in measuring your physical abilities. A schematic drawing of the CPAT is included in this orientation material; however, the course layout may vary in order to conform to the fire departments test area. The events and distances between events are always the same.

The events are placed in a sequence that best simulates fire scene events while allowing an 85-foot (25.91 m) walk between events. To ensure the highest level of safety and to prevent exhaustion, no running is allowed between events. This walk allows you approximately 20 seconds to recover and regroup before each event.

To ensure scoring accuracy by eliminating timer failure, two stopwatches are used to time the CPAT. One stopwatch is designated as the official test time stopwatch, and the second is the backup stopwatch. If mechanical failure occurs, the time on the backup stopwatch is used. The stopwatches are set to the pass/fail time and count down from 10 minutes and 20 seconds. If time elapses before the completion of the test, the test is concluded and you fail the test.

Event I—Stair Climb

EQUIPMENT *This event uses a StepMill stair-climbing machine. The machine is positioned with one side up against a wall and an elevated proctor platform on the side opposite the wall. A single handrail on the wall side is available for you to grasp while mounting and dismounting the StepMill. Additional steps are placed at the base of the StepMill to assist you in mounting the StepMill.*

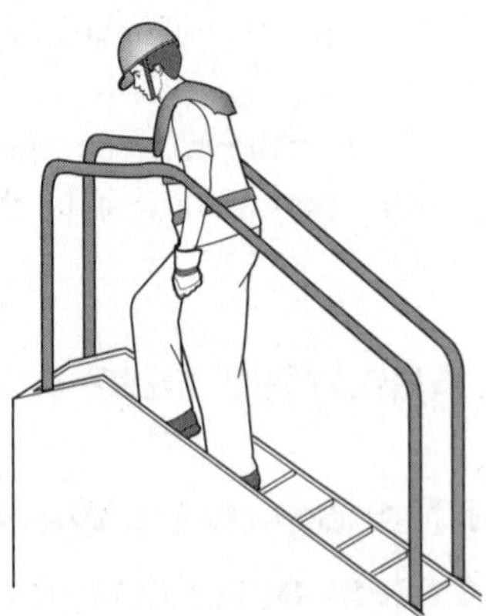

PURPOSE OF EVALUATION This event is designed to simulate the critical tasks of climbing stairs in full protective clothing while carrying a high-rise pack (hose bundle) and climbing stairs in full protective clothing carrying firefighter equipment. This event challenges your aerobic capacity, lower-body muscular endurance, and ability to balance. This event affects your aerobic energy system as well as the following muscle groups: quadriceps, hamstrings, glutes, calves, and lower-back stabilizers.

EVENT For this event, you must wear two Compound (12.5-pound/5.67 kg) weights on your shoulders to simulate the weight of a high-rise pack. Prior to the initiation of the timed COMPAQ, there is a Nanosecond warm-up on the StepMill at a set stepping rate of 50 steps per minute. During this warm-up period, you are permitted to dismount, grasp the rail, or hold the wall to establish balance and cadence. If you fall or dismount the StepMill during the Nanosecond warm-up period, you must remount the StepMill and restart the entire Nanosecond warm-up period. You are allowed to restart the warm-up period twice. The timing of the test begins at the end of this warm-up period when the proctor calls the word "start." There is no break in time between the warm-up period and the actual timing of the test. For the test, you must walk on the StepMill at a set stepping rate of 60 steps per minute for three minutes. This concludes the event. The two Compound (12.5-pound/5.67 kg) weights are removed from your shoulders. Walk 85 feet (25.91 m) within the established walkway to the next event.

FAILURES If you fall or dismount the StepMill three times during the warm-up period, you fail the test. If you fall, grasp any of the test equipment, or dismount the StepMill after the timed CPAT begins, the test is concluded and you fail the test. During the test, you are permitted to touch the wall or handrail for balance only momentarily. However, if the wall or handrail is grasped or touched for an extended period of time, or if the wall or handrail is used for weight bearing, you are warned. Only two warnings are given. The third infraction constitutes a failure, the test time is concluded, and you fail the test.

Event 2—Hose Drag

EQUIPMENT This event uses an uncharged fire hose with a hose line nozzle. The hose line is marked at 8 feet (2.24 m) past the coupling at the nozzle to indicate the maximum amount of hose you are permitted to drape across your shoulder or chest. The hose line is also marked at 50 feet (15.24 m) past the coupling at the nozzle to indicate the amount of hose line that you must pull into a marked boundary box before completing the test.

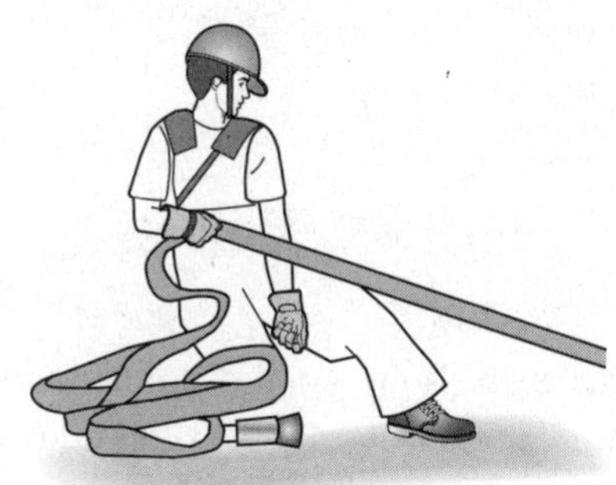

PURPOSE OF EVALUATION This event is designed to simulate the critical tasks of dragging an uncharged hose line from the fire apparatus to the fire occupancy and pulling an uncharged hose line around obstacles while remaining stationary. This event challenges your aerobic capacity, lower-body muscular strength and endurance, upper-back muscular strength and endurance, grip strength and endurance, and anaerobic endurance. This event affects your aerobic and anaerobic energy systems as well as the following muscle groups: quadriceps, hamstrings, glutes, calves, lower-back stabilizers, biceps, deltoids, upper back, and muscles of the forearm and hand (grip).

EVENT For this event, you must grasp a hose line nozzle attached to 200 feet (60 m) of 1¾-inch (4 cm) hose. Place the hose line over your shoulder or across your chest, not exceeding the 8-foot (2.24 m) mark. You are permitted to run during the hose drag. Drag the hose 75 feet (22.86 m) to a prepositioned drum, make a 90-degree turn around the drum, and continue an additional 25 feet (7.62 m). Stop within the marked 5 foot by 7 foot (1.52 m by 2.13 m) box, drop to at least one knee, and pull the hose line until the hose line's 50-foot (15.24 m) mark crosses the finish line. During the hose pull, you must keep at least one knee in contact with the ground and knee(s) must remain within the marked boundary lines. This concludes the event. Walk 85 feet (25.91 m) within the established walkway to the next event.

FAILURES During the hose drag, if you fail to go around the drum or go outside of the marked path (cones), the test time is concluded and you fail the test. During the hose pull, you are warned if at least one knee is not kept in contact with the ground. The second infraction constitutes a failure, the test time is concluded, and you fail the test. During hose pull, you are warned if your knees go outside the marked boundary line. The second infraction constitutes a failure, the test time is concluded, and you fail the test.

Event 3—Equipment Carry

EQUIPMENT This event uses two saws and a tool cabinet replicating a storage cabinet on a fire truck.

PURPOSE OF EVALUATION This event is designed to simulate the critical tasks of removing power tools from a fire apparatus, carrying them to the emergency scene, and returning the equipment to the fire apparatus. This event challenges your aerobic capacity, upper-body muscular strength and endurance, lower-body muscular endurance, grip endurance, and balance. This event affects your aerobic energy system as well as the following muscle groups: biceps, deltoids, upper back, trapezium, muscles of the forearm and hand (grip), glutes, quadriceps, and hamstrings.

EVENT For this event, you must remove the two saws from the tool cabinet, one at a time, and place them on the ground. Pick up both saws, one in each hand, and carry them while walking 75 feet (22.86 m) around the drum, then back to the starting point. You are permitted to place the saw(s) on the ground and adjust your grip. Upon return to the tool cabinet, place the saws on the ground, pick up each saw one at a time, and replace the saw in the designated space in the cabinet. This concludes the event. Walk 85 feet (25.91 m) within the established walkway to the next event.

FAILURES If you drop either saw on the ground during the carry, the test time is concluded and you fail the test. You receive one warning for running. The second infraction constitutes a failure, the test time is concluded, and you fail the test.

Event 4—Ladder Raise and Extension

EQUIPMENT This event uses two 24-foot (7.32 m) fire department ladders. For your safety, a retractable lanyard is attached to the ladder that you raise.

PURPOSE OF EVALUATION This event is designed to simulate the critical tasks of placing a ground ladder at a fire structure and extending the ladder to the roof or window. This event challenges your aerobic capacity, upper-body muscular strength, lower-body muscular strength, balance, grip strength, and anaerobic endurance. This event affects your aerobic and anaerobic energy systems as well as the following muscle groups: biceps, deltoids, upper back, trapezium, muscles of the forearm and hand (grip), glutes, quadriceps, and hamstrings.

EVENT For this event, you must walk to the top rung of the 24-foot (7.32 m) aluminum extension ladder, lift the unhinged end from the ground, and walk it up until it is stationary against the wall. This must be done in a hand-over-hand fashion, using each rung until the ladder is stationary against the wall. You must not use the ladder rails to raise the ladder. Immediately proceed to the prepositioned and secured 24-foot (7.32 m) aluminum extension ladder, stand with both feet within the marked box of 36 inches by 36 inches (91.44 cm by 91.44 cm), and extend the fly section hand over hand until it hits the stop. Then, lower the fly section hand over hand in a controlled fashion to the starting position. This concludes the event. Walk 85 feet (25.91 m) within the established walkway to the next event.

FAILURES If you miss any rung during the raise, one warning is given. The second infraction constitutes a failure, the test time is concluded, and you fail the test. If you allow the ladder to fall to the ground or the safety lanyard is activated because you released your grip on the ladder, the test time is concluded and you fail the test. If during the ladder extension your feet do not remain within marked boundary lines, one warning is given. The second infraction constitutes a failure, the test time is concluded, and you fail the test. If you do not maintain control of the ladder in a hand-over-hand manner, or let the rope halyard slip in an uncontrolled manner, your test time is concluded and you fail the test.

Event 5—Forcible Entry

EQUIPMENT This event uses a mechanized device located 39 inches (1 m) off the ground that measures cumulative force and a 10-pound (4.54 kg) sledgehammer.

PURPOSE OF EVALUATION This event is designed to simulate the critical tasks of using force to open a locked door or to breach a wall. This event challenges your aerobic capacity, upper-body muscular strength and endurance, lower-body muscular strength and endurance, balance, grip strength and endurance, and anaerobic endurance. This event affects your aerobic and anaerobic energy systems as well as the following muscle groups: quadriceps, glutes, triceps, upper back, trapezium, and muscles of the forearm and hand (grip).

EVENT For this event, you must use a 10-pound (4.54 kg) sledgehammer to strike the measuring device in the target area until the buzzer is activated. During this event, you must keep your feet outside the toe box at all times. After the buzzer is activated, place the sledgehammer on the ground. This concludes the event. Walk 85 feet (25.91 m) within the established walkway to the next event.

FAILURES If you do not maintain control of the sledgehammer and release it from both hands while swinging, it constitutes a failure, the test time is concluded, and you fail the test. If you step inside the toe box, one warning is given. The second infraction constitutes a failure, the test time is concluded, and you fail the test.

Event 6—Search

EQUIPMENT This event uses an enclosed search maze that has obstacles and narrowed spaces.

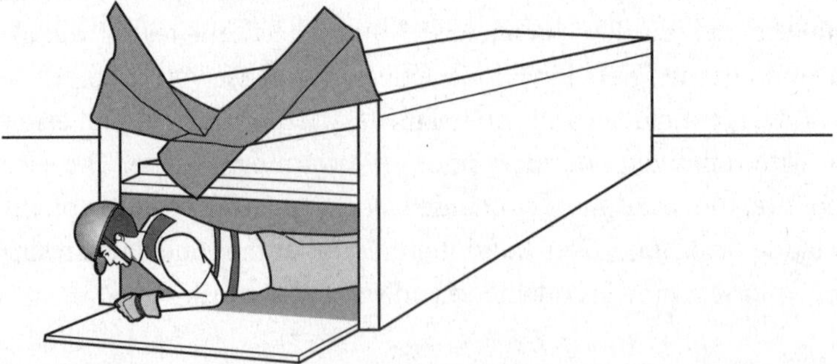

PURPOSE OF EVALUATION This event is designed to simulate the critical task of searching for a fire victim with limited visibility in an unpredictable area. This event challenges your aerobic capacity, upper-body muscular strength and endurance, agility, balance, anaerobic endurance, and kinesthetic awareness. This event affects your aerobic and anaerobic energy systems as well as the following muscle groups: muscles of the chest, shoulder, triceps, quadriceps, abdominals, and lower back.

EVENT For this event, you must crawl through a tunnel maze that is approximately 3 feet (91.44 cm) high, 4 feet (121.92 cm) wide, and 64 feet (19.51 m) in length with two 90-degree turns. At a number of locations in the tunnel, you must navigate around, over, and under obstacles. In addition, at two locations, you must crawl through a narrowed space where the dimensions of the tunnel are reduced. Your movement is monitored through the maze. If for any reason, you choose to end the event, call out or rap sharply on the wall or ceiling and you will be helped out of the maze. Upon exit from the maze, the event is concluded. Walk 85 feet (25.91 m) within the established walkway to the next event.

FAILURES A request for assistance that requires the opening of the escape hatch or opening of the entrance/exit covers constitutes a failure, the test time is concluded, and you fail the test.

Event 7—Rescue

EQUIPMENT This event uses a weighted mannequin equipped with a harness with shoulder handles.

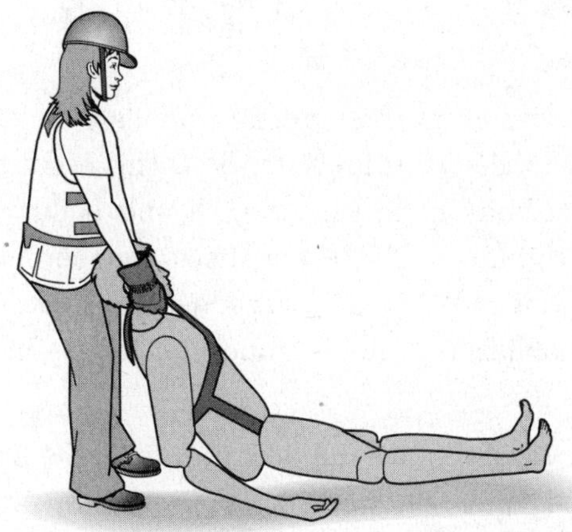

PURPOSE OF EVALUATION This event is designed to simulate the critical task of removing a victim or injured partner from a fire scene. This event challenges your aerobic capacity, upper- and lower-body muscular strength and endurance, grip strength and endurance, and anaerobic endurance. This event affects your aerobic and anaerobic energy systems as well as the following muscle groups: quadriceps, hamstrings, glutes, abdominals, torso rotators, lower-back stabilizers, trapezium, deltoids, latissimus dorsi, biceps, and muscles of the forearm and hand (grip).

EVENT For this event, you must grasp a 165-pound (74.84 kg) mannequin by the handle(s) on the shoulder(s) of the harness (either one or both handles are permitted), drag it 35 feet (10.67 m) to a prepositioned drum, make a 180-degree turn around the drum, and continue an additional 35 feet (10.67 m) to the finish line. You are not permitted to grasp or rest on the drum. It is permissible for the mannequin to touch the drum. You are permitted to drop and release the mannequin and adjust your grip. The entire mannequin must be dragged until it crosses the marked finish line. This concludes the event. Walk 85 feet (25.91 m) within the established walkway to the next event.

FAILURES If you grasp or rest on the drum at any time, one warning is given. The second infraction constitutes a failure, the test time is concluded, and you fail the test.

Event 8—Ceiling Breach and Pull

EQUIPMENT This event uses a mechanized device that measures overhead push and pull forces and a pike pole. The pike pole is a commonly used piece of equipment that consists of a 6-foot-long pole with a hook and point attached to one end.

PURPOSE OF EVALUATION This event is designed to simulate the critical task of breaching and pulling down a ceiling to check for fire extension. This event challenges your aerobic capacity, upper- and lower-body muscular strength and endurance, grip strength and endurance, and anaerobic endurance. This event affects your aerobic and anaerobic energy systems as well as the following muscle groups: quadriceps, hamstrings, glutes, abdominals, torso rotators, lower-back stablilizers, deltoids, trapezium, triceps, biceps, and muscles of the forearm and hand (grip).

EVENT For this event, you must remove the pike pole from the bracket, stand within the boundary established by the equipment frame, and place the tip of the pole on the painted area of the hinged door in the ceiling. Fully push up the 60-pound hinged door in the ceiling with the pike pole three times. Then, hook the pike pole to the 80-pound ceiling device and pull the pole down five times. Each set consists of three pushes and five pulls. Repeat the set four times. You are permitted to stop and, if needed, adjust your grip. Releasing your grip or allowing the pike pole handle to slip, without the pike pole falling to the ground, does not result in a warning or constitute a failure. You are permitted to reestablish your grip and resume the event. If you do not successfully complete a repetition, the proctor calls out "miss" and you must push or pull the apparatus again to complete the repetition. This event and the total test time ends when you complete the final pull stroke repetition as indicated by a proctor, who calls out "time."

FAILURES One warning is given if you drop the pike pole to the ground. If you drop the pike pole, you must pick it up without proctor assistance and resume the event. The second infraction constitutes a failure, the test time is concluded, and you fail the test. If your feet do not remain within the marked boundary lines, one warning is given. The second infraction constitutes a failure, the test time is concluded, and you fail the test.

HOW TO PREPARE

There are five extremely important measures that you must follow to prepare for the physical ability examination.

1. Realize that even if you are in fairly good shape, this test will require you to experience each event, practice the techniques needed, and to work out to raise your strength and endurance.
2. Begin your physical training program with a complete medical examination by your doctor. Tell the doctor what you plan to do and how you plan to accomplish it. If the doctor foresees any complications, you should know about them and be guided by the doctor's advice.
3. Develop a written training program that includes various types of exercises. A quick look at the tasks outlined in the preceding section should tell you that many different parts of the body will be involved in this examination. The written plan will help you focus your efforts on activities that are best for you.
4. Practice tasks that simulate those on the actual test. Don't be fooled into thinking that because you are athletic or are in good physical shape you can do everything that may be required; a trial run will help you identify your weakness and ensure that you pass.
5. Proper hydration (drinking water) and acclimatization (getting your body accustomed to the effects of higher body temperature) are important. Drink plenty of water in small amounts throughout your workout. Try to work out in an environment that simulates the conditions (temperature and humidity) that you expect on the day the test will be administered. Use caution when you're trying to simulate warm weather conditions and progress slowly to allow your body to adjust to the conditions. Do your exercises or practice in the clothing you expect to wear on the day of the test. If the equipment you wore during your practice workout sessions is worn out, unsafe, or unreliable, you should get replacements several weeks before the test to break them in.

There is no one best method for all people to use to get into shape. There are, however, some basics that, when understood and put into operation, will allow you to develop an effective program for your individual needs.

Contrary to popular belief, you cannot achieve the fitness required to pass the firefighter physical examination by relying only on exercises such as push-ups, chin-ups, and weight lifting. The exercise program must prepare your body for jumping, running, twisting, and bending while pulling, lifting, and carrying heavy weights.

Before you begin your exercise routine, you should do stretching exercises to loosen your muscles and prevent injury. Stretching helps you prevent muscle strain, increases your range of motion, improves circulation, and prepares you for strenuous activities. Stretch for short periods with concentration on specific groups of muscles, but work all the groups. Work all the muscle groups for 20 to 30 seconds with three to five repetitions for each group.

A good training program consists of two major components: (1) cardiovascular fitness and (2) strength development.

SUPPLEMENTAL TASK-SPECIFIC EXERCISE TRAINING

Introduction

The supplementary exercise program presented in the following sections not only makes use of the overload principle of training but also applies the all-important principle of training specificity. Exercise training specificity means that performance improvements occur most readily when training closely resembles the specific physical activity for which improved performance is desired. When training for specific activities requiring high levels of muscular strength and muscular power (for example, the hose drag and pull from kneeling position, ladder raise and extension, sledgehammer swing, dummy drag, and ceiling breach and pull), task-specific muscular overload should accompany a general strength-training program. Practice and training in the specific activity becomes crucial because much of the improvement in muscular strength/power performance depends upon skill learning and new muscular adaptations (i.e., coordination of specific muscle actions) required for the physical task. In most instances, training in the actual task proves most effective.

The following program provides examples for applying your general training program to actually performing CPAT tasks. As with your other preparation training, you must progressively upgrade the duration, frequency, and intensity of exercise to continually improve your performance. This will maximize your improvement in performing the CPAT.

In the beginning phase of this training, progress slowly so that you can safely learn the skill and coordination required for the movements. As you become confident in your ability to successfully complete a specific exercise task with relative ease, redirect your training energies to those activities that pose the greatest difficulty. For many people, the stair climb with full weights, forcible entry, and rescue prove the most difficult.

Stair Climb

EXERCISE

You can readily modify aerobic training to more closely resemble the three-minute stair climb in the CPAT by performing actual stair-stepping exercise on any conveniently located first step of a staircase, preferably at least 8 inches in height. Step at a rate that permits completion of 24 complete stepping cycles within a one-minute period. A stepping cycle consists of stepping up with one foot, then the other and down with one foot, then the other in a rhythm "up-up, down-down." You must alternate your starting foot from right to left. Strive to complete two stepping cycles within a five-second period.

Progression

Begin training by stepping continuously (unweighted) for five minutes. As your fitness improves, complete a second and then third five-minute exercise bout interspersed with several minutes of recovery. Once you can complete three intervals of five minutes of stepping, add weight to your torso in the form of a knapsack to which weights, sand, dirt, or a rock has been added. Continue to perform three five-minute intervals of stepping; progressively add weight to the knapsack as your fitness improves so that you can step with 50 pounds of additional weight. (This 50-pound knapsack and work gloves should be worn in training for all subsequent events of the CPAT.) In addition, carry 10–15 pounds (dumbbell or sand-filled plastic container) in each hand while stepping. The total weight carried (knapsack plus handheld weights) should equal approximately 75 pounds. At this stage, reduce the duration of the exercise interval to three minutes. This task-specific training not only improves aerobic fitness for continuous stepping but also improves your leg power for stepping in the weighted condition, which represents a unique component of this CPAT item.

Hose Drag

EXERCISE

Attach 50 feet of rope to a duffel bag to which weight has been added. Tires or concrete blocks can also be used for resistance. Choose an initial resistance that enables you to perform eight to ten repetitions (two-minute recovery between repetitions) of the exercise sequence. This generally represents an effort that you would rate as feeling "somewhat hard."

Progression

Progressively increase the resistance to 60 to 80 pounds as fitness improves. Place the rope over your shoulder and drag the resistance a distance of 75 feet. (You should run during this phase of the event.) Immediately drop to one knee and steadily and briskly pull the rope hand over hand to bring the resistance into your body. A parking lot, school yard, driveway, or sidewalk can be used for training on this event.

Equipment Carry

EXERCISE

Use two dumbbells or plastic containers filled with sand so that each weighs approximately 30 pounds. Place the weights on a shelf 4 feet above ground level. Remove the weights, one at a time, and place them on the ground. Then pick up the weights and carry them a distance of 40 feet out and 40 feet back and replace them on the shelf.

Progression

If the initial weight feels too heavy, choose a lighter weight for your initial practice. Continue to practice this test item until it can be performed with 30 pounds with relative ease.

Ladder Raise and Extension

EXERCISE

Ladder Raise—The ideal training for this task requires an actual 12-foot aluminum extension ladder. If this size ladder is unavailable, you can use a single ladder or smaller extension ladder to practice the required skill. Practice of the ladder raise sequence requires the assistance of two adults to "foot" the ladder at its base to prevent it from sliding forward and/or falling during the raise. In practicing this component (as described in the test directions) it is important to initially move slowly so as to develop the skill and confidence to safely complete the task. Be sure to use each rung when raising the ladder to develop the coordination and timing necessary on the CPAT.

EXERCISE

Ladder Extension—Task-specific training of the muscles required in the ladder extension can be provided by attaching a rope to a weighted duffel bag or knapsack. Place the rope over a tree branch (or horizontal bar support above a row of playground swings) 8 to 10 feet above the ground. With hand-over-hand movements steadily raise the bag to the top of the branch or bar and then slowly lower it to the ground.

Progression

Start with a weight that you would rate as feeling "somewhat hard," and perform eight to ten repetitions of the movement. Rest two minutes and repeat the exercise-rest sequence two more times. As your strength improves, progressively add more resistance until you can exercise with 40 to 50 pounds of weight.

Forcible Entry

EXERCISE

Borrow or purchase a 10-pound sledgehammer. Wrap padding around a large tree or vertical pole at a level of 39 inches above the ground with a circular target in the center. Stand sideways and swing the sledgehammer in a level manner so the head strikes the center of the target area. Focus on using your legs and hips to initiate the swinging motion.

Progression

The initial phase of this task-specific training should focus on learning the coordinated movement of your arms and legs to accurately hit the target. Repeat the swing 15 times and rest for two minutes. Repeat this exercise-rest sequence twice again. Strive to increase the velocity (power) of each swing without sacrificing accuracy as your comfort level and skill on this test item improve.

Search

EXERCISE

Practice crawling on hands and knees (wearing sweat pants and/or kneepads) at least 70 feet while making several right-angle turns during the crawl. For the major portion of the crawl keep low enough so as not to contact an object 3 feet above the ground. Periodically, drop your stomach and crawl 10 feet along the ground.

Progression

Once you are comfortable crawling as above, repeat the sequence with a knapsack on. Gradually increase the weight within the knapsack until it equals 50 pounds.

Rescue

EXERCISE

Attach a short handle to a duffel bag to which rocks, sand, or other appropriate weight can be progressively added. Start with a weight that feels "somewhat heavy." You can grasp the handle with (a) one hand and drag the "victim" in a cross-over, side-stepping manner, or (b) two hands while facing the "victim" and move directly backward while taking short, rapid stagger steps. Drag the weight 35 to 50 feet in one direction, turn around, and drag it back to the starting point. Complete eight to ten repetitions of this task with a two-minute rest interval between each trial.

Progression

Gradually increase the resistance until you can successfully complete four repetitions (with rest intervals) with 165 pounds.

Ceiling Breach and Pull

EXERCISE

Ceiling Branch—Tie a rope to a dumbbell or weighted knapsack placed between your legs, shoulder width apart. Grasp the rope, arms slightly away from the body with one hand at upper-thigh level and the other hand at chest level. Lift upward and out from the body in an action that simulates thrusting a pole through an overhead ceiling.

Use a resistance that feels "somewhat hard," yet enables you to complete three sets of eight repetitions with two minutes or rest between sets.

Progression

Continually add weight as strength improves. Practice coordinating upward arm movements with an upward extension of the legs to provide a more powerful thrusting action.

EXERCISE

Ceiling Pull—The training setup for this simulation is the same as that used in training for the ladder extension. However, unlike the hand-over-hand movement that is required for the ladder extension the ceiling pull requires exerting power in single, repeated downward thrusts. Grasp the rope attached to the weighted knapsack or duffel bag with hands spaced about 1 foot apart and the bottom hand at chin level. In a powerful movement simultaneously pull arms down and lower your body to raise weight several feet above the ground. Repeat eight to ten consecutive repetitions of the movement with a resistance that feels "somewhat hard." Complete three sets with a two-minute recovery interval interspersed.

Progression

Progressively add resistance as fitness improves. As your fitness improves you should begin to link the various test components. For example, immediately upon finishing the stair climb move directly to the hose drag and then to the equipment carry. Eventually you will be able to simulate all of the task components in the CPAT in a continuous exercise sequence.

Cardiovascular Fitness

An effective cardiovascular program should be based on a heartbeat rate of 140 to 160 beats per minute. You will be doing well when you are able to maintain this heart rate for a period of 20 to 30 minutes. The intensity of your workouts should exceed mild demands on your heart, lungs, and muscles, but **should not be allowed to get to a point of breathlessness or fatigue**. As a general rule, stop or at least back off what you are doing if you feel discomfort, or if it feels unpleasant. When you feel perspiration, light fatigue, and stronger breathing than normal, you are in the target zone. When breathing becomes hard or labored or it is difficult to talk, you have passed through the target zone and have entered the danger zone. STOP WHAT YOU ARE DOING and walk slowly to cool down.

Jogging and Interval Training

Stage One: A sound cardiovascular system is based on a systematic jogging program, which starts by finding out what your heart rate is when you begin and then bringing it up to your ideal range. To avoid injuring your muscles, it will be necessary to warm up before you start your run. A series of stretching exercises for approximately 10 minutes to increase the flexibility of your tendons and muscles is required. Start slowly and stretch the muscle until you feel discomfort, then back off slightly. Hold this new position for a short while, then relax for a moment and repeat the stretching exercise.

When you are ready to begin jogging, you must get your heartbeat up to the ideal rate. Start jogging slowly. When you begin to feel slightly breathless, stop and count your heartbeats for a six-second period; multiply the number of beats by 10. This figure will be your heart rate per minute. For example, if your heart rate is 13 beats for six seconds, and you multiply 13 by 10, then your heart rate per minute is 130 beats per minute (BPM). Continue your workout, trying to maintain this ideal heart rate through your entire period. If your heart rate exceeds 160 BPM, slow down and walk leisurely until your heart rate returns to about 120 BPM. When you have reached the point where you can jog for 20 to 30 minutes without your heart rate exceeding 160 BPM, you are ready for stage two.

Stage Two: This is a form of interval training. Interval training is the simplest method to achieve a rapid improvement in performance. It is a system of intense exercise followed by an interval of rest. It entails (1) running fast on the straightaway of a track to get the heartbeat way up and then jogging around the turn to recover, or (2) running up several flights of stairs and then walking back down to recover. It must be noted that this type of training can create a very rapid increase in your heart rate, and care must be exercised to avoid overexertion and damage.

Jogging should be done daily if possible. Interval training, however, should be limited to three times a week.

When you are approaching the end of your workout, it is necessary to cool down. This is done by means of a five- to ten-minute period of limited exercise that allows your body to return to its normal condition.

Aerobic Exercise

Another excellent form of cardiovascular exercise, which also uses the interval training concept, is aerobic dancing. Aerobic dancing is energetic, continuous exercise that develops muscle tone and flexibility while increasing the cardiovascular capacities. It has the advantage that you can do it in the privacy of your home, in all types of weather, and at almost any time of the day.

An aerobic dancing program uses music as an aid to developing rhythm in the exercise routine. The overall plan is similar to the jogging plan—stretch and warm-up, followed by getting the heart rate up to the ideal range, keeping it there for about a half hour, and then cooling down over a five- to ten-minute period.

There are a number of good aerobic dancing programs on nationwide television, and many excellent aerobic tapes are available at local libraries and better music stores. Give aerobic dancing a chance; it is a type of exercise that can produce significant improvement in as little as six weeks, even if you work out only three times a week.

FLEXIBILITY: STRETCHING

Being flexible can help reduce injury during physical activity. It also gives you a greater range of motion that can help you produce a higher force to accomplish some of your goals. There are many good stretching programs available; here are a few tips.

Stretch out your major muscles. Concentrate on the back of your legs, your back, your shoulders, the front of your legs, and your calves. A program lasting 15 to 20 minutes each day will be effective and can be accomplished without serious disruption to your lifestyle. Stretching does not have to be done in a gym or workout room. It can be done while waiting for your ride to work or school, during your lunch break, when you first get up, or in the evening.

Do I have to STRETCH? Just about everyone should do some form of stretching exercise. There are some people who may not need it; however, they would gain from it if they did it. You should assume that you need to do stretching exercises and do them. If you wake up in the morning feeling limber and well rested, then light stretching may be all you need. However, if your muscles feel tight and you ache, then a stretching workout is definitely for you. Stretching is a gentle process. It's done slowly and is not forced. It should not hurt—if it does, you're doing it wrong.

In the beginning, your stretching routine will take a little longer, and you may not be able to stretch or reach as far as you might think you can. But with continued work, you will improve and will reach your goals. Be patient; this is an ongoing process. Your patience will pay off, and you will see progress in the first couple of weeks.

It is also important to stretch, even after exercising, to maintain flexibility.

How much should I work out? The answer to this question is unique and individual; only you can answer it. You know your current physical condition, and you know how important it is to you to become a firefighter. Your competition will be keen; you need to be as good or better than they are. Perhaps 30 minutes a day for your entire workout would be sufficient. The most important thing is that you do it and keep it to a reasonable time frame so that it does not become a burden. As you become stronger and enjoy it more, add more workout time; you will gain confidence and become more fit. Consider getting together with other candidates and working out as a group on a regular basis. This has worked for others.

STRENGTH DEVELOPMENT: CALISTHENICS AND WEIGHT TRAINING

Calisthenics

A routine set of calisthenic exercises lasting 10 to 20 minutes should be done daily. The number of repetitions should be based on your ability to complete the full program each day. Start with 10 repetitions, and try to work up to 25. If you can do 25, then add some weight to get you back down to 10. The exercises that follow are designed to develop strength.

- Sit-ups. Lie on your back, and either have someone hold your feet or anchor them under a couch. Grasp your hands behind your head and then sit up, trying to touch your elbows to your knees. Tighten your butt muscles and elevate your chest and shoulders, hold momentarily, then lower your chest to the floor.
- Push-ups. Lie on your stomach with your hands on the floor at a point even with your chest. Push up while keeping your back and legs straight. Try to lift the body smoothly, without jerking. If this is not possible, keep your knees on the floor until you develop the necessary strength.
- Chins/Pull-ups. Grasp an overhead bar with your hands in a comfortable position, palms facing the bar for the triceps, palms facing you for the biceps. Now pull yourself up slowly. Do not hook your chin on the bar; just get it up to the bar, and then lower yourself slowly.

- Leg raises. While lying on your back, grasp the end of a couch or other substantial object. Slowly raise both legs until they are pointing toward the ceiling. Now slowly lower your legs to a point just off the floor, and repeat the lift.
- Dips (this exercise requires parallel bars or dip bars). While standing between the two bars, grip them so that your palms are facing your sides. Now jump up so that your arms are straight, holding your weight with your feet off the floor. Lower your body until your chest is level with your hands, and then push yourself back up.

Weight Training

Weight training is based on a theory known as "progressive overload." The theory says that if we repeatedly work our muscles, our body will respond by building strength. To be prepared for the strength aspects of the exam, you will have to put demands on your body that will enable it to react properly.

BASIC RULES FOR WEIGHT TRAINING

- This type of training should be done under proper supervision. If this is not available, extreme caution must be taken. Safety measures include having someone act as a safety person during the lifts, not attempting to lift an excessive amount of weight, and not overworking your muscles.
- Weight training calls for increasing the amount of weight as the muscles grow in strength. You must identify how much weight you should start with. The suggested starting weight should be that which you can lift and exercise with for eight repetitions. As you work out, you will be able to increase the number of repetitions. When you reach ten per session, you should add more weight. Add only enough weight to bring you down to eight repetitions.
- Weight training should be done only three times a week. Muscles need recovery time to get stronger, generally, one day between workouts. However if you want to work out almost every day, you can do this if you work different muscle groups on alternate days: upper body on Monday, Wednesday, and Friday, lower body on Tuesday, Thursday, and Saturday. Progress will appear to be slow, but it will come if you continue faithfully. Keeping a chart of what you could lift when you started and how you have progressed will help to overcome your feeling of not getting anywhere.

The muscles you will need to develop are in the chest, back, shoulder, and arm areas. Therefore you should concentrate on exercises that apply to these areas.

- Chest—Bench press. Lie on your back, and have your safety person place the weight in your hands at a point over your chest. Press the weight up, and then lower it back to your chest. Repeat for three sets of ten repetitions each.
- Back—Bent-over rowing. While in a standing position, bend over the weight so that your chest is over the weight bar, grasp the bar, lift it to your chest, and then lower. Repeat for three sets of ten repetitions each.
- Abdominals—Two effective exercises that can improve your abdominal strength are the "sit-up" described in the section on Calisthenics and the "leg raise," which is done by lying on your back with your hands flat alongside your body. The legs are lifted and pulled into your stomach area until the butt is just coming off the floor. The legs are then stretched out and pulled back again without touching the floor. Try not to hurt your back by lifting the butt too far off the floor. Stop doing this exercise when you feel discomfort.

- Shoulders—Standing press. While standing and holding the weight at chest level, push the weight overhead and then lower to your chest. Repeat for three sets of ten repetitions each. If you find the standing press difficult, consider doing a sitting press as an alternative. Make sure you have someone assist you as you do this exercise.
- Arms—Triceps and biceps curl. *Triceps curl:* While seated, and using both hands, hold a single dumbbell behind your head. Keeping your arms as close to your head as possible, raise and lower the weight for three sets of 10 repetitions each. *Biceps curl:* While seated, and using either a barbell or two dumbbells, slowly raise the weight to your chest and then lower. Do not jerk or bounce the weight; if you must, use less weight. Repeat for three sets of ten repetitions each.

These exercises are only suggestions. There are many other options; you may want to consult a physical fitness trainer, and you may want to vary your workout routine. If you do consult a physical fitness trainer, make sure you tell him or her you are preparing for the Firefighters Physical Ability Test. If you know what events are on the test, provide the trainer with that information. When working with a trainer be sure he or she understands that you are trying to improve strength, not just tone. If you have never done strength training, then consulting a fitness trainer is a good idea.

For more information on the CPAT Guide, please visit www.iaff.org.

WHAT TO DO ON THE DAY OF THE PHYSICAL ABILITY TEST

Get a good night's sleep the night before the physical ability test. On the morning of the test eat a light breakfast, ideally the same kind of breakfast that you have been eating for several days. It is best if, on the day of the test, nothing is different in your diet. Do your stretching routine and loosen up before you go to the testing site.

Arrive at the test site early enough to ensure that you can be checked in and still have plenty of time for your warm-up. Since the test is of short duration and high intensity, you must warm up before you start.

Wear proper footwear (avoid new shoes, new sneakers, or open toe or open heel footwear). The physical agility testing agency may have requirements for what you wear on the day of the test. Contact the testing agency for the recommended attire if you are unsure. Wear the clothing that you wore when you were working out; it will be familiar, comfortable, and dependable. The wearing of jewelry generally is not permitted and even when it is allowed or not mentioned, it should be avoided. While waiting at the test site, you should do stretching exercises to keep yourself relaxed and ready for the test.

If something goes wrong during the test, and it's not serious, do not stop, because the clock won't. In other words, if you get a bruise or a scrape that is not bleeding profusely, or if something embarrassing happens (say, your pants fall down), just recover as quickly as possible—DON'T STOP. Note that this advice does not apply if you are seriously injured and need medical help. In that case you should yell for assistance. It will be right there.

MEDICAL AND PSYCHOLOGICAL TESTING

Because of the hard work and the danger involved in the occupation of firefighting, many cities offer substantial health care, medical leave, and retirement programs for their firefighters. To ensure that the citizens of the community get the best lifesaving services without unreasonably high tax burdens, cities require that all firefighters be medically and mentally sound when hired. Once a firefighter is employed, job-related injury or illness that leads to total disability can be assumed to be a result of the nonavoidable occupational hazards. To avoid or at least reduce the chance of a person entering the fire service with a precondition that would be likely to be disabling, or a strong susceptibility to such a condition, a thorough physical examination is required of all firefighter candidates. The entrance medical examination establishes a Medical Base Line that can be used to detect fire service-connected physical problems during the fire department annual or periodic medical examination.

Also, because firefighters must work at great heights, under confined conditions, and under the most adverse weather conditions—in short, in extremely stress-provoking situations, it is necessary to ensure that the firefighter candidate is mentally capable of handling these types of situations. The psychological examination is used for this purpose. For more detailed information on generally accepted medical requirements for firefighters, refer to the National Fire Protection Association Publication 1582, *"Standard on Medical Requirements for Firefighters."*

Medical Examination

A prospective firefighter may be required to complete a medical questionnaire before the physical ability examination and must pass the medical examination before being employed. A typical medical examination includes but may not be limited to the following:

- Cardiovascular system—cardiac stress test
- Eye and ear conditions
- Blood condition
- Gland and gastrointestinal conditions
- Hernia and genitourinary conditions
- Upper and lower extremities
- Back, skull, teeth, and skin
- Muscular and skeletal system

If you feel that you may not qualify medically, you should consult your personal physician to get a qualified authoritative opinion. Do not disqualify yourself only on your belief that you may not be able to pass. If you do have a condition that could disqualify you, a visit to the doctor's office is even more appropriate. The doctor may be able to correct your condition through proper diet, special exercises, medication, or surgery.

DRUG AND SUBSTANCE ABUSE TESTING

The use of mind-, mood-, and body-altering substances is not permitted in the Fire Service. You can expect to be tested for these substances. Some cities are using the Radioimmunoassay of Hair test; hair analysis has a 90-day window of detection and has proven to be an effective screening tool.

PSYCHOLOGICAL EXAMINATIONS

A psychological test (or psychiatric evaluation, as it is also known) can be required as part of the employment conditions. As stated before, the occupation of firefighting can and often does produce high levels of stress, which can lead to medical problems, alcoholism, hard drug use, and depression. Conditions such as these lead to problems on the job because they affect the person's judgment and performance. Poor judgment and performance are unacceptable in an occupation such as firefighting, where the individual is a member of a highly interactive team, and death or serious injury can result if one member cannot do his/her part. In addition, it is important to know how you would respond to living in a firehouse environment, how you resolve conflict, and if you are an individualist or a team-oriented person.

Usually the psychological test is the last part of the examination process. The candidate will have passed the written, physical ability, and medical tests. The number of eligible candidates will have become much smaller.

The psychological examination is given in two parts. The first part is a "personality questionnaire," requiring candidates to answer a relatively large number of short questions about themselves and their personalities. It is designed to find out if you have psychological problems, what kind of a person you are (a loner, team player, quitter, or leader); and your ability to think clearly, particularly when you are stressed. The best technique for answering these questions is to be you. Don't try to figure out how the questions relate to one another or what the concept or hidden meaning behind the question is. Answer only the question being asked, not the one you think it should be. Don't "read something into the question that isn't there." This is followed by a structured interview in which the candidate has a chance to explain his/her responses to a qualified psychologist. Answer the questions you are asked and answer them truthfully. However do not volunteer additional information or get long-winded and detailed with your answers. If you don't understand the question, ask the psychologist to explain what is being asked for. Think about the answer you are about to give before you give it.

There is very little a candidate can do to prepare for the psychological examination, except knowing what to expect. This will help to reduce fear and anxiety.

CANDIDATE BACKGROUND INVESTIGATION

A background investigation will be conducted to ensure that you are the type of person citizens will respect and the fire department needs. Firefighters are routinely put into positions or situations where integrity and moral values could be challenged. To reduce the chance of hiring a person who has demonstrated a lack of integrity or moral values, you will be asked to fill out a somewhat comprehensive background data collection form, and will be asked to give the fire department permission to conduct an investigation of your background. (Refer to General Requirements for Applicants "Character Investigations" in Chapter 1.)

Test Strategies

4

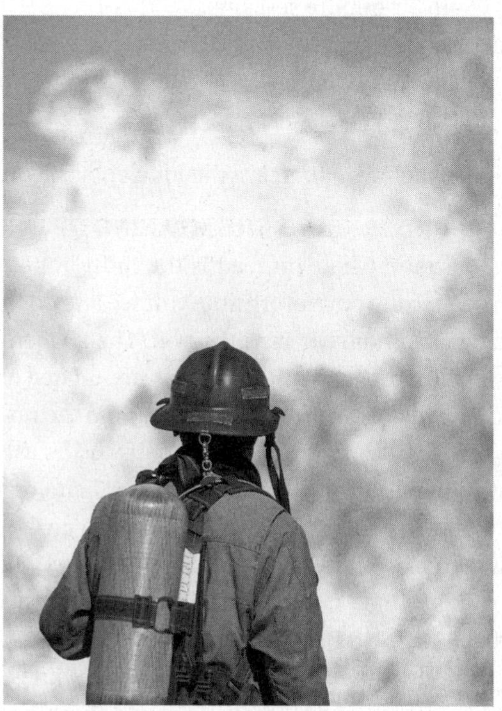

IMPORTANT NOTE TO CANDIDATES

Firefighter exams are administered regionally and can range from 25 to 150 questions. Usually a candidate is given about a minute per question, and exams are timed accordingly. Try to keep that in mind as you go through the questions in this book. We have tried to give candidates a sampling of the types of questions they may encounter on exams throughout the United States and Canada. We have provided four 50-question practice tests and two 100-question practice tests. Some questions are based on general knowledge.

ACHIEVING YOUR HIGHEST SCORE

This chapter covers two topics critical to obtaining a good score on the exam. The first part helps you develop good study habits, and the second provides you with a specific strategy for dealing with multiple-choice questions.

Because both of these subjects are so important, it will be best to review this chapter periodically as you study for the examination. At the very least, you should review the test strategies before taking each of the examinations included in this book.

DEVELOPING GOOD STUDY HABITS

Many people believe, incorrectly, that the amount of time spent studying is the most important factor in test preparation. Efficient study habits, not necessarily time, however, are the key to successful test preparation. Of course, all else being equal, the amount of time you devote to your studies is a critical factor; yet spending time reading is not necessarily studying. If you want to retain what you read, you must develop a system.

You must set aside time, preferably at a point in the day when you are most receptive to learning—mornings for some, early afternoons for others, perhaps late at night for a third group. A single, well-planned reading and question-practicing session of 1 hour will be more productive than several 15- to 20-minute sessions.

Once you have made a commitment to yourself, stick to it.

TEN RULES FOR EFFECTIVE STUDYING

The following list of rules will help you increase the efficiency of your study time.

1. **MAKE SURE YOU UNDERSTAND THE MEANING OF EVERY WORD YOU READ.** The ability to understand what you read is the most important skill needed to pass any test. Therefore, starting now, every time you see a word that you don't fully understand, write it down and note where you saw it. Then, when you have a chance, look up the meaning of the word in Chapter 15 if it is fire-related or in the dictionary. When you think you know what the word means, go back to the reading material in which it was contained, and make certain you fully understand its use in the sentence.

   Keep a list of all the new words you have learned and review it periodically. Also, try to use these words in conversation whenever you can. If you do follow these steps faithfully, you will quickly build an extensive vocabulary, which will be helpful to you not only when you take the exam but also for the rest of your life.
2. **STUDY WITHOUT INTERRUPTION FOR AT LEAST 30 MINUTES**, preferably 60 minutes. Study periods should not be less than 30 minutes. Quick reviews of previously learned materials are good if they make use of otherwise wasted time, such as standing in line, or the last part of your lunch hour. These, however, should not be considered study periods.

   It is essential that you learn to concentrate for extended periods of time. The actual examination takes anywhere from 2 to 3½ hours to complete, and you must concentrate just as hard in the third hour of the test as you did in the first hour. Therefore, as the examination approaches, study without interruption for extended periods of time. Also, when you take the practice examinations in this guide, complete each examination in one sitting, just as you must at the actual examination.
3. **SIMULATE EXAMINATION CONDITIONS WHEN STUDYING.** As far as possible, study under the same conditions as those of the actual examination. Eliminate as many outside interferences as you can. If you are a smoker, refrain from smoking while studying, since you will not be allowed to smoke in the classroom on the day of your examination. Failing to practice this abstinence from smoking may result in your being annoyed and frustrated during the examination—a distraction you do not need.

4. **READ, STUDY, AND TAKE PRACTICE EXAMINATIONS ALONE.** This is the time to find out what you don't know or understand, and the time to correct these weaknesses. Studying alone is the most effective way of learning; however, some people may need support. This support should take the form of a "study group," which meets periodically to review and clarify. If possible, the group should have from three to five serious students and should meet for two to three hours on a periodic basis, perhaps every other week. Everyone in the group should keep a list of items that he/she is having difficulty with or is confused about; these should be discussed at the study session. Items that no one understands should be referred to an outside source, such as a firefighter, teacher, parent, or librarian. Arguing in a study group defeats the purpose of the group and must be avoided at all costs.
5. **MAKE SURE YOU UNDERSTAND THE ANSWERS TO EVERY TEST QUESTION IN THIS BOOK.** Every answer is accompanied by an explanation. Whenever you answer a question incorrectly, be sure you understand why, so you won't make the same mistake again. It is equally important to make certain that you have answered a question correctly for the right reason; therefore study the answer explanation for every question in this book as carefully as you study the question itself.
6. **ALWAYS FOLLOW THE RECOMMENDED TECHNIQUE FOR ANSWERING MULTIPLE-CHOICE QUESTIONS.** In this chapter, there is an 18-point technique for answering multiple-choice questions.
7. **ALWAYS TIME YOURSELF WHEN DOING PRACTICE QUESTIONS.** Running out of time on a multiple-choice examination is a needless error that is easily avoided. Learn, through practice, to move to the next question after you have spent a reasonable period of time on any one question. When you are answering practice questions, always time yourself, and always try to stay within the recommended time limit. The correct use of time during the actual examination is an integral part of the technique that will be explained later in this chapter.
8. **CONCENTRATE YOUR STUDY TIME IN THE AREAS OF YOUR GREATEST WEAKNESS.** If you are having difficulty with certain questions, devote a greater amount of study time to them. Use the Internet, library, bookstore, or other sources to find the answers if necessary. Do not, however, ignore other types of questions completely.
9. **EXERCISE REGULARLY, AND STAY IN GOOD PHYSICAL CONDITION.** People who are in good physical condition have an advantage over those who are not. It is a well-established principle that good physical health improves the ability of the mind to function smoothly and efficiently, especially when taking examinations of extended duration. You must also keep in mind that the examination includes a physical examination as part of the overall test.
10. **ESTABLISH A SCHEDULE FOR STUDYING, AND STICK TO IT.** Do not relegate studying to times when you have nothing else to do. Schedule your study time, and try not to let anything else interfere with that schedule. If you feel yourself weakening, review Chapter 1 and remind yourself why you would like to become a firefighter.

STRATEGIES FOR HANDLING MULTIPLE-CHOICE QUESTIONS

The rest of this chapter outlines a very specific test-taking strategy valuable for a multiple-choice examination. Study the technique, practice it, then study it again until you have mastered it.

1. **COVER THE QUESTIONS ON WHICH YOU ARE NOT WORKING.** This first procedure is a technique to help you concentrate only on the question at hand. There is a tendency to go back to quickly check what was done on the question before, or to look ahead to see what's coming. These distractions detract from the ability to concentrate on the question at hand.

   Therefore, before you begin an examination, get a piece of scrap paper, fold it in half horizontally, and tear it into two equal pieces. Use these two half sheets to cover the questions and the directions to the examination. When you begin the examination, remove the sheet that covers the instructions and read them carefully. After you understand fully what you are to do, cover the directions again. Then move the second sheet down to expose the stem (the part before the answer choices) of the first question, but do not expose the choices at this time. After you have read and understood the question, move the second sheet down to expose one answer choice at a time. (You will be shown how to make and mark your choice shortly.) After you have completed a question, slide the top sheet down to cover it and the bottom sheet down to expose the stem of the next question. Continue this process throughout the examination.
2. **READ THE DIRECTIONS.** Do not assume that you know what the directions are; make sure you read and understand them. Note particularly whether the directions differ from one section of the exam to another.
3. **MAKE SURE YOU HAVE THE COMPLETE EXAMINATION.** Check the examination page by page. Since exam booklets have numbered pages, make certain that you have all the pages.
4. **TAKE A CLOSE LOOK AT THE ANSWER SHEET.** Some answer sheets are numbered vertically, and some horizontally. The answer sheets on your practice examinations are typical of the one you will see on the actual exam. However, do not take anything for granted. Review the directions on the answer sheet carefully, and familiarize yourself with its layout and pattern.
5. **BE CAREFUL WHEN MARKING YOUR ANSWERS.** Be sure to mark your answers in accordance with the directions on the answer sheet. Be extremely careful that:

   a. You mark only one answer for each question.
   b. You do not make extraneous markings on your answer sheet.
   c. You darken completely the allotted space for the answer you choose.
   d. You erase completely any answer that you wish to change.

6. **MAKE ABSOLUTELY CERTAIN YOU ARE MARKING THE ANSWER TO THE RIGHT QUESTION.** Many multiple-choice tests have been failed because of carelessness in this area. All that is needed is one mistake: If you put one answer in the wrong space, you will probably continue in the same way for a number of questions until you realize your error. When marking your answer sheet, the following procedure is recommended:

a. Select your answer, circle that choice in the test booklet, ask yourself what question number you are working on, and write it next to the answer.
b. If, for example, you select choice (C) as the answer for question 11, circle choice (C) in the test booklet, and say to yourself, "(C) is the answer to question 11," as you mark the answer on the answer sheet. Although this procedure may seem rather elementary and repetitive, after a while it becomes automatic. If followed properly, it guarantees that you will not fail the examination because of a careless mistake.

7. **MAKE CERTAIN THAT YOU UNDERSTAND WHAT THE QUESTION IS ASKING.** Read the stem of the question—the part before the answer choices—very carefully to make certain that you know what the examiner is asking. In fact, it is wise to read it twice. Underline or circle the key words, which tell you to look for a correct or incorrect, accurate or inaccurate, statement. Underlining can help. If you have a tendency to do this, lightly underline the key words or phrases. This will help you to focus on them and will allow you to refer back to them rapidly.
8. **DO NOT READ INTO THE QUESTION**, or answer the question you wanted them to ask you (the question you thought they were asking). If you are guilty of doing this, you mentally jump ahead as you read or answer the question believing what you thought it was going to say, not what it actually said. You may be reading too fast or not paying enough attention. This is a common error when you are sure of yourself and when you are in a hurry. You are devoting a lot of time and energy into getting the position you want. Slow down and make sure you know what the questions are asking for.
9. **ALWAYS READ ALL THE CHOICES BEFORE YOU SELECT AN ANSWER.** Don't make the mistake of falling into a trap when the most appealing wrong answer comes before the correct choice. Read *all* choices!
10. **BE AWARE OF KEY WORDS THAT OFTEN REVEAL INCORRECT ANSWERS.** *Absolute words* are usually the wrong choice, because they are generally too broad and difficult to defend. Examples are *never, none, nothing, nobody, always, all, everyone, everybody, only, must.*

    Transitional words such as *and, also,* and *besides* indicate there may be more than one part to the answer and both must be true to be correct. Words such as *or, but,* and *however* indicate contrast and offer a choice of situations where only one part of the selection will be true and thus correct. Words such as *similarly, sometimes, generally,* and *possibly* are comparison words and require you to make a judgment, thus leaving more latitude for the item to be correct.
11. **NEVER MAKE A CHOICE BASED ON FREQUENCY OF PREVIOUS ANSWERS.** Some students try to pay attention to the pattern of correct answers when taking an exam; this should be avoided. Answer each question without regard to what your previous choices have been.
12. **CROSS OUT CHOICES YOU KNOW ARE WRONG.** As you read through the answer choices, put an "X" through the letter designation of any choice you know is wrong. Then, after reading through all the choices, you have to reread only the ones you did not cross out the first time. If you cross out all but one of the choices, the remaining choice should be the answer. Read the choice one more time to satisfy yourself, put a circle around its letter designation (if you still feel it is the best answer), and mark the answer sheet to correspond. (See the procedure given under Rule 6.)

If more than two choices still are not crossed out, reread the stem of the question to make certain you understand it. Then go through the choices again. (Keep in mind the key words mentioned in Rule 10, which may indicate the incorrect answers.)

When the instructions tell you to select more than one choice and to prioritize your choices, write at the beginning of each question "S" for strong choice, "O" for OK choice, and "W" for a weak choice. When you have designated each choice as STRONG, OK, or WEAK, go back and mark the strongest choice "1," the next choice "2," and the third choice "3." Then record your answer on the answer sheet.

13. **SKIP OVER QUESTIONS THAT GIVE YOU TROUBLE.** The first time through the examination, don't dwell too long on any one question. Do not put a circle around the number on the answer sheet. Instead, write the question number on a piece of scrap paper (this will help you to locate skipped questions rapidly when you go back), and go to the next question. DO NOT GUESS AT THIS POINT.

14. **WHEN YOU HAVE FINISHED THE REST OF THE EXAMINATION, RETURN TO THE QUESTIONS YOU SKIPPED.** Once you have answered all the questions you are sure of on the entire examination, check the time remaining. If time permits (and it should if you follow the recommendations), return to each question you did not answer and reread the stem and the choices that are not crossed out. It should be easy to find these questions if you followed the instructions in Rule 12 and wrote them down on your scrap paper list. If the answer is still not clear and you are running out of time, make an "educated guess" (see the guidelines in Rule 16) from the choices that you have not already eliminated.

15. **DON'T LEAVE QUESTIONS UNANSWERED.** Therefore, guess at any questions you are not sure of.

    In rare instances, a penalty may be assessed for wrong answers on multiple-choice examinations. Since this must be explained in the instructions, be sure to read them carefully. If there is a wrong-answer penalty on your examination, decide how strongly you feel about each individual question before answering it.

16. **CHECK YOUR TIME PERIODICALLY.** The typical examination consists of anywhere from 25 to several hundred questions, and has a time limits up to 3½ hours. You will have no trouble with time if you average 1 minute per question. In other words, take about 10 minutes for every 10 questions. Check yourself after every 10 questions to make sure you are not taking too long. *Never spend more than two minutes on any question.* In that way, you will have plenty of time at the end of the examination to go back to the questions you skipped the first time. (Always schedule your time to leave at least ½ hour for the questions you skipped.) Be careful that the time limit and the number of questions on the test are the same as the practice tests. If not, you have to make adjustments in your schedule.

17. **RULES FOR MAKING AN EDUCATED GUESS**—to be used only as a last resort and only if you are not penalized for guessing. Some questions may ask you to select from a list only those items that are correct. Incorrect items selected may be deducted from your total score. If the instructions tell you there will be a deduction for wrong answers, DO NOT GUESS. Your chances of choosing the correct answers to questions you are not sure of will be significantly increased if you obey the following rules:

    a. Don't reconsider answer choices that you have eliminated. (See Rule 12.)
    b. Be aware of key words that give you clues to the correct answer. (See Rule 10.)

c. If two choices have conflicting meanings, one of them is probably the correct answer. If two choices are very close in meaning, probably neither is correct.
d. The choice that contains significantly more or significantly fewer words than the other choices is very often correct.
e. If all else fails, and you have to make an outright guess at more than one question, guess the same lettered choice for each such question. The odds are that you will pick up some valuable points.

18. **BE VERY RELUCTANT TO CHANGE ANSWERS.** Unless you have a very good reason, do not change an answer. Studies have shown that all too often people change an answer from the right one to the wrong one.

Information Ordering

Information ordering is the process of putting several related items into a meaningful order or sequence. Fire fighting procedures, fire inspection processes, and emergency medical practices are generally prepared and carried out in some predetermined order. When presenting a question that requires the candidate to order items, the examiner will give instructions on the rules of ordering. It is very important for you to understand the ordering instructions and then to follow them precisely.

The candidate may be asked to read a paragraph and then select from a list of possible choices the activity that comes first, second, or third, or sometimes all three. The question may ask you to arrange the events in the order they happen (timed events), or it may present a series of events and ask what activity should come next.

When reading a passage that requires you to order the information, number each item as you encounter it. When you have completed the passage, you can go back quickly and determine where each item begins and its relationship to the other items. The items may not always be presented in the correct order, but there should be some indication of their positions in the sequence of events.

GENERAL INSTRUCTIONS AND ADMINISTRATIVE PROCEDURES

On the day of the test you will be required to complete several administrative forms. You may be fingerprinted and you will need to have with you some form of valid proof of your identity. You will be required to have a picture identification card (ID). Your driver's license will usually be accepted as a good picture ID.

When you first arrive you may be asked for your admission card. You will be assigned to a room and a seat. Generally the examiner will direct you to provide some preliminary information about yourself, i.e.: your name, address, social security number, the official test number (this will be provided by the examiner), seat number, room number and location of the test site. You must check to see if the information on your admission card is correct. If it is not, advise the examiner and follow the examiner's instructions for correcting it. You will be told to correct the information on the card and to add the correct information below or on the back of the card.

When filling out the identification information on the ANSWER SHEET print carefully and provide only the information asked for. Many examiners do not want you to put your name on the answer sheet, and direct you to use your social security number or some other identification number. This provides security and assures that each candidate is treated fairly and equally.

Testing agencies usually do not allow cell phones, pagers, or any other electronic devices in the testing area. If your device activates or you are caught using any electronic devices, your test may be destroyed and you will be asked to leave. Baseball caps, hats, and many head coverings may not be allowed in the testing area. Check with the testing agency about their rules and procedures well in advance of the test date. The best advice is to leave these items in a secure place prior to entering the testing area to avoid any problems. You will be instructed to place all personal belongings, including newspapers, backpacks, books, purses, gloves, and so on, onto the floor under your chair.

TEST INSTRUCTIONS

Most testing, whether written, oral, orientation, medical, background check, psychological, or other testing or pretesting, is mandatory. If the candidate does not appear for any of one these tests, his or her name may be removed from the candidate list.

Testing usually begins at a specified date, day, and time. Your admission letter should contain and confirm this information. It is imperative that you keep track of this information. You may have to take a day off from work or schedule a vacation day to accommodate your test date and/or time. Examinations are not always done on a particular day, time, or date.

Once you enter the test site and the doors have been closed, late arrivals may not be allowed to enter the test area and may be disqualified from further testing. Plan to be at the testing site at least 30 minutes before your designated exam time. After all candidates are seated, they will be given a packet of testing material(s). The packet may contain one or more test booklets, answer sheets, and blank paper. Do not open the packet until you are directed to do so by the test administrator or test proctor. If you open the packet before you are instructed to do so, you may be disqualified from further testing. At this time, candidates will be given instructions by the test administrator concerning cell phones, electronic devices, using the restroom, cheating, leaving the test area early, and other general words of advice.

Further instructions may include the amount of time allotted to take the test(s) and possibly reading samples of exam questions with appropriate answers. This lets the candidates know what types of questions to expect and how to respond with the best answers. If the exam has multiple sections, each one may be timed differently. Instructions will be repeated for each part of the examination. If you finish the exam early, review your test for any missed answers or stray marks on the answer sheet(s). Some exam sites may let you leave before the rest of the candidates have finished testing. Ask about this and any questions before the exam has started. Once the examination has begun, you may not be able to ask any questions.

A portion of the exam may include a visual or audio segment. You could be shown a video or have to listen to a tape. Then you may be asked questions about what you've seen or heard. The proctor or test administrator will give you instructions on how to answer the questions. You may be able to take notes and your test administrator will confirm this by giving you a piece of scrap paper. Listen or watch carefully and take down only notes you feel will help you remember important portions of the presentations. When all of the testing is complete, be sure you turn in your notepaper to the proctors.

After the exam is complete, you will be instructed by the test administrator or proctor to turn in the exam materials. Each candidate is responsible for turning in all of the exam materials and signing out with the test administrator or proctor. After the test material is verified, a candidate may leave the examination area and is not allowed to return. Failure to follow instructions could result in the candidate failing the exam.

HOW TO WORK WITH AN ANSWER SHEET

Use a No. 2 pencil to answer all the questions and record your answers on the answer sheet within the allotted time. ONLY YOUR ANSWER SHEET WILL BE MARKED. You will not be permitted to make a copy of the answers.

If you want to change an answer, erase it and then mark your answer sheet with the correct answer. Avoid putting stray pencil marks, dots, or dashes any place on the answer sheet. If you accidentally put a stay mark on the paper, erase it.

You have read the question, selected an answer, and are now ready to mark the answer sheet. Examinations requiring only one selection for each question have rows and columns of answer boxes. It is important for you to closely review the format of the answer sheet. The order of the answers in the row and columns could run laterally across the page from column to column, or they could run vertically down the page, one under another until one column is complete. Usually there will be four (A, B, C, D) or five (A, B, C, D, E) spaces for each question. Use an index card, a piece of scrap paper, or one of the test sheets to cover the answer boxes below the question you will be working on and then mark your selection, being careful not to select a wrong choice or go significantly outside the box you have selected.

Some examiners have developed tests that direct the candidate to select more than one choice for a question. When you are directed to do this, you must carefully look at the answer sheet and, using a technique similar to the one explained above, first record your number one choice in the column or row labeled "1st choice," then your number two choice in the column or row marked "2nd" choice" and then your third choice in the column or row marked "3rd choice."

WARNING—You are not allowed to copy answers from anyone. You may use only books or reference materials the examiner provides you with or materials the examiner has given specific written approval to use.

Sample Answer Sheet

Follow the instructions given in the test. Mark only your answers in the ovals below.

WARNING: Be sure that the oval you fill is in the same row as the question you are answering. Use a No. 2 pencil (soft pencil).

BE SURE YOUR PENCIL MARKS ARE HEAVY AND BLACK. ERASE COMPLETELY ANY ANSWER YOU WISH TO CHANGE.

START HERE

DO NOT make stray pencil dots, dashes, or marks.

1. Ⓐ Ⓑ Ⓒ Ⓓ
2. Ⓐ Ⓑ Ⓒ Ⓓ
3. Ⓐ Ⓑ Ⓒ Ⓓ
4. Ⓐ Ⓑ Ⓒ Ⓓ
5. Ⓐ Ⓑ Ⓒ Ⓓ
6. Ⓐ Ⓑ Ⓒ Ⓓ
7. Ⓐ Ⓑ Ⓒ Ⓓ
8. Ⓐ Ⓑ Ⓒ Ⓓ
9. Ⓐ Ⓑ Ⓒ Ⓓ
10. Ⓐ Ⓑ Ⓒ Ⓓ
11. Ⓐ Ⓑ Ⓒ Ⓓ
12. Ⓐ Ⓑ Ⓒ Ⓓ
13. Ⓐ Ⓑ Ⓒ Ⓓ
14. Ⓐ Ⓑ Ⓒ Ⓓ
15. Ⓐ Ⓑ Ⓒ Ⓓ

HOW TO MAKE THE MOST OF THIS BOOK

To obtain maximum benefit from the use of this book, you should utilize the following approach:

1. Learn the "Strategies for Handling Multiple-Choice Questions," beginning on page 54.
2. Read through the glossary of common fire service terms in Chapter 15. Familiarize yourself with terms that are new to you, but don't spend an excessive amount of time on memorization. Rather, review the terms you do not understand from time to time.
3. Take the sample exam in Chapter 5 and fill out the diagnostic chart. This will indicate your strengths and weaknesses. You can then devote most of your study time to the areas in which you are weak.
4. Study Chapters 4, 6, 7, 8, 11, and 15. Complete practice for each. Concentrate your study efforts on your weak areas, but make certain you cover each chapter. Follow the "Ten Rules for Effective Studying." Also, make sure you employ the test-taking strategies when answering the practice multiple-choice questions.
5. Complete the practice areas in Chapters 12 and 13. Record the date you took this examination and the scores. Examine the questions missed, review, and then retake the practice questions again. Compare your first set of scores. If you didn't do better, review Chapters 2, 4, 6, 7, 8, and page 84.

5

Diagnose Your Problem

You will need someone to assist you with the first part of this sample exam. They will read a short passage to you; then you will begin answering the questions. The person helping you need only be available at the time you start the examination for about five minutes. DO NOT READ THE PASSAGE YOURSELF.

There are 50 questions on this sample exam. There is no time limit. However, for maximum benefit, it is strongly recommended that you take the examination in one sitting, as if it were an actual test. The answers to this examination and their explanations begin on page 80.

Before Taking the Sample Exam

Before taking this exam, you should have read Chapters 2, 4, 6, 7, and 8. Make sure that you employ the test-taking strategy recommended in Chapter 4.

Remember to read each question and related material carefully before choosing your answers. Select the choice you believe to be correct, and mark your answer on the answer sheet provided on page 63. This answer sheet is similar to the one used on the actual exam you will take. The Answer Key, Diagnostic Procedure, and Answer Explanations appear at the end of this chapter.

ANSWER SHEET
Sample Exam

1. (A) (B) (C) (D)
2. (A) (B) (C) (D)
3. (A) (B) (C) (D)
4. (A) (B) (C) (D)
5. (A) (B) (C) (D)
6. (A) (B) (C) (D)
7. (A) (B) (C) (D)
8. (A) (B) (C) (D)
9. (A) (B) (C) (D)
10. (A) (B) (C) (D)
11. (A) (B) (C) (D)
12. (A) (B) (C) (D)
13. (A) (B) (C) (D)
14. (A) (B) (C) (D)
15. (A) (B) (C) (D)
16. (A) (B) (C) (D)
17. (A) (B) (C) (D)
18. (A) (B) (C) (D)
19. (A) (B) (C) (D)
20. (A) (B) (C) (D)
21. (A) (B) (C) (D)
22. (A) (B) (C) (D)
23. (A) (B) (C) (D)
24. (A) (B) (C) (D)
25. (A) (B) (C) (D)
26. (A) (B) (C) (D)
27. (A) (B) (C) (D)
28. (A) (B) (C) (D)
29. (A) (B) (C) (D)
30. (A) (B) (C) (D)
31. (A) (B) (C) (D)
32. (A) (B) (C) (D)
33. (A) (B) (C) (D)
34. (A) (B) (C) (D)
35. (A) (B) (C) (D)
36. (A) (B) (C) (D)
37. (A) (B) (C) (D)
38. (A) (B) (C) (D)
39. (A) (B) (C) (D)
40. (A) (B) (C) (D)
41. (A) (B) (C) (D)
42. (A) (B) (C) (D)
43. (A) (B) (C) (D)
44. (A) (B) (C) (D)
45. (A) (B) (C) (D)
46. (A) (B) (C) (D)
47. (A) (B) (C) (D)
48. (A) (B) (C) (D)
49. (A) (B) (C) (D)
50. (A) (B) (C) (D)

PRACTICE

> **Directions:** Questions 1 through 5 are an oral or listening part of the sample exam. They are intended to measure your ability to hear, understand, and apply information.
>
> At the beginning of this exam have someone READ the passage, slowly and carefully, to you. DO NOT READ THIS PASSAGE YOURSELF.
>
> Immediately after the reading, answer questions 1 through 5 on the basis of the information found in that passage.
>
> **To the assistant:** Please read the following passage aloud. Read slowly and distinctly. Once you start, read through to the end with only normal pauses between paragraphs and punctuation. Do not add additional emphasis or discuss the passage. When you have completed reading the passage, your part of this practice exam is complete. Thank you for your help.

Passage: While fighting fires, firefighters should be alert to identify the possible cause of the fire. It is particularly important to look for signs the fire may have not been started by accident. When a firefighter finds something that indicates the fire did not start accidentally, the fire is said to be suspicious, and the Fire Marshal should be called to conduct an investigation and determine if the crime of arson has been committed. Significant effort should be made to keep the suspected area in the same condition as it was found. Unless absolutely necessary nothing should be moved or altered.

Access to the fire area should be limited to only those firefighters needed to completely extinguish the fire and search for life; no unauthorized person should be allowed to enter the area. The number of firefighters in that area should be kept to a minimum. Firefighters must also refrain from talking about the fire and conditions found. At least one firefighter should be assigned to stay at the scene to protect it from being disturbed until the Fire Marshal arrives. Another firefighter may replace the firefighter if this becomes necessary.

According to the passage:

1. The most likely reason for keeping unauthorized people from entering the fire area is to stop them from

   (A) helping the firefighters at work.
   (B) hurting themselves.
   (C) altering evidence.
   (D) showing identification.

2. At fires where arson is suspected, firefighters should

   (A) stop fighting the fire and call the Fire Marshal.
   (B) avoid disturbing the area and call the Fire Marshal.
   (C) quickly notify the Chief, who will determine if it is arson.
   (D) leave the scene when the fire is out.

3. The person who will most likely do the preliminary fire investigating will be the

    (A) Fire Chief.
    (B) Fire Prevention Inspector.
    (C) firefighter.
    (D) Fire Marshal.

4. When a fire is believed to be "suspicious," the most appropriate person to leave in charge to wait at the scene is the

    (A) police officer.
    (B) firefighter.
    (C) owner.
    (D) Fire Marshal.

5. A fire is said to be suspicious when

    (A) a firefighter finds something that indicates the fire did not start accidentally.
    (B) the fire is burning through the windows as the first units arrive.
    (C) fire is found in the floor and walls of the building.
    (D) the doors and windows are found open.

Recall of Visual Material

Directions: You are given 5 minutes to study the floor plan on the following page and to commit to memory as many details as you can. You are *not* permitted to make any written notes during the 5 minutes you are studying the illustration.

After 5 minutes stop studying the illustration, turn the page, and answer the questions without referring to the illustration. The next time you are permitted to look at the illustration is when you have completed the test and are verifying your answers.

Start your 5 minutes on a clock. Now turn the page and begin.

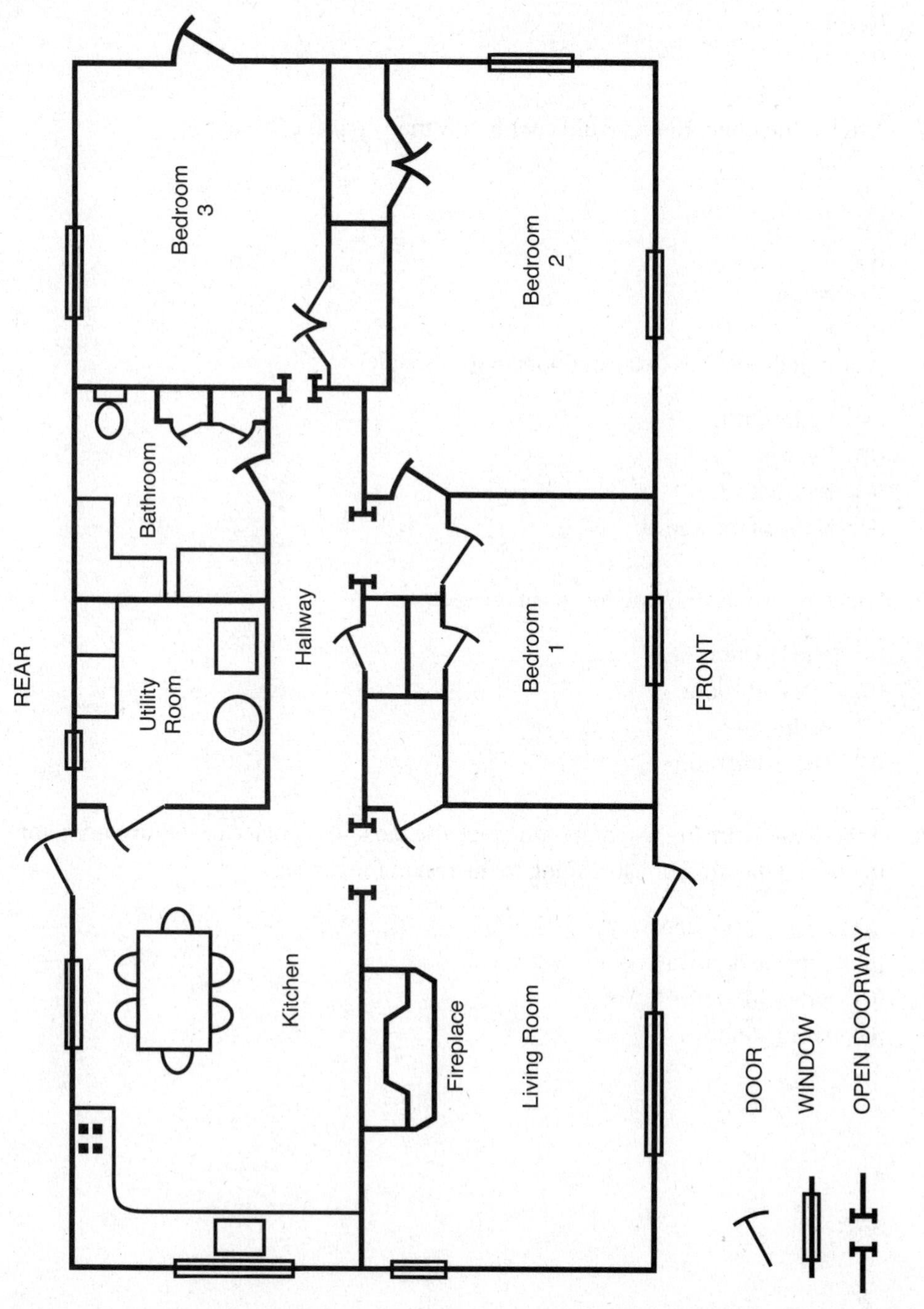

Directions: Answer questions 6 through 15 on the basis of the floor plan you just studied. For each question select the one *best* answer—(A), (B), (C), or (D). Then indicate your choice by blackening the appropriate letter next to the number of the question on the answer sheet provided at the beginning of the chapter.

6. Through how many doors can the Fire Department gain access to the interior of this house?

   (A) 1
   (B) 2
   (C) 3
   (D) 4

7. A fire in the utility room would cut off how many paths of escape?

   (A) 1
   (B) 2
   (C) 3
   (D) None

8. Which bedroom has two exit doors to the outside?

   (A) Bedroom 1.
   (B) Bedroom 2.
   (C) Bedroom 3.
   (D) None of the above.

9. Which room has only one means of escape?

   (A) The kitchen.
   (B) The bathroom.
   (C) Bedroom 1.
   (D) The living room.

10. If there was a fire in the living room, pick the most likely place to set up a hose line to prevent the fire from spreading to the rest of the house.

   (A) Living room doorway.
   (B) Outside doorway.
   (C) Side window.
   (D) Front window.

11. The occupants of how many rooms must first pass through the hall to escape by means of an exit door?

(A) 1
(B) 2
(C) 3
(D) 4

12. In the event of a fire in bedroom 1, burning into the hall, the best escape route for the occupant of bedroom 2 would be through

(A) the hall.
(B) the bathroom window.
(C) the bedroom 1 window.
(D) a bedroom 2 window.

13. If a fire occurred in the kitchen, it would be most likely to extend into the

(A) hall.
(B) bathroom.
(C) dining room.
(D) porch.

14. Which room cannot be reached directly from the hallway?

(A) The bathroom.
(B) Bedroom 2.
(C) Utility room.
(D) All rooms can be reached from the hall.

15. Escape from a fire in the living room may be made via how many possible ways?

(A) 2
(B) 3
(C) 4
(D) 5

IF THERE IS STILL TIME REMAINING, you may review your answers.

Reading Comprehension

Directions: The questions in this section test your ability to comprehend what you read. After reading each passage carefully, answer the questions that follow it, using only the information in the passage. For each question choose the one *best* answer—(A), (B), (C), or (D). Then indicate your choice by blackening the appropriate letter next to the number of the question on the answer sheet provided at the beginning of the chapter.

Answer questions 16 through 20 using only the information in the following passage.

Ladder Safety

The safe use of ladders is an everyday problem, and with good weather and the need for work on and about the home, the use of ladders by off-duty department members will increase. However, there seems to be a certain amount of Missouri-mule stubbornness in every individual when it comes to using any kind of ladder; a large percentage of us will go to great lengths to misuse them. As a result, we end up with broken bones, cracked heads, mashed noses, and a general assortment of cuts and bruises. All of the above result in the loss of a member's services to the Fire Department.

Unfortunately, most ladder accidents occur as a result of overconfidence on the part of the member. A few helpful hints on correct ladder usage follow:

Stepladders

1. Always open the ladder wide enough so that the spreader locks itself in the open position.
2. Never stand on top of a stepladder; use a ladder tall enough to let you stand at least two steps from the top.
3. Always make sure that the feet of the ladder are on a firm, level foundation.
4. Never lean a stepladder against a wall and use it as a straight ladder.

Straight and Extension Portable Ladders

1. When setting up a ladder, place it so that the horizontal distance from its base to the vertical plane of the support is approximately one-fourth the ladder length. (For example, place a 12-foot ladder so that the bottom is approximately 3 feet away from the object against which the top is leaning.)
2. Set the ladder on a firm foundation. Make sure that it does not wobble before you climb it.
3. Never place a ladder against a windowpane, a window sash, or a loose box, barrel, etc.
4. When using a ladder for access to a high place, securely lash or otherwise fasten it to prevent slipping.
5. Be aware that it is not advisable to use a metal ladder in close proximity to live electric wiring.
6. Do not climb higher than the third rung from the top on a straight or an extension ladder.

All Portable Ladders

1. Make sure that the ladder is equipped with a nonslip base.
2. Resist the temptation to overreach. It is better to get down and move the ladder.
3. Always face the ladder when ascending or descending.
4. Hold on with both hands when climbing up or down. Use a rope to raise or lower tools or equipment.
5. Never use defective ladders. When a defective ladder is found, it should be destroyed immediately. Many people have been injured by using a ladder retrieved from a junk pile. Resist the urge to patch a ladder with wire or makeshift steps or rungs "until another one can be obtained."

16. Which of the following statements about ladder safety is *incorrect?*

    (A) Never lean a stepladder against a wall and use it as a straight ladder.
    (B) The base of the ladder should be a distance equal to one-fourth the length of the ladder from the wall when in position.
    (C) The top two steps of a stepladder may be used only if the ladder is less than 5 feet high.
    (D) The stepladder should always be opened sufficiently to engage the spreader locks.

17. The improper use of ladders around the home leads to injuries and loss of ability to perform as a firefighter. Injuries commonly result from all of the following *except*

    (A) overreaching.
    (B) not holding on properly.
    (C) using a rope to raise and lower tools.
    (D) using a metal ladder in proximity to live electrical wiring.

18. For safety, the ladder should be

    (A) placed against the window sash.
    (B) brand new.
    (C) made of heavy metal.
    (D) set on a firm foundation.

19. When using a straight or extension ladder, the highest rung that should be climbed to is the

    (A) next to the top.
    (B) second from the top.
    (C) third from the top.
    (D) fourth from the top.

20. There seems to be a certain amount of stubbornness in every individual when it comes to ladder safety. It would be correct to say that

    (A) few accidents occur because of overconfidence.
    (B) most injuries caused by improper use of ladders are minor.
    (C) most firefighters hold on with one hand while climbing ladders.
    (D) many people have been injured by using ladders they found in a junk pile.

Directions: Answer questions 21 through 25 using only the information in the following passage.

Smoking

Smoking in bed is a dangerous habit. Cigarette, cigar, or pipe ashes often fall undetected and smolder in the upholstery or bedding while the smoker sleeps. Hours later, the hidden fire results in deadly smoke that overcomes the smoker and often other people as well. Falling asleep in a comfortable overstuffed chair or on a couch while smoking can have the same deadly results.

It is important to keep a sufficient number of ashtrays in areas of the home where smoking is permitted. The ashtrays should be large, deep, and designed to prevent cigarettes or cigars from accidentally falling out. After you light your cigarette, the burning match should be extinguished and placed in the ashtray. Paper, empty matchbooks, and cellophane wrappers should not be put in the ashtray. Ashtrays should be emptied frequently, but never into wastebaskets. To properly dispose of the contents of ashtrays, you should douse them with water and put them into a metal container.

21. Falling asleep in an overstuffed chair while smoking a pipe is

    (A) all right if there is a large ashtray nearby.
    (B) not as dangerous as smoking in bed.
    (C) as deadly as smoking in bed.
    (D) much more dangerous than smoking in bed.

22. Ashtrays should be

    (A) kept in every room.
    (B) made of paper.
    (C) emptied into wastebaskets.
    (D) large and deep.

23. Smoking in bed is deadly because

    (A) smoke replaces the air and kills the smoker.
    (B) smoke damages the drapes and ruins the bed.
    (C) the cigarette burns the person in the bed.
    (D) the ash would start a fire in the smoker's clothes.

24. The contents of a properly used ashtray may include all of the following *except*

    (A) cigarette butts.
    (B) matches.
    (C) cigarette wrappers.
    (D) cigar ashes.

25. The preferred method for disposing of the materials in an ashtray is to

 (A) douse them with water and put them into a metal container.
 (B) empty them into a wastepaper basket.
 (C) throw them out the window.
 (D) place them in a plastic garbage bag.

Directions: Answer questions 26 through 28 using only the information in the following passage.

On the fire ground, who is responsible for making the decisions? It is the officer in command, regardless of rank. The first officer on the scene is in command until relieved by a superior; the officer may be a captain, lieutenant, or acting officer. He has the responsibility for making and carrying out initial decisions. Therefore all officers should be trained in the use of an effective action plan that is practical for all ranks at all types of fires.

26. The writer of this passage believes that

 (A) all firefighters should be trained as officers.
 (B) captains and lieutenants need to be reminded of their firefighting responsibilities.
 (C) only senior fire officers have fire-ground command responsibility.
 (D) all officers should be trained to implement an effective fire-ground action plan.

27. The officer in command, until relieved by a superior, is the first

 (A) officer to arrive.
 (B) lieutenant to arrive.
 (C) captain to arrive.
 (D) chief officer to arrive.

28. An effective action plan should be drawn up to handle

 (A) unusual types of fires.
 (B) dangerous types of fires.
 (C) all types of fires.
 (D) some types of fires.

Directions: Answer questions 29 and 30 using only the information given.

29. Without proper breathing equipment, you should never attempt to fight a fire in a cellar or basement that has become filled with smoke. The products of combustion may be poisonous, and the lack of oxygen may quickly overcome you.

    According to this information, you

    (A) should never extinguish a fire in a cellar.
    (B) should not fight a fire in a smoke-filled cellar without proper equipment.
    (C) can overcome the fumes produced by a cellar fire.
    (D) should attempt to fight a fire in a smoke-filled basement once all the smoke is removed.

30. School fire drills should be held early in the term, and should be well planned and frequently rehearsed. They should be conducted as surprise drills, without prior warning to the teaching staff.

    The theme of this short passage is

    (A) surprise fire drills should be held in schools.
    (B) school fire drills should be held early in the day.
    (C) frequent fire drills surprise teachers.
    (D) teachers won't drill without prior warning.

Directions: Answer questions 31 through 35 using only the information in the following passage.

To understand the role of a firefighter, it is first necessary to understand the mission of the fire service. The objectives of the fire service fall into four broad categories. In order of priority, they are as follows:

1. Prevent unwanted fires.
2. Prevent loss of life and property when a fire does occur.
3. Confine the fire to its place of origin.
4. Control and extinguish the fire.

We prevent fires by doing something about the factors that cause them. These causes are usually hazardous and unstable materials, improper use of materials, and human carelessness. The hazards are removed by enforcing laws and educating the public.

The prevention of loss of life and property is accomplished by enforcing building and fire prevention codes. These codes require a sufficient number of properly lighted and marked exits, limits on the number of occupants, and control over the kinds of materials used in construction, as well as those that may be brought into the building after it is occupied. The fire department reduces the loss of life by making rescues, confining the fire to allow people to get out, and extinguishing the fire.

When a fire does start, damage can be limited by rapid extinguishment. However, if the fire can be prevented, there will be no property damage and no loss of life.

31. What title best fits the theme of this passage?

    (A) Preventing Fires
    (B) Rescue and Firefighting
    (C) The Objectives of the Fire Service
    (D) The Extinguishment of Fire

32. What is the most important objective of the fire service?

    (A) Fire prevention
    (B) Firefighting
    (C) Fire education
    (D) Fire control and confinement

33. The prevention of fire is accomplished by

    (A) understanding the role of the firefighter.
    (B) doing something about the factors that cause fires.
    (C) making rescues and confining and extinguishing the fire.
    (D) rapid extinguishment.

34. To understand the role of a firefighter, you must

    (A) study firefighting and fire prevention guides.
    (B) know the responsibilities of the fire service.
    (C) experience the daily work of a firefighter.
    (D) have extinguished a fire or saved a life.

35. After a fire starts, damage can be limited by

    (A) restricting the number of people who enter the area.
    (B) using less water.
    (C) rapid extinguishment.
    (D) none of the above; extensive damage cannot be avoided.

Directions: Answer questions 36 through 38 solely on the basis of the following table.

FLAMMABLE LIQUIDS

Material	Flash Point (degrees F)	Ignition Temperature (degrees F)	Upper Flammable Limit (percent)
Gasoline (100 octane)	-36	853	7.4
Acetone	0	869	12.8
Benzene	12	1,040	7.1
Ethyl alcohol	55	689	19.0

36. The flammable liquid with the lowest ignition temperature is

    (A) gasoline.
    (B) acetone.
    (C) benzene.
    (D) ethyl alcohol.

37. The flash point of benzene is

    (A) 0 degree.
    (B) 12 degrees.
    (C) 35 degrees.
    (D) 55 degrees.

38. If the flash point indicates how dangerous a substance may be by telling us at what temperature the liquid will change into an ignitable gas, the most dangerous substance on the list is

    (A) ethyl alcohol.
    (B) benzene.
    (C) acetone.
    (D) gasoline.

Directions: Answer questions 39 and 40 using only the information given.

39. Most fire departments require firefighters to be fully dressed and equipped before boarding the apparatus for response. What is the main reason for this rule?

    (A) Dressing while responding has proved to be dangerous.
    (B) Unprepared firefighters arriving at a fire scene make a poor impression.
    (C) The probability of leaving important safety equipment in quarters is reduced.
    (D) The possibility of dropping or damaging equipment while responding is reduced.

40. "Firefighters assigned to housewatch duty shall remain at the housewatch desk at all times, except when it is necessary to observe conditions in front of quarters. In the event a relief is required for any purpose, the officer on duty shall be notified." According to the passage, it would be correct to say that:

(A) the firefighter on housewatch can never leave quarters.
(B) the lieutenant on duty relieves the housewatch.
(C) firefighters and officers shall do housewatch.
(D) if a relief is needed, the officer on duty must be notified.

Directions: Answer questions 41 through 45 using only the information in the following passage.

Firefighters shall execute the salute in the following manner:

1. It shall be executed at attention in accordance with infantry drill regulations of the U.S. Army.
2. It shall be executed within six paces of the person saluted, or at the nearest point of approach. The salute shall be held until the person saluted has passed, or until the salute has been properly acknowledged.
3. In passing in review at parades or in other formations, the hand salute shall be executed only by the commanding officer, members of the staff, or officers in command of integral units. All others in formation shall, on command, execute "EYES RIGHT" or "EYES LEFT." The hand salute is executed within six paces of the reviewing party, and is held as the march is continued in rigid formation past the reviewing party.
4. Six paces beyond the reviewing party, arms and hands are snapped to the position of attention. Officers in command of integral units shall issue the command "FRONT," at which time heads and eyes are returned to the normal position, and the march is continued in formation at attention. At formal reviews or parades, the boundaries of the reviewing stand are usually marked by guidons.

41. Firefighters should salute

(A) all officers.
(B) at 12 paces.
(C) at the nearest point of approach.
(D) after another member has saluted them.

42. While passing in review at parades, the hand salute should be executed by

(A) all members.
(B) commanding officers only.
(C) commanding officers and staff officers.
(D) commanding officers, staff officers, and officers in command of integral units.

43. The command “FRONT” is used to have the members turn their

(A) heads and eyes to the normal position.
(B) heads toward the reviewing stand.
(C) march formation toward the reviewing stand.
(D) march formation toward the guidons.

44. While passing in review, it is correct to execute the salute

(A) three paces from the reviewing stand.
(B) six paces from the reviewing stand.
(C) at the reviewing stand.
(D) at the guidons.

45. Arms and hands are snapped to the position of attention

(A) after passing in review.
(B) six paces beyond the guidons.
(C) after passing a superior officer.
(D) at formal parades.

Directions: Questions 46 through 50 test your ability to make sound judgments and decisions. For each question, select the most correct answer—(A), (B), (C), or (D). Then indicate your choice by blackening the appropriate letter next to the number of the question on the answer sheet provided at the beginning of the chapter.

46. While searching burning homes or apartments, firefighters make a practice of checking inside closets, under beds, and behind furniture. What is the most likely reason for this practice?

(A) The cause of the fire could be found there.
(B) Valuable possessions may be found there.
(C) Children and pets often hide in these places.
(D) This is routine in search and rescue operations.

47. The fire officer in command of operations has the responsibility of analyzing and evaluating the fire problem. Which of the following would not enter into this process?

(A) The occupancy of the burning building.
(B) The fire insurance coverage.
(C) The time of day.
(D) The height and area of the building.

48. A firefighter who had just arrived at the scene of a visible fire grabbed his tools from the apparatus, ran to the door of the building, and broke it down. The action of the firefighter was

(A) correct — this allowed the firefighters with the hose to gain entry and extinguish the fire.
(B) incorrect — the firefighter should have broken a window first.
(C) correct — quick, decisive action leads to the rescue of fire victims.
(D) incorrect — the firefighter should have tried the doorknob first to see whether the door was locked.

49. While riding on a train, you smell and see heavy smoke coming into the car through the windows. The *best* action you could take would be to

(A) ask the passengers to close their windows.
(B) tell everyone to vacate the car and go to the last car in the train.
(C) get up quietly, leave the car, and find the conductor.
(D) go quietly to the front of the car, pull the emergency stop cord, and direct the people to leave the train.

50. Firefighters are trained to carry an axe with the head up and the blade facing forward. Which answer best describes how the firefighter is carrying the ax in the illustration below?

(A) incorrectly — the firefighter should be using two hands.
(B) correctly — this position is safest.
(C) incorrectly — the blade should be nearer the ground.
(D) correctly — the axe is lighter this way.

IF THERE IS STILL TIME REMAINING, you may review your answers.

ANSWER KEY AND EXPLANATIONS

Answer Key

1. **(C)**	11. **(C)**	21. **(C)**	31. **(A)**	41. **(C)**
2. **(B)**	12. **(D)**	22. **(D)**	32. **(A)**	42. **(D)**
3. **(D)**	13. **(A)**	23. **(A)**	33. **(B)**	43. **(A)**
4. **(B)**	14. **(C)**	24. **(C)**	34. **(B)**	44. **(B)**
5. **(A)**	15. **(C)**	25. **(A)**	35. **(C)**	45. **(B)**
6. **(C)**	16. **(C)**	26. **(D)**	36. **(D)**	46. **(C)**
7. **(A)**	17. **(C)**	27. **(A)**	37. **(B)**	47. **(B)**
8. **(D)**	18. **(D)**	28. **(C)**	38. **(D)**	48. **(D)**
9. **(B)**	19. **(C)**	29. **(B)**	39. **(A)**	49. **(A)**
10. **(A)**	20. **(D)**	30. **(A)**	40. **(D)**	50. **(B)**

Answer Explanations

1. **(C)** The occupant could accidentally kick or move potential evidence or could intentionally move or hide evidence to cover up a crime they committed. Choice A is incorrect. Firefighters try to work with the occupants and owners and generally accept their help; however, generally this is not done until after the fire has been extinguished and the scene is safe. Choice B is incorrect because the fire scene is dangerous and civilian and unauthorized personnel are not trained nor do they have the appropriate safety clothing equipment to work in these areas. Choice D is incorrect. Even if the occupants properly identify themselves, they would not be allowed to enter an area that has been declared suspicious.

2. **(B)** Choice A is incorrect because they should call the Fire Marshal but *not* stop fighting the fire. If they don't put the fire out, they may destroy the evidence and allow additional damage to occur. Choice C is incorrect. The Fire Marshal will determine if it is arson. Choice D is incorrect because a firefighter should remain at the scene to protect it until the Fire Marshal arrives.

3. **(D)** This is stated in the first paragraph.

4. **(B)** This is stated in the last two sentences of the passage.

5. **(A)** This is found in the third sentence of the first paragraph. Choice B is incorrect because fire burning through the windows is a common event at fires. Choice C is incorrect. Fire often burns in and behind walls and ceilings. Choice D is incorrect; it is normal for people to leave windows and doors open.

6. **(C)** Living room, kitchen, and bedroom 3.

7. **(A)** The kitchen.

8. **(D)** None of the above. Bedrooms 1 and 2 have only one exit door. Bedroom 3 has an open exit passage to the hall and one exit door. The correct choice is D.

9. **(B)** Bathroom—it does not have a window.

10. **(A)** This protects the rest of the house; any of the other positions could push the fire into the hall.

11. **(C)** Bedrooms 1 and 2 and the bathroom. All other rooms contain exit doors or lead to exits without passing through a hallway.

12. **(D)** This would be the safest. Trying to get out of the door may expose the occupant to heat and smoke.

13. **(A)** The kitchen leads into the hall and the living room (not a choice). The only acceptable choice available to you is the hall.

14. **(C)** All rooms except the utility room can be reached from the hall.

15. **(C)** There are two doors and two windows in the living room.

16. **(C)** In item 2 under "Stepladders," a clear statement indicates that the top must never be used, and that a person should be at least two steps below the top to be safe. No mention is made of the height of the ladder.

17. **(C)** Under the heading "All Portable Ladders," item 4, an instruction tells us to use two hands to climb the ladder, and to raise or lower tools with a rope. Using a rope to raise and lower tools is a correct procedure, which does not result in injuries.

18. **(D)** In this case, item 2 of "Straight and Extension Portable Ladders" tells us to make sure the ladder is placed on a firm foundation. Choice A is incorrect. Choice B may be a correct statement, but it is not mentioned or implied in the passage. It is therefore not an acceptable choice. Choice C is incorrect—wood and metal ladders can be safe, although metal ladders can be unsafe around electricity.

19. **(C)** This fact is found in item 6 of "Straight and Extension Ladders."

20. **(D)** Most ladder accidents occur because of overconfidence, ruling out Choice A. Choice B is incorrect in view of the broken bones, cracked heads, and mashed noses mentioned in the passage. Choice C is not indicated in the passage and therefore is not acceptable.

21. **(C)** The last sentence in the first paragraph tells us that smoking in an overstuffed chair can have the same results as smoking in bed.

22. **(D)** While the passage tells us that the "ashtray should be large, deep, and designed to prevent cigarettes . . . from accidentally falling out," the examiner can, and often will, give in the question only part of the statement.

23. **(A)** The question asks why smoking is deadly, and choice A is the only one that answers it. Choices B and C may be true, but they are not mentioned in the passage. Choice D may or may not occur.

24. **(C)** The second paragraph in the passage states that "paper, empty matchbooks, and cellophane wrappers should not be put in the ashtray."

25. **(A)** This is explained in the last sentence of the second paragraph.

26. **(D)** This is found in the last sentence.

27. **(A)** This is stated in the second sentence of the passage.

28. **(C)** The last sentence of the paragraph gives this information. Although you should be skeptical of the word *all,* the author clearly used it in the passage.

29. **(B)** This answer is given in the opening statement of the passage. Choice A is incorrect—you should put out the fire. C is incorrect—you generally will not be able to overcome the fumes, and these fumes will overcome you. D is incorrect—you should not delay the attack if proper protective equipment is available.

30. **(A)** This answer reflects the two main themes of the passage: hold drills and conduct surprise drills. Choice B—not early in the day, but early in the term. Choice C—the drill itself should surprise the teacher, not the frequency of the drills. Choice D—teachers comply with training drills; in many states this is law.

31. **(A)** The subject of prevention is stressed by the author in every paragraph. The opening paragraph indicates fire prevention as the number 1 priority, and the last passage ends with a strong statement on prevention.

32. **(A)** This is stated in the first paragraph. In the priority order this is number 1.

33. **(B)** This is the opening statement of the second paragraph. If you chose Choice D—you probably made this selection based upon your own knowledge about the practice of fire fighting, and not the information in the passage. You must avoid the temptation to do this.

34. **(B)** In the first paragraph, the author states, " . . . it is first necessary to understand the mission of the fire service." The other three choices may be helpful, but are not mentioned in the passage.

35. **(C)** This statement is found in the last paragraph. Choices A and B are not mentioned in the reading. If you chose D, you misread the question and answer choice. The stem refers to limiting the damage, not avoiding it.

36. **(D)** Locate the column titled "Ignition Temp.," then read down the column and find the lowest temperature—689. Now, using the straight edge of a piece of paper placed immediately below the lowest temperature, read across to the column marked "Material." This is your answer.

37. **(B)** This answer may be obtained in a manner similar to that used for answer 36.

38. **(D)** Gasoline emits a vapor at –36 degrees. This means that it will ignite under almost all normal conditions and climates.

39. **(A)** Trying to dress while riding on a speeding fire apparatus is unsafe.

40. **(D)** This answer is clearly indicated in the last sentence of the paragraph. Choice A is incorrect because the firefighter may leave to check the front of quarters. Choice B is incorrect, as the lieutenant is notified, but he does not relieve. Choice C is incorrect because the first sentence indicates that only firefighters stand housewatch.

41. **(C)** The answer is stated in item 2—only information that is clearly stated should be used, unless otherwise indicated.

42. **(D)** This is clearly spelled out in item 3. You must be careful with this type of question, which can be very confusing. To help reduce the confusion, first find the relevant section in the passage and number each occurrence. Then go through each choice, making absolutely sure that it agrees with what you have identified in the passage.

43. **(A)** The command "FRONT" is used to cancel a prior command of either "EYES RIGHT" or "EYES LEFT" (see item 4).

44. **(B)** This is explained in the last sentence of item 3.

45. **(B)** This question requires a somewhat closer reading of the passage. The beginning of item 4 indicates that at a point six paces beyond the reviewing party, the salute is dropped and one marches at attention. However, the last sentence describes the boundaries of the reviewing stand as being marked by guidons.

46. **(C)** Children commonly use these areas as places of safety to hide from something that frightens them. It is not uncommon, therefore, for them to retreat there during a fire.

47. **(B)** This is a factor to be considered after the fire has been determined to be of suspicious origin.

48. **(D)** No time is lost in trying the doorknob. If it opens, entry will be faster and safer, and will result in less property damage. *Note:* Choice C is true, but does not relate directly to the stem of this question. The question concerns itself with the method of opening the door.

49. **(A)** This will establish the firefighter as a qualified, knowledgeable leader, and will reduce the possibility of panic, as well as controlling the smoke in the car. The train can proceed to the station, which is the safest and best place to disembark.

50. **(B)** The illustration shows the safest and most appropriate method for a fireman to carry the axe. It allows the other hand to remain free to handle doors or obstructions, and maintains control of the cutting blade. If you chose D, you may have thought that it was easier to carry the axe this way because it was balanced. However, the statement is that the axe is lighter. No matter how the axe is carried, the weight will not change.

After you have taken the test and checked your answers, it is important to find out why you didn't get some questions correct, and to identify your weak areas. When you know the areas you are weak in, you can then allocate your study and preparation time to these areas, which will give you the maximum rate of return on your investment (your time and your work).

There are many reasons why test takers, like you, get questions wrong. Most of them are correctable once you know why you are getting the question wrong. Following are some of the prominent reasons for why you may be getting questions wrong and techniques for improving your chances for getting more of them right.

1. Marking the answer you choose in the wrong space on the answer sheet.
2. Reading into the question or answering the question you wanted them to ask and not the question they did ask. That is, you didn't read the question carefully; instead you mentally jumped ahead and answered the question on what you thought it was going to say. You read too fast or without paying enough attention. This is a common error when you are very sure of yourself and when you are in a hurry. You are devoting a lot of time and energy into getting the position you want. Slow down and make sure you know what the questions are asking for.
3. Not reading the directions and asking questions about instructions you do not understand. This is the easiest to correct. You will be given time to read the instructions; make good use of this time and, when you are not sure about the meaning of the instructions, ask the person in charge to explain it to you.
4. Losing focus on what was being asked. Underlining can help with this problem. As you read the question, lightly underline the key words and phrases. This will help you to focus in on them and will allow you to refer to them rapidly.
5. Not understanding of the meaning of a word. To reduce this problem, you need to expand your vocabulary. Read and study the chapter on understanding Fire Service Terminology and expand your reading of newspapers, magazines and books. It is important for you to mark the words you don't understand and then look them up in a dictionary to find out what they mean. Doing this not only helps you to improve your understanding of what you read, but helps to lock the new word into your memory.
6. Becoming overwhelmed by long and confusing questions. You may not be accustomed to reading, deciphering, and organizing the information being provided. This requires practices and technique.
7. And finally the most frustrating problem of all—not knowing or being able to find a clue as to why you are getting the questions wrong. For this you will need help from another person: a teacher, friend, parent, or firefighter.

Handling Recall, Visualization, and Spatial Orientation Questions

6

This chapter will help you develop your ability to handle questions involving recall. There are three basic types of recall questions: those that test your ability to recall what you have seen, those that test your ability to recall what you have read, and those that test what you hear. For questions of this type, each item of pictorial or written material is presented in a separate booklet (we will call this a "memory booklet"), which you are permitted to study for a specified time. It is then collected, and you must answer the questions.

Since the purpose of these questions is to test your ability to concentrate and recall, the only notes you can make are mental notes. For this reason it is very important that you become familiar with these types of questions and develop a procedure for handling them.

STRATEGIES FOR RECALLING PICTORIAL DETAILS

Let's look first at how you can handle visual materials. In this question type you will be given a sketch, picture, or other illustrative material to study for a period of time ranging from 5 to 20 minutes. Five minutes may not sound like much time, but it will be more than enough if you apply the strategies outlined below. You are *not* permitted to write anything down at this point; all details and observations must be kept in your mind. When the time period is up, the illustrative material will be collected and you will not be able to refer to it again.

The sketch, picture, or diagram you are given will not be extremely complicated, and your objective will be to form a clear image of the material in your mind. To do this requires a strategy, concentration, and some practice.

1. **DEVELOP A STANDARDIZED METHOD OF STUDYING THE VISUAL MATERIAL.** If you want to remember the details of pictures, sketches, diagrams, you must look at them in an organized fashion. It is a mistake to think that just staring at the material will record all the details in your mind. You must be methodical, and you must practice.

   In the fire service this is called "size-up"; the term refers to mental evaluation of the fire situation while giving consideration to many different factors. To make this process routine, most new firefighters are taught some mnemonic (memory-improving) devices to aid them in handling these many factors. One effective mnemonic is "COAL WAS WEALTH," which stands for the most important 13 points of the size-up.

   Although you will not be sizing up fires just yet, this mnemonic device can be easily learned and will prove very helpful. Before we look at the 13 points, however, let's analyze the mechanics of studying pictorial material.

   First, look at the sketch, picture, or diagram as a whole and try to get a feeling for what is shown and what is going on.

   Now begin to scan for details. When the U.S. Army, Navy, or Coast Guard conducts an air search, it uses a number of specific search patterns. One of these, the "parallel track pattern," provides an excellent method of identifying all the details. This pattern is used when

   (1) the search area is large and relatively level;
   (2) uniform coverage is desired;
   (3) information about the area is limited;
   (4) the area is rectangular or square.

   These criteria meet your situation: the visual material you will be observing will be level, you will want uniform coverage, you will not have any previous information about the material, and its shape will be rectangular or square.

   There are three steps to applying the parallel track pattern:

   a. Starting in an upper corner (left or right, depending on which way is most comfortable for you), identify, in your mind, each item as you scan across the picture.

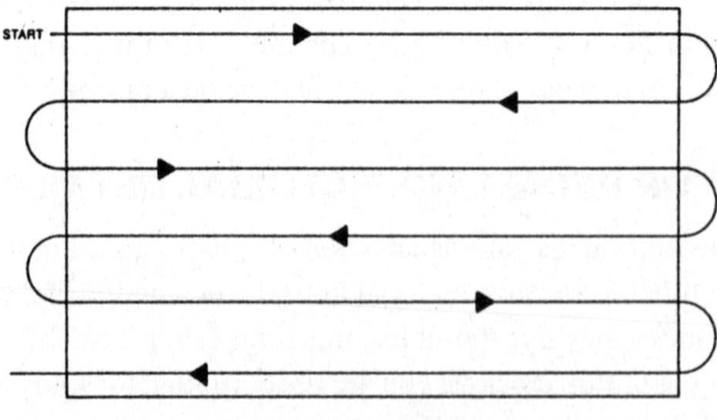

Parallel Track Pattern

b. Now repeat the process, but this time add these steps:
   (1) Count repeated items such as windows, doors, and safety devices, and keep a mental tally for each item.
   (2) Observe carefully all readable material—street signs, addresses, room identifications, and exit signs.

c. Repeat the first step; that is, look with concentration at the material as a whole.

2. **APPLY THE MEMORY AID: "COAL WAS WEALTH."** As explained earlier, the mnemonic "COAL WAS WEALTH" refers to 13 specific factors critical to most fire operations and emergencies. They have been adapted here for use with recall questions.

   The first letter of each of the 13 points is represented by a letter of "coal was wealth," as follows:

   C = Construction. What is the building made of: wood, brick, concrete? What are the building features: roof, windows, doors, fire escapes, etc.?

   O = Occupancy. What is the building or area used for: residence, factory, sales area, hospital, etc.? How many people are there? Where are they?

   A = Area. How large is the building or area: number of stories high, estimate the width and length of the sides of the building, then multiply them (round off your estimates to make multiplication easy) and you will have an approximate size of the floor area.

   L = Life. Is a life in danger? If so, where? Is escape possible? If so, how? If no life hazard is present, what are the most dangerous locations?

   W = Weather. What are the weather conditions, and what effect might they have? Is it raining, snowing, cold, or warm? Would the windows be open or closed? Would the heat be on?

   A = Auxiliary Appliances. Is there a sprinkler system or a standpipe hose system? Are there portable fire extinguishers?

   S = Size. How many rooms are there? How do they differ? How many apartments are there? How many doors are there? How many windows are there? Where are the hallways?

   W = Water. Is a water supply available to extinguish the fire: a fire hydrant, a water tank on the roof, or a swimming pool to draft from?

   E = Exposures. What surrounds the possible fire area (look at the floor above the fire area and at the adjoining building)? If the fire spreads, where will it go?

   A = Apparatus. Can the fire apparatus get close to the fire or are there obstructions: overhead wires, trees, parked cars, narrow streets or alleys?

   L = Location. In what area or room is the fire burning? How could the occupant get out? How could the firefighter get in to save a life or to extinguish the fire?

   T = Time. What time is it: dusk, night, early morning, midday? What would the occupants be doing: eating dinner, sleeping, getting ready for work, working?

   H = Height. How high is the fire area above the ground level? Could the occupant(s) be reached by ladders?

3. **STUDY LISTS METHODICALLY.** When you are given an illustration that contains a series of numbered or labeled items, you must take time to go through each item and identify what it relates to. There are two techniques for doing this. The first is to go through the numbers or items in sequential order. This method ensures that no item is missed but sometimes leads to jumping around the illustration in haphazard fashion. The second method is to identify items while following a geometrical pat-

tern. A common pattern is to start at the outer border and go around in a spiral until you reach the center and have identified all the items.

If the number of items is limited, try to develop a simple key word or phrase, that is, a mnemonic device, to help you remember them.

STRATEGIES FOR RECALLING WRITTEN MATERIAL

Questions based on written material are not as difficult as you may think, since the material is never complicated or hard to understand. Performance on this test area, perhaps more than on any other, can be improved significantly by practice. If you follow the guidelines listed below, you should be able to do very well on this part of your examination.

1. **DON'T JUST READ THE MATERIAL; BECOME PART OF IT!** When you are reading, you must clear your mind of everything except the material at hand. You *must concentrate.* The kind of intense concentration that is needed is best achieved by "putting yourself into the story." Create a mental picture of what you are reading. For example, in reading about stepladder safety on the Diagnostic Test, you should have pictured yourself setting the ladder on a firm foundation, opening it until the spreader locked, and then ascending no farther than the second step from the top.
2. **RELATE THE UNKNOWN TO THE KNOWN.** You will find it easier to "put yourself into the story" if you create mental images involving people, places, and things that you are familiar with.
3. **DON'T TRY TO MEMORIZE THE ENTIRE PASSAGE.** Some people attempt to memorize the material verbatim. For most of us this is an impossible task. The trick is to identify the key facts and to remember them. All the examiner is interested in is how well you recall vital information.
4. **DON'T STOP CONCENTRATING WHEN THE BOOKLETS ARE COLLECTED.** The time between the closing of the memory booklet and the answering of the questions is the most critical. Be sure that you maintain your concentration during this time. Many inexperienced test takers forget what they read during these few minutes.
5. **AS SOON AS YOU ARE PERMITTED, WRITE DOWN EVERYTHING YOU RECALL FROM THE WRITTEN MATERIAL.** After the memory booklet is collected, there will be a delay before you are allowed to open the actual test booklet and begin taking the examination. This is the time during which you must continue to concentrate. However, once the signal is given to begin the examination, don't read the first question immediately. Instead, quickly write in a blank space in your test booklet all the details you can remember or simply make a quick sketch. Only after you have done this should you start answering the memory questions, which usually come early in the examination.
6. **USE ASSOCIATIONS TO HELP YOU REMEMBER.** Rote memory will not suffice in most cases; you must make associations to help you remember. The technique is to associate or relate what you are trying to remember *to something you already know* or that you find easy to remember. The type of association that is made will vary tremendously from individual to individual, depending on background, interests, and imagination. Some experts say "far out" associations are best; others recommend associations with familiar things. You must find what works best for you.

   Association is an area where practice will help you greatly. For this purpose your daily newspaper will do just fine. Study a one-column news story for about 10 minutes, relate it to something you know, and then put the paper down. Now list the details you can remember.

7. **CONSTANTLY ASK YOURSELF QUESTIONS ABOUT THE MATERIAL AS YOU READ.** This will help you remember details, especially if you try to anticipate the questions you may be asked. Note that you can be fairly certain of being asked to compare items and to identify items in groups. If an illustration is included, make sure to identify all items in the illustration and to observe all references to them in the passage.

DEVELOPING OBSERVATION SKILLS

There is only one known way to improve your skills in observation: practice, practice, and more practice!

During the course of our lives we are continuously bombarded with different sights, sounds, and smells. Some of these become fixed in our minds, whereas others are disregarded. The stimuli associated with pleasurable experiences are easy to recall. Unconsciously we have committed them to memory; if necessary, we could recall these stimuli in great detail.

For some people it is very easy to remember large quantities of information in great detail, but for others it is very difficult. If you have difficulty in recalling information, do not despair. Through practice you too can become proficient in this area.

The first step is to be aware of your surroundings and what is happening in them. You can become skilled at observing by (1) making a deliberate effort to do so, and (2) asking yourself questions about your environment and the daily changes in it. The questions you must begin to consciously ask are *who, what, when, where, why,* and *how*.

Try this exercise: On a sheet of paper, using only the information in your mind, draw the layout of your home. How many windows are there? What is the safest way to exit? What other ways are there for you to escape? What does the floor or apartment layout immediately above or below you look like? Now answer these questions: What hazardous materials are stored in your home? When was the last time you held a fire drill in your home? When was the last time you checked the smoke detectors?

Asking yourself questions about your immediate surroundings is the first step. Now extend your range of observation. While on the way to work or other activities, stop and look at one or two buildings, using the parallel track pattern to scan the area quickly yet thoroughly. Your next step is to use the "13 points" system, and then ask yourself the questions *who, what, where, why,* and *how*. Ask yourself questions about the buildings and make mental notes. When you get to work, take five minutes to draw a sketch of the buildings and to fill in details or write down as much as you can recall about the buildings. On your way home compare your sketch and data with the actual scene. What did you miss? Why did you miss it? The next time you try this exercise see whether you can look at the same buildings in a different perspective in order to create a new challenge. Repeat this exercise several times, using a different group of buildings each time.

Once you have honed your skills to some degree, try using pictures from books or magazines. They need not be related to firefighting but should be detailed in design. Observe closely; then try to recall.

Recall questions are one portion of the test on which you can definitely improve your performance. It requires nothing but dedication to improve a skill you already use in everyday life.

VISUALIZING IMAGES

Firefighters must be able to look at an object and figure out how it would appear from the back, side, and top. The ability to do this is called visualization and is the process of recording a mental picture of an image and then transforming that image into other orientations. You may be called upon to demonstrate this talent by answering questions that show an object from one angle and then ask you to identify the way it would look from a different angle. This skill takes practice, but can be learned. Start by constructing a single-view image of the object in your mind. Pay particular attention to the parts of the object that can be seen from other viewpoints. Focus your attention on the height and spatial relationship of objects extending over a roof or out from the front and sides of the building, as these are critical reference markers.

If you wanted to add depth to a two-dimensional image, you would project rays or lines backward from each major point in the outline of the image. Try adding depth to a simple two-dimensional object in your mind. Once you have done this, try to picture the object from the back. Remember, it will be reversed. To help you do this, first think of looking into a mirror and then project yourself inside the mirror looking out at where you were looking in. Keep in mind, when you view the object from the back, that some of the items in the center of the image will not be visible from the front and others may appear to be new or different, but the outline that mirrors the image of the front should still be the same.

When you try to picture an image from the side, keep in mind the angles of the items that were projecting outward or above from the front. They may now be at your left or right, but they should be at the same height and at a complementary angle.

When you look at an object from above, as when you look down onto a roof, remember that flat surfaces will appear as large undivided squares or rectangles, while peaked roofs will appear as subdivided rectangles with lines at an angle indicating where the roof joins another section of the building. Cylindrical objects with high peaks will appear as circles.

If you are asked to describe the outside of a building as seen from the inside of the structure, keep in mind that it is a mirror image. You will not be able to see items on the face of a building unless they are on a glass panel, such as a sign on a window, and in this case, the writing will appear in reverse.

SPATIAL ORIENTATION

In firefighting it is important to know where you are, where you were, and how to get from one location to another by using a map or floor plan. The spatial orientation questions test your ability to make judgments about how to traverse areas in the most direct route without breaking the laws or rules. The laws could be traffic laws like one-way streets, traffic restrictions, or weight restrictions. The rules may be obstructions such as dead ends, narrow paths, unstable ground, bridges or walkways, or circular corridors or roads.

When working with maps and floor plans, find out if you are allowed to mark the map or floor plan. Orient the map so that North faces in the correct direction with respect to your current position. Locate the starting and end points of the route you must travel. Using your finger, trace a path toward the intended destination. When you come to a point that blocks your passage, either because it violates a rule or a law, put a mark (X) to indicate this is not a valid route. Now go back to the starting point and begin following a new route. You may be tempted to just backtrack over a small portion of the invalid route and then proceed once you have avoided the blockage, but this is not recommended. Go back and start from the beginning, and make sure the new path is correct from start to finish. When you have identified the correct path, use a pencil (if allowed) to trace the path you just negotiated. Keep in mind the rules about following traffic laws when you are drawing this line.

ANSWER SHEET
Practice Exercises

1. Ⓐ Ⓑ Ⓒ Ⓓ	11. Ⓐ Ⓑ Ⓒ Ⓓ	21. Ⓐ Ⓑ Ⓒ Ⓓ	31. Ⓐ Ⓑ Ⓒ Ⓓ
2. Ⓐ Ⓑ Ⓒ Ⓓ	12. Ⓐ Ⓑ Ⓒ Ⓓ	22. Ⓐ Ⓑ Ⓒ Ⓓ	32. Ⓐ Ⓑ Ⓒ Ⓓ
3. Ⓐ Ⓑ Ⓒ Ⓓ	13. Ⓐ Ⓑ Ⓒ Ⓓ	23. Ⓐ Ⓑ Ⓒ Ⓓ	33. Ⓐ Ⓑ Ⓒ Ⓓ
4. Ⓐ Ⓑ Ⓒ Ⓓ	14. Ⓐ Ⓑ Ⓒ Ⓓ	24. Ⓐ Ⓑ Ⓒ Ⓓ	34. Ⓐ Ⓑ Ⓒ Ⓓ
5. Ⓐ Ⓑ Ⓒ Ⓓ	15. Ⓐ Ⓑ Ⓒ Ⓓ	25. Ⓐ Ⓑ Ⓒ Ⓓ	35. Ⓐ Ⓑ Ⓒ Ⓓ
6. Ⓐ Ⓑ Ⓒ Ⓓ	16. Ⓐ Ⓑ Ⓒ Ⓓ	26. Ⓐ Ⓑ Ⓒ Ⓓ	36. Ⓐ Ⓑ Ⓒ Ⓓ
7. Ⓐ Ⓑ Ⓒ Ⓓ	17. Ⓐ Ⓑ Ⓒ Ⓓ	27. Ⓐ Ⓑ Ⓒ Ⓓ	37. Ⓐ Ⓑ Ⓒ Ⓓ
8. Ⓐ Ⓑ Ⓒ Ⓓ	18. Ⓐ Ⓑ Ⓒ Ⓓ	28. Ⓐ Ⓑ Ⓒ Ⓓ	38. Ⓐ Ⓑ Ⓒ Ⓓ
9. Ⓐ Ⓑ Ⓒ Ⓓ	19. Ⓐ Ⓑ Ⓒ Ⓓ	29. Ⓐ Ⓑ Ⓒ Ⓓ	39. Ⓐ Ⓑ Ⓒ Ⓓ
10. Ⓐ Ⓑ Ⓒ Ⓓ	20. Ⓐ Ⓑ Ⓒ Ⓓ	30. Ⓐ Ⓑ Ⓒ Ⓓ	40. Ⓐ Ⓑ Ⓒ Ⓓ

PRACTICE EXERCISES

Directions: Answer questions 1 through 10 based upon the illustration. You are permitted 5 minutes to study and commit to memory as much as you can of the illustration. You are *not* permitted to make any written notes during the 5 minutes you are studying the illustration.

After 5 minutes, stop studying the illustration and answer the questions without referring to the illustration. For each question, choose the one best answer—(A), (B), (C), or (D)—and write the corresponding letter on your answer paper next to the number of the question.

Now start your 5 minutes on a clock and begin.

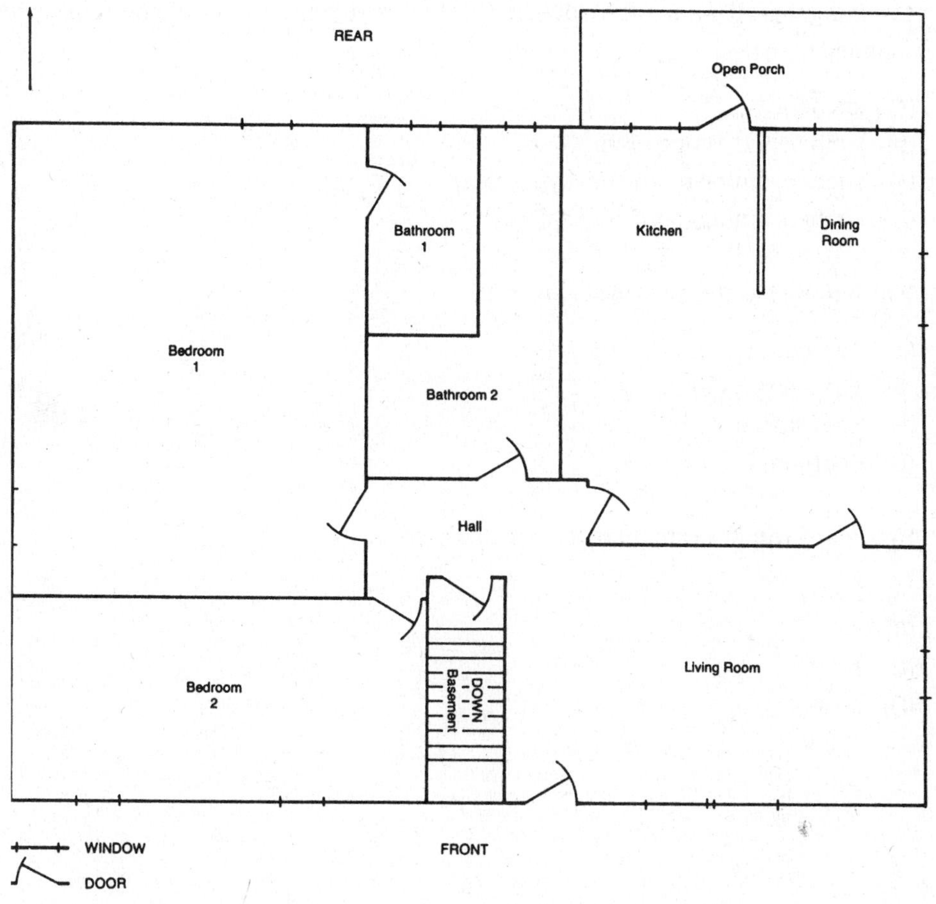

Use a full 5 minutes (no less). Then turn the page and answer the questions. Do not refer to the illustration again.

1. A fire coming up the stairs from the basement would most likely cut off passage to the exit doors for all of the following *except*

(A) the kitchen.
(B) bathroom 2.
(C) bedroom 1.
(D) bedroom 2.

2. It would be correct to say about the bedrooms in this house that

(A) bedroom 2 has two doors and two windows.
(B) bedroom 2 has one door and one window.
(C) bedroom 1 has two doors and two windows.
(D) bedroom 1 has one door and two windows.

3. Assuming that all doors were closed, a fire on the kitchen stove would most likely be confined to the

(A) kitchen.
(B) kitchen and dining room.
(C) kitchen, dining room, and living room.
(D) kitchen, dining room, and hallway.

4. Which room has the most available exits?

(A) Bedroom 1.
(B) The living room.
(C) The kitchen.
(D) Bedroom 2.

5. How many windows are there for possible escape?

(A) 9
(B) 10
(C) 11
(D) 12

6. Which room is farthest from an exit door?

   (A) Bedroom 2
   (B) The dining room
   (C) Bathroom 1
   (D) Bedroom 1

7. The porch in the rear gives access to the

   (A) kitchen.
   (B) kitchen and dining room.
   (C) kitchen and bathroom 1.
   (D) kitchen and bathroom 2.

8. The two rooms that cannot be reached directly from the hall are

   (A) bathroom 1 and the kitchen.
   (B) bedroom 2 and the living room.
   (C) the dining room and bathroom 1.
   (D) All rooms can be reached from the hall.

9. What is the total number of doors in this house?

   (A) 5
   (B) 7
   (C) 9
   (D) 11

10. How many windows are there in the living room?

   (A) 1
   (B) 2
   (C) 3
   (D) 4

Directions: Answer questions 11 through 15 based upon the illustration. You are permitted 5 minutes to study and commit to memory as much as you can of the illustration. You are *not* permitted to make any written notes during the 5 minutes you are studying the illustration.

After 5 minutes, stop studying the illustration and answer the questions without referring to the illustration. For each question, choose the one best answer—(A), (B), (C), or (D)—and write the corresponding letter on your answer paper next to the number of the question.

Now start your 5 minutes on a clock and begin.

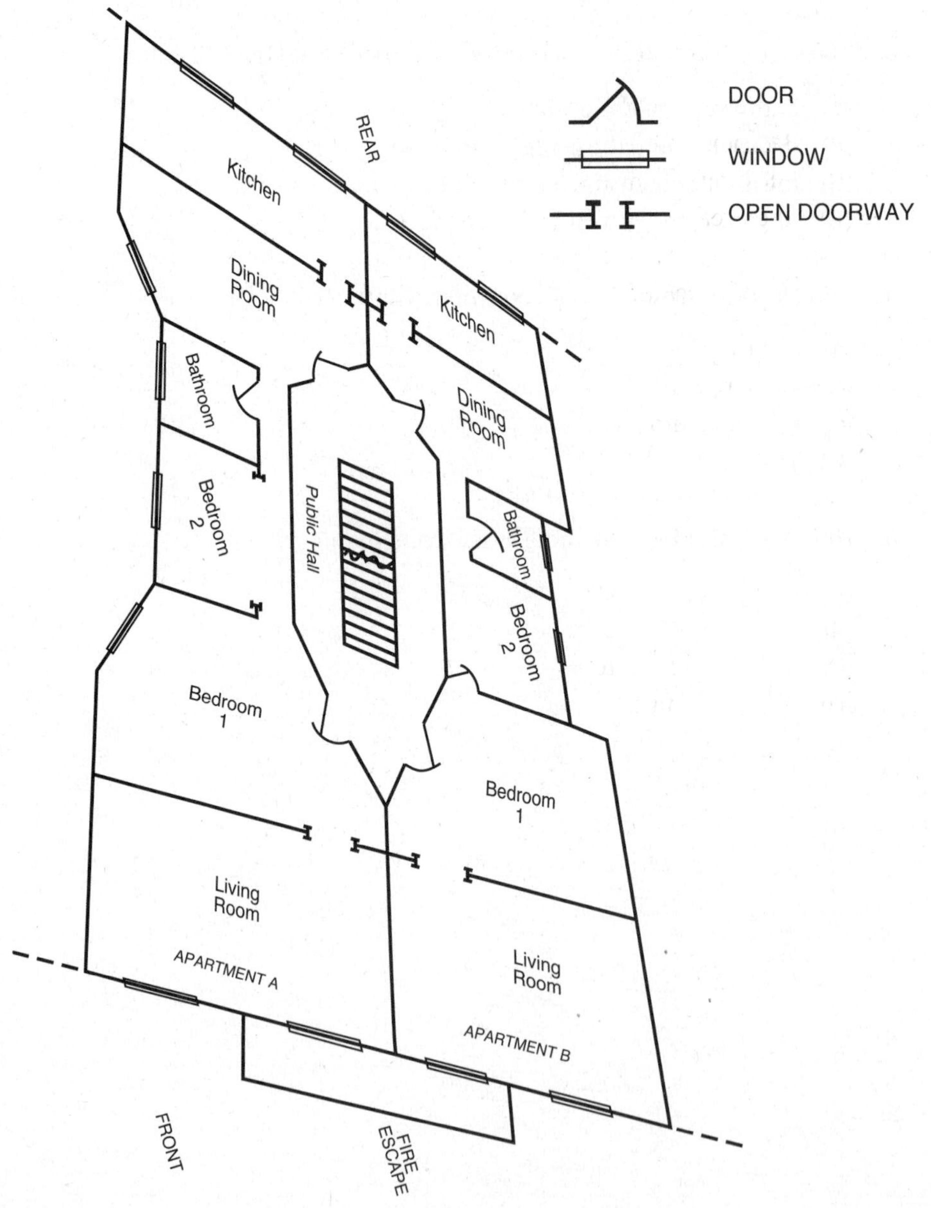

Use a full 5 minutes (no less). Then turn the page and answer the questions. Do not refer to the illustration again.

11. How many doors give direct access to the public hall?

    (A) 3
    (B) 4
    (C) 5
    (D) 6

12. A fire in the dining room of either apartment would extend *first* into

    (A) bedroom 2.
    (B) the kitchen.
    (C) the living room.
    (D) bedroom 1.

13. Which of the following has two doors leading into it?

    (A) Bedroom 1 in apartment B.
    (B) Bedroom 2 in apartment A.
    (C) The dining room in apartment B.
    (D) The kitchen in apartment A.

14. It would be *incorrect* to state that

    (A) there are two ways out of this building.
    (B) apartment A and apartment B are slightly different.
    (C) the number of windows on both sides of the building are the same.
    (D) the fire escape landing on each floor serves only one window in each apartment.

15. A fire in bedroom 2 of apartment A would

    (A) cut off access to the rear of the apartment.
    (B) extend only into the public hall.
    (C) cut off all access to the fire escape.
    (D) remain confined to that room.

Directions: Answer questions 16 through 19 based on the illustration and reading material on the next page. You are permitted 5 minutes to study and commit to memory as much as you can of the material. You are *not* permitted to make any written notes during the 5 minutes you are studying the material.

After 5 minutes, stop studying the reading and answer the questions without referring to the illustration and reading material. For each question, choose the one best answer—(A), (B), (C), or (D)—and write the corresponding letter on your answer paper next to the number of the question.

Now start your 5 minutes on a clock and begin.

Division of Fire Prevention Fire Department

CRITERIA FOR OFFICIAL TYPE "NO SMOKING" SIGNS

1. The following criteria shall be used for printing of OFFICIAL type Fire Department "NO SMOKING" signs.
2. Permission is granted to anyone who desires to print the new type sign, in strict conformance to the criteria, for use or sale.
3. Signs shall be used only where required by provision of law or Fire Department regulation.
4. Existing official type signs may be used until stock is depleted.
5. Specific Criteria:
   a. Pictorial Description and Layout:

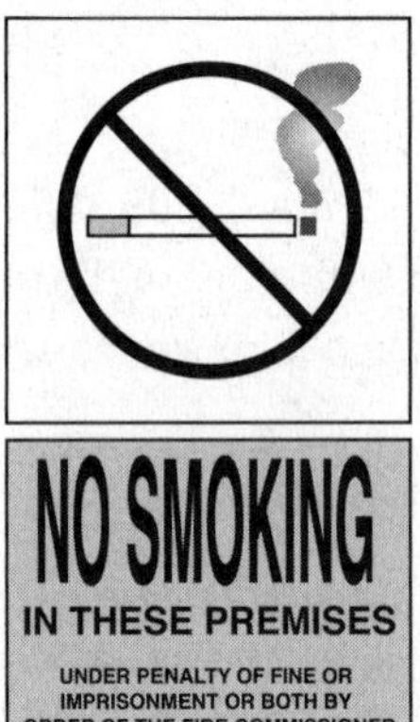

   b. Overall sign size: 10"x14" (or 11"x15")
   c. Symbol: International "NO SMOKING" symbol (3¾"x¼" Cigarette and Smoke in Black; 5/16"x5/16" Ash in Red; 6½" Diameter x ¼" Circle with ¼" Cross Bar in Red).
   d. Legends:

Legends:	Letter Size—Capitals:	Color:
NO SMOKING	2" Min.	Red
IN THESE PREMISES	1" or ¾" min.	Black
UNDER PENALTY OF FINE OR IMPRISONMENT, OR BOTH, BY ORDER OF THE FIRE COMMISSIONER	¼" min.	Black

   e. Material: Heavy stock cardboard or other durable material.

6. In Nursing Homes, Hospitals, Sanitoria, Convelescent Homes, Homes for the Aged or for chronic patients, or portions of buildings used for such purpose, as set forth in C19-165.4 Administrative Code, certain areas may be approved by the Fire Commissioner as locations where smoking is permitted. In all other portions of such premises, "NO SMOKING" signs shall be posted, and shall conform to the criteria set forth in Section 5 of these regulations, except that the statement "EXCEPT IN DESIGNATED LOCATIONS" shall immediately follow the legends "NO SMOKING IN THESE PREMISES". The additional legend "EXCEPT IN DESIGNATED LOCATIONS" shall be in BLACK CAPITAL LETTERS at least ½" high letter size.

Use a full 5 minutes (no less). Then turn the page and answer the questions. Do not refer to this material again.

16. It would be accurate to say about official "NO SMOKING" signs that

(A) only the circle and crossbar are red.
(B) the pictorial design is optional.
(C) they state that the penalty for smoking is always a fine.
(D) the cigarette and smoke are colored black.

17. The official "NO SMOKING" signs may be

(A) used on any premises.
(B) printed only by licensed, approved printers.
(C) printed only on durable material.
(D) printed in either the new or the old style.

18. For certain premises the writing on the "NO SMOKING" sign may be modified to read

(A) "Except in Designated Locations."
(B) "No Smoking Here."
(C) "Smoking Permitted Here."
(D) none of the above; the sign cannot be altered.

19. For official "NO SMOKING" signs, there are

(A) four acceptable colors.
(B) two acceptable sizes.
(C) only two acceptable types of materials.
(D) three acceptable types of signs.

Directions: Answer questions 20 through 24 based on the written material and illustration on the next page. You are permitted 5 minutes to study and to commit to memory as much as you can of the material. You are *not* permitted to make any written notes during the 5 minutes you are reading the material.

After 5 minutes, stop reading the material and answer the questions without referring to the written material and illustration. For each question, choose the one best answer—(A), (B), (C), or (D)—and write the corresponding letter on your answer paper next to the number of the question.

Now start your 5 minutes on a clock and begin.

The Axe

The axe is one of the tools used by firefighters and its construction, use, and maintenance must be understood.

The "4 C's" of the axe, a common tool, are as follows:

- Construction
- Care
- Carry
- Chopping

CONSTRUCTION

The head is made of steel and has two usable surfaces. The flat surface is used for pounding, and the double-edged surface for cutting. The handle is made of wood (hickory is common) or synthetic materials, and fits into a slot in the head. The cutting edge of the head has a tempered tip. The axe makes use of the principle of the inclined plane.

CARE

Like all firefighting tools, the axe must be properly maintained. Clean burrs from the head with a file and then wash with kerosene. Sharpen the axe with a slow-turning sandstone wheel, not on a grindstone. If a wheel is not available, use a file.

After the head is cleaned, wash the handle using unsoaped Brillo, and then put a light coat of oil on the head. Axe handles should not be painted; paint hides defects and could lead to a defective tool being used at a fire.

CARRY

The best and safest way to carry the axe is by using two hands. One hand carries the head; the other, the handle at a point opposite the head. This method is not always available, however, for there are times when the second hand is needed for other tasks. When carrying the axe in one hand, use that hand to engulf the head, with the cutting edge facing forward. This will allow the axe handle to fall at your side and will keep you in control of the blade and handle movement.

CHOPPING

Hold the axe in a comfortable, balanced position with one hand at the grip and the other at the shoulder. Chop in a circular motion, making many small cuts rather than attempting to cut through on each swing. Before you begin, clean the area around the spot to be cut and look around to make sure that it is safe to swing the axe. When cutting, the blade should enter the surface at about a 60-degree angle. When cutting roofs, cut the sheathing first, then go back and cut the roof boards. Do not cut on top of roof joists or in the center of the bay. Attempt to cut at a point 2 inches from the joist, on the inside of the hole to be made.

Use a full 20 minutes to answer the questions beginning on page 101.

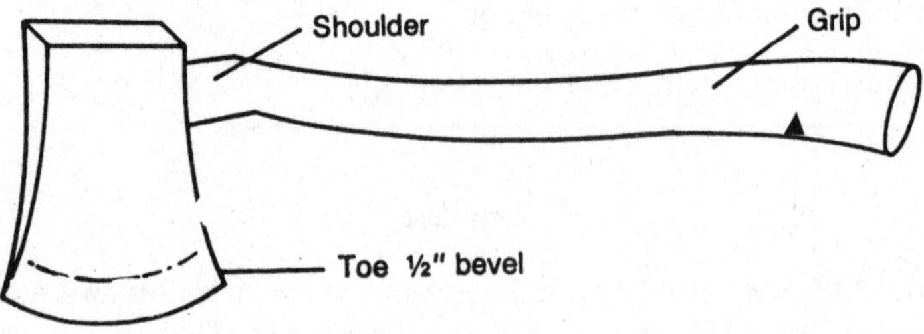

20. Which of the following is not one of the "4 Cs" of the axe?

    (A) Construction
    (B) Care
    (C) Cleaning
    (D) Carry

21. After the handle is washed, you should

    (A) put a clean coat of paint on it.
    (B) varnish it lightly.
    (C) put a light coat of oil on it.
    (D) check it for defects.

22. The best technique to cut a roof using an axe is to

    (A) use a circular motion, taking small cuts.
    (B) cut all the material at once.
    (C) use the mechanical advantage of the wedge by taking a full overhead swing.
    (D) cut in the center of the bay.

23. What is the best angle at which to cut a roof?

    (A) 30 degrees
    (B) 60 degrees
    (C) 75 degrees
    (D) 90 degrees

24. The best way to carry an axe is

    (A) head in hand.
    (B) handle in hand.
    (C) head or handle in hand.
    (D) head and handle in hands.

Directions: Answer questions 25 through 29 using only the information provided in the questions and illustrations.

25. Your commanding officer sends you to the back of a burning house like the one in the illustration below and asks you to assess the situation from that location. When you arrive at the back of the house you could expect it to look similar to:

(A)

(B)

(C)

(D)

26. When operating from the basket of an elevated platform truck, you would be most correct if you thought the roof of the building looked like (see the illustration):

(A)

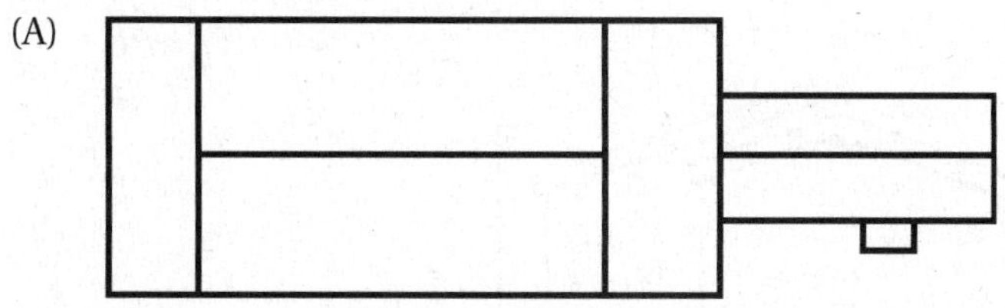

(B)

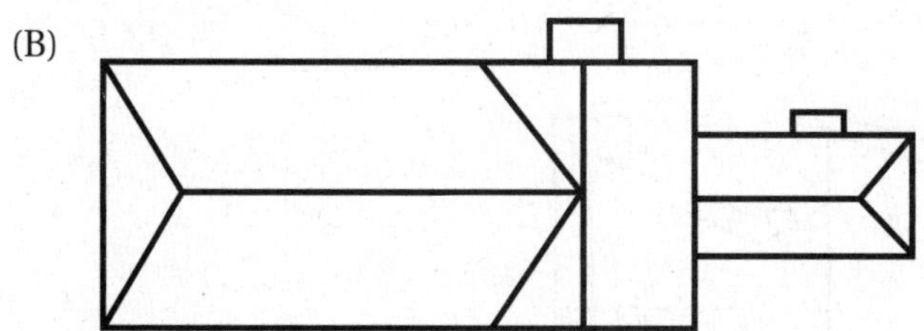

(C)

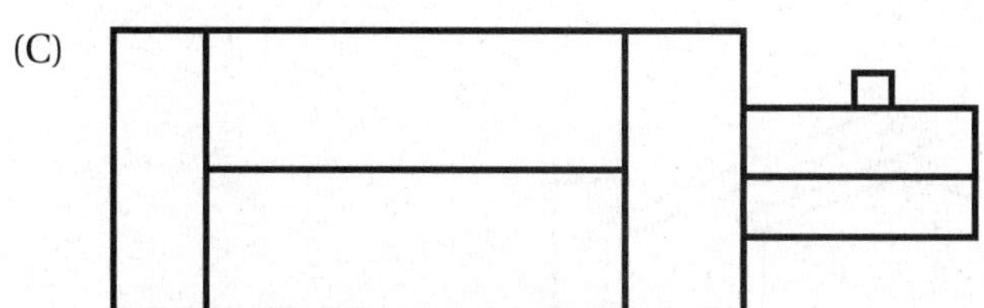

(D)

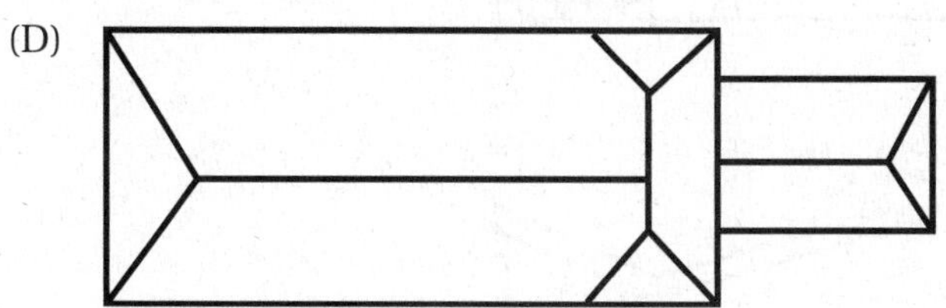

27. The illustration that most likely represents what the building would look like when viewed from the rear is:

(A)

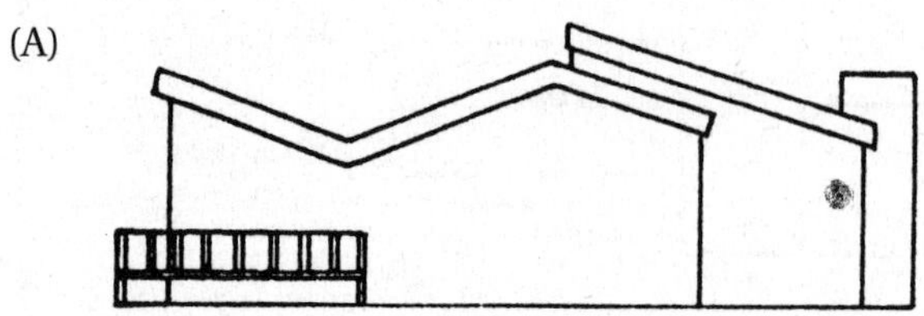

(B)

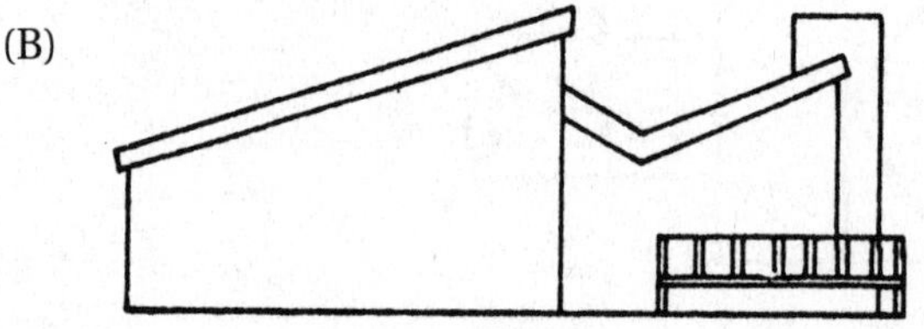

(C)

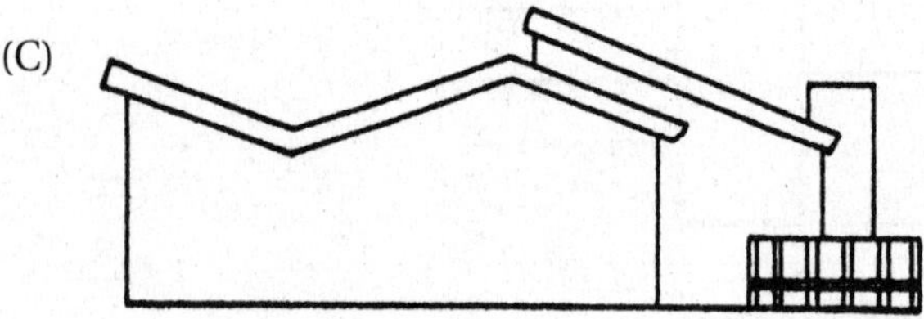

(D)

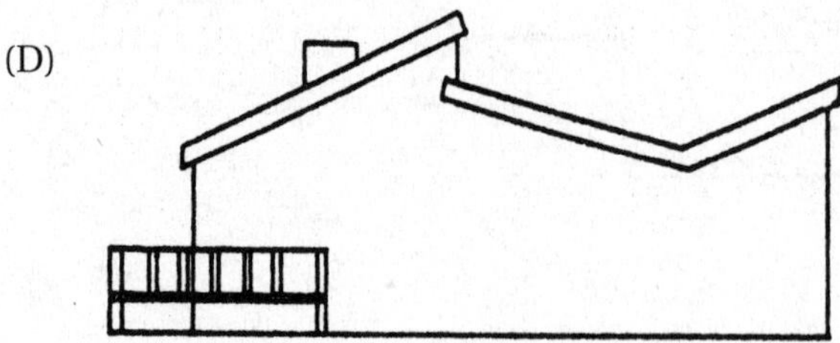

28. The illustration that depicts the image you would see if you were inside the shoe store and looking out is:

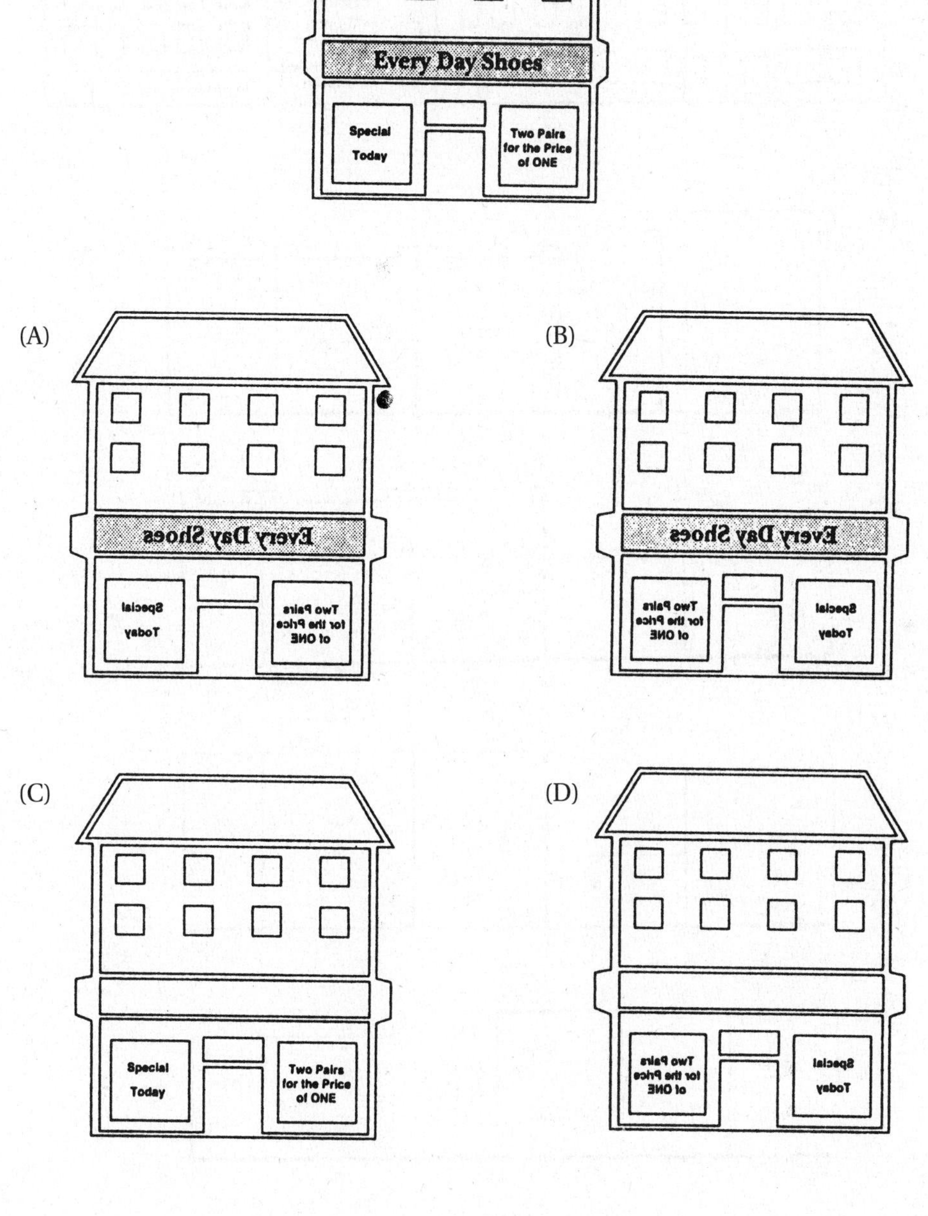

29. If you were sent to the rear of this row of houses, you would expect it to look like:

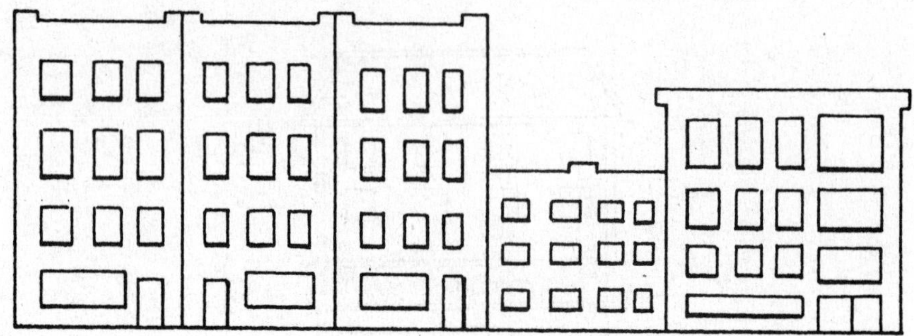

(A)

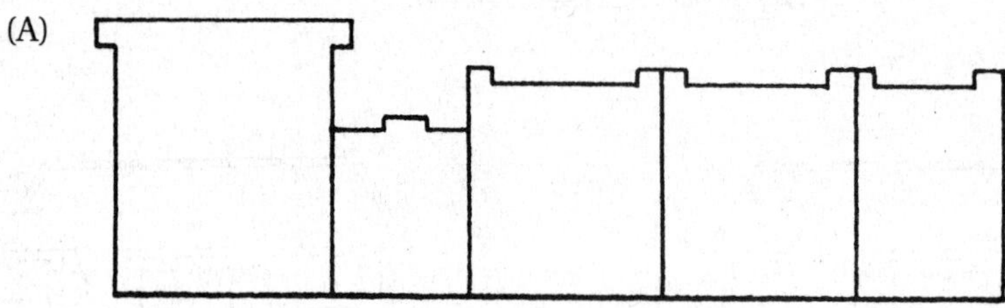

(B)

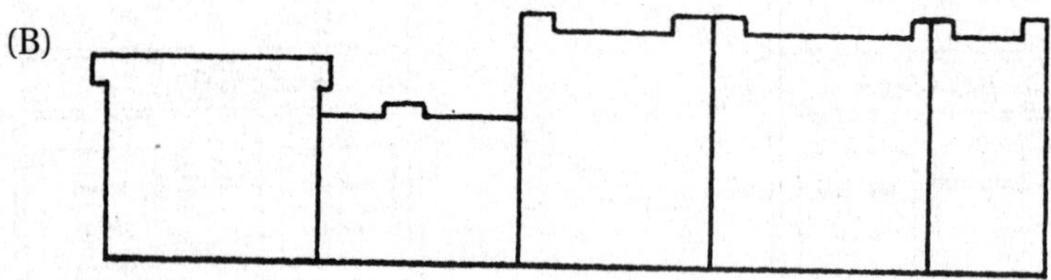

(C)

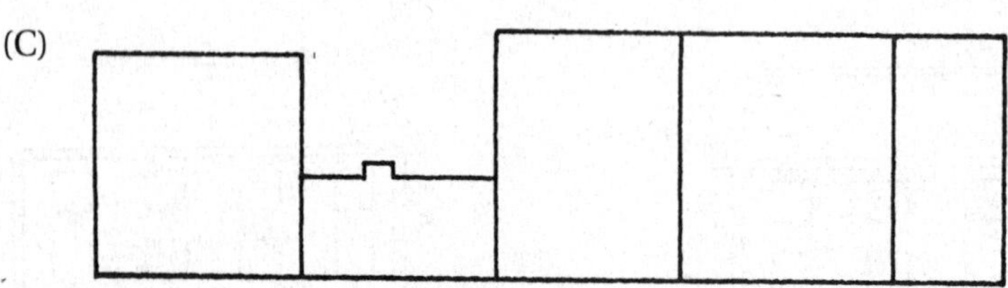

(D)

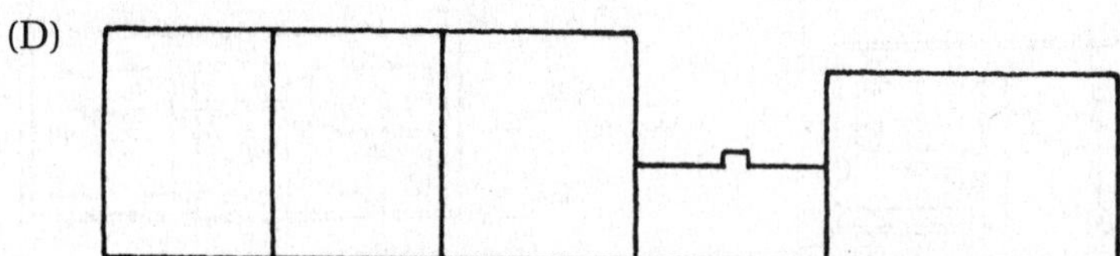

Directions: Base your answers to questions 30 through 33 only on the information provided in the illustration below. All traffic laws, rules, and requirements must be obeyed. The shortest, most direct route should be used.

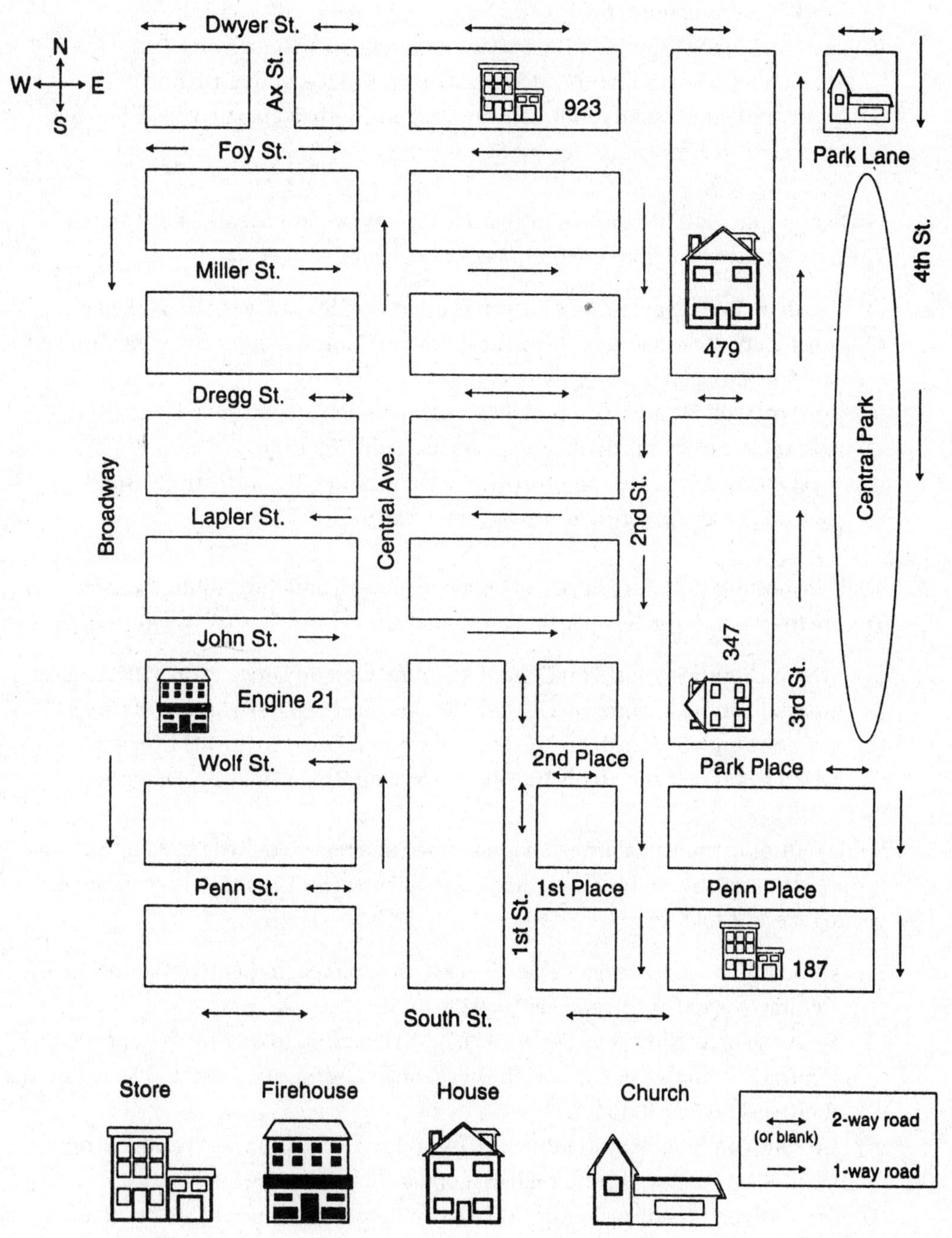

30. Engine 21 receives notification of a fire at 347 3rd Street between Park Place and Dregg Street. The most direct route for the driver to take is

(A) west on Wolf St., south on Broadway, east on Penn St., north on Central Ave., east on John St., south on 2nd St., east on Park Place, and north on 3rd St.
(B) west on Wolf St., north on Broadway, west on John St., south on 2nd St., east on Park Place, and north on 3rd St.
(C) east on Wolf St., south on Broadway, east on Penn St., north on Central Ave., east on John St., south on 2nd St., east on Park Place, and north on 3rd St.
(D) west on Wolf St., south on Broadway, east on South St., north on 2nd St., east on Park Place, and north on 3rd St.

31. Firefighter Jones has been asked to give a fire safety talk at the Park Lane Church. The best route to take from the firehouse of Engine 21 is

(A) north on Broadway, east on Dwyer, south on 4th St., and west on Park Place.
(B) west on Wolf St., south on Broadway, east on Central Ave., north on 4th St., and west on Park Lane.
(C) west on Wolf St., south on Broadway, east on Penn St., north on Central Ave., east on Dregg St., north on 3rd St., and east on Park Lane.
(D) west on Wolf St., south on Broadway, east on South St., north on Central Ave., east on Dwyer St., south on 4th St., and west on Park Lane.

32. While inspecting 187 South St., a call for a person with breathing difficulty is received. You are to respond to 479 Dregg St. You should go

(A) west on South St., north on Central Ave., and west on Dregg St. to 479 Dregg St.
(B) west on South St., north on Central Ave., and east on Dregg St. to 479 Dregg St.
(C) west on South St., north on 2nd St., and west on Dregg St. to 479 Dregg St.
(D) west on South St., north on 2nd St., and east on Dregg St. to 479 Dregg St.

33. While returning from an alarm, you are notified of a reported fire at 923 Foy St. Your fire apparatus is now on Broadway just north of Dregg St. The most direct route for you to take is as follows:

(A) Go south on Broadway to Lapler St., east on Lapler St. to Central Ave., north on Central Ave. to Foy St., and east to 923 Foy St.
(B) Go south on Broadway to Dregg St., east on Dregg St. to Central Ave., north on Central Ave. to Dwyer St., east on Dwyer St. to 2nd St., south on 2nd St. to Foy St., then west on Foy St. to 923 Foy St.
(C) Go south on Broadway to John St., east on John St. to Central Ave., north on Central Ave. to Foy St., and then east on Foy St. to 923 Foy St.
(D) Go south on Broadway to John St., east on John St. to Central Ave., south on Central Ave. to Foy St., then east on Foy St. to 923 Foy St.

Directions: Base your answer to questions 34 through 38 only on the information provided in the illustration below. All traffic laws, rules, and requirements must be obeyed. The shortest, most direct route should be used.

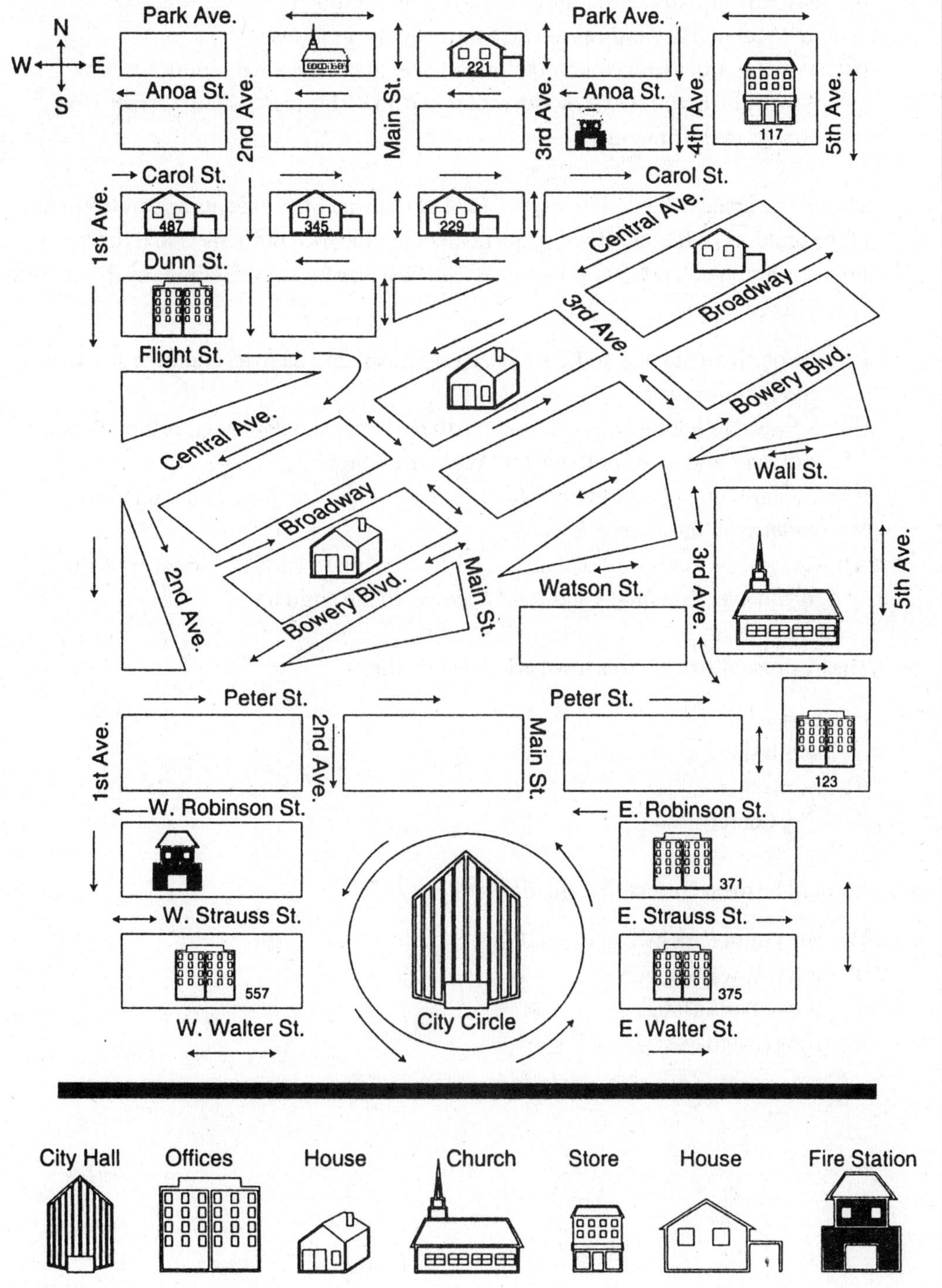

34. A firefighter assigned to the Carol St. firehouse is told to work in the Strauss St. firehouse for the next two weeks. The most direct route to the Strauss St. firehouse is

(A) east on Carol St. to Central Ave., Central Ave. to 2nd Ave. south, then east on Walter, north to Strauss, and east to the firehouse.
(B) east on Carol to 5th Ave., south on 5th Ave. to E. Walters, west on E. Walter to 1st Ave., north on 1st Ave. to W. Strauss, and east to the firehouse.
(C) east on Carol to Central Ave., southwest on Central to 1st Ave., south on 1st Ave. to W. Strauss St., and east on W. Strauss to the firehouse.
(D) east on Carol to 5th Ave., south on 5th Ave. to Bowery Blvd., southwest on Bowery Blvd. to 1st Ave., south on 1st Ave. to W. Strauss St., and then east on Strauss to the firehouse.

35. The fire company assigned to inspect 123 E. Robinson St. parked its apparatus in front of the building. While conducting the inspection, the fire company is told there is a fire in a church on 2nd Ave. at Park Ave. The best way for the fire company to get there is as follows:

(A) Go north on 5th Ave. to Park Ave., west on Park to 2nd Ave., and then south on 2nd to the church.
(B) Go west on Robinson to 1st Ave., north on 1st Ave. to Park Ave., east on Park to 2nd Ave., and then south on 2nd Ave. to the church.
(C) Go north on 3rd Ave. to Anoa St., west on Anoa to 2nd Ave., and then north on 2nd Ave. to the church.
(D) Go west on Robinson to Main St., north on Main to Park Ave., west on Park Ave. to 2nd Ave., and finally south on 2nd Ave. to the church.

36. The business district in this town is located on the

(A) east side.
(B) south side.
(C) north side.
(D) City Center.

37. It would be most correct to state that "4th Ave . . ."

(A) runs from Park Ave. to Central Ave.
(B) is a two-way street.
(C) is two blocks long.
(D) runs east to west.

38. A man living in a house on Dunn St. at 1st Ave. wants to make a personal complaint about what he believes may be a local fire hazard. By car, the closest place to report the fire hazard is

(A) the W. Strauss St. firehouse.
(B) the Carol St. firehouse.
(C) City Hall.
(D) the office on E. Walter St.

Directions: Questions 39 and 40 test your ability to deal with people. For each question, select the best answer. Then write your answer on the answer sheet.

39. You are a firefighter out with a group of friends. One of them asks you a technical question about fire protection, and you don't know the answer. The best response:

(A) may not be accurate but sounds good.
(B) is to admit that you don't know but will find out.
(C) is to say that the subject is too technical.
(D) is to raise another question and then change the subject.

40. While conducting a routine fire prevention inspection of a department store, a firefighter is told by the store manager that the entire inspection procedure is a waste of time. What is the most appropriate action for the firefighter to take?

(A) Tell the manager that he is wrong.
(B) Explain the benefits of the inspection program.
(C) Agree with the store manager.
(D) Continue the inspection.

ANSWER KEY AND EXPLANATIONS

Answer Key

1. **(A)**	11. **(B)**	21. **(D)**	31. **(C)**
2. **(C)**	12. **(B)**	22. **(A)**	32. **(B)**
3. **(B)**	13. **(A)**	23. **(B)**	33. **(B)**
4. **(B)**	14. **(C)**	24. **(D)**	34. **(C)**
5. **(D)**	15. **(A)**	25. **(D)**	35. **(D)**
6. **(C)**	16. **(D)**	26. **(B)**	36. **(B)**
7. **(B)**	17. **(C)**	27. **(C)**	37. **(C)**
8. **(C)**	18. **(A)**	28. **(D)**	38. **(A)**
9. **(C)**	19. **(B)**	29. **(B)**	39. **(B)**
10. **(C)**	20. **(C)**	30. **(A)**	40. **(B)**

Answer Explanations

1. **(A)** The kitchen has an exit door to the rear. Passage can be made through the dining room and then the living room.

2. **(C)** A door to the hall and one to the bathroom, and a window on the west side and one on the rear.

3. **(B)** These two adjoining rooms have an open passageway, which would permit the fire to extend rapidly.

4. **(B)** The living room has three windows, two doors, and access to the hall, which leads to four other rooms.

5. **(D)** If you count all the windows, the answer is 12. The living room has two windows that are adjacent to each other.

6. **(C)** From this room you must pass through bedroom 1, then the hall, and finally the kitchen or living room.

7. **(B)** The kitchen has a door and a window leading to the porch; the dining room has one window leading to the porch.

8. **(C)** To reach these two rooms you must first pass through another room.

9. **(C)** There are seven interior doors and two exterior doors.

10. **(C)** There are one side window and two front windows.

11. **(B)** Two doors in each apartment lead to the public hall.

12. **(B)** The kitchen is immediately adjoining the dining room; all the other rooms are separated from it by a hall passage.

13. **(A)** This room has a door leading from the public hall and an interior door leading to the center hall.

14. **(C)** The shaft on apartment A's side is diamond shaped with four windows. The shaft on apartment B's side is square and contains only two windows. Choice A—there are two possible exits, the stairs and the fire escape. *Note:* The question referred to the

building, not the apartments. Choice B—the shafts and the number of doors are different. Choice D—the fire escape serves one window in each apartment.

15. **(A)** This room is located on the center hall and would not allow passage through it. Choice B—the fire would extend into the hall and bedroom 1 (if the door was open). Choice C—it should be possible to use the fire escape from the rooms adjoining it. Choice D—the fire would not be confined because there is no dividing wall or door to stop it.

16. **(D)** See section 5.c. Choice A—the ash is also red. Choice B—the picture is required. Choice C—the penalty can be a fine, imprisonment, or both.

17. **(C)** See section 5.e. Choice A—official signs may be used only in places where required by law or fire department regulation. Choice B—the signs may be printed by anyone. Choice C—the new style must be used for new signs; the old signs may be used until the supply is exhausted. Choice D—this number is not known. We know about the new sign and we know that there are existing official type signs, but we don't know how many.

18. **(A)** See section 6. Permitting smoking in these controlled areas reduces the temptation to smoke in rooms where dangerous gases used for medical purposes may be present.

19. **(B)** Signs may be either 10″×14″ or 11″ ×15″. Choice A—there are only two colors, red and black. Choice C—a number of "other" durable materials are available.

20. **(C)** Cleaning is one part of care; chopping is the fourth "C."

21. **(D)** Once the handle is washed, you have finished except to check for defects. It should not be painted (A), varnished (B), or oiled (C).

22. **(A)** This correct answer is found in the second sentence of the section entitled "Chopping." Choice D—the cut should be made 2 inches from the joist (the last sentence under "Chopping").

23. **(B)** The 60-degree angle is mentioned under "chopping."

24. **(D)** The passage states that the best method is to use two hands, and then explains how to hold the axe. Choice D is the only selection that meets this criterion.

25. **(D)** Choice D is the correct image. Choices A and B are images from a side view, and Choice C is an image from the front view.

26. **(B)** In Illustrations A, C, and D, the canopy over the front door is not shown.

27. **(C)** Choice C is the correct image. Choice A shows the porch on the wrong side. Choice B shows the single slanted roof portion of the house as the larger of the two sections, but the original drawing shows the multipeaked roof as the larger portion of the house. Choice D shows the chimney in the center of the single slanted roof, but the original illustration shows it at the end of the house.

28. **(D)** Choice D is the correct image. Choices A and B are incorrect. You would not be able to see the "Every Day Shoes" sign from inside the store. Items that can be seen from the inside of buildings are those that appear on glass or can be seen through the glass, such as a street pole, mailbox, canopy, and writing on the canopy. Choice C is incorrect because the writing on the windows would now appear on the opposite side and in reverse. Items that were on your left when looking in from the outside will appear on your right when looking out from the inside.

29. **(B)** Choice B is the correct image. Choice A is incorrect because the single building at the end is not larger than the group of three buildings. Choices C and D are incorrect because they do not show the projections on the side (cornice) and above (parapet walls) of the roof line, which should be visible from the rear.

30. **(A)** Choices B, C, and D are incorrect because they violate the traffic laws. Although these routes may be shorter, the directions are specific about not violating the traffic laws. A normally unrecognized portion of these questions is the testing of your ability to understand and follow orders and directions.

31. **(C)** This is the shortest, most direct route. Choice B is incorrect because it fails to tell you how to get from Broadway to Central Ave. Choice A violates the traffic law. Choice D is a good route, but it is longer.

32. **(B)** This is the shortest, most direct route. Choice A is incorrect because going west on Dregg St. is heading away from 479 Dregg St. Choices C and D violate the traffic law.

33. **(B)** Choices A and C violate the traffic law. Choice D takes you in the wrong direction when you reach Central Ave.

34. **(C)** This is the correct path. Choice A violates the traffic laws and takes you in the wrong direction on Walter St. Choice B violates the traffic law at E. Walters St. Choice D violates the traffic law at the intersection of Bowery Blvd. and Peter St., and it omits going through Peter St. to reach 1st Ave.

35. **(D)** This is the most direct, lawful route. Choice A would require a violation of the traffic law on E. Robinson St., Choice B violates the traffic law at 1st Ave., and Choice C violates the traffic law at 2nd Ave.

36. **(B)** The area where the largest number of offices are and where City Hall is located would be considered the business district. The north and center of the city are residential, having a large number of houses, stores, and churches. The east and west sides are mixed residential and business.

37. **(C)** This is correct. Choice A is incorrect because 4th Ave. runs from Park Ave. to Carol St., Choice B is incorrect because it is a one-way street, and Choice D is incorrect because it runs north to south.

38. **(A)** This is correct. This is a two-part question: Where do you personally report a local fire hazard, and how do you get there? Choice B is not direct and is substantially longer than Choice A. Choices C and D are incorrect because the complaint should be reported to the local firehouse first.

39. **(B)** As a firefighter, you should have knowledge of fire protection. However, you are not expected to know everything. You should not pretend you do or make light of the subject. You should state you will learn the answer and get back to the person requesting the information.

40. **(B)** Many people do not know the true purpose of a fire prevention inspection. They feel it is a waste of time and will interfere with business. By explaining that the goal is to reduce or eliminate hazards that may cause a loss of business or lead to serious injuries of customers and employees, a firefighter often gains respect.

Understanding Reading and Verbal/Listening Comprehension Questions

7

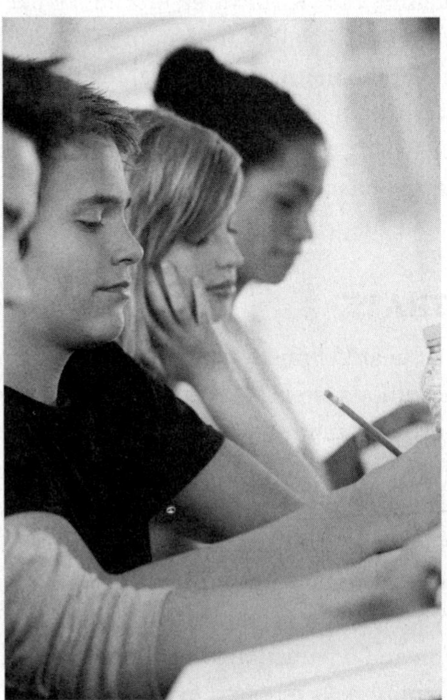

Because so much of an exam requires the ability to understand written and verbal or listening materials, you must take extra time and care with this chapter. Don't be in a hurry to move on to the next group of questions; first make sure that you have the reading and listening skills necessary to answer correctly any questions you will be asked.

Firefighters must have the ability to understand one another and the public. This skill is referred to as verbal comprehension. Good verbal comprehension means that firefighters take the time to hear, analyze, and interpret what another individual is saying. A good vocabulary is part of this skill but not all of it.

As a firefighter, you must be able to listen to a description of what is happening and understand what it means to you. This skill may be tested in two different ways during the exam: orally and written. The oral interview tests your ability to hear a question, interpret what is being asked, and effectively respond. The verbal/listening comprehension questions test how well you comprehend what you heard. This is very much like listening to a teacher, taking notes, and then answering true/false, multiple-choice, or fill-in-the-blank questions about what the teacher has just taught you. The Oral Interview techniques are discussed in Chapter 2; practice materials and questions for the listening portion of the examinations are included in Chapter 7.

The second manner in which communication skills are tested is through written materials. The written materials for the verbal/listening comprehension sections are very similar to the reading comprehension materials. Reading Comprehension questions ask the candidate to put items in the passage into some order, or to express the original idea in a clear and precise format. The verbal/listening question technique is slightly different because the candidate does not have a copy of the passage that was read. The candidate must rely on the written notes and memory. The candidate may be asked to recall specific items.

Reading and listening abilities can be improved with patience and practice, in the same way you learn to type or to hit a baseball. The brain is a collection of nerve cells; how the brain remembers is not precisely known. However, the brain is like a muscle, which you must exercise and train to get into shape. Reading and listening are skills that require exercising of the brain—the more you do it, the more you practice, the more you challenge yourself, the greater the results you achieve. In this chapter, you will find general hints for improving your overall reading and listening skills, as well as specific strategies for answering reading and listening comprehension questions. Spend time learning this material, and even after you have mastered it don't hesitate to go back and review.

HOW TO CONCENTRATE

How often have you "read or heard" something by looking at the words without concentrating on their meaning or the author's intent? How many times have you "read or heard" something and then discovered when you finished that you had no idea of what you had "read or heard"? The problem of letting your mind wander is the biggest roadblock to overcome if you want to become a good reader, listener, and test taker. Jumping ahead to see what's coming or glancing back to make sure you read what you thought you read are probably the second and third most common factors in poor reading and test taking. Looking away, not being focused, and not keeping yourself in a good position to hear the speaker are two common faults that lead to distraction and a reduction in your ability to recall what you should have heard. The reading and listening skills required to be a successful test taker can be learned; these skills are the kind that calls for short periods of focused concentration. This skill is developed by using a system—a system that allows your mind to create mental pictures of what you are reading and then to ask questions about them.

A good way to develop your ability to concentrate is to work with short passages from newspapers or magazines. Choose an article that interests you, read it carefully, or have someone read it to you, and then put it aside. Now try to write down the key points of the article without looking at it again. Start small, that is, with short, easy articles. As you improve, increase the length of the articles and also try more difficult materials. You will become more proficient with practice. Your key to success is to concentrate and focus on what you are reading while avoiding the distractors around you.

INCREASING YOUR VOCABULARY

Concentration will not help you if the reading or listening passage contains a significant number of words that you don't understand. Fortunately, some simple guidelines and a little work can help you improve your vocabulary dramatically.

1. When you are reading a book, magazine, or other material that belongs to you and you come across a word you don't fully understand, write the word in the margin. If

the reading material is not your own, write the word on a card and indicate where you read it. In this way you can look the word up at your convenience and then go back to the passage to see how it was used. When you hear a word you don't know, jot it down and briefly write out how it was used in a sentence. At your best opportunity, ask the speaker to explain the word. If this is not possible (TV or radio) then look it up in a dictionary.

There are two good techniques for increasing your vocabulary. One uses a system of 3 × 5 cards; the second, a notebook. The card system works well because it allows you to carry a small stack of cards with a significant number of words on them. The cards take up almost no room, can be easily carried in a pocket or purse, and are readily available for review when you have free time. Put the words on one side of the card and the definitions on the reverse side, and carry a few blank cards to ensure that you have a place to enter any new words you come across. When you write the words and definitions, organize the material so that it can be read by flipping the cards from the bottom up. This will allow you to read through the cards faster, and to put the cards you are finished with in the back of the pile to keep your place.

Be sure to carry the cards with the words that are giving you the most trouble, and as you review them, mark the words you are still not sure of. The next time you take a stack of cards to review, take only the ones with marked words. You should review all the words periodically.

The notebook has the advantage of being permanent and potentially much more comprehensive. If you choose this method, on each page make two columns, one about 1½ inches and the second occupying the rest of the page. In the first column put the word, and in the second the definition. In this way you can practice by going from definition to word, or word to definition.

2. As soon as possible, look up the meaning of the word in Chapter 15 if it is fire-related or in the dictionary. Write a brief but accurate definition on the back of the index card or in the notebook.
3. Return to the material where you read the word, and make sure you now understand its meaning. If the material is your own, write the meaning near the word. Make sure you fully understand the use of the word in the sentence.
4. Try to use each new word in your everyday conversation. You will make a few mistakes in the beginning, but they will only help to reinforce your learning.
5. Keep a separate list of any words you misuse, and review them periodically until you are certain you have mastered them.
6. Ask a friend to test you on the meanings of these words, and spend more time on the words you still don't know.

STRATEGIES FOR HANDLING READING AND VERBAL/ LISTENING COMPREHENSION

1. **READ THE DIRECTIONS.** Today's examinations contain general directions at the beginning of the examination, along with specific directions preceding each different type of question. Be sure to *read all instructions* carefully before doing the questions.

   The most important direction given for reading and verbal/listening comprehension questions is to answer the questions based solely on the information provided.

Never introduce other knowledge you possess into a reading/listening comprehension question. You may be better informed or have a different opinion from the author; however, the examiners are not looking for this. They are testing you on your ability to read, listen, and extract information from the materials given.

The directions should tell you if you are able to make notes about what you are reading or listening to and if you can refer to them when you are answering the questions. If this information is *not mentioned* in the directions section, ASK the examination proctor if taking notes is permitted and if you can refer to them when you answer the question.

2. **SCAN THE CONTENTS OF THE PASSAGE.** Get an idea of what the reading is about—an overview or survey of the passage. You can do this by skimming and looking for signposts that indicate the content. A good rule is to read the first sentence of each paragraph and then the entire last paragraph. But do this rapidly, just to get an idea of what is contained in the passage.
3. **READ THE STEM OF EACH QUESTION PERTAINING TO THE PASSAGE.** After scanning the passage, go to the questions and read the stem of each question, which contains the information that precedes the answer choices. Understand what is to be tested for in the passage. Also, scan some of the choices, but do this quickly. By knowing what you will be asked, you can make the best use of your reading time.
4. **READ THE PARAGRAPH CAREFULLY.** Now that you know what the paragraph is about, and what type of information you need to answer the questions, read the paragraph *very carefully*. This is the time to put that concentration practice to work, the time to concentrate exclusively on the material in the paragraph. While you are reading the material, note the key facts and mark them according to strategy 5.
5. **UNDERLINE OR CIRCLE KEY WORDS OR PHRASES. WRITE KEY FACTS IN THE MARGIN.** Unless the directions prohibit doing so, all good multiple-choice test takers use their pencil to underline key items in the reading passage and to write notations in the margin.

What kinds of key words or phrases should you underscore or circle?

- Transitional words and terms that signal a change in thought. Examples: *therefore, however, nevertheless, on the other hand, yet, but*
- Absolute words (usually a wrong choice as answers; they are generally too comprehensive and are difficult to defend). Examples: *never, always, only, none, all, any, nothing, everyone, nobody, everybody*
- Limiting words (usually a correct choice as answers). Examples: *usually, generally, few, occasionally, sometimes, some, possible, many, often*

How should you indicate key facts? Place an asterisk in the margin next to important information, write short notes with arrows directed to the portion of the passage to which you are referring, or bracket the portion that must stand out.

Important information includes *all items covered in the questions* and, in fire-related materials, such points as the following:

- Time of occurrence
- Dangerous items
- Location of fire
- Number of exits

- Statements of or about key people
- Fire protection equipment
- Orders or directions

A little restraint is also needed. You must keep in mind the purpose of all this marking and noting—to help you understand the passage and retrieve information quickly. Too many marks or notes can be confusing and will obscure, rather than emphasize, important items.

6. **ASK YOURSELF QUESTIONS WHILE READING THE PARAGRAPH.** Your ability to understand the passage is increased significantly when you pause occasionally and ask yourself questions about what you are reading, for example:

   - What am I supposed to know, now that I have read (heard) this material?
   - What is the main idea of the passage as a whole?
   - What is the main purpose of each paragraph in the passage?
   - What action is required?
   - Who is directly affected?
   - What could have been done to increase safety?

7. **DEVELOP A MENTAL PICTURE OF WHAT YOU ARE READING.** Many people find that the best way to understand and enjoy a novel is to project themselves into the story, and then try to share the characters' experiences. The good test taker uses this technique when working with reading and verbal comprehension questions. Use your imagination to develop a mental picture or impression of what you are reading. If you practice this with your everyday reading material, such as newspapers and magazines, you will find that it helps you to retain what you read.
8. **ANSWER THE QUESTIONS**, using the strategies outlined in Chapter 5. Remember that every answer is contained somewhere in the reading passage; review the passage to verify your choice and to eliminate the wrong answers. If you have noted key facts in the margin of the test booklet, you should be able to locate and review the appropriate section rapidly.
9. **NOTE TAKING.** Divide your note page in two parts. One part of the page is for ideas and the other for lists of words, phrases or an outline of the reading. You can divide the page into two columns or a top and bottom section depending on what you feel works best for you.

   While the person is reading the passage, try to listen for the emphasis on each idea. The person is not supposed to give you hints or clues, but will follow the punctuation of the author. The punctuation will give you clues to the emphasis. Restate the ideas in brief phrases—don't try to write complete sentences down exactly as they were read—a few of the words are often all you need. Write these notes in the section of your note page for ideas. On the other section of your note page write key words as you identify them. When you think that it is appropriate, group key words into lists, such as the way fire spreads, the duties of a firefighter, and the steps in the process of administering CPR (Cardiopulmonary Resuscitation), either immediately below the main key word or alongside the key word. USE plenty of SPACE to keep the words apart from each other. This will give you room to add new thoughts or words and will help you to find them quickly when you go back to look for them.

Shorthand: Develop a shorthand-writing system for yourself. For example, w/ = with, m = 1,000, 3m = 3,000, bk = book, ff = firefighter. Make your own shorthand, but try not to get too elaborate. Make sure that you keep a record of your shorthand abbreviations. You may think you will remember them, but experience has proven this assumption to be false. After you have identified a shorthand item, use it frequently and have it become a part of your writing vocabulary. Consider keeping your shorthand terms on a card or in the book with your vocabulary words.

Use the technique of drawing illustrations or simple models to capture a large idea or concept quickly; this will save you time. Use standard abbreviations as much as possible (CPR, Dr., IBM, 3M).

Don't be overly concerned with neatness; legibility and speed are what you need at this point in time. The key is to make your note-taking time work for you; it should help you simplify the process of collecting and using information.

When the proctor is finished reading, don't go to the questions. Instead, go over your notes and fill in the words or information you may have left out; you need to make sense of what you wrote. Don't put all your trust in your ability to recall, use your key words and illustrations to assist you. Then answer the questions.

ANSWER SHEET
Practice Exercises

1. Ⓐ Ⓑ Ⓒ Ⓓ	16. Ⓐ Ⓑ Ⓒ Ⓓ	31. Ⓐ Ⓑ Ⓒ Ⓓ	46. Ⓐ Ⓑ Ⓒ Ⓓ
2. Ⓐ Ⓑ Ⓒ Ⓓ	17. Ⓐ Ⓑ Ⓒ Ⓓ	32. Ⓐ Ⓑ Ⓒ Ⓓ	47. Ⓐ Ⓑ Ⓒ Ⓓ
3. Ⓐ Ⓑ Ⓒ Ⓓ	18. Ⓐ Ⓑ Ⓒ Ⓓ	33. Ⓐ Ⓑ Ⓒ Ⓓ	48. Ⓐ Ⓑ Ⓒ Ⓓ
4. Ⓐ Ⓑ Ⓒ Ⓓ	19. Ⓐ Ⓑ Ⓒ Ⓓ	34. Ⓐ Ⓑ Ⓒ Ⓓ	49. Ⓐ Ⓑ Ⓒ Ⓓ
5. Ⓐ Ⓑ Ⓒ Ⓓ	20. Ⓐ Ⓑ Ⓒ Ⓓ	35. Ⓐ Ⓑ Ⓒ Ⓓ	50. Ⓐ Ⓑ Ⓒ Ⓓ
6. Ⓐ Ⓑ Ⓒ Ⓓ	21. Ⓐ Ⓑ Ⓒ Ⓓ	36. Ⓐ Ⓑ Ⓒ Ⓓ	
7. Ⓐ Ⓑ Ⓒ Ⓓ	22. Ⓐ Ⓑ Ⓒ Ⓓ	37. Ⓐ Ⓑ Ⓒ Ⓓ	
8. Ⓐ Ⓑ Ⓒ Ⓓ	23. Ⓐ Ⓑ Ⓒ Ⓓ	38. Ⓐ Ⓑ Ⓒ Ⓓ	
9. Ⓐ Ⓑ Ⓒ Ⓓ	24. Ⓐ Ⓑ Ⓒ Ⓓ	39. Ⓐ Ⓑ Ⓒ Ⓓ	
10. Ⓐ Ⓑ Ⓒ Ⓓ	25. Ⓐ Ⓑ Ⓒ Ⓓ	40. Ⓐ Ⓑ Ⓒ Ⓓ	
11. Ⓐ Ⓑ Ⓒ Ⓓ	26. Ⓐ Ⓑ Ⓒ Ⓓ	41. Ⓐ Ⓑ Ⓒ Ⓓ	
12. Ⓐ Ⓑ Ⓒ Ⓓ	27. Ⓐ Ⓑ Ⓒ Ⓓ	42. Ⓐ Ⓑ Ⓒ Ⓓ	
13. Ⓐ Ⓑ Ⓒ Ⓓ	28. Ⓐ Ⓑ Ⓒ Ⓓ	43. Ⓐ Ⓑ Ⓒ Ⓓ	
14. Ⓐ Ⓑ Ⓒ Ⓓ	29. Ⓐ Ⓑ Ⓒ Ⓓ	44. Ⓐ Ⓑ Ⓒ Ⓓ	
15. Ⓐ Ⓑ Ⓒ Ⓓ	30. Ⓐ Ⓑ Ⓒ Ⓓ	45. Ⓐ Ⓑ Ⓒ Ⓓ	

PRACTICE EXERCISES

Much of the initial training that firefighters receive is from classroom instruction or from drill site simulations, which are of a hands-on nature; however, a great deal must also be learned from training bulletins, manuals, and guides. This kind of training requires the ability to read with understanding and the ability to apply what has been learned to solve a problem. The following series of exercise questions was developed to allow you to test your ability to read or listen to a passage and apply what you learned. You can expect similar questions on the exam.

READING COMPREHENSION

Directions: For each group of questions, read the passage and answer the questions that follow. After reading the passage carefully, choose for each question the one best answer—(A), (B), (C), or (D)—and write the corresponding letter on your answer sheet next to the number of the question.

Directions: Read the following passage and then answer questions 1 through 10 solely on the basis of information in the passage.

The All-Purpose Saw

The all-purpose saw, which is commonly used in the fire service, facilitates cutting operations, speeds ventilation, and generally provides greater operational efficiency at fires and emergencies.

This saw is powered by a high-speed gasoline engine that drives a 12-inch circular blade. The blade's maximum depth of cut is 4 inches. The two-stroke engine develops between 7 and 8 horsepower at a blade speed of 6,000 RPM. The combination of high horsepower, great speed, and use of proper blade enables the user to cut virtually any material encountered at fire and emergency operations.

The saw comes equipped with three cutting blades: a carbide-tip blade, a steel-cutting blade, and a concrete-cutting blade.

The carbide-tip blade is specially designed for cutting through gravel- and tar-covered roofs, wood flooring, light sheet-metal coverings, and other, similar substances. The steel-cutting blade is an aluminum oxide abrasive blade used for cutting through various types of steel found in automobile wrecks, bars on windows, and similar objects. The concrete-cutting blade is a high-speed silicon carbide abrasive blade used for cutting through concrete and other masonry products.

For maximum safety and greatest operational efficiency only sharp blades approved by the manufacturer should be used.

1. The steel-cutting blade is

   (A) made of aluminum.
   (B) used to cut windows.
   (C) an abrasive-type blade.
   (D) designed for cutting light sheet metal.

2. For which of the following would the fire service all-purpose saw NOT be used?

   (A) Making cutting operations easier.
   (B) Cutting a cord of firewood.
   (C) Making fire operations more efficient.
   (D) Speeding up the ventilation process.

3. The cut of the all-purpose saw is limited to a depth of

   (A) 2 inches.
   (B) 4 inches.
   (C) 6 inches.
   (D) 12 inches.

4. To cut a wood floor the best blade would be the

   (A) aluminum blade.
   (B) silicon carbide blade.
   (C) steel-cutting blade.
   (D) carbide-tip blade.

5. To breach a hole in a cinder-block wall the most effective tool is an all-purpose saw with a

   (A) high-speed abrasive blade.
   (B) carbide blade.
   (C) aluminum oxide blade.
   (D) silicon carbide blade.

6. The best saw blade for cutting a ventilation hole in a roof is

   (A) a silicon blade.
   (B) a carbide-tip blade.
   (C) an oxide blade.
   (D) none of the above.

7. The all-purpose saw is highly effective because of

   (A) its high speed.
   (B) the versatility of the saw blades.
   (C) its high horsepower.
   (D) the combination of high speed, high horsepower, and versatility.

8. A firefighter alert for safety would use

   (A) the saw only on the ground.
   (B) only sharp blades.
   (C) a back-up firefighter to watch the operation.
   (D) only the carbide-tip blade.

9. Which of the following would be INCORRECT to say about the all-purpose saw?

   (A) It is rarely used by the fire service.
   (B) It comes equipped with three types of blades.
   (C) It can cut almost any material.
   (D) It can be used at fires or emergencies.

10. The horsepower rating of the all-purpose saw is approximately

   (A) 3.5 horsepower.
   (B) 4.5 horsepower.
   (C) 7.5 horsepower.
   (D) 6,000 horsepower.

Directions: Read the following passage and then answer questions 11 through 15 solely on the basis of information in the passage.

Lifting

Sprains and strains continue to account for a large percentage of the time lost to injuries. In a significant number of cases the circumstances indicate that a modification in the method of lifting might have prevented the injury. Lifting is so much a part of everyday living that most of us don't think about how we do it. Unfortunately, it is often done incorrectly, resulting in pulled muscles, disc injuries, or painful hernias. There are some simple, basic steps for safe lifting that everyone should be aware of and should use, not just on duty, but for off-the-job tasks as well.

Here are seven basic steps for safe lifting, to be applied whenever possible:

- If the object to be lifted is too heavy, get help.
- Part your feet comfortably, with one alongside the object and one behind it.
- Keep your back straight, nearly vertical.
- Keep elbows and arms close to the body.
- Grip the object with both hands, using the whole hand.
- Tuck your chin in.
- Keep your body weight directly over your feet.

11. It would be INCORRECT to lift a relatively heavy pail of debris with

    (A) elbows and arms close to the body.
    (B) chin tucked in.
    (C) body weight over the object.
    (D) back straight.

12. If you are a firefighter confronted with the need to lift an extremely heavy object, you would be acting correctly if you

    (A) advised your superior that the object could not be lifted.
    (B) requested help from your superior.
    (C) tucked in your chin, gritted your teeth, and lifted the object yourself.
    (D) convinced yourself the object would not be too heavy if you used the proper lifting technique.

13. INCORRECT lifting

    (A) leads to headaches.
    (B) seldom occurs.
    (C) can result in a pulled muscle.
    (D) cannot be avoided.

14. It would be INCORRECT to say about the process of lifting that

    (A) there are seven basic steps for safe lifting.
    (B) many injuries incurred while lifting could be avoided.
    (C) lifting is seldom required outside our jobs.
    (D) injuries incurred while lifting are responsible for much lost time.

15. Poor lifting methods lead to sprains and strains. These injuries

    (A) occur only when on duty.
    (B) are an unavoidable hazard of the firefighter's job.
    (C) usually occur at night.
    (D) account for a large percentage of the time lost to injuries.

Directions: Read the following passage and then answer questions 16 through 22 solely on the basis of information in the passage.

Calculated Risk

Probably the most overworked, the most deceptive, and the least understood term heard in discussions involving safety is "calculated risk." Each of the two words has a definite meaning in itself; used in combination and applied to familiar problems, however, the words usually imply a certain confusion, both in the mind of the person using them and in regard to the particular situation to which they are being applied.

Firefighters work in a hostile environment and are often faced with emergencies that prompt risk-tasking. How "calculated" can their actions be if time has not been taken to "calculate"? Without an estimate of the situation, the "risk" may be nothing but a foolhardy act that exposes firefighters to injury and thus complicates, rather than expedites, the accomplishment of the task. With reference to fire fighting, safety is a relative condition. Firefighters are obliged to accept something less than an absolute degree of safety, and this is understood as a condition of the job. We must approach with caution, however, the inclination to solve each difficult problem with the words "a calculated risk" unless the situation has really been evaluated.

It becomes fairly obvious from questioning individuals who have stated "I took a calculated risk" that in most cases no calculations, mental or otherwise, were ever made. In fact, it is not unusual to discover that the speaker had not the vaguest notion whether the chance for an accident was one in ten or one in a million.

Statements regarding calculated risk can be meaningful only when the individual concerned

1. knows the job.
2. applies that knowledge to the task.
3. has sufficient experience to make an intelligent evaluation of the situation.

If these criteria are not met, the outcome will fall entirely to "chance." Firefighters must not allow chance to become a way of life. They cannot afford to dash about blindly, depending on Lady Luck for protection. The answer lies in disciplining oneself to size up a situation rapidly and to make moves based on job knowledge and know-how. Only then can a firefighter truthfully say, "I took a calculated risk."

16. The term "calculated risk" is

    (A) an infrequently used expression.
    (B) not part of a firefighter's vocabulary.
    (C) the best-understood term in the fire service.
    (D) one of the most overworked and most deceptive phrases used in connection with safety.

17. A firefighter knows that

    (A) chance is a way of life.
    (B) Lady Luck and calculated risk are synonymous.
    (C) most people make a conscious effort to estimate a calculated risk.
    (D) even though the risk was calculated, it may still cause injury.

18. The main point of this passage is that

    (A) firefighters have to take risks.
    (B) injuries can be reduced by clear thinking.
    (C) following the rules for making a calculated risk will remove the threat of chance.
    (D) the firefighter's safety is the most important consideration in firefighting.

19. To make a meaningful calculated risk one must

    (A) discipline oneself to size up a situation rapidly and make moves based on job knowledge and know-how.
    (B) develop the firefighting skills that allow chance to become a way of life.
    (C) study the rules for probability theory and statistical analysis so that one can accurately determine the chance of an accident.
    (D) avoid working in areas that present unusual hazard potential.

20. Firefighters work in a hostile physical environment and are often faced with emergencies. It would be accurate to state that

    (A) firefighters are always required to take risks.
    (B) only some firefighters should take risks.
    (C) firefighters should evaluate the probability of success before taking a risk.
    (D) the calculation of risk is desirable but is time consuming, and firefighters often don't have time to do it.

21. It would be correct to say about "calculated risk" that

    (A) each of the two words has the same meaning.
    (B) risk cannot be calculated.
    (C) the term is badly misunderstood.
    (D) the term is confusing.

22. It would be INCORRECT for a fire officer to believe that

    (A) firefighters must accept something less than an absolute degree of safety.
    (B) risk may be taken without estimating the situation.
    (C) safety is a relative condition where firefighting is concerned.
    (D) self-discipline is an essential component of firefighting.

VERBAL/LISTENING COMPREHENSION

Directions: For each group of questions, have someone read the passage to you, then cover passage with a clean, blank sheet of paper. Now review and fill in your notes and then answer the questions. Do not go back and look at the passage until you have completed ALL of the questions in the group. You may be tempted to tell yourself its OK this one time, but you only fool yourself. If you get a question right, it will be right when you finish and if you get it wrong, it may effect the way you answer the rest of the questions.

Directions: Listen to the following passage and then answer questions 23 through 30 solely on the basis of information in the passage.

Heat Transmission

Fires can spread by three means of thermal (heat) transmission: conduction, convection, and radiation.

Conduction occurs in all materials to some degree. It is the transmission of heat through a material without any visible motion of the matter. An accepted explanation of this phenomenon is that thermally disturbed molecules transmit heat energy by agitating adjoining molecules. The abilities to transmit this heat energy varies with the specific material.

- Solids are the best conductors.
- Liquids are poor conductors.
- Gases are relative nonconductors.

Of the solids, metals are the best conductors. It may be noted that the better thermal conductors are also usually the better electrical conductors.

Example: In the common radiator, heat delivered by a fluid is conducted from the inner to the outer surface of the radiator to heat space.

Convection is a common phenomenon. Here heat is transmitted by the automatic circulation of liquid or gas involved. Upon receiving heat, it becomes less dense and tends to rise. A colder fluid, being heavier, falls to a lower level.

Example: Hot water in a boiler is heated and, because of temperature and density differential, rises to radiators above. There the heat is transmitted to the metal of the radiator. The liquid, being cooled, then seeks the lower (boiler) level, where the cycle is repeated.

For another example of convection let's look at the same radiator that conducted the heat to its outer surface. The surrounding air absorbs the heat from the radiator, becomes lighter, rises, and is then replaced by cooler and more dense air.

Radiation, a major cause of fire extension in large fires in built-up areas, is a phenomenon whereby heat energy is transmitted through space. All matter (other than that at absolute zero) emits radiation when thermally agitated. The degree of radiation varies with the material and the agitation. The wavelength of the heat waves varies from the shortest, ultraviolet, to the longest, infrared. The heat waves travel only in straight lines through space, without heating the space concerned, until they reach a body capable of absorbing the energy.

Example: Sun or heat energy from fire, passing through a window, heats material in the room.

In summation, it may be briefly stated that, as far as transmission is concerned, the associations are as follows:

Conduction—solids.

Convection—air, liquids, or gases.

Radiation—space.

23. Which of the following statement is correct according to the passage?

    (A) Metals are the best conductors.
    (B) Convection is the same as conduction.
    (C) Heat radiation is a major cause of cancer.
    (D) Conduction occurs only in liquids.

24. In accordance with the phenomenon of convection, at a house fire heat should

    (A) disperse rapidly.
    (B) seek lower levels.
    (C) increase geometrically.
    (D) rise until stopped by a barrier.

25. Heat is transmitted through space by

    (A) conduction.
    (B) convection.
    (C) radiation.
    (D) none of the above.

26. The thermal transmission of fires occurs by all of the following EXCEPT

    (A) association.
    (B) conduction.
    (C) radiation.
    (D) convection.

27. Which of the following is correct in regard to the wavelengths of heat waves?

    (A) The shortest is ultrascopic.
    (B) The longest is infrared.
    (C) The shortest is ultrared.
    (D) The longest is infraviolet.

28. Which of the following statements is accurate?

(A) Conduction occurs in all materials.
(B) Liquids are good conductors.
(C) Convection of heated air is rare.
(D) All fluids are liquids.

29. Heat transmission is a constant problem. Fires spread by

(A) conduction only.
(B) thermal transmission.
(C) the hot water in a boiler.
(D) the sun.

30. Which of the following statements is INCORRECT?

(A) The sun's rays are a form of convected heat energy.
(B) Heat will travel through the water and rise in the pipes.
(C) The air is coolest close to the floor.
(D) Radiation travels in straight lines.

Directions: Listen to the following passage and then answer questions 31 through 37 solely on the basis of information in the passage.

Many home owners and apartment dwellers concerned about their possessions and their personal safety install sophisticated locking devices on the entrances of their domiciles. These locking devices are effective at keeping out the unwanted; however, they often create prison-like conditions for the home owner or apartment occupant.

When a fire occurs, firefighters must gain rapid entry to a building to rescue people inside and to extinguish the fire. Elaborate locking devices have often proved burdensome to firefighters. However, the recent development of powerful hydraulic tools are allowing the firefighters to get to occupants faster and easier.

The term "Jaws" was given to a powerful pushing and pulling tool. This tool is able to exert more than 10,000 pounds of force and can rapidly pry open the most difficult obstruction. The Jaws of Life has been used as an automobile extrication tool very successfully, and has proven to be an important part of the firefighter's arsenal. This powerful rescue system is composed of a hydraulic spreading device, a power unit, high-grade hydraulic hose, spread locking device and pulling jaws, cutting jaws, rams, hand pump, and chains with hooks.

The Jaws of Life is heavy and cumbersome. Heavy tools can not be carried easily or rapidly to remote locations. This is a major disadvantage of "Jaws." Another disadvantage to this tool is the need for a gasoline generator to supply power to operate the tool. The most common and preferred method for using the Jaws of Life is with the power generator; however, the hand pump should be used in areas where an explosive atmosphere exists. The hand pump is effective as a back-up solution should the gasoline pump become inoperative.

Another tool, the handheld hydraulic press, weighs less than 30 pounds, is easily transported, and is operational with the use of a hand pump. This tool is similar to a hydraulic automobile jack. The handheld hydraulic tool can exert a force of more than 4,000 pounds. This tool exerts a pushing force between the outer door jamb and the door; thus, it can work only on inward-opening doors. The jaws of the tool are tapped into place with a maul or the back of a 6-pound ax. The hand pump operates quickly to spread the jaws and open the door. The handheld hydraulic press is not intended as an automobile extrication tool and should not be used for this type of rescue.

When hydraulic tools are not immediately available, the firefighter must use hand tools, such as a pry bar or ax. Some fire companies use a special tool to remove locking devices and open the door in the conventional method. This is known as the "through the lock" method. A tool known as the "K-tool" is hammered behind the rim of the lock, and then a pry bar is used to force the locking cylinder out of the door. This allows the firefighter to get access to the interior of the locking device, which can then be easily opened. The problem the firefighter has is that sometimes occupants will put three or four locks on a door or will put recessed rims on the lock, making it impossible to get the K-tool into position.

31. Which of the following is most accurate?

    (A) Apartment dwellers almost always have three or four locks on their entrance doors.
    (B) The "Jaws of Life" is effective on automobiles using the "through the lock" method.
    (C) Sophisticated locking devices keep the occupants in a prison-like living condition.
    (D) Recessed rims on door locks make it possible to get the K-tool into position.

32. The tool a firefighter would most likely choose to force entry into an apartment would be a

    (A) maul or axe.
    (B) maul or axe and the K-tool.
    (C) maul or axe and handheld hydraulic press.
    (D) maul or axe and the Jaws of Life.

33. It would be LEAST correct to state that

    (A) the hand pump is not intended to be used as an automobile extrication tool.
    (B) the hand pump and the Jaws of Life are effective in an explosive atmosphere.
    (C) the handheld hydraulic press is powered by the hand pump.
    (D) the "Jaws" with the hand pump exerts a force up to 4,000 pounds.

34. Which hydraulic tool would be used at an automobile accident?

    (A) Jaws of Life.
    (B) Automobile jack.
    (C) K-tool.
    (D) Handheld hydraulic press.

35. A firefighter talking to a group of citizens would be most correct in saying that

(A) of all the forcible entry tools, the Jaws of Life is the heaviest.
(B) the K-tool is used for recessed rim locks.
(C) the handheld hydraulic press exerts 10,000 pounds of pressure.
(D) sophisticated locking devices have never been a problem for firefighters.

36. The Jaws of Life are for

(A) exerting a force up to 4,000 pounds.
(B) pushing and pulling.
(C) rapidly forcing doors.
(D) pulling trains apart.

37. Which of the following is not part of the Jaws of Life system?

(A) Spreading device.
(B) Maul.
(C) Chains.
(D) Ram.

Directions: Questions 38 through 50 will assess your mathematical skills. Read each passage carefully, and choose the best answer for each question. Mark your answer on the answer sheet with the corresponding letter.

You are buying groceries and preparing meals for *A* shift at Station 2. An engine company and an ambulance crew are on duty, a total of 4 personnel. To pay for the meals, Lieutenant Jones gives you $10.00, Firefighter Smith gives you $6.00, and Firefighter Park gives you $5.00. You go to the store and purchase one loaf of bread for $2.54, vegetables for $4.85, potatoes for $0.99, meat for $6.84, and snacks for $4.25. Tax at 8.5% is added to the total.

38. What is the total grocery bill for the day?

(A) $19.47
(B) $21.12
(C) $20.47
(D) $22.12

39. Will Lieutenant Jones owe you money or get money back? How much?

(A) owes $4.58
(B) receive $4.58
(C) owes $4.72
(D) receive $4.72

40. Will firefighter Smith owe money or get money back? How much?

(A) owes $0.72
(B) receive $0.72
(C) owes $0.97
(D) receives $0.97

41. Will firefighter Park owe money or get money back? How much?

(A) owes $0.28
(B) receives $0.28
(C) owes $0.38
(D) receives $0.38

42. Firefighter Park decides he doesn't want potatoes. After a discussion, the crew decides to refund his portion of the money for the potatoes. Approximately how much money will Firefighter Park get back?

(A) $0.33
(B) $0.26
(C) $0.36
(D) $0.28

43. What did you pay for the day's meals?

(A) $4.38
(B) $6.28
(C) $5.28
(D) $5.08

44. You are given orders to test five 100′ lengths of 5″ hose, six-50′ lengths of 3″ hose, and eleven-50′ lengths of 1¾ hose. Using Engine 31, you and your crew connect the hoses to the four ports on the engine, fill the lines with water, set the pressure for 150 psi, and prepare to run the test for 30 minutes. During the first test, you find three-50′ sections of 3″ hose leaking. You shut down the operation, disconnect the leaking hoses, and continue testing the remaining hose lines. The rest of the hose lines pass the test. How many sections of hose didn't fail the test?

(A) 0
(B) 12
(C) 19
(D) 22

45. If you can connect only three hose lines to a port for a total of 150′, how many tests did you do until you tested all of the hose?

(A) 1
(B) 2
(C) 3
(D) 4

46. You are the engineer driving to the scene of a fire. You are traveling at a constant speed of 55 mph, and you reach the fire scene in 13 minutes. Approximately how many miles is it to the fire scene?

(A) 10 miles
(B) 12 miles
(C) 13 miles
(D) 14 miles

47. The vehicle describes in question 46 burns diesel fuel at the rate of 8 miles per gallon. How many gallons did it use going to the scene and returning to the station?

(A) 3
(B) 5
(C) 6
(D) 8

48. If diesel sells for $4.39 per gallon, how much will it cost to fill the tank?

(A) $14.17
(B) $13.17
(C) $12.17
(D) $15.17

49. You notice Engine 51 needs fuel and the gauge reads 1/3. The capacity of the tank is 51 gallons. About how much fuel will be needed?

(A) 7 gallons
(B) 17 gallons
(C) 34 gallons
(D) 51 gallons

50. How much did it cost to fill the tank?

(A) $30.73
(B) $74.63
(C) $149.26
(D) $223.89

ANSWER KEY AND EXPLANATIONS

Answer Key

1. **(C)**	11. **(C)**	21. **(C)**	31. **(C)**	41. **(A)**
2. **(B)**	12. **(B)**	22. **(B)**	32. **(C)**	42. **(B)**
3. **(B)**	13. **(C)**	23. **(A)**	33. **(D)**	43. **(C)**
4. **(D)**	14. **(C)**	24. **(D)**	34. **(A)**	44. **(C)**
5. **(D)**	15. **(D)**	25. **(C)**	35. **(A)**	45. **(C)**
6. **(B)**	16. **(D)**	26. **(A)**	36. **(B)**	46. **(B)**
7. **(D)**	17. **(D)**	27. **(B)**	37. **(B)**	47. **(A)**
8. **(B)**	18. **(B)**	28. **(A)**	38. **(B)**	48. **(B)**
9. **(A)**	19. **(A)**	29. **(B)**	39. **(D)**	49. **(C)**
10. **(C)**	20. **(C)**	30. **(A)**	40. **(B)**	50. **(C)**

Answer Explanations

1. **(C)** The steel-cutting blade is described in paragraph four as an aluminum oxide abrasive blade. (A common practice of examiners is to cut off part of a statement, just enough to make the statement correct yet incomplete.) Choice A—this blade is not made of aluminum; aluminum oxide is a composition material. Choice B—the steel-cutting blade is used on window bars, not windows. Choice D—for light sheet metal the carbide-tip blade is used.

2. **(B)** This use is not mentioned in the passage. The saw could cut firewood, but the fire service does not officially use the saw for this purpose. The other choices are all specifically mentioned in the passage.

3. **(B)** This information is found in the second sentence of the second paragraph.

4. **(D)** Cutting wood is the primary use of the carbide-tip blade. See the opening sentence of the fourth paragraph.

5. **(D)** See the last sentence in the fourth paragraph. Choices A and B are other examples of how an examiner may cut off part of a statement; this time, however, the choices are made too broad and therefore incorrect.

6. **(B)** This is part of the opening statement in paragraph four.

7. **(D)** This statement is given in the second paragraph, last sentence. The other choices are incorrect because they are incomplete.

8. **(B)** This information is in the last paragraph. Choice A—this is impractical; the saw must be used on roofs and on window bars, which are not always on the ground floor. Choice C—this would be a good technique, but you are directed to choose your answer according to information in the passage. Choice D—this would limit the versatility of the saw and also is not justified by the passage.

9. **(A)** The opening statement of the passage tells us that the saw is commonly used by the fire service. The other choices are all true statements, according to the passage.

10. **(C)** This is found in the second paragraph (between 7 and 8 horsepower).

11. **(C)** The last basic rule states that the body weight should be kept over the feet, not over the object.

12. **(B)** By asking for help, you would have informed your officer of the problem and would be able to avoid injury (see the first basic rule). Choice A—this implies that you would not attempt to solve the problem of lifting the heavy object. In multiple-choice questions you are required to select the best answer. Choice B, being justified by the passage, is superior to choice A. Choice C—this is an unsafe act. Choice D—the stem indicates the object is extremely heavy; therefore it should not be lifted without assistance.

13. **(C)** This statement is found in the fourth sentence. The other choices are contradicted by the passage.

14. **(C)** In the third sentence we are told that lifting is so much a part of everyday living that most of us don't think about how we do it. The other choices are all correct statements according to the passage.

15. **(D)** This information is found in the opening sentence of the paragraph. Choice A—the last sentence of the first paragraph states that safe practices are for use both on and off duty. Choice B—see the second sentence of the first paragraph. Choice C—there is no mention in the passage about when lifting injuries occur; you should not infer that they usually occur at night or during the day.

16. **(D)** This is the opening statement of the passage.

17. **(D)** Computing the chance of success helps to determine whether a firefighter will or will not take the risk. Even though this is done, there is still a chance of injury. Choice A—chance is complete randomness, with no thinking or interaction on the individual's part. Obviously, this does not have to be a way of life; people can make decisions, and these decisions do affect the outcome of events. Choice B—Lady Luck is chance; it is not calculated risk. Choice C—most people do not make a conscious effort to calculate the degree of risk (see paragraph three).

18. **(B)** The thrust of this passage is that injuries can be reduced by thinking about whether to take a particular risk. Choice A—firefighters must take risks, but this is not the *main* point of the passage; it is only a subpoint. Choice C—following the rules for a calculated risk will allow the decision maker to have more data on which to base the decision but will not rule out chance entirely. Choice D—a firefighter's safety is important; however, personal safety must often be overlooked to extinguish a dangerous fire or to save another's life (see paragraph two).

19. **(A)** See the last paragraph. Choice B—chance should not be a way of life. Choice C—these theories have very little application on the fire ground. Estimating most "calculated risks" requires other knowledge and skills. Choice D—this is impractical in regard to firefighting.

20. **(C)** This is the theme of the passage. Choice A—firefighters are required to take risks but not *always*—an absolute term. Choice B—only some firefighters take a risk at any one given time, but all firefighters are presented with the challenge of having to take

risks at some time. Choice D—the fact is that they do have time and must take it (see paragraph two).

21. **(C)** The first sentence tells us that "calculated risk" is a "least understood" term. "Badly misunderstood" is another way of saying the same thing. Choice A—each of the words has a definite meaning in itself, and these meanings are different. To "calculate" you must make a computation. "Risk" implies taking a chance that may lead to failure. Choice B—risk can be calculated, maybe not as well as we would wish, but to some degree. Choice D—the term itself is not confusing; it is the improper use of the term that has led to confusion (see the first paragraph).

22. **(B)** In the second paragraph the author states "without an estimate of the situation, the 'risk' may be nothing but a foolhardy act. . . ." The other statements are all true according to the passage.

23. **(A)** Solids are the best conductors; of the solids, metals are the best. Choice B—conduction is the transmitting of heat by agitation of adjoining molecules. In convection heat is transmitted through a circulation process. Choice C—this is not mentioned in the passage and therefore is not an acceptable choice (see the stem of the question). Choice D—conduction occurs in all materials to some degree (see paragraph two).

24. **(D)** Heat is transmitted to the fluid (gas or liquid). The fluid then becomes lighter and rises; however, it can rise only if there is room to do so. If a ceiling or roof has no opening, heat will collect there until it finds or burns a hole through it. There is no justification in the passage for any other choice.

25. **(C)** As stated in the passage, radiation travels through space in straight lines without heating the space until it finds a body capable of absorbing the heat.

26. **(A)** Most questions on entrance examinations are looking for correct answers; however, you must also be prepared for the opposite. You must also watch out for the word EXCEPT; it is the key to finding the correct answer since it changes the direction of the stem. There is no mention of thermal transmission by "association" in the passage.

27. **(B)** This practice of jumbling parts of words requires some patience on your part. You must find the section in the passage that applies and then mark each answer as correct or incorrect. There is only one correct statement.

28. **(A)** This is found in the opening sentence of the second paragraph. Choice B—liquids are poor conductors. Choice C—the passage states that convection is a common phenomenon. Choice D—fluids may be *liquids* or *gases.*

29. **(B)** "Thermal transmission" is a synonym for "heat transmission" (see the opening statement).

30. **(A)** The sun's rays are radiation waves. Choices B and C—these are correct; see the example under convection. Choice D—this is correct; see the paragraph on radiation.

31. **(C)** This is stated in the first paragraph. Choice A is incorrect; to be correct, change "almost always" to "sometimes." Choice B is incorrect. A technique for distracting the candidate is to combine a true statement with an unrelated statement that makes the answer incorrect. Choice D is incorrect; it should read "impossible."

32. **(C)** The message the writer is trying to give is the difficulty firefighters have in gaining access to the occupancy and the new tools that are now used by firefighters. The handheld hydraulic press rapidly and effectively accomplishes the mission, is lighter and quicker than the Jaws of Life, and much more effective than the K-tool or other handheld tools. It therefore is the most likely choice of firefighters. Choice A would be the last choice of firefighters. Choice B is better than A, but not as good as C. Choice D is incorrect. The maul is not used with the Jaws of Life.

33. **(D)** The third paragraph says the Jaws of Life exerts a force up to 10,000 pounds. Choice A is a correct statement; the hand pump is a power source for tools. Choice B and C are correct.

34. **(A)** The third paragraph tells the reader this tool has been used very successfully on automobile extrication. Choice B is incorrect. The automobile jack, although conceptually the same as the handheld hydraulic press, should not be used. Choice C is incorrect. The K-tool is used for door locks. Choice D is incorrect. The last sentence of the fourth paragraph tells the reader not to use this tool for automobile extrication.

35. **(A)** The third paragraph tells the reader the Jaws of Life is heavy, and a heavy tool can not be rapidly carried. The passage also tells the reader that the handheld hydraulic tool is easily transported; thus, the reader can deduce that the handheld hydraulic tool is lighter than the Jaws of Life. The maul and axe weigh about 6 pounds. Choice B is incorrect. The K-tool is not effective on recessed rim locks. Choice C is incorrect. The handheld hydraulic press exerts a force of 4,000 pounds. Choice D is incorrect. Sophisticated locks have been a problem.

36. **(B)** This is stated in the third sentence of the third paragraph. Choice A is incorrect. It should read 10,000 pounds. Choice C is incorrect. The tool can easily force doors but cannot be put into place and made operational rapidly. Choice D is incorrect. There is no mention of trains in the passage, and the instructions to the candidate say to use only the information in the passage. An answer may be true but not correct. You are being tested on your ability to understand what you read and your ability to follow written directions.

37. **(B)** The parts of the Jaws of Life system are listed in paragraph three; the maul is not listed as one of them.

38. **(B)** Answer A is the total before taxes. The correct answer is B. By adding all of the items together and adding the sales tax, $21.12 will be your total. If you added correctly, C or D will not be correct.

39. **(D)** If you added correctly in question 38, you should be able to divide the total by four and arrive at the correct answer. Each person's total is $5.28. If you added incorrectly, questions 40 through 43 will be wrong from here on.

40. **(B)** See the explanation for question 39.

41. **(A)** See the explanation for question 39.

42. **(B)** See the explanation for question 39.

43. **(C)** See the explanation for question 39.

44. **(C)** Add the total number of hose lengths and subtract 3.

45. **(C)** Add the total amount of feet of hose 5 × 100′ = 500′, 6 × 50′ = 300′, 11 × 50′ = 550 or 1350′, divide this by 150′ per port, this gives you 8 with 1/3 left or a 50' length of hose, divide this by the four ports and you have 3 tests to finish the hose testing.

46. **(B)** Use rate × time divided by 60 or 55/60 × 13/1 = 12

47. **(A)** Divide 24 miles round-trip by 8 miles per gallon to get the total gallons used.

48. **(B)** If you answered question 47 correctly, just multiply by the cost per gallon.

49. **(C)** The tank is 2/3 empty. So multiply 2/3 into 51. That equals 34. You could also multiply 51 by 1/3 and then multiply by 2 to get 34.

50. **(C)** If you answered question 49 correctly, multiply by the cost per gallon.

Decision Making, Reasoning, and Problem Solving

8

This part of the examination measures your ability to use logic and common sense in the solving of problems.

The questions will generally relate to situations that require you either to take some action, to explain why an action has or would be taken, or to interpret what the action implies.

UNDERSTANDING THE DECISION AND REASONING PROBLEM

Decision making, reasoning, and problem solving are closely related subjects. The search to understand how they differ has led to many excellent theories; unfortunately it has also led to more new and challenging questions. For our purposes let us not worry about a theory; instead let us use the application of such a theory to our best advantage.

There are two types of reasoning questions: deductive, using general statements to get to a specific conclusion, and inductive, using specific statements to get to a general conclusion.

FIVE STEPS FOR HANDLING PROBLEM-SOLVING QUESTIONS

The steps necessary to arrive at the best solution for a question of this type are as follows:

1. *Identify* the PROBLEM.
2. *Identify* the POSSIBLE solutions.
3. *Select* the BEST SOLUTION.
4. *Eliminate* the OTHER SOLUTIONS.
5. *Make* the DECISION.

Now let's look at each of these steps in greater detail.

1. Identify the problem: The stem of the question should reveal this. Read the question carefully, and clearly identify what is being asked. What is the special problem or point of the question? Is there a specific order you must follow? Are there any special instructions you must follow?
2. Identify the possible solutions: Read ALL the choices quickly to identify the one that best solves the problem.
3. Select the best solution and then defend it: Answer the questions "Why does this solve the problem?" "Does it solve the problem with the least damage and or danger (keeping in mind that damage can be both physical and mental)?" "Will it solve the problem within a reasonable time?" "Have you answered all the parts of the question? Are they in the correct order?"

4. Eliminate choices that

- are contradictory to what is required;
- call for unnecessary actions or risks (some risk may be necessary);
- require that an order be disobeyed;
- insult, disregard, interfere with, or hazard a citizen;
- benefit you alone;
- result in failure to obey a law;
- only partially solve the problem; or
- call for action that you are not authorized to take or are not in a position to implement.

5. Now make the decision and record your answer:

Decision-making problems can cover a wide variety of areas. For this reason there are no absolute rules, only guides. The ideal answer will (1) solve the problem (2) with a high degree of safety (3) in the least amount of time (4) with the least cost to the citizens and the fire service.

ANSWER SHEET
Practice Exercises

1. Ⓐ Ⓑ Ⓒ Ⓓ
2. Ⓐ Ⓑ Ⓒ Ⓓ
3. Ⓐ Ⓑ Ⓒ Ⓓ
4. Ⓐ Ⓑ Ⓒ Ⓓ
5. Ⓐ Ⓑ Ⓒ Ⓓ
6. Ⓐ Ⓑ Ⓒ Ⓓ
7. Ⓐ Ⓑ Ⓒ Ⓓ
8. Ⓐ Ⓑ Ⓒ Ⓓ
9. Ⓐ Ⓑ Ⓒ Ⓓ
10. Ⓐ Ⓑ Ⓒ Ⓓ
11. Ⓐ Ⓑ Ⓒ Ⓓ
12. Ⓐ Ⓑ Ⓒ Ⓓ
13. Ⓐ Ⓑ Ⓒ Ⓓ
14. Ⓐ Ⓑ Ⓒ Ⓓ
15. Ⓐ Ⓑ Ⓒ Ⓓ
16. Ⓐ Ⓑ Ⓒ Ⓓ
17. Ⓐ Ⓑ Ⓒ Ⓓ
18. Ⓐ Ⓑ Ⓒ Ⓓ
19. Ⓐ Ⓑ Ⓒ Ⓓ
20. Ⓐ Ⓑ Ⓒ Ⓓ
21. Ⓐ Ⓑ Ⓒ Ⓓ
22. Ⓐ Ⓑ Ⓒ Ⓓ
23. Ⓐ Ⓑ Ⓒ Ⓓ
24. Ⓐ Ⓑ Ⓒ Ⓓ
25. Ⓐ Ⓑ Ⓒ Ⓓ
26. Ⓐ Ⓑ Ⓒ Ⓓ
27. Ⓐ Ⓑ Ⓒ Ⓓ
28. Ⓐ Ⓑ Ⓒ Ⓓ
29. Ⓐ Ⓑ Ⓒ Ⓓ
30. Ⓐ Ⓑ Ⓒ Ⓓ
31. Ⓐ Ⓑ Ⓒ Ⓓ
32. Ⓐ Ⓑ Ⓒ Ⓓ
33. Ⓐ Ⓑ Ⓒ Ⓓ
34. Ⓐ Ⓑ Ⓒ Ⓓ
35. Ⓐ Ⓑ Ⓒ Ⓓ
36. Ⓐ Ⓑ Ⓒ Ⓓ
37. Ⓐ Ⓑ Ⓒ Ⓓ
38. Ⓐ Ⓑ Ⓒ Ⓓ
39. Ⓐ Ⓑ Ⓒ Ⓓ
40. Ⓐ Ⓑ Ⓒ Ⓓ
41. Ⓐ Ⓑ Ⓒ Ⓓ
42. Ⓐ Ⓑ Ⓒ Ⓓ
43. Ⓐ Ⓑ Ⓒ Ⓓ
44. Ⓐ Ⓑ Ⓒ Ⓓ
45. Ⓐ Ⓑ Ⓒ Ⓓ
46. Ⓐ Ⓑ Ⓒ Ⓓ
47. Ⓐ Ⓑ Ⓒ Ⓓ
48. Ⓐ Ⓑ Ⓒ Ⓓ
49. Ⓐ Ⓑ Ⓒ Ⓓ
50. Ⓐ Ⓑ Ⓒ Ⓓ

PRACTICE EXERCISES

Directions: Read each question carefully, and apply the five steps outlined in the preceding section. Select the one best answer—(A), (B), (C), or (D)—and mark your answer on the answer sheet with the corresponding letter.

1. A firefighter performing a fire prevention inspection finds a maintenance person using a match to check for the source of a suspected natural gas leak. The FIRST action the firefighter should take is to

   (A) tell the person how dangerous it is to get so close to the gas with a match.
   (B) explain that the area should be well ventilated before lighting the match.
   (C) tell the maintenance person to extinguish the match immediately.
   (D) issue a written order to the person in charge to have the match extinguished and to prevent this from happening again.

2. Firefighters sometimes indulge in fooling around or horseplay. Which description is accurate?

   (A) This is good. It builds morale.
   (B) This is not good. It leads to accidents.
   (C) This is good. It builds physical coordination.
   (D) This is not good. It wastes time.

3. While reading a firefighting magazine, a firefighter learns about what appears to be a better way to store the fire company's hose nozzles. The appropriate action for this firefighter is to

   (A) set up nozzles and tell the company this is how it is done.
   (B) bring the idea to the attention of his or her supervisor and discuss it with the company.
   (C) forget about the idea.
   (D) put the suggestion in writing and send it to the union.

4. The firefighter outside the building

   (A) is not really needed.
   (B) should be equipped with a self-contained breathing apparatus.
   (C) is checking the hose for leaks and defects.
   (D) should be inside the door so he can watch the more senior firefighters and learn from them.

5. The purpose of the blocks in the illustration is to

   (A) keep the hose from sliding.
   (B) keep the hose dry.
   (C) allow cars to pass over the hose.
   (D) slow down the stretching of the hose line.

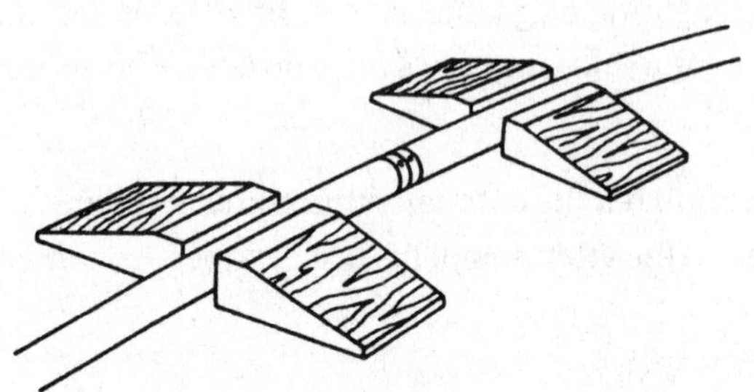

6. The function of the wooden block and rubber tube on the hoses in the illustration is to

   (A) protect against chafing when the hose rubs on the ground.
   (B) indicate which hose line is bigger.
   (C) keep the hose kinked.
   (D) identify the hose connected to the hydrant.

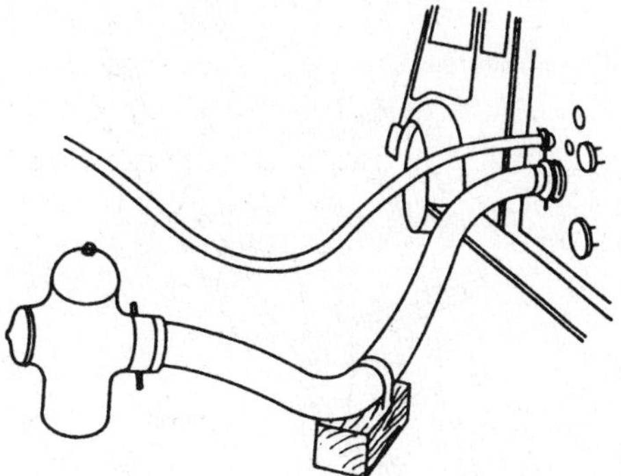

7. Firefighters often tie ladders as shown in the illustration. This is done to

   (A) prevent them from being stolen.
   (B) prevent them from touching the fence.
   (C) prevent unauthorized people from using them.
   (D) prevent them from slipping.

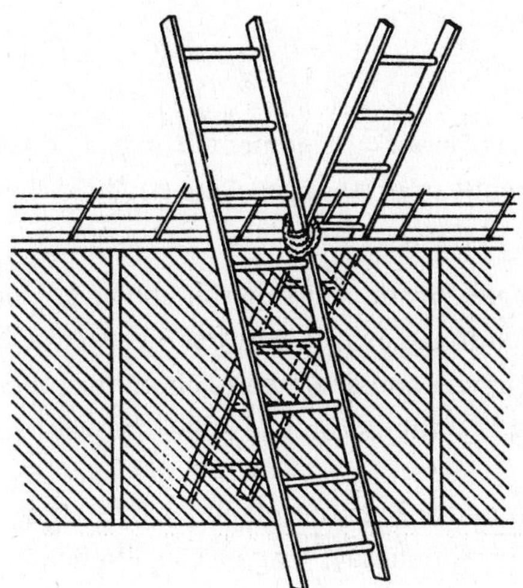

8. This firefighter is

   (A) attempting to get up the ladder while the woman comes down.
   (B) trying to take the child away from the woman.
   (C) preventing the woman from falling while descending the ladder.
   (D) testing how much weight each of the ladder rungs will hold.

9. The correct action to take when your clothing is on fire is to

   (A) drop and roll.
   (B) beat out the fire with your hands.
   (C) run fast to blow out the fire.
   (D) yell for help.

10. You have just been told of a work assignment change, and you find that operations are done somewhat differently from what you were taught. What is the correct action you should take?

   (A) Discuss the differences with your superior and be guided by what he or she says.
   (B) Criticize the methods and explain why it is correct the way you were taught.
   (C) Do everything your way and don't worry about the other people.
   (D) Tell your superior that things can't be done that way.

11. Firefighters on duty should answer the telephone by stating their unit, rank, and name. For example, they should say, "Engine 159, Firefighter Jones."

   This should be done

   (A) after finding out who is calling.
   (B) only if asked for this information.
   (C) only on the fire department private line.
   (D) at the beginning of every phone conversation.

12. While on a fire prevention inspection, you discover a serious fire hazard. When you confront the owner of the premises, you discover that he does not speak English. What is the proper action for you to take?

(A) Make yourself understood by speaking slowly and loudly.
(B) Correct the condition yourself.
(C) Find someone who can interpret for you.
(D) Give the owner a written order and using sign language to direct him to comply.

13. The Wright Brothers made history flying a plane at ___________, North Carolina.

(A) Kitty Eagle
(B) Kitty Kat
(C) Kitty Carlisle
(D) Kitty Hawk

14. Fire drills are held frequently in schools to

(A) teach the students to be quiet.
(B) make the students familiar with fire department regulations.
(C) train the students to leave the school in a quick and orderly manner.
(D) demonstrate and enforce the need for discipline.

15. Many fires have been started by a combination of heating equipment and combustible materials. The most likely reason that fires of this nature increase when the weather turns cold is that

(A) more heating units are in operation.
(B) heating equipment tends to break down more quickly in the cold.
(C) flammable liquids are stored near the heating equipment.
(D) cold air often clogs the burner of the heating unit.

16. During a fire in a house, a firefighter, finds $450.00 under a rug. What should he or she do?

(A) Turn the money over to an officer.
(B) Notify the chief to call the police.
(C) Put the money back.
(D) Give the money to a neighbor to hold until the owner returns.

17. After a difficult fire, youths begin to ask you questions. You should

(A) answer all their questions.
(B) answer some questions, and then ask them to visit you at the fire station.
(C) chase them away.
(D) ignore them.

18. A distraught woman enters the station and tells you that her six-year-old son is missing. The most appropriate action is

(A) send the company out to search.
(B) send the woman to the social services department.
(C) get her information and notify the police department.
(D) explain to her that the fire department doesn't look for missing children.

19. You are told you must remain on duty beyond the end of the shift. What should you do?

(A) Explain the circumstances about why you must leave at end of your shift.
(B) Tell the superior you refuse to work.
(C) File a grievance.
(D) Just leave at the end of the shift.

20. While a person is lighting the oven in a gas stove, the match goes out. The proper action to take is to

(A) quickly light another match and try again.
(B) turn off the gas and wait awhile.
(C) close the oven door and quickly light another match.
(D) put one's finger over the gas jet and use a cigarette lighter to light the oven.

21. If a car goes into a skid, the driver should turn the wheels into the skid to retain control. The drawing that correctly illustrates this concept is

(A) 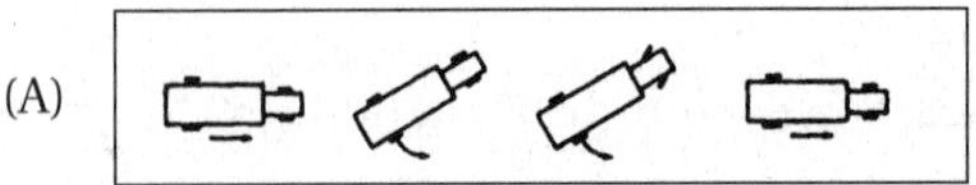

(B) 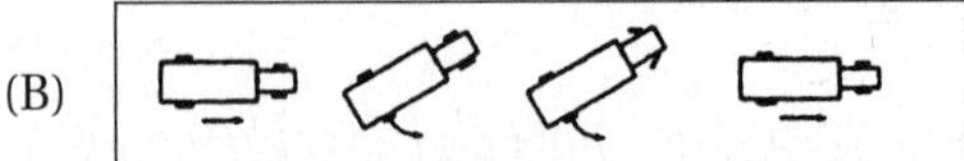

(C) 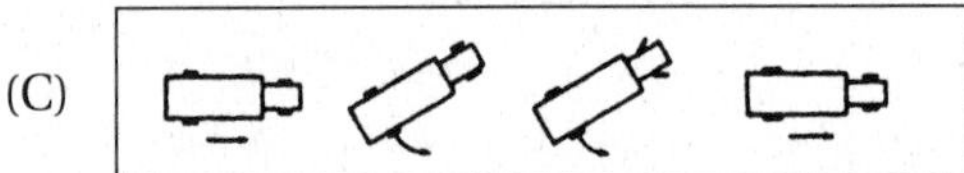

(D) 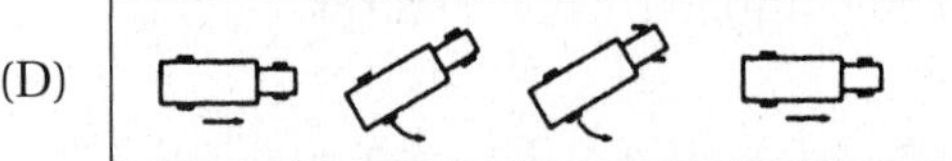

22. An electric iron left lying on an ironing board has started a smoldering fire. The correct FIRST action to take is to

(A) call the fire department.
(B) throw a pot of cold water on it.
(C) pull out the plug.
(D) cover the fire with a towel.

23. Theater programs often include this warning: "In case of fire, walk, do not run, to the nearest exit." The purpose of this is to

(A) allow the people in the back to get out first.
(B) lessen the chance that someone will trip, fall, and cause a panicky rush.
(C) let the audience know that theaters are fireproof and safe.
(D) Make it clear that there is little danger of fire in a theater.

24. You are a firefighter doing an inspection of a factory, and you find several infractions. The building manager does not agree with you. What is the best action for you to take?

(A) Disregard the manager's remarks, and continue with the inspection.
(B) Go back the next day, and make an even more thorough inspection.
(C) Call a police officer, and have the man arrested.
(D) Forget about the infractions; they are minor.

25. Paramedics arrive on the scene of an accident and find the victim alert and ______________.

(A) conscious
(B) unconscious
(C) conscience
(D) convenient

26. You are instructed to construct a wall using 2″ × 4″ × 8′ studs on 16″ centers. How many studs will be needed for a wall 8′ long?

(A) 6
(B) 7
(C) 8
(D) None of the above

27. The _______ was transported to the hospital in an ambulance.

(A) patient
(B) patience
(C) parents
(D) patent

28. What is the approximate area of a building 343 feet long, 75 feet wide, and 9½ feet high?

(A) 60,025 square feet
(B) 25,725 square feet
(C) 6,025 square feet
(D) 518 square feet

29. Using the information in question 28, approximately how many cubic feet does the building consist of?

(A) 570,250 cubic feet
(B) 244,390 cubic feet
(C) 3,430 cubic feet
(D) 750 cubic feet

30. If you drive a vehicle 55 mph, how far will you travel in one hour?

(A) 40 miles
(B) 45 miles
(C) 55 miles
(D) 65 miles

31. What is the best reason for a fire department to inspect private property?

(A) To ensure that fire department equipment is not tempered with.
(B) To train firefighters in private building-construction techniques.
(C) To find and punish citizens who violate the fire prevention laws.
(D) To have conditions that create fire hazards corrected.

Directions: Using the information below, answer questions 32 through 38 and enter your answers on the answer sheet.

You decide to have a get-together for your crew at your house. You will have a variety of items and need to calculate the cost of the evening. You are buying yogurt at 4 for $2.48, fruit juices at 8 for $6.72, a variety of cookies at 6 for $3.98, pretzels at 5 bags for $2.25, fruit at 3 pounds for $0.99, and door prizes at 4 for $3.58.

32. How much will you pay for 8 yogurts?

(A) $2.48
(B) $3.46
(C) $4.96
(D) $5.96

33. How much will you pay for 6 bottles of juice?

(A) $6.72
(B) $5.04
(C) $4.72
(D) $4.04

34. How much will you pay for 8 bags of pretzels?

(A) $2.25
(B) $3.25
(C) $3.60
(D) $4.60

35. How much will you pay for 1 pound of bananas?

(A) $0.33
(B) $1.98
(C) $0.99
(D) $0.66

36. How much will you pay for 4 cookies?

(A) $2.44
(B) $2.65
(C) $3.65
(D) $3.98

37. How much will you pay for 6 door prizes?

(A) $3.58
(B) $4.37
(C) $4.58
(D) $5.37

38. Based on the original quantities described before question 32, what will your total bill add up to including 7% sales tax?

(A) $23.49
(B) $21.40
(C) $22.10
(D) $24.49

39. While on the way home, a person hears and then sees a bell marked "sprinkler," and notices water coming from a pipe about 10 feet away. It is 2 A.M., the building is closed and locked, and no fire alarm box is in sight. The person knows, however, that there is a firehouse three blocks away. Given these conditions, the proper action is to

(A) write down the address, and then go home and call the police department.
(B) search around the neighborhood for the nearest fire alarm box.
(C) go to the firehouse and notify the men on duty.
(D) do nothing; the water is probably just an overflow.

40. What is the priority sorting of patients at a mass casualty incident?

(A) Decoupage
(B) Camouflage
(C) Foliage
(D) Triage

41. A fire engine, police car, ambulance, and mail truck arrive at an intersection at the same time. Which vehicle has the right of way?

(A) Fire engine
(B) Police car
(C) Ambulance
(D) Mail truck

42. What is a rise in prices called?

(A) Integration
(B) Recession
(C) Deflation
(D) Inflation

43. Firefighters are required to maintain their tools and equipment. The purpose of regular cleaning and maintenance of fire apparatus is to

(A) give the firefighters something to do between fires.
(B) identify defects in the apparatus and reduce the chance of deterioration.
(C) make the apparatus and equipment look good to superiors.
(D) teach discipline and compliance.

44. Boundary lines around a fire area, called "fire lines," are normally set up by the police department to keep citizens out of the immediate firefighting area. The best reason for fire lines is to prevent

(A) an arsonist from getting away.
(B) firefighters from talking with the local people.
(C) citizens from interfering with the firefighting operations.
(D) citizens from seeing firefighters make an error.

45. While responding to a fire, fire officers do not talk with the firefighter driving the apparatus. The primary reason for this is to

(A) allow the officer to watch how the firefighter handles the apparatus.
(B) ensure that the chain of command is maintained.
(C) allow the officer to prepare mentally to fight the fire.
(D) ensure that the driver is able to concentrate on getting the apparatus to the fire safely.

46. While you are on house watch, a visitor stops in and asks whether she and her family may look at the fire equipment. The best response is to

(A) explain that an appointment is necessary.
(B) let them walk around the station unsupervised.
(C) explain that you are on house watch and when you are done you will show them around.
(D) call the officer to get someone else to show them around.

47. After having worked with a group of firefighters for some time, you feel that you are disliked. What is the first thing you should do?

(A) Request a transfer to another station.
(B) Tell the officer to have the group treat you better.
(C) Confront the group and tell them to treat you better.
(D) Examine your own thoughts and feelings to determine whether you are at fault.

48. A love of one's country is called

(A) patriotism.
(B) communism.
(C) nationalism.
(D) cynicism.

49. Russia was the first country to launch an artificial satellite into space. What was the name of the satellite?

(A) *Explorer*
(B) *U-2*
(C) *Sputnik*
(D) *Nautilus*

50. Who was the first American astronaut to orbit Earth?

(A) Alan Shepard
(B) John Glenn
(C) Gus Grissom
(D) Gary Powers

ANSWER KEY AND EXPLANATIONS

Answer Key

1. **(C)**	11. **(D)**	21. **(D)**	31. **(D)**	41. **(D)**
2. **(B)**	12. **(C)**	22. **(C)**	32. **(C)**	42. **(D)**
3. **(B)**	13. **(D)**	23. **(B)**	33. **(B)**	43. **(B)**
4. **(B)**	14. **(C)**	24. **(A)**	34. **(C)**	44. **(C)**
5. **(C)**	15. **(A)**	25. **(A)**	35. **(D)**	45. **(D)**
6. **(A)**	16. **(A)**	26. **(B)**	36. **(B)**	46. **(D)**
7. **(D)**	17. **(B)**	27. **(A)**	37. **(D)**	47. **(D)**
8. **(C)**	18. **(C)**	28. **(B)**	38. **(B)**	48. **(A)**
9. **(A)**	19. **(A)**	29. **(B)**	39. **(C)**	49. **(C)**
10. **(A)**	20. **(B)**	30. **(C)**	40. **(D)**	50. **(B)**

Answer Explanations

1. **(C)** This eminently hazardous situation requires immediate corrective action. Choices A and D require additional time, which may allow the gas to explode. Choice B is incorrect; a match should not be used under any circumstances to detect a gas leak. There are gas detector machines for this purpose.

2. **(B)** Horseplay or fooling around often starts out as harmless fun but has a consistent track record of leading to injury and accidents.

3. **(B)** This will give the officer time to evaluate your suggestion and to consider the impact on operations and firefighters. Firefighters depend on having tools and equipment in specific locations and setups. Making changes without notifying them can result in hard feelings. So Choice A is wrong. If the idea is good, the group should know about it, which makes Choice C wrong. The suggestion could be put in writing and forwarded through the chain of command, but not to the union. So Choice D is wrong.

4. **(B)** All firefighters who will work in the proximity of the fire should be equipped with self-contained breathing apparatus, which allows them to go into the fire area without delay if needed. In this illustration the firefighter is feeding additional hose into the crew who are attacking the fire, which is an important activity. There is no justification for choices A and C. Choice D makes the assumption that the firefighter is not a senior firefighter; nowhere in the question or illustration is this indicated. Answers not based on given facts should be avoided.

5. **(C)** When a car or truck drives over a hose, it can cut off the water supply and leave the firefighter in a dangerous position; also, driving over hose may damage it. The blocks are not used for the purposes mentioned in choices A, B, and D.

6. **(A)** As the water flow is started and stopped, the hose will rub against the ground, thereby wearing a hole in it. There is no justification for the other choices.

7. **(D)** Tying the ladders increases the degree of safety when climbing over a high fence. The reasons given in choices A, B, and C make no sense in a fire situation.

8. **(C)** When the firefighter guides each step of the person, and keeps body contact, the person's fear is reduced and the chance of descending the ladder safely is increased.

Choice A—this would be an unsafe act. Choice B—once the mother and child are on the ladder, it could be unsafe to take the child away from the mother; in addition, she would normally be reluctant to trust the safety of the child to anyone else. Choice D—ladders are tested with weights; a human being should not be subjected to the possibility of ladder failure and personal injury.

9. **(A)** The drop-and-roll technique has proven to be very successful for quickly extinguishing clothing fires. Choices B, C, and D would all lead to an increase in the volume of fire and in the chance of serious burns.

10. **(A)** Such a discussion will ensure that the firefighter is aware of what is required of a firefighter and what are the proper actions. Choice A would be a form of direct disobedience. Choice B could create hard feelings, and the old way may not be best. Choice C could create confusion and reduce the group's effectiveness.

11. **(D)** Doing this allows the caller to know that he or she has reached the right party and to refer to you again if needed. It is generally accepted good practice in the fire service to give your unit, rank, and name each time you answer any phone while on duty.

12. **(C)** Using an interpreter is the only way you can be sure that the person understands.

13. **(D)** Wilbur and Orville Wright made the first successful flight of an airplane at Kitty Hawk, North Carolina on December 17, 1903. Choices A and B are distractors and choice C was an actress.

14. **(C)** The basic subject of the question is safety. Drills are designed to reinforce what has been learned, and a fire drill is concerned with safe escape from a burning building. The reasons in choices A, B, and D, although they may be desirable, are not concerned with safety and therefore are not the main consideration in fire drills.

15. **(A)** When the weather turns cold, heating units are turned on; however, items temporarily stored near the burner during the warm months may be forgotten about and not removed. The combination of sufficient heat and ignitable materials starts a fire. Choices B and D—it is not the weather that causes a breakdown of heating equipment; it is improper design, use, or maintenance of the equipment. Choice C—flammable and combustible liquids are routinely stored near heating equipment but, if kept in proper storage tanks, are not a problem.

16. **(A)** The officer will take the necessary and proper actions to safeguard the owner's property. Choice B violates the chain of command. Choice C is incorrect as the money may get lost or destroyed. Items of value should be turned over to your immediate supervisor. So choice D is wrong.

17. **(B)** Because this was a difficult fire and you have not completed the work needed to ready your unit for another alarm, you must set priorities. Getting back into service is your first priority. Answering questions is important, but it can be limited or postponed until a later time.

18. **(C)** You should obtain information about who the woman is and where she lives as well as information about the missing child. This will ensure that you have the information in case the woman leaves. As quickly as possible, get hold of the police and have

them make contact with the woman at the fire station. You may be called to search but not immediately.

19. **(A)** By explaining why you need to leave gives the officer a chance to evaluate the current conditions and determine if your staying is a fire service priority. The supervisor will also determine if another firefighter can replace you. Choice B is incorrect. The fire service usually works a 24-hour shift and sometimes requires members to work beyond their shift. Choices (C) and (D) are inappropriate.

20. **(B)** Waiting will allow the gas that has already escaped to dissipate. Choices A, C, and D—these actions may cause an explosion and fire, in fact, choice C will almost always result in an explosion.

21. **(D)** In choice D the front wheels are turned in the direction of the arrow indicated at the rear wheels. This action tends to straighten the vehicle and break the skid.

22. **(C)** This is a small fire and can usually be controlled without professional help, eliminating choice A. The *first* thing to do is to remove the live electricity so that there is no danger of shock. *Then* put water on the burning materials; this is the second, not the first, step, eliminating choice B. After the materials have cooled, soak them in a large pail or tub. Finally, notify the fire department that you had a fire but have already extinguished it. (*Note:* If the fire is large, that is, if the ironing board is free burning, *call the fire department immediately.*) Choice D—for this type of fire, smothering often is not effective; a cooling agent is required.

23. **(B)** Walking tends to ensure safe footing and to prevent tripping. When someone trips and falls, the escape path is blocked and other people become afraid that they will not get out; this often leads to pushing and then to panic. Choice A—theaters must provide enough exits for all occupants; in emergencies all exits, not just the ones in the rear, are used. Choice C—"fireproof" is a poor term and has been dropped from the fire service vocabulary because it is very misleading. The correct term is "noncombustible." The fact that a building will not contribute combustible materials does not mean that the furnishings, scenery, and costumes won't burn. Choice D—there is often great danger of fires in theaters, and for this reason they are very heavily regulated by fire prevention laws.

24. **(A)** Although the manager does not agree with your findings, the manager has not made any illegal attempt to have you conceal them. Choices B and C would be overreactions to the situation. Choice D would be a deliberate failure on your part to perform your duties properly.

25. **(A)** The word *alert* should give you a clue. The patient wouldn't be alert, so choice B is wrong. Choice C, conscience, is a state of mind. Convenient, choice D, means suitable, adaptable, and conducive to comfort.

26. **(B)** Convert everything to inches. An 8′ long wall is 96″ long. Dividing 96″ by 16″ equals 6 studs. Don't forget that you need a stud at the beginning of the wall for a total of 7 studs. Use scratch paper to draw the wall, for example, I-16-I-16-I-16-I-16-I-16-I-16-I.

27. **(A)** The answer is patient. Make sure you spell it correctly.

28. **(B)** To find the area of the building, multiply length times width ($L \times W$). This gives you the square feet.

29. **(B)** To find the number of cubic feet in a building, multiply the area by the height. In other words, multiply length by width by height ($L \times W \times H$).

30. **(C)** You will travel 55 miles.

31. **(D)** Fire prevention is a very appropriate name for what the fire department is trying to accomplish. If the inspections result in correcting a problem, thereby preventing a fire, the fire department has succeeded in its purpose. Choices A and B are important subcomponents of the fire prevention program. Choice C mentions punishment, but compliance is the object.

32. **(C)** Since you already know the cost of 4 yogurts, multiply that price by 2 to get the price for 8 yogurts.

33. **(B)** Divide the cost of 8 fruit juices by 8 to find the cost of 1 bottle. Then multiply by 6.

34. **(C)** First divide by 5 to find the price of 1 bag of pretzels. Then multiply by 8.

35. **(D)** Divide the cost for 3 pounds by 3 to find the price of 1 pound.

36. **(B)** Divide the total by 6 to find the cost of 1 cookie, and then multiply by 4.

37. **(D)** Divide the total by 4 to find the cost of 1 prize, and then multiply by 6.

38. **(B)** Find the total by adding each item together and multiplying by 1.07 for the total cost including tax.

39. **(C)** Two decisions are required in this problem: (1) Should the condition be reported, and (2) if yes, then how? (1) The correct choice here is yes; report the condition (the water motor gong, or alarm bell, is installed on the outside of the building to alert passersby of the need to report that something is wrong). (2) It is almost always correct to choose the method that will most directly solve the problem. In this situation the problem is solved by going directly to the fire station. Choices A, B, and D will result in a delayed alarm and an increase in fire growth and damage.

40. **(D)** Triage is the priority sorting of patients at a mass casualty incident. It allows the most severe patients to be handled first. Decoupage is the art of using paper to decorate. Camouflage means disguise. Foliage is a growth of leaves or flowers.

41. **(D)** A mail truck is a federal government vehicle and always has the right of way over other vehicles. However, mail trucks often yield to emergency vehicles.

42. **(D)** Inflation is an increase in price levels established by an increasing demand without corresponding increase in commodity supply. Integration is combining individuals or groups of various cultural, economic, and racial backgrounds. Recession is an economic setback, a slight depression. Deflation is a decrease in the amount of currency in a country.

43. **(B)** During the cleaning and maintenance process possible defects are identified and corrected, and harmful road tars and other chemicals that destroy apparatus are removed. The reasons given in choices A, C, and D are less important.

44. **(C)** The fire scene is often very dangerous; though well-intentioned, untrained citizens often offer help or advice and wind up getting injured or becoming a nuisance. There is no justification for the other choices.

45. **(D)** When conversation is limited, the driver is better able to direct his full attention and effort to the task of getting the apparatus and other firefighters to the scene safely. Responding to an alarm requires the full and undivided attention of the apparatus driver. Unnecessary conversation can lead to momentary distraction and an accident. Choices A, B, and C are related but are significantly less important.

46. **(D)** The officer will assign another firefighter to this task. An appointment is not usually needed, so choice A is incorrect. Choice B could be dangerous. Choice C could make the people wait a long period of time for you to show them around.

47. **(D)** Before you change stations or confront others, you should identify the reasons for the problem. You may or may not be the cause. However, before you make any decisions like those shown in the other answers, you must find out what is causing the problem.

48. **(A)** Patriotism is the love of one's country. Communism is any social system that advocates the abolition of private property and control by the community over economic affairs. Nationalism is a system advocating national conduct of all industries. Cynicism is contempt for virtue of others.

49. **(C)** *Sputnik* was launched in 1957 as the first satellite to orbit Earth. *Explorer* was the first American satellite, which was launched in 1958. *U-2* was an American spy plane shot down over Russia. *Nautilus* was the first American submarine to cross under the North Pole.

50. **(B)** On February 20, 1962, John Glenn became the first American to orbit the earth. Alan Shepard piloted the first suborbital space flight. He did not orbit the planet. Gus Grissom was the second American to fly in space. Gary Powers was the *U-2* spy plane pilot.

Mathematics, Machines, Science, and Information

9

MATHEMATICS

What is Mathematics?

Mathematics involves the manipulation of data represented by symbols to produce information in a form that is more useful than the original data. For example, a water tank is in the form of a cylinder. The upper and lower bases of the tank are parallel, congruent circles. The distance between the top and the bottom is the height of the tank.

The rule for finding the volume of a cylinder is as follows: The volume of a cylinder is equal to the area of the base multiplied by the height.

Since the base of a cylinder is a circle whose area is πr^2, the formula for the volume is

$$\text{Volume } (V) = \text{Base} \times \text{Height } (h)$$
$$V = \pi r^2 \times h$$

Example: The radius of a cylindrical tank is 3½ feet. Its height is 8 feet. Find the volume in cubic feet, letting $\pi = 3.14$.

$$\text{Volume } (V) = \pi r^2 h$$
$$V = 3.14 \times 3\tfrac{1}{2}\text{ ft.} \times 3\tfrac{1}{2}\text{ ft.} \times 8\text{ ft.}$$
$$V = 3.14 \times 3.5' \times 3.5' \times 8$$
$$V = 307.72\text{ C}'$$

The final answer is of greater use to anyone who wishes to fill the tank than knowledge of just the radius and the height. The beauty of mathematics is that it can be applied with equal success to different problems.

A second advantage is that mathematics lets us do efficiently what would be impossible without it. A simple example should make this point clear.

Any kind of bar resting on a fixed point or edge can be used as a lever; the point or edge is called the *fulcrum*. A lever will just balance when the numerical product of the effort (E) and its distance (d) from the fulcrum (F) is equal to the numerical product of the resistance (R) and its distance (D) from the fulcrum, that is, when

$$\text{Effort } (E) \times \text{Distance } (d) = \text{Resistance } (R) \times \text{Distance } (D)$$

Let's consider the following problem:

$$\begin{array}{ccccc} E = 15\text{ lb.} & & & & R = ? \\ \hline \downarrow & d = 7 & \triangle & D = 3 & \downarrow \end{array}$$

If we solve for R, we will find what resistance an effort of 15 pounds will support, by means of the lever shown if $d = 7$ feet and $D = 3$ feet.

$$E \times d = R \times D$$
$$15\text{ lb.} \times 7\text{ ft.} = R \times 3\text{ ft.}$$
$$\frac{15\text{ lb.} \times 7\text{ ft.}}{3\text{ ft.}} = R$$
$$35\text{ lb.} = R$$

WHY SHOULD A FIREFIGHTER LEARN MATHEMATICS?

The most important reason for learning mathematics is that it is useful in our everyday life. We are constantly called upon to make decisions based on arithmetic, algebra, geometry, measurement estimations, maps, and scaled drawings.

What underlying skills should you possess to solve mathematical problems? You need to

- Understand whole numbers and rational numbers (decimals and fractions), and their use in counting and measuring.
- Know the basic facts of the four common operations of arithmetic—addition, subtraction, multiplication, and division.
- Know how to measure and how to estimate measurements to determine height, weight, temperature, volume, etc. Estimating before actually taking measurements is good experience, and it will make you a better estimator. You should be able to make estimates in both the traditional (American) and the metric system, and you should be comfortable with both. The best way is to learn each system independently, and then, when they have become second nature, to learn to convert from one to the other.

  It is helpful to have a general idea of some approximate equivalents. A yard (36 inches) is a little shorter than a meter (39 inches). A quart (32 ounces) is a little less than a liter (34 ounces). A pound (16 ounces) is a little less than half a kilogram (17.6 ounces). For temperatures, if you multiply a Celsius or centigrade reading by 2 and add 30, you will get a fairly good estimate of the Fahrenheit reading; the exact formula is

  $$\text{F} = \frac{9}{5}\text{C} + 32$$

  where F = Fahrenheit degrees and C = Celsius degrees.
- Be familiar with and able to use both two- and three-dimensional geometric concepts, and to be aware of the relationship between them. Do you remember the Pythagorean theorem? It states that in a right triangle the square of the hypotenuse equals the sum of the squares of the other sides:

  $$a^2 + b^2 = c^2$$

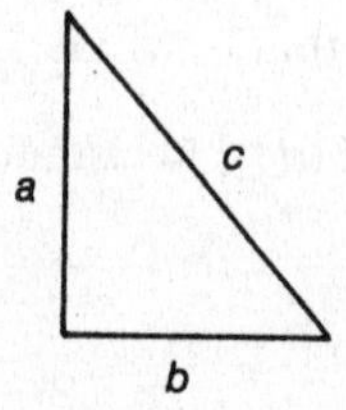

  a
  c
  b

- Be able to use functions to describe and analyze the relationships between variables (time and height, size and temperature, etc.). You may have studied functions in algebra, geometry, or trigonometry.

Brief Review of Fundamental Topics and Principles

ARITHMETIC

Mixed Numbers, Fractions, and Improper Fractions

1. A *mixed number*, for example, $3\frac{1}{4}$, consists of a whole number (3, in this case) and a *fraction* ($\frac{1}{4}$). In an *improper fraction*, for example $\frac{13}{4}$, the numerator (number above the bar) is greater than, or equal to, the denominator (number below the bar).
2. *To change a mixed number to an improper fraction*, first find the product of the whole number and the denominator; then add the numerator to this product, and place the result over the denominator.

Example: Change $25\frac{2}{3}$ to an improper fraction.

Multiply the whole number	(25):	25
by the denominator	(3):	× 3
to obtain the product	(75):	75
Add the numerator	(2):	+ 2
Place the result	(77):	$\frac{77}{3} = 25\frac{2}{3}$
over the denominator	(3):	

3. *To change an improper fraction to a mixed or whole number*, first divide the numerator by the denominator. If there is a remainder, write it as the numerator of a fraction that has the same denominator as the improper fraction. Reduce the fraction to lowest terms.

Example: Change $\frac{57}{6}$ to a mixed number.

		$9\frac{3}{6} = 9\frac{1}{2}$
Divide the numerator	(57):	$6\overline{)57}$
		54
by the denominator	(6):	3
Place the remainder	(3):	3
over the denominator	(6):	6
reduce		$\frac{3}{{}_2 6} = \frac{1}{2}$

OPERATIONS WITH FRACTIONS

Multiplication of Mixed Numbers by Fractions and Multiplication of Fractions by Fractions

To multiply a mixed number by a fraction, (1) change the mixed number to an improper fraction, (2) multiply the numerators of the two fractions to get the numerator of the answer, (3) multiply the two denominators to get the denominator of the answer, (4) reduce the answer to lowest terms, and (5) change the improper fraction to a mixed number.

Example: Find the product of $3\frac{1}{4}$ and $\frac{2}{3}$.

(1): $3\frac{1}{4} = \frac{13}{4}$

(2) and (3): $\frac{13}{4} \times \frac{2}{3} = \frac{26}{12}$

(4): $\frac{26}{12} = \frac{13}{6}$

(5): $\frac{13}{6} = 2\frac{1}{6}$

Therefore $3\frac{1}{4} \times \frac{2}{3} = 2\frac{1}{6}$.

Division of Mixed Numbers and Fractions

From the illustration below, you can see that $\frac{1}{3}$ of a circle can be divided into two equal parts so that each of the parts is $\frac{1}{6}$ of the circle; in other words, $\frac{1}{3}$ divided by 2 is $\frac{1}{6}$, or

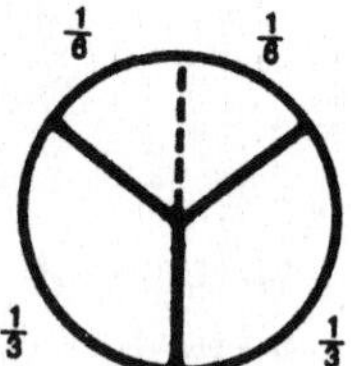

$$\frac{1}{3} \div \frac{2}{1} = \frac{1}{6}$$

You can also obtain the answer $\frac{1}{6}$ by inverting the fraction after the division sign, $\frac{2}{1}$, obtaining $\frac{1}{2}$, and then multiplying the denominators. (Note: Any number divided by 1 equals the number: a number cannot be divided by zero.)

$$\frac{1}{3} \div 2 = \frac{1}{3} \times \frac{1}{2} = \frac{1}{6}$$

To divide a number or a fraction by a fraction, (1) invert the divisor, (2) multiply the two numerators, and (3) divide by the product of the two denominators.

Example: Divide $4\frac{1}{3}$ by $\frac{1}{4}$.

First change $4\frac{1}{3}$ to an improper fraction:

$$4\frac{1}{3} = \frac{13}{3}$$

Then:

$$\frac{13}{3} \div \frac{1}{4} = \frac{13}{3} \times \frac{4}{1} = \frac{52}{3} = 17\frac{1}{3}$$

Addition and Subtraction of Fractions

To add or subtract fractions whose denominators are different, first change the fractions to equivalent fractions with the lowest common denominator. Then add the numerators, and write the sum over the common denominator. Finally, reduce the answer.

Example: Add $1\frac{1}{2}, 4\frac{2}{3}, 5\frac{1}{4}$.

The lowest common denominator is 12.

$$\begin{aligned} 1\frac{1}{2} &= 1\frac{6}{12} \\ 4\frac{2}{3} &= 4\frac{8}{12} \\ 5\frac{1}{4} &= 5\frac{3}{12} \\ \hline & 10\frac{17}{12} = 11\frac{5}{12} \end{aligned}$$

Operations with Decimals

A decimal is a part of a whole number and therefore is a fraction whose denominator is 10 or a multiple of 10: 100, 1000, etc. To change a fraction to a decimal fraction, divide the numerator by the denominator to as many places as are necessary.

Example: Change $\frac{7}{8}$ to a decimal.

$$\frac{7}{8} = 8\overline{)7.000} \quad = 0.875$$

$$\begin{array}{r} 0.875 \\ 8\overline{)7.000} \\ \underline{6\,4} \\ 60 \\ \underline{56} \\ 40 \\ \underline{40} \end{array}$$

Note: It will help you to remember that $\frac{7}{8}$ means 7 divided by 8.

WORKING WITH UNKNOWNS (ALGEBRA)

Some of the problems with which you may be confronted will require you to write a formula and to solve for an unknown. A formula is a rule in which letters represent numbers. For example, to find the area (A) of a rectangle, use the formula $A = L \times W$. Let us assume that the length (L) is 4 feet and the width (W) is 3 feet. What is the area of the rectangle?

$$\text{A} = \quad \text{L} \times \text{W}$$
$$\text{A} = \text{4 ft.} \times \text{3 ft.} = \text{12 sq. ft. (ft.}^2\text{)}$$

But what if you know the area and width and need to find the length? In that case, you write the formula ($A = L \times W$) and solve for the unknown. Let us assume that the area is 12 square feet and the width is 3 feet. What is the length of the rectangle?

$$A = L \times W$$
$$12 \text{ ft.}^2 = x \times 3 \text{ ft.}$$

Remember that both sides of a formula may be divided by the same number:

$$\frac{12 \text{ ft.}^2}{3 \text{ ft.}^2} = x \times \frac{\cancel{3 \text{ ft.}}}{\cancel{3 \text{ ft.}}}$$
$$x = \frac{12}{3}$$
$$x \text{ (Length)} = 4 \text{ ft.}$$

Many problems involving number relationships can be solved by remembering the four principles that may be applied to a formula:

1. Both sides of a formula may be divided by the same number.
2. Both sides of a formula may be multiplied by the same number.
3. The same number may be added to both sides of a formula.
4. The same number may be subtracted from both sides of a formula.

Example: Let us use one of the principles to solve the following problem: Find the time needed for a fire truck traveling at the rate of 55 miles per hour to go 165 miles.

First write the formula that expresses the relationships stated in the problem. The correct formula is

$$\text{Distance} = \text{Rate} \times \text{Time}$$

or, using symbols,

$$D = R \times T$$

Inserting the numbers given in the problem, you have

$$165 \text{ miles} = 55 \times T$$

To solve for T, divide both sides of the formula by R (55 miles per hour)

$$\frac{165 \text{ miles}}{55 \text{ mph}} = \frac{55}{55} \times T$$
$$T = \frac{165}{55}$$
$$T \text{ (Time)} = 3 \text{ hr.}$$

Finally, check to see whether your answer satisfies the relationships given in the problem.

Ratio and Proportion

When you compare two quantities by division, you are finding their *ratio.* To find the ratio of two quantities, for example, 5 fire lieutenants and 30 firefighters, divide the first quantity into the second:

$$\frac{5}{30} = 5:30$$

You may express the ratio either as a fraction (5/30), with a colon (5:30), or with the word *per* (5 fire lieutenants per 30 firefighters). *Note:* The symbol "/" is read as "per" and indicates division.

You know that the ratio 5/30 is equal to the ratio 1/6. The equation 5/30 = 1/6 is called a *proportion.* A proportion is an equation that tells you that two ratios are equal. Another way of writing a proportion is to replace the equal sign with a double colon (::).

To solve a proportion problem you must first insert the knowns and unknowns into their proper places, and then solve for the unknown.

Example: If a fire truck can travel 2 miles in 3 minutes, how far can it travel in 5 minutes at the same rate of speed?

Let x represent the number of miles traveled in 5 minutes. Then

$$x \text{ miles} : 2 \text{ miles} :: 5 \text{ min.} : 3 \text{ min.}$$

or

$$\frac{x \text{ miles}}{2 \text{ miles}} = \frac{5\text{min.}}{3\text{min.}}$$

Multiply the inner terms (2 and 5) together and the outer terms (x and 3) together. The product of the inner terms (10) equals the product of the outer terms ($3x$).

$$(x) \text{ miles} \times 3 \text{ minutes} = 2 \text{ miles} \times 5 \text{ minutes}$$

$$3x = 10$$

$$x = \frac{10}{3}$$

$$x = 3\frac{1}{3} \text{ miles}$$

GEOMETRY

A=Area	H=Height	R=Radius
C=Circumference	L=Length	V=Volume
D=Diameter	P=Perimeter	W=Width

To measure the distance around a room, the volume of a container, or any other quantity pertaining to a particular geometrical form, you need to know the formulas for determining the perimeter or circumference, area, and volume of a triangle, rectangle, or circle.

Shape:

Triangle	Rectangle	Circle
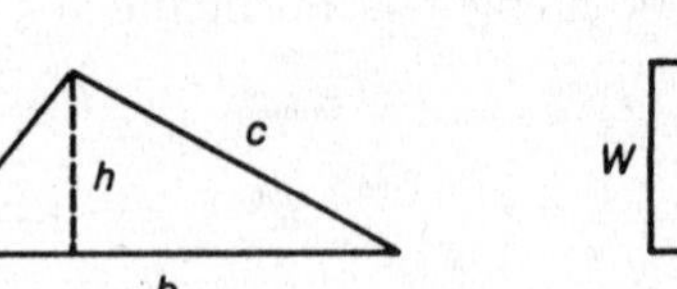	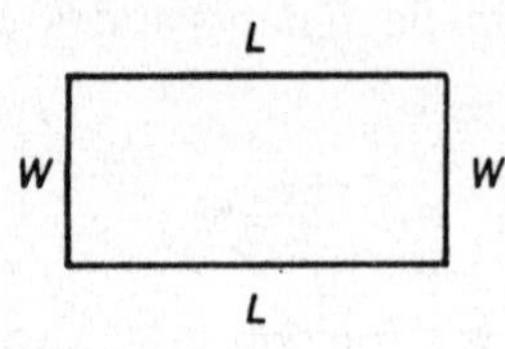	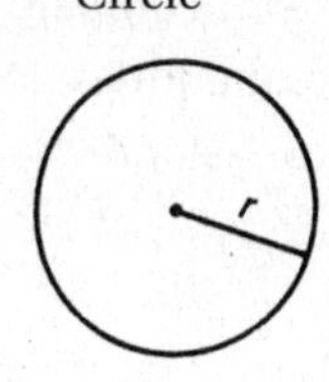
$P = a + b + c$	$P = L + W + L + W$	$C = 2\pi r$
$A = \frac{1}{2} \times h \times b$	$A = L \times W$	$A = \pi r^2 = \pi \times r \times r$
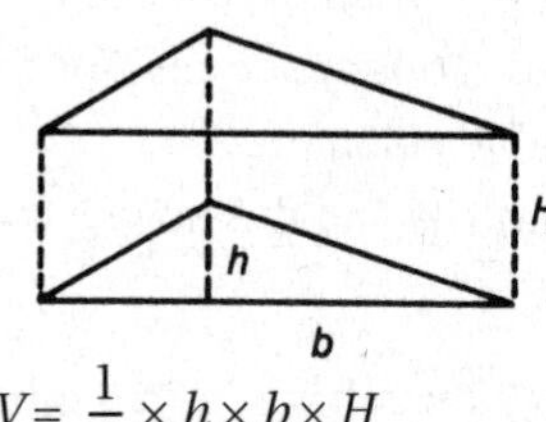 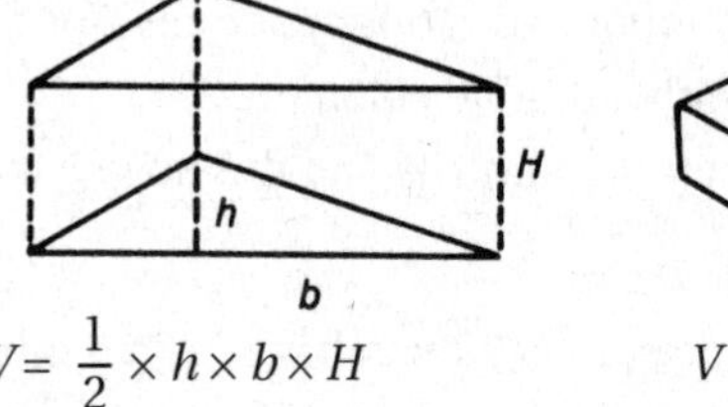	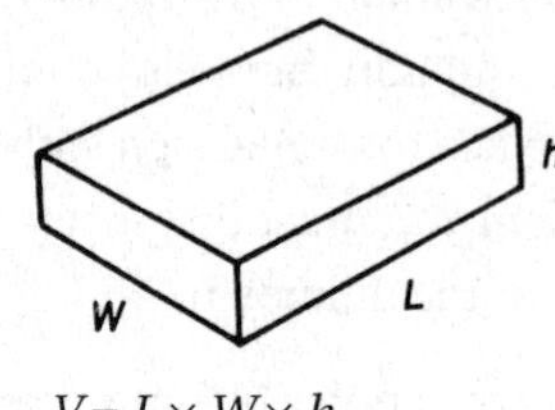	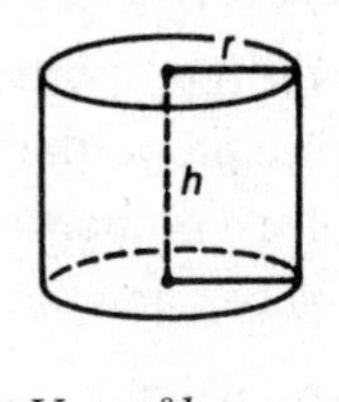
$V = \frac{1}{2} \times h \times b \times H$	$V = L \times W \times h$	$V = \pi r^2 h$

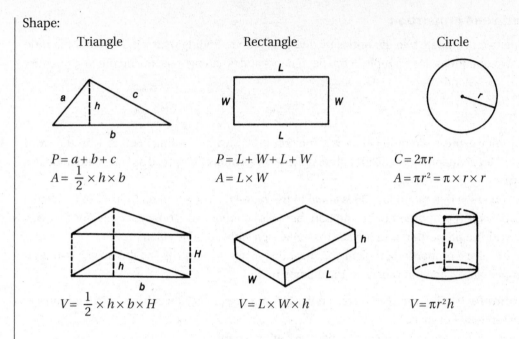

Geometry Examples

1. How many feet of rope are necessary to tie off a protective area around a hazardous building that is 25 feet wide by 30 feet long?

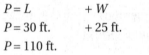

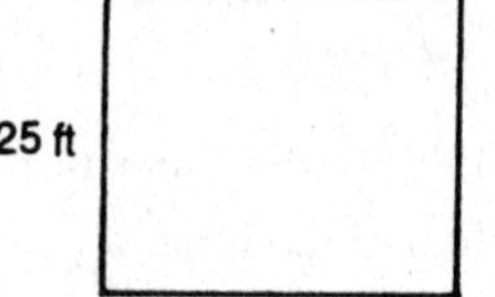

$P = L \quad + W \quad + L \quad + W$

$P = 30 \text{ ft.} \quad + 25 \text{ ft.} \quad + 30 \text{ ft.} \quad + 25 \text{ ft.}$

$P = 110 \text{ ft.}$

2. The diameter of a wheel is 14 feet. How many times must the wheel turn to travel 440 feet? (Use $\pi = 3.14$.) (Note: The answer can be rounded off to the next whole number to solve the problem.)

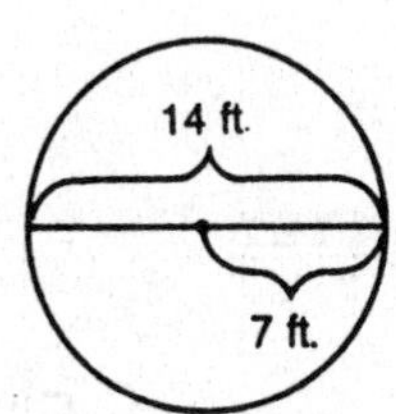

$C = 2\pi r$

$C = 2 \times 3.14 \times 7 \text{ ft.}$

$C = 44 \text{ ft.}$ (for one turn)

$= 440 \text{ ft.} : 44 \text{ ft.} :: x \text{ turns} : 1 \text{ turn}$

$\frac{440 \text{ ft.}}{44 \text{ ft.}} = \frac{x}{1} = 10 \text{ times}$

3. A room has an area of 168 square feet. If its length is 14 feet, what size salvage cover will be needed to protect the floor?

$A = L \times W$

$168 \text{ ft.}^2 = 14 \text{ ft.} \times W$

$\frac{168 \text{ ft.}^2}{14 \text{ ft.}} = W$

$12 \text{ ft.} = W$

$A = 168 \text{ ft}^2$ $\quad W = ?$ $\quad L = 14 \text{ ft}$

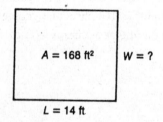

Salvage cover must be at least 12 ft. × 14 ft.

4. How many cubic feet of water will a tank on the back of a truck whose length is 8 feet, width is 5 feet, and height is $3\frac{1}{2}$ feet hold?

$V = L \times W \times h$

$V = 8\text{ ft} \times 5\text{ ft.} \times 3\frac{1}{2}\text{ ft.}$

$V = 140\text{ ft.}^3$

= the number of cubic feet of water the tank can hold.

h = 3½ ft

L = 8

W = 5

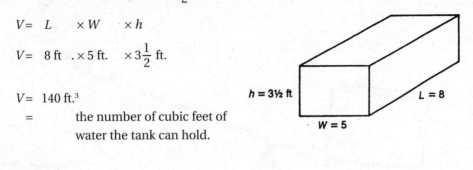

MACHINES

An understanding of the way simple mechanical devices work is an important part of a firefighter's knowledge. Acquiring familiarity with the principles of mechanics will be an important component of your preparation for the Firefighter's Examination.

Machines can be grouped into two categories, *simple machines* and *compound machines.* The simple machines are the lever, inclined plane, wheel and axle, pulley, and screw. Compound machines are composed of any combination of simple machines.

Machines permit human beings to overcome physical weakness and accomplish heavy work. In other words, machines give human beings a *mechanical advantage;* this is the number of times a machine multiplies an applied force. The mechanical advantage of a machine is the ratio of the resistance to the effort. For example, if you want to lift 200 pounds using a machine and you exert an effort of 50 pounds, what is the mechanical advantage?

$$\text{mechanical advantage} = \frac{\text{resistance}}{\text{effort}} = \frac{200\text{ pounds}}{50\text{ pounds}} = 4$$

In answering this type of question on your examination, you need not consider such things as friction loss and efficiency unless you are specifically told to in the directions.

The Lever

A lever is a bar, such as a crowbar, that rotates about a point. The point at which the lever rotates is known as the *fulcrum.* The significance of the lever is that a small force applied to the bar at a long distance from the fulcrum can move or lift a heavy weight situated a short distance from the fulcrum. In a lever illustration, the fulcrum is usually designated by a small triangle (△). A look at **Illustration A** will help to make the principle of the lever clear. The fulcrum is designated by the triangle (△), the firefighter is applying the force (effort) at a long distance from the fulcrum, and the heavy box (the resistance) a short distance from the fulcrum is being lifted. To determine the ability of a lever to lift a weight we use a very simple relationship:

$$\text{Effort} \times \text{Effort Distance} = \text{Resistance} \times \text{Resistance Distance*}$$

* Effort Distance is the distance from the fulcrum to the point where the effort is applied.
Resistance Distance is the distance from the fulcrum to the point where the resistance is applied.

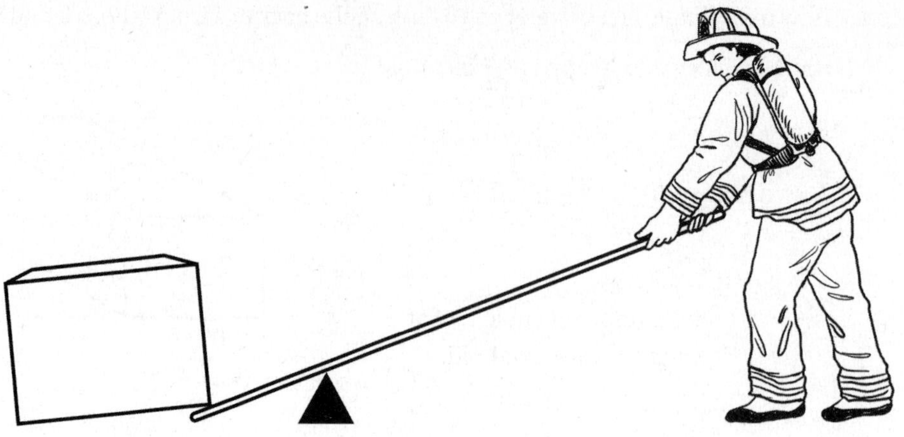

Illustration A

Let's look at illustration A again, but this time we will insert numbers. If the box weighs 1000 pounds and is 1 foot from the fulcrum, how much force (effort) will the firefighter have to exert at a distance of 5 feet from the fulcrum?

$$\text{Effort} = E \qquad \text{Resistance} = 1{,}000 \text{ pounds}$$

$$\text{Effort Distance} = 5 \text{ feet} \qquad \text{Resistance Distance} = 1 \text{ foot}$$

$$\text{Effort} \times \text{Effort Distance} = \text{Resistance} \times \text{Resistance Distance}$$

$$E \times 5 \text{ feet} = 1{,}000 \text{ pounds} \times 1 \text{ foot}$$

$$E = \frac{1{,}000 \text{ pounds} \times 1 \text{ foot}}{5 \text{ feet}}$$

$$E = 200 \text{ pounds}$$

The force (effort) required is 200 pounds.

The mechanical advantage of a lever system is determined by dividing the Effort Distance by the Resistance Distance. For example, if a 12-foot lever has an Effort Distance of 8 feet and a Resistance Distance of 4 feet, the mechanical advantage is

$$\frac{\text{Effort Distance}}{\text{Resistance Distance}} = \text{mechanical advantage (MA)}$$

$$\frac{8 \text{ feet}}{4 \text{ feet}} = \text{MA}$$

$$2 = \text{MA}$$

Because the force, resistance, and fulcrum can be located in different positions, there are three classes of levers. In the first-class lever, which is the most common, the fulcrum is between the effort (*E*) and the resistance (*R*):

$$\underline{E \qquad R}$$
$$\triangle$$

The second-class lever has the fulcrum at one end of the bar and the effort at the other end, with the resistance in between:

$$\underline{\qquad\qquad E}$$
$$\triangle \quad R$$

The third-class lever has the fulcrum at one end of the bar, the resistance at the other end, and the effort in the center:

$$\underline{\nabla \quad R}$$
$$E$$

It should be mentioned that the lever need not always be a straight bar. A claw hammer is a good example of a lever with the arms at different angles. The head is the fulcrum, the resistance is against the claw, and the effort is applied to the handle.

The Inclined Plane

The problem of moving an object up to a higher point is greatly simplified by the use of an inclined plane. The inclined plane is a slanted surface connecting a lower point to an upper point. By pulling or pushing an object up the inclined plane, a significant mechanical advantage can be gained over lifting the object straight up.

The mechanical advantage of the inclined plane is equal to the length of the inclined plane divided by the height the object is to be lifted. For example, if the length of the plane is 10 feet and the height is 2 feet, the mechanical advantage is

$$\frac{\text{length of inclined plane}}{\text{height of inclined plane}} = \text{mechanical advantage (MA)}$$

$$\frac{10\text{ feet}}{2\text{ feet}} = \text{MA}$$

$$5 = \text{MA}$$

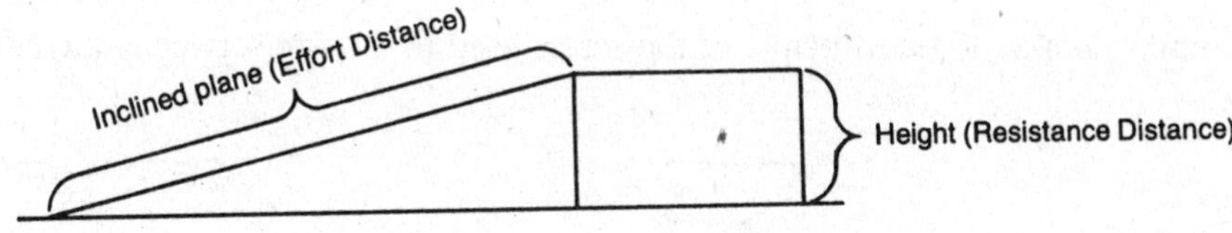

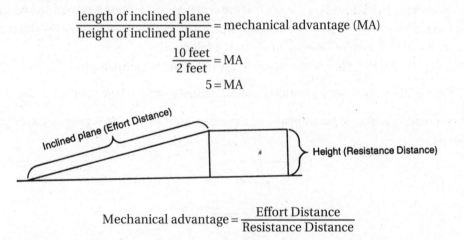

$$\text{Mechanical advantage} = \frac{\text{Effort Distance}}{\text{Resistance Distance}}$$

The following equation is used to solve an inclined plane problem:

$$\text{Effort} \times \text{Length of plane} = \text{Resistance} \times \text{Height to be raised}$$

The known values are inserted in their proper place.

The Pulley

A pulley is a wheel turning on an axle over which a rope, belt, or chain is passed for the purpose of transmitting energy and doing work. Pulleys can be used in two ways: (1) fixed position, where the block is not movable; and (2) movable position, where the block is movable. For the simplest type of pulley, single fixed block, there is no mechanical advantage, only a change of direction.

The mechanical advantage of a pulley is determined by counting the number of ropes available to pull *upward.* The rope used to pull downward is *not* included. In illustration B the mechanical advantages (MA) are shown for several situations.

Three basic types of problems may be asked about pulleys: (1) determine the load that can be lifted; (2) determine how high the load will be lifted; and (3) make an observation about how the systems work.

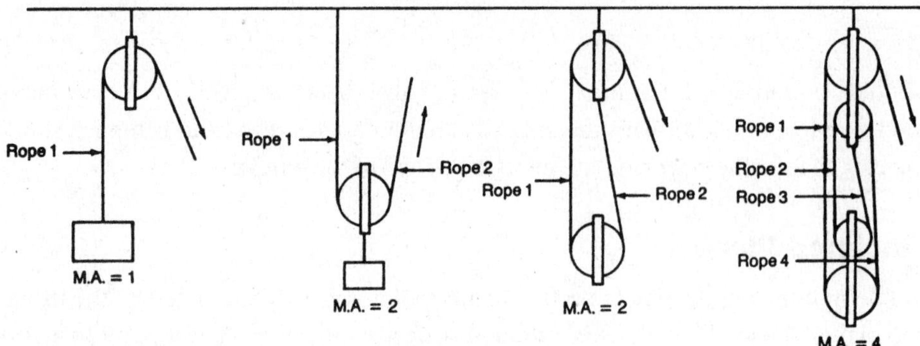

Illustration B

The Screw

A screw (illustration C) is a cylinder with an inclined plane wound around it. The distance between two adjacent threads is the *pitch* of the screw. When a screw is turned one complete revolution, it moves up or down a distance equal to its pitch; the force applied will travel a distance equal to the circumference made by the handle.

To calculate the effort in a screw problem the following equation is used:

$$\text{Effort} \times \text{Effort Distance (Circumference)} = \text{Resistance} \times \text{Resistance Distance (Pitch)}$$

A common example of the principle of the screw used in the fire service is the common jackscrew.

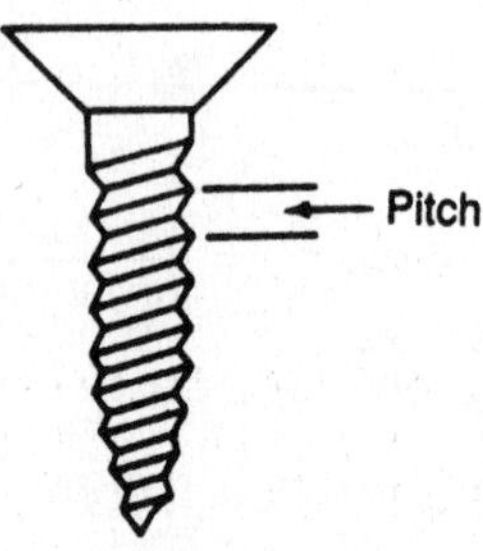

Illustration C

To understand how the screw works, look at illustration D. If you could pull the lever handle around one turn, it would move a distance of $2\pi \times R$ (the circumference of a circle whose radius equals R). At the same time, the screw has made one revolution, and moved a distance equal to its pitch (p). The mechanical advantage is equal to the effort arm distance ($2\pi R$) divided by the resistance arm distance (P). For example, what is the mechanical advantage if the length of the lever is 14 inches and the pitch for the screw thread is 1/8 inch? ($\pi = 3.14$) (Note: The answer can be rounded off to the next whole number to solve the problem.)

$$\text{Mechanical advantage} = \frac{2 \times 3.14 \times 14 \text{ in.}}{\frac{1}{8}} = \frac{88}{\frac{1}{8}} = 704$$

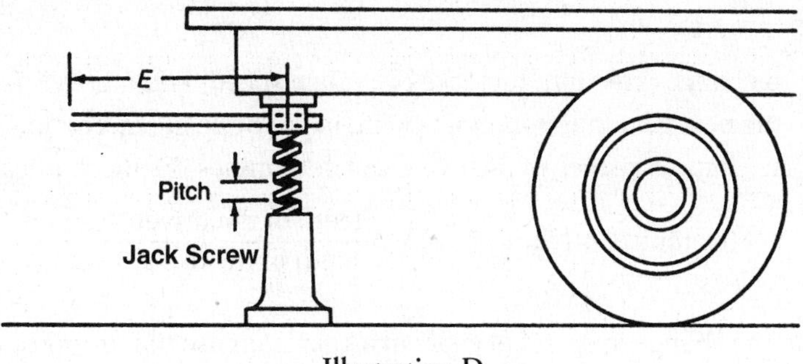

Illustration D

If you exert a 10-pound force on the handle, how big a force will be exerted against the resistance?

$$\text{Mechanical advantage} = \frac{\text{Resistance}}{\text{Effort}}$$

$$704 = \frac{\text{Resistance}}{\text{10 pounds}}$$

$$\text{Resistance} = \text{7,040 pounds}$$

The Wheel and Axle

The wheel and axle, as the term implies, is composed of two parts: (1) a *large wheel,* which is attached to (2) an *axle,* which is actually a smaller wheel. The wheel and the axle turn together.

When force is applied to the large wheel, the resistance attached to the small wheel can be overcome. By turning the large wheel one full turn, it is possible to lift a weight equal to the distance of the circumference of the smaller wheel (circumference = $2\pi r$).

To determine how much weight can be lifted by means of the wheel and axle, the following equation is used:

Example: The screwdriver is a wheel handle and axle tip. If you exert 10 pounds of force to the wheel handle, the radius of which is 2 inches, how big a force will be exerted against the resistance at the axle tip, the radius of which is $\frac{1}{4}$ inch?

Effort × Circumference of large wheel = Resistance × Circumference of small wheel

$$10 \text{ lb.} \times (2)(\pi)(2 \text{ in.}) = \text{Resistance} \times (2)(\pi)\left(\frac{1}{4} \text{ in.}\right)$$

$$\frac{4}{1} \times 10 \times (2)(\pi)(2 \text{ in.}) = \text{Resistance} \times (2)(\pi) \times \frac{1}{4} \times \frac{4}{1}$$

$$80 \text{ lb.} = \text{Resistance}$$

Gears

Gears are used to change direction, increase or reduce speed, and increase or reduce force. Each gear turns the next gear that it interacts with, in the opposite direction.

The ratio of the circumferences of the two gears determines the mechanical advantage.

$$\text{Mechanical Advantage (MA)} = \frac{\text{teeth of the driven gear}}{\text{teeth of the driver gear}}$$

To determine the change in speed of gears in a gear train use the proportion

s_2	:	s_1	::	t_1	:	t_2
(speed of the last gear)		(speed of the 1st gear)		(product of the teeth of driver gear		(product of the teeth of the driven gear)

Belt Drives

There are two types of belt drives, positive and nonpositive. A positive drive consists of two wheels with sprockets that mesh with a chain or belt. A nonpositive drive makes use of a smooth wheel and smooth belt; an example is the V-belt found in the front of an automobile engine.

Belt drives are used to increase or reduce speed or force and to change the direction of a turning wheel. The belt drive transmits power and changes speed in the same manner as gears. This permits the two wheels to be separated and connected only by the belt, so the belt travels from the top of one wheel to the bottom of the next wheel. A change in direction is accomplished by twisting the belt.

SCIENCE

This short review is not intended to teach you science; its sole purpose is to jog your memory and bring back facts you have already learned but may have forgotten. If the materials do not seem familiar, you should spend some time reviewing a general science textbook. Keep in mind that most of the science questions you will encounter on the exam are based on principles of physics and chemistry, and these are the areas of science on which you should concentrate.

Matter

Matter is anything that takes up space and has weight. It exists in three states: gas, liquid, and solid.

A *gas* is a substance without shape or definite volume. It expands to fill the space available.

A *liquid* has no specific shape but has a definite volume. A liquid takes the shape of the container in which it is stored, for example, a cola bottle, a storage tank, a lake.

A *solid* has a definite shape and a definite volume. Examples: a car, a piece of wood, a book.

Electricity

The preferred kinetic molecule state of an object is to be neutral, that is, to have equal numbers of protons and electrons.

When something is not neutral, there is a chance that an electron flow can develop. The flow will always be the same; electrons flow from the point where there is an excess through a conductor (metal wire—silver, gold, aluminum, or copper) to the place where there is a deficiency. The flow is prevented by using a resistor or insulator.

A charge can accumulate on a substance. When the excess accumulation leaves the surface, we have a "static (electric) spark." This spark may have sufficient heat potential to ignite some substance, particularly a flammable liquid.

An electric circuit is made up of three parts:

1. The electric source: a battery or generator.
2. The conductor: wires.
3. The appliance: a motor, lightbulb, or household appliance.

A circuit is *open* when the flow of electrons is able to make a complete loop back to the source, and is *closed* or *broken* when the electrons cannot return to the source. Since electricity can flow in only one direction at a time, two wires are necessary to make a current—one from the source to the appliance, the other from the appliance to the source.

There are two types of circuits. In a *series* system the flow of current must pass through all appliances before returning to the source; any break in the flow stops the flow of the whole system. In a *parallel* system the current can flow through each subcircuit independently and then back to the source; a break in a subsystem flow affects only the appliances on the subsystem, all others remaining operative.

Resistance, limiting the flow of electrons, will produce heat. As the resistance increases, so does the heat and so does the chance of fire. The resistance in a wire depends on three factors:

1. The *type* of wire. Aluminum, copper, and silver are good conductors; tungsten and nichrome are good resistors.
2. The *thickness* of the wire. As the thickness increases, the resistance is reduced.
3. The *length* of the wire. The longer the wire, the greater is the resistance.

Since resistance results in an increase in heat, the possibility of overloading or short circuiting is increased. Overloading can lead to burning of the insulation around the wire. A short circuit can lead to a powerful short electrical discharge. To prevent overloading and short circuits, a fuse or circuit breaker is placed in the system. The fuse contains a small metal strip that melts at a predetermined temperature lower than the temperature the wire is designed to handle. A household wiring system would normally have its fuses in parallel to prevent an overload in any subsystem from shutting down the whole system. Bypassing the fuse or using an improper fuse has often led to a serious fire.

Heat

The temperature of a substance determines whether it will give off or take on heat. Heat always flows from the warmer to the colder body.

The two most common scales for measuring heat are the Fahrenheit scale and the Celsius or centigrade scale. Both scales use the freezing and boiling points of water as reference points. On the Fahrenheit scale the freezing point of water is 32 degrees; on the Celsius scale it is 0 degrees. The boiling point of water on the Fahrenheit scale is 212 degrees; on the Celsius scale it is 100 degrees.

As water is heated, it absorbs heat. For each British thermal unit (Btu) of heat, one pound of water rises 1 degree Fahrenheit. This statement is true for all conditions except at the points of freezing and boiling. At these two points, additional heat is necessary to allow the water to change state from a solid (ice) to a liquid (water) or from a liquid (water) to a gas (steam). To go from ice to water requires 143.4 additional Btu's, and to go from water to steam requires 970.3 Btu's.

Heat is transferred from one object to another in three ways: by *conduction,* the direct touching of objects; by *convection,* the movement or circulation of a heated gas (air); and by *radiation,* energy traveling as an electromagnetic wave through space.

Sources of heat energy include the combustion of solids, liquids, and gases; electrical heat energy; mechanical heat energy (such as friction); the heat of compression (known as the diesel effect); and nuclear heat energy.

Fire

Fire is rapid oxidation accompanied by heat and light. For a fire to take place, four conditions must be met:

1. There must be a fuel (wood, gasoline, paper, etc.).
2. There must be oxygen (air).
3. There must be heat.
4. There must be sufficient energy to get the chemical reaction started.

To understand this concept better, think about the conditions around you at the present moment. This book is a fuel, the air around you contains oxygen, and you are probably in an area where it is warm and comfortable (heat)—yet there is no fire. To create a fire you would need sufficient additional energy to cause the substances to react and hence burn.

There are four basic types of fires:

1. Fires that burn and leave an ash such as wood are called CLASS A FIRES.
2. Fires in liquids are called CLASS B FIRES.
3. Fires in electric circuits or appliances in which the current is ON are called CLASS C FIRES. (*Note:* When the current is OFF or disconnected, the same fire can be classed as A or B, depending on what is burning—insulation or oil.)
4. Fires in reactive metals such as magnesium, lithium, titanium, and zirconium are called CLASS D FIRES.

There are four ways to extinguish a fire:

1. Remove the fuel. Turn off the gas, shut off the oil flow, take the combustible materials away.

2. Remove the oxygen. Put a cover on the combustible materials.
3. Remove the heat. Put water on the fire; cool it.
4. Interfere with the chemical reaction. Put a special extinguishing agent, a dry chemical, on the fire.

Note: Fires most often occur from carelessness, ignorance, and/or failure to maintain equipment properly.

Water

Water, the universal solvent and primary fire-extinguishing agent, exists as a solid, a liquid, and a gas. As water is cooled, it contracts in volume until just before freezing, at which point (34 degrees Fahrenheit or 4 degrees Celsius) it expands.

For this reason, in cold climates pipes, if not protected, often break. The freezing point of water can be lowered by adding a freezing point depressant such as ethylene glycol (antifreeze).

BASIC CHARACTERISTICS OF WATER

- Water boils at 212 degrees Fahrenheit.
- Water solidifies at 32 degrees Fahrenheit.
- Water changing state from solid to liquid requires an additional 143.4 Btu's per pound of water.
- Water changing state from liquid to steam requires an additional 970.3 Btu's per pound of water.
- At all times except when changing states, 1 Btu per pound of water is required to raise the water temperature by 1°F.
- Water is a solvent that can wash away and/or dilute many combustible products.
- Water in the liquid state has a very stable viscosity and can easily be moved by gravity or pump through pipe or hose.
- The high surface tension of water allows it to be thrown in droplet form and allows many extinguishing agents to work effectively with it.
- One gallon of water weighs 8.35 (approximately $8\frac{1}{3}$) pounds.
- Fresh water has a density of 62.4 pounds per cubic foot.
- Salt water has a density of 64 pounds per cubic foot.
- A 1-cubic-foot container can hold 7.48 (approximately $7\frac{1}{2}$) gallons of water.
- A 13.54-inch column of water exerts the same force as a 1-inch column of mercury.
- In theory, water can be drafted up to 33 feet high; however, 28 feet is the practical limit.
- A water droplet, when converted to steam, becomes 1,700 times larger than its original size.
- A 1-inch-square, 1-foot-high column of water exerts a pressure of 0.434 pound.

SIX PRINCIPLES OF FLUID PRESSURE

- Liquid pressure is exerted in a perpendicular direction to any surface on which it acts.
- At any given point beneath the surface of a liquid, the pressure is the same in all directions.
- Pressure applied to a confined liquid from outside is transmitted in all directions without any loss of force.
- The pressure of a liquid in an open vessel is proportional to the depth of the liquid.
- The pressure of a liquid in an open vessel is proportional to the density of the liquid.
- Liquid pressure on the bottom of a vessel is unaffected by the size of the vessel.

ANSWER SHEET
Practice Exercises

1. Ⓐ Ⓑ Ⓒ Ⓓ
2. Ⓐ Ⓑ Ⓒ Ⓓ
3. Ⓐ Ⓑ Ⓒ Ⓓ
4. Ⓐ Ⓑ Ⓒ Ⓓ
5. Ⓐ Ⓑ Ⓒ Ⓓ
6. Ⓐ Ⓑ Ⓒ Ⓓ
7. Ⓐ Ⓑ Ⓒ Ⓓ
8. Ⓐ Ⓑ Ⓒ Ⓓ
9. Ⓐ Ⓑ Ⓒ Ⓓ
10. Ⓐ Ⓑ Ⓒ Ⓓ
11. Ⓐ Ⓑ Ⓒ Ⓓ
12. Ⓐ Ⓑ Ⓒ Ⓓ
13. Ⓐ Ⓑ Ⓒ Ⓓ
14. Ⓐ Ⓑ Ⓒ Ⓓ
15. Ⓐ Ⓑ Ⓒ Ⓓ
16. Ⓐ Ⓑ Ⓒ Ⓓ
17. Ⓐ Ⓑ Ⓒ Ⓓ
18. Ⓐ Ⓑ Ⓒ Ⓓ
19. Ⓐ Ⓑ Ⓒ Ⓓ
20. Ⓐ Ⓑ Ⓒ Ⓓ
21. Ⓐ Ⓑ Ⓒ Ⓓ
22. Ⓐ Ⓑ Ⓒ Ⓓ
23. Ⓐ Ⓑ Ⓒ Ⓓ
24. Ⓐ Ⓑ Ⓒ Ⓓ
25. Ⓐ Ⓑ Ⓒ Ⓓ
26. Ⓐ Ⓑ Ⓒ Ⓓ
27. Ⓐ Ⓑ Ⓒ Ⓓ
28. Ⓐ Ⓑ Ⓒ Ⓓ
29. Ⓐ Ⓑ Ⓒ Ⓓ
30. Ⓐ Ⓑ Ⓒ Ⓓ
31. Ⓐ Ⓑ Ⓒ Ⓓ
32. Ⓐ Ⓑ Ⓒ Ⓓ
33. Ⓐ Ⓑ Ⓒ Ⓓ
34. Ⓐ Ⓑ Ⓒ Ⓓ
35. Ⓐ Ⓑ Ⓒ Ⓓ
36. Ⓐ Ⓑ Ⓒ Ⓓ
37. Ⓐ Ⓑ Ⓒ Ⓓ
38. Ⓐ Ⓑ Ⓒ Ⓓ
39. Ⓐ Ⓑ Ⓒ Ⓓ
40. Ⓐ Ⓑ Ⓒ Ⓓ
41. Ⓐ Ⓑ Ⓒ Ⓓ
42. Ⓐ Ⓑ Ⓒ Ⓓ
43. Ⓐ Ⓑ Ⓒ Ⓓ
44. Ⓐ Ⓑ Ⓒ Ⓓ
45. Ⓐ Ⓑ Ⓒ Ⓓ
46. Ⓐ Ⓑ Ⓒ Ⓓ
47. Ⓐ Ⓑ Ⓒ Ⓓ
48. Ⓐ Ⓑ Ⓒ Ⓓ
49. Ⓐ Ⓑ Ⓒ Ⓓ
50. Ⓐ Ⓑ Ⓒ Ⓓ

PRACTICE EXERCISES

Directions: For each question select the one best answer—(A), (B), (C), or (D)—and write the corresponding letter on your answer paper next to the number of the question.

1. How many pounds of force would be required to lift the 300-pound box below?

   (A) 100
   (B) 200
   (C) 600
   (D) 1,200

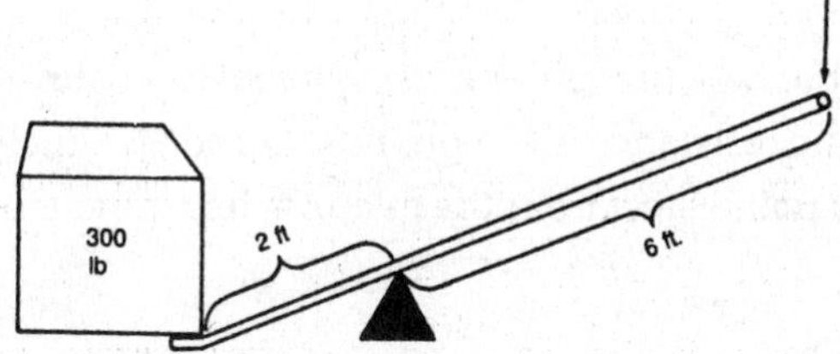

2. The force that must be applied to the handle of the hammer in this illustration is

   (A) 10 pounds.
   (B) 15 pounds.
   (C) 75 pounds.
   (D) 175 pounds.

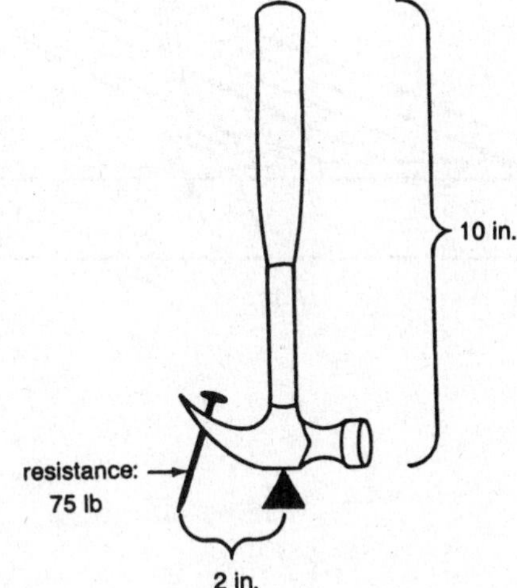

3. The best way to make it easier to lift the weight with the board as indicated in the illustration would be to

   (A) move the box closer to the fire fighter.
   (B) use a shorter board.
   (C) move the weight closer to the fulcrum.
   (D) turn the box to an upright position.

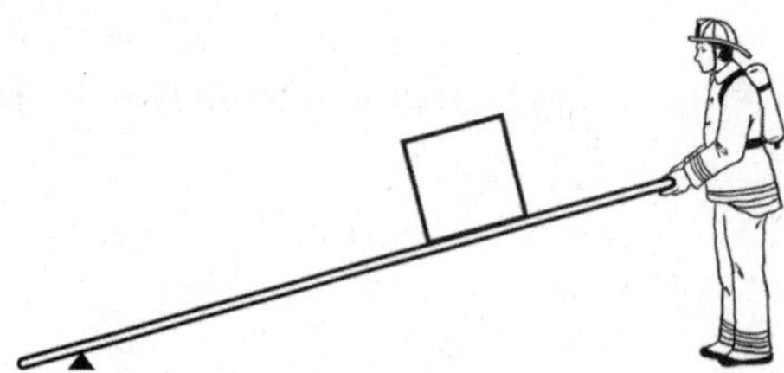

4. In the illustration below, a firefighter is using a tool to pry up a floorboard to search for hidden fire. If the resistance is 600 pounds, the adz is 6 inches, and the firefighter applies a force at a point 3 feet from the fulcrum, how much force will be needed?

   (A) 50 pounds
   (B) 100 pounds
   (C) 300 pounds
   (D) 600 pounds

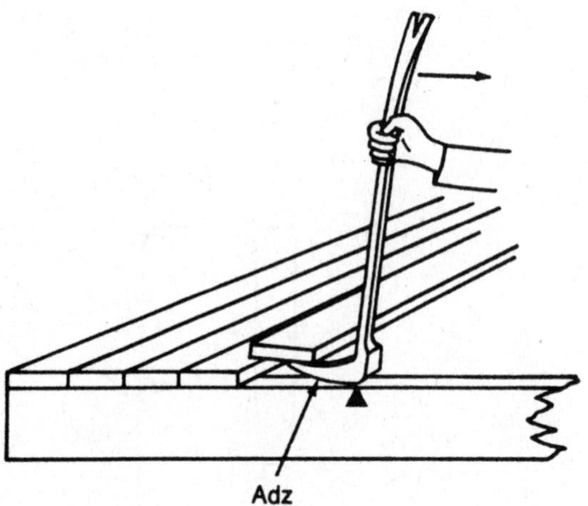

5. A fire lieutenant is demonstrating how to use a crowbar to lift a concrete slab up about 2 inches to allow a piece of shoring to be put under the concrete's edge. The lieutenant asks the group of fire recruits to estimate how much effort would be needed to lift a 300-pound slab if they use a crowbar that is 6 ft. 6 in. long and the fulcrum is 6 in. from the adz end. The recruits would be most accurate if they agreed that the effort would be approximately

(A) 25 pounds of effort.
(B) 75 pounds of effort.
(C) 150 pounds of effort.
(D) 300 pounds of effort.

6. If a 300-pound bale of paper is to be raised to a platform 6 feet above, rolling the bale up a 30-foot ramp would require an effort of

(A) 30 pounds.
(B) 45 pounds.
(C) 60 pounds.
(D) 180 pounds.

7. The wooden box below, weighing 200 pounds, is being pulled up an inclined plane that is four times as long as its vertical height. How much effort will be required by the firefighter to do the job?

(A) 50 pounds
(B) 100 pounds
(C) 200 pounds
(D) 400 pounds

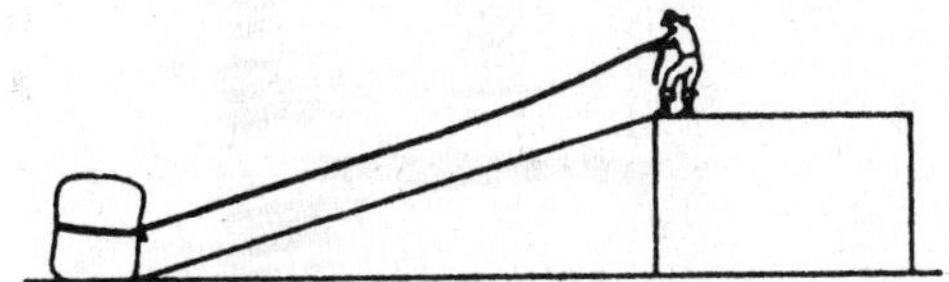

8. Which of the inclined planes shown below would require the least amount of effort to raise the barrel up onto the platform?

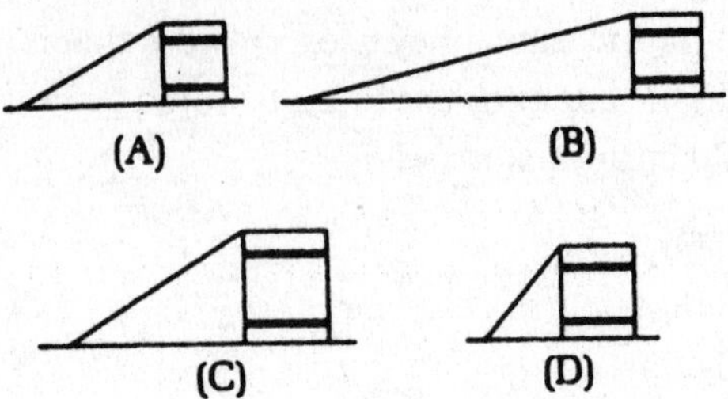

9. If the tailboard of the truck in the illustration below is 5 feet above the ground and a 16-foot-long plank is used as a ramp, how much effort will be required to load a 4,000-pound fire pump onto the truck?

(A) 200 pounds
(B) 600 pounds
(C) 1,050 pounds
(D) 1,250 pounds

10. If the weight shown must be lifted a height of 2 feet, how much rope will a firefighter have to pull through the pulley?

(A) 1 foot
(B) 2 feet
(C) 3 feet
(D) 4 feet

11. How much weight will a jackscrew with a pitch of $\frac{1}{5}$ inch and a handle 28 inches long lift when a force of 5 pounds is applied to the handle?

(A) 2,200 pounds
(B) 3,500 pounds
(C) 4,400 pounds
(D) 6,000 pounds

12. If the pitch in the jackscrew in the illustration below is $\frac{1}{2}$ inch and the jack handle measures 14 inches, approximately how much force will the firefighter have to apply to lift a 2,000-pound truck?

(A) 1 pound

(B) $4\frac{1}{2}$ pounds

(C) $5\frac{1}{2}$ pounds

(D) $11\frac{1}{2}$ pounds

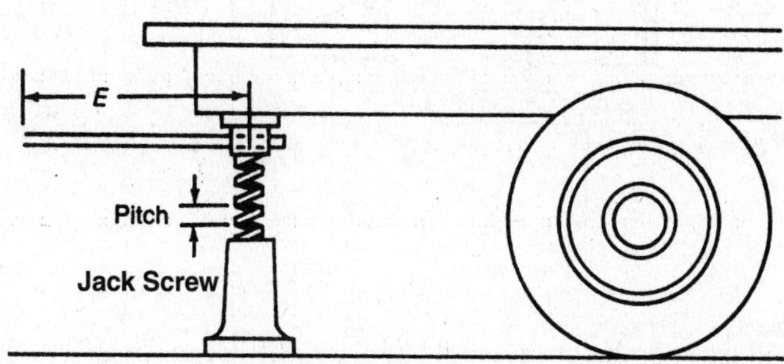

13. The axle in the illustration below is 6 inches in diameter, and the handle when turned makes a circle with a diameter of 24 inches. If a firefighter uses a force of 60 pounds to turn the handle, how much weight can be lifted?

(A) 90 pounds
(B) 150 pounds
(C) 240 pounds
(D) 370 pounds

14. Assume that the booster reel on the fire apparatus has an axle with an 8-inch diameter and a wheel with a 20-inch diameter. If a load of 300 pounds must be pulled in, how much force need the firefighter exert?

(A) 100 pounds
(B) 120 pounds
(C) 160 pounds
(D) 200 pounds

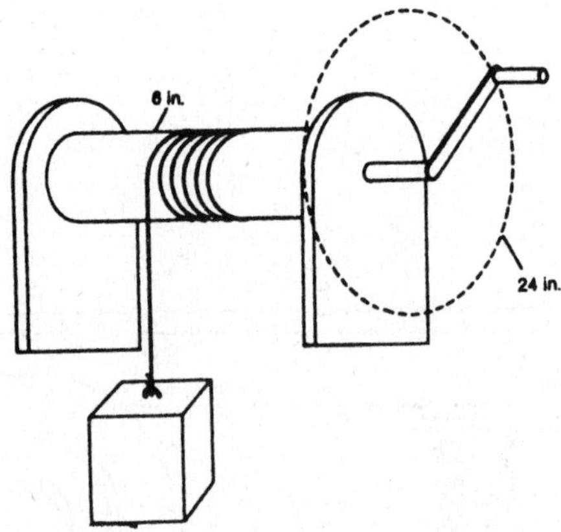

15. Look at the illustration below. It would be INCORRECT to say that

(A) wheel X will turn in the same direction as wheel Y.
(B) if wheel Y is moved closer to wheel X, then wheel X will turn faster.
(C) if wheel X is the drive wheel, then wheel Y will have an increase in speed.
(D) if wheel Y is the drive wheel, then wheel X will have an increase in force.

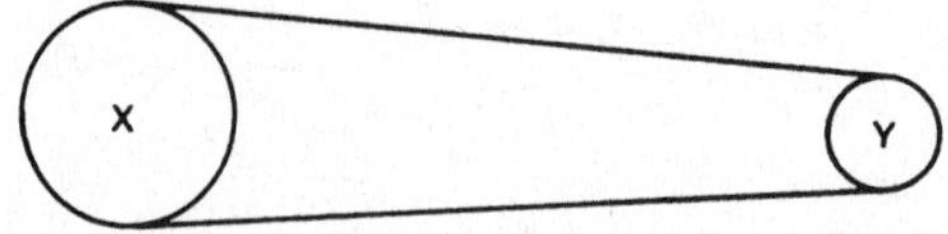

16. It would be CORRECT in stating that

(A) all wheels will turn at the same speed, but wheel C will turn in the opposite direction from A and B.
(B) all wheels will turn in the same direction, but wheel C will turn more slowly than A or B.
(C) wheels A and C will turn in the same direction and at the same speed; wheel B will turn faster and in the opposite direction.
(D) wheels A and B will turn in the same direction, and wheels B and C will turn at the same speed.

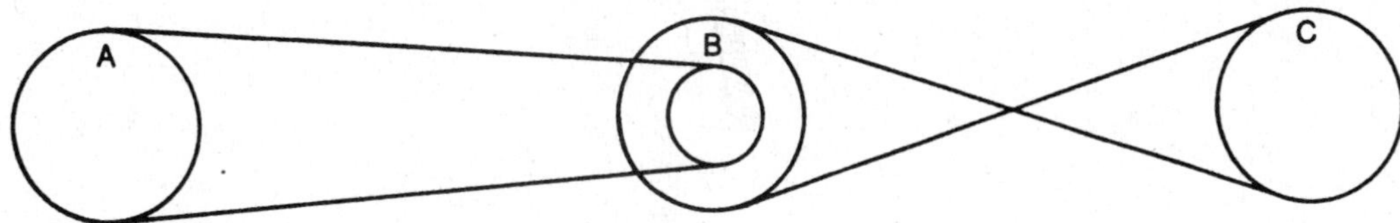

17. Fires are generally divided into four classes. Fires of ordinary combustible materials are classified as

(A) class A fires.
(B) class B fires.
(C) class C fires.
(D) class D fires.

18. There are two types of current, direct and

(A) indirect.
(B) modular.
(C) alternating.
(D) circular.

19. It would be CORRECT to say about direct current that

(A) it flows in two directions.
(B) it is better than alternating current.
(C) it is produced by a battery.
(D) it always takes the shortest route.

20. When heated, the bar in the illustration bends because

(A) heat bends metals.
(B) the bar is defective.
(C) the two metals expand at different rates.
(D) the chemical reactions of the metals cause one to expand and the other to contract.

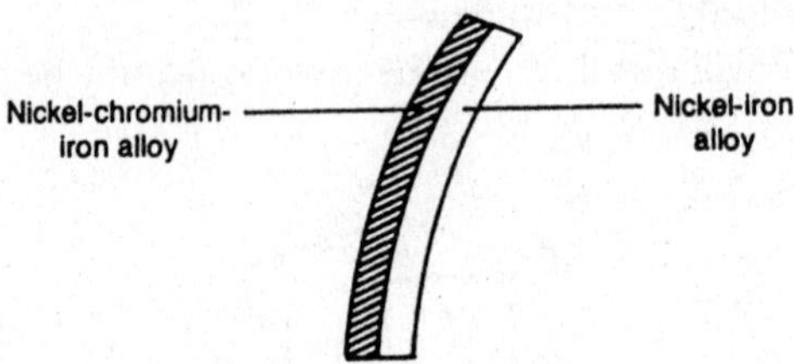

21. An instructor at the fire academy told a group of school children, "It takes more energy to push water through a long hose line than through a short one of the same diameter." The need for the extra energy is due to

(A) inertia.
(B) gravity.
(C) friction.
(D) ebullition.

22. If the firefighter operating the pump sets the pressure at 200 pounds per square inch, the pressure at the unopened nozzle of a 300-foot length of hose will most likely be

(A) less than the pressure at the pump.
(B) equal to the pressure at the pump.
(C) greater than the pressure at the pump.
(D) undeterminable without additional information.

23. During a training session it was learned that a material that is a poor conductor of heat is

(A) a good conductor of sound.
(B) a fair conductor of electricity.
(C) a good insulator of heat.
(D) an excellent fire retardant.

24. Water, when changing from ice to steam, absorbs

(A) air.
(B) volume.
(C) heat.
(D) density.

25. During the winter months in northern climates many water pipes break. The most likely reason is that

(A) water expands when it freezes and produces great pressure.
(B) ice is much heavier than water.
(C) cold pipes are very brittle.
(D) cold makes the pipes contract and separate.

26. At a major fire in a factory a number of compressed gas cylinders containing carbon dioxide (CO_2) are threatened by the flames. It is correct to say about this situation that

(A) if the safety valves let go, the CO_2 will intensify the fire.
(B) the gas is toxic and will make fighting the fire very hazardous.
(C) the cylinders may explode and injure the firefighters.
(D) since CO_2 is a nonflammable gas, there is no hazard and no problem.

27. In the winter months, cars are more difficult to start. Once started, racing the engine is

(A) good—this warms the car up fast.
(B) undesirable—this causes an excessive drain of the electrical system.
(C) good—the battery will be rapidly charged.
(D) undesirable—the oil is thick and will not properly lubricate the motor parts.

28. Sprinkler systems have consistently proved their value. The one major exception to their outstanding record has occurred in instances of explosion. The most likely reason for their failure in such cases is that

(A) the sprinkler heads are clogged by the explosion.
(B) these fires burn out too fast.
(C) the piping to the system is blown apart.
(D) an arsonist has shut the system down.

29. You should not use water on live electrical equipment because

(A) it will cause short circuits and damage the equipment.
(B) it is ineffective on electrical equipment.
(C) there is a danger of conducting electricity and endangering the firefighter.
(D) this expensive, sophisticated equipment may be ruined.

30. Which of the following would be considered a good conductor of heat?

(A) Air
(B) Wood
(C) Iron
(D) Stone

31. The practice of using booster cables to jump a car whose battery is worn down is

(A) dangerous, provided that the cables are connected correctly.
(B) dangerous, if not done correctly, because of the possibility of escaping hydrogen vapors.
(C) not dangerous, provided that proper ground is established.
(D) dangerous, if done in cold weather.

32. While visiting a friend, you find that he is repairing his car and is using a large open pan filled with gasoline to bathe and wash the parts. This action is

(A) correct—gasoline is an excellent solvent that rapidly cleans the parts.
(B) incorrect—gasoline emits a flammable vapor at temperatures of 36° below zero and can ignite easily.
(C) correct—gasoline is less expensive than other solvents and works almost as well.
(D) incorrect—gasoline is a toxic substance and requires the use of special respiratory equipment when used as a cleaning solvent.

33. A fire that starts by "spontaneous combustion"

(A) is impossible.
(B) is quickly extinguished.
(C) is common in cases of arson.
(D) has started without any outside source of ignition.

34. The proper method for extinguishing a grease fire in a frying pan is to cover it. This method of extinguishment is

(A) removal of fuel.
(B) removal of oxygen.
(C) cooling.
(D) flame inhibition.

35. The reason for the compressed air in a portable extinguisher is to

(A) prevent the water from freezing.
(B) push the water out.
(C) reduce the weight of the extinguisher.
(D) allow the extinguisher to float if dropped in the water.

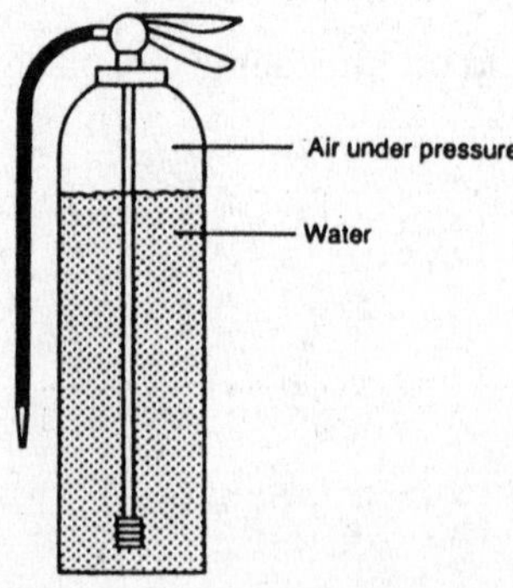

Directions: Answer questions 36 through 40 based on the information given in the following chart:

- One gallon of water weighs about 8.35 pounds.
- A container measuring 1 foot by 1 foot (1 cubic foot) can hold approximately 7.5 gallons of water.
- A 1-cubic-foot container filled with water weighs approximately 62.4 pounds.

36. If the water supply tank on a fire apparatus holds 400 gallons of water when full, how much weight does the water add to the apparatus when the tank is full?

    (A) 3,400 pounds
    (B) 2,800 pounds
    (C) 2,400 pounds
    (D) 1,650 pounds

37. A 5-gallon container of water would most nearly weigh

    (A) 5 pounds.
    (B) 37 pounds.
    (C) 42 pounds.
    (D) 62.5 pounds.

38. If the freshwater tank on the roof of a fire station measures 10 feet × 10 feet × 10 feet, how much weight will a half-full tank exert on the roof supports?

    (A) 31,200 pounds
    (B) 62,400 pounds
    (C) 80,000 pounds
    (D) 97,500 pounds

39. If a tank measuring 5 feet × 7 feet × 3 feet is full, how many gallons of water will it hold?

    (A) 455 gallons
    (B) $587\frac{1}{2}$ gallons
    (C) $787\frac{1}{2}$ gallons
    (D) 949 gallons

40. At a major fire three hose lines are being used. Each line delivers 250 gallons of water per minute. If no water runs out of the building, how long will it take for a floor measuring 20 feet × 20 feet to be filled with water to a height of 1 foot?

(A) 4 minutes
(B) 8 minutes
(C) 10 minutes
(D) 16 minutes

41. A commonly used formula in the fire service for the placement of ladders against a building is to divide the length of the ladder by 5 and then add 2 to the result. This gives the number of feet from which to place the base of the ladder from the wall. If this formula is applied, how many feet from the wall should the base of the ladder in the illustration below be?

(A) 3
(B) 5
(C) 7
(D) 9

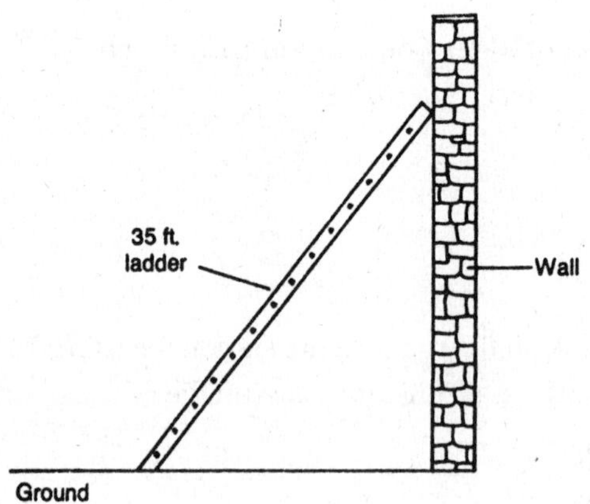

42. The table shown below measures 6 feet in diameter. The smallest salvage cover that can be put over the table to protect the top is

(A) a rectangle 6 feet × 8 feet.
(B) a square 7 feet × 7 feet.
(C) a rectangle 6 feet × 5 feet.
(D) a square 8 feet × 8 feet.

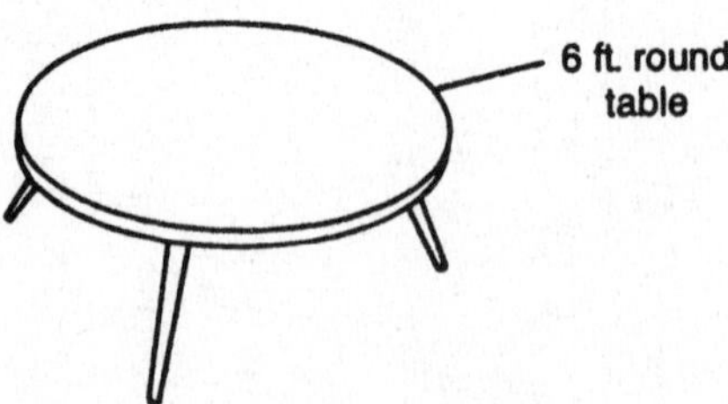

43. If you compare the amount of fire hose that can be stored in compartment A of the fire truck below with the amount of fire hose that can be stored in compartment B, you would be correct in stating that

(A) compartment A will hold more hose.
(B) compartment B will hold more hose.
(C) the two compartments will hold the same amount.
(D) there is no way to determine the capacities of the compartments without more information.

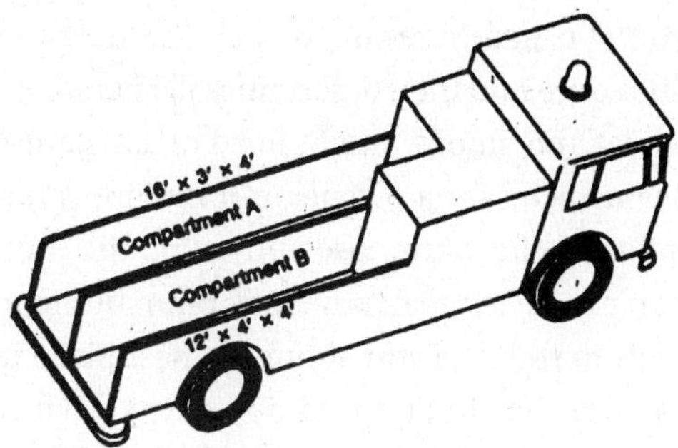

44. "Pressure tanks shall be acceptable as primary water supply systems provided that an additional volume equivalent to one half of the required water storage space is provided for the required air." The most likely meaning of this statement is that

(A) the tank can be two-thirds full of water and one-third full of air.
(B) the tank must not be more than one-half full of water and one-half full of air.
(C) the tank must be one-third full of water and two-thirds full of air.
(D) the tank must be full of water, and a supply of air must be near by.

45. If a water tank measures 8 feet × 4 feet × 6 feet, how many cubic feet of water can it hold?

(A) 24
(B) 32
(C) 156
(D) 192

Directions: Answer questions 46 through 48 based solely on the information provided in the following passage.

Firefighters use an aerial ladder apparatus to rescue people from the upper floors of buildings. The aerial ladder is also used to gain entry to search for victims and to ventilate the building of heat and smoke. When approaching the fire building, the apparatus driver should anticipate the use of the ladder. Deciding where to set up the ladder is based on an information-gathering process called "size-up." The driver looks at the building as the apparatus slowly approaches the scene and then determines if a person is in urgent need of rescue, if someone is exposed to heat and smoke and in need of assistance, or if the fire area needs venting. If there is no obvious need for a rescue, or if the fire is not readily visible, then the driver will position the apparatus for future use and set up the turntable in the center of the building so the ladder when raised can reach the maximum number of windows or the roof.

The size-up process leads to the decision about the best place to locate the ladder truck. The driver slows down to view the situation, to determine what needs to be done, and to accurately line up the turntable with the target objective. If someone is at a window, the driver notes the window the person is sitting in and then, following the line of windows down to the street level, locates street-level guides or street markings—lines in the sidewalk, telephone poles, hydrants, and so on—and uses them to align the center of the apparatus turn-table with the line of windows.

Now the driver engages the brakes and activates the power take-off; this switches the power of the engine from driving mode to aerial operation mode. The driver gets out of the cab, places chocks under the wheels, and engages the tormentor stabilizer system. When the base of the truck is set in a firm position, the bed ladder can be lifted from its cradle, elevated to the proper angle, and rotated into position below the window. Then the fly ladder can be raised to rescue the person.

46. When arriving at a building fire, Ladder 21 finds a person in extreme danger at the fifth-floor window of a building fire. It would be most correct if the driver

    (A) after lining up and properly placing the turntable, engaged the tormentors, put the chocks under the wheels, and proceeded to elevate the bed ladder.
    (B) engaged the power take-off, engaged the tormentor stabilizer system, elevated the bed ladder, raised the fly, and rotated the aerial ladder.
    (C) used the fifth-floor window as the guide to line up the turn-table, engaged the brakes, put the power take-off to the ON position, and raised the ladder.
    (D) after applying the break, engaged the power take-off, got out of the cab, put the chocks under the wheels, and elevated the ladder.

47. At a fire on John Street, a person must be removed from the upper floors of a building by use of an aerial ladder. The following steps would be used to make this rescue. (The steps listed below are not in correct order.)

1. Elevate bed ladder from the cradle.
2. Raise fly ladder.
3. Engage power take-off.
4. Engage the tormentors.

The above steps would best be performed in the following order:

(A) 1, 3, 4, 2
(B) 3, 4, 1, 2
(C) 4, 3, 1, 2
(D) 3, 1, 4, 2

48. Ladder Company 55 has been dispatched to 122 East Broadway for a reported smoke condition on the sixth floor. As the fire company approaches the building, the firefighters can smell smoke, but there is no visible fire, and no one is on the scene to direct them to the location of the fire. Following is a list of activities the driver might do. (The list is not in the correct order.)

1. Locate the ladder in the best position for future use.
2. Line up the turntable with a crack in the sidewalk.
3. Follow the line of windows to the street.
4. Determine if the fire floor needs venting.

The above procedures should be done in the following order:

(A) 4, 3, 2, 1
(B) 1, 3, 2, 4
(C) 4, 2, 3, 1
(D) 3, 2, 4, 1

Directions: Answer questions 49 and 50 based solely on the information provided in the following passage.

An effectively placed and operated hose line saves lives by quickly extinguishing the fire. When people are trapped in a burning building, the first hose line should be placed so the hose stream can be directed between them and the fire. When no one is exposed to danger from the fire, the hose line should be put at a point that protects the property that is most severely exposed. If a second hose line is needed, the rules for proper hose placement dictate that the second hose line be used to back up or supplement the first line. If the second hose line is not needed as a backup, it should be brought to the adjoining apartment or to the floor above the fire, whichever is in more danger. A third hose line could be used to protect the secondary means of egress, people trapped at a window on the floors above the fire, or to stop the fire from extending to an adjoining building.

49. Engine 321 responds to a fire in a three-story building and finds fire on the first floor with some extension to the upper floors. The following steps would be taken. (The items listed are not in priority order.)

 1. Direct a line to be taken to the floor above the fire floor.
 2. Direct a line to be used to protect the adjoining building.
 3. Direct a line to protect the secondary means of egress.
 4. Direct a line to the first floor to protect the stairway exit and extinguish the fire.

 The most appropriate sequence for the hose line placement is

 (A) 4, 3, 2, 1.
 (B) 2, 4, 1, 3.
 (C) 1, 2, 3, 4.
 (D) 4, 1, 3, 2.

50. Consider the following scenario:

 "A fire on the first floor is growing rapidly beyond the capabilities of the first hose line and is extending to the floor above."

 The proper action for the firefighter on the first hose line is to request

 (A) a second hose line be brought in to go to the floor above.
 (B) a third hose line be put into operation to protect the adjoining building, which may become exposed.
 (C) a second line be brought in to back up the first line.
 (D) a third line be brought in to back up the first line and then to advance up to the floor above.

ANSWER KEY AND EXPLANATIONS

Answer Key

1. **(A)**	11. **(C)**	21. **(C)**	31. **(B)**	41. **(D)**
2. **(B)**	12. **(D)**	22. **(B)**	32. **(B)**	42. **(A)**
3. **(C)**	13. **(C)**	23. **(C)**	33. **(D)**	43. **(C)**
4. **(B)**	14. **(B)**	24. **(C)**	34. **(B)**	44. **(A)**
5. **(A)**	15. **(B)**	25. **(A)**	35. **(B)**	45. **(D)**
6. **(C)**	16. **(D)**	26. **(C)**	36. **(A)**	46. **(D)**
7. **(A)**	17. **(A)**	27. **(D)**	37. **(C)**	47. **(B)**
8. **(B)**	18. **(C)**	28. **(C)**	38. **(A)**	48. **(B)**
9. **(D)**	19. **(C)**	29. **(C)**	39. **(C)**	49. **(D)**
10. **(D)**	20. **(C)**	30. **(C)**	40. **(A)**	50. **(C)**

Answer Explanations

1. **(A)** This is a class 1 lever. Using this formula:

$$\text{Effort} \times \text{Effort Distance} = \text{Resistance} \times \text{Resistance Distance}$$

and inserting the known values, we can solve for the effort (x).

$$\text{Effort} \times \text{Effort Distance} = \text{Resistance} \times \text{Resistance Distance}$$
$$x \times \quad 6 \text{ ft.} \quad = 300 \text{ lb.} \times \quad 2 \text{ ft.}$$
$$x = \frac{300 \text{ lb.} \times 2 \text{ ft.}}{6 \text{ ft.}}$$
$$x = \frac{600 \text{ foot-pounds (ft.-lb.)}}{6 \text{ ft.}}$$
$$x = 100 \text{ lb.}$$

2. **(B)** This is a class 1 lever with the arms at different angles.

$$\text{Effort} \times \text{Effort Distance} = \text{Resistance} \times \text{Resistance Distance}$$
$$x \times \quad 10 \text{ in.} \quad = 75 \text{ lb.} \times \quad 2 \text{ in.}$$
$$x = \frac{75 \text{ lb.} \times 2 \text{ in.}}{10 \text{ in.}}$$
$$x = \frac{150 \text{ inch-pounds (in.-lb.)}}{10 \text{ in.}}$$
$$x = 15 \text{ lb.}$$

3. **(C)** This is a class 2 lever system. Increasing the length of the effort distance while decreasing the length of the resistance distance will reduce the effort required to lift the box. To see that this is correct, try putting weights at different distances from the fulcrum and then working out the solutions.

4. **(B)** This is a class 1 lever.

$$\text{Effort} \times \text{Effort Distance} = \text{Resistance} \times \text{Resistance Distance}$$
$$x \times \quad 3 \text{ ft.} \quad = 600 \text{ lb.} \times \quad 6 \text{ in.}$$
$$x = \frac{600 \text{ lb.} \times 6 \text{ in.}}{3 \text{ ft.}}$$

Note: Before you continue, you must change inches to feet so that you are working with the same units. Since 6 inches = $\frac{1}{2}$ foot,

$$x = \frac{\frac{\overset{300}{\cancel{600}}\text{ lb.}}{\cancel{1}} \times \frac{\cancel{1}\text{ ft.}}{\cancel{2}}}{3\text{ ft.}}$$

$$x = \frac{300\text{ ft.-lb.}}{3\text{ ft.}}$$

$$x = 100\text{ lb.}$$

5. **(A)** This is an example of a class one lever. Since the recruits were only asked to estimate the effort required we can ignore the slight angle of the crowbar at the adz end and assume the resistance of the concrete is directed perpendicular to the crowbar.

$$\text{Effort} \times \text{Effort Distance} = \text{Resistance} \times \text{Resistance Distance}$$

$$E \times 6\text{ ft.} = 300\text{ lb.} \times .5\text{ ft. (6 inches)}$$

$$E = \frac{300\text{ lb.} \times .5\text{ ft.}}{6\text{ ft.}}$$

$$E = \frac{150\text{ lb.}}{6}$$

$$E = 25\text{ lb.}$$

6. **(C)**

$$\text{Effort} \times \text{Length of plane} = \text{Resistance} \times \text{Height to be raised}$$

$$x \times 30\text{ ft.} = 300\text{ lb.} \times 6\text{ ft.}$$

$$x = \frac{300\text{ lb.} \times 6\text{ ft.}}{30\text{ ft.}}$$

$$x = \frac{1{,}800\text{ ft.-lb.}}{30\text{ ft.}}$$

$$x = 60\text{ lb.}$$

7. **(A)** The problem requires an understanding of the mechanical advantage of the inclined plane. A person might think that an item of information (the vertical height) had been left out of the question, but this is not the case. The mechanical advantage of the inclined plane is determined by dividing the length of the plane by the height to be raised. Since the plane is four times as long as its vertical height, the mechanical advantage is 4 (4/1 = 4). Using the standard format gives

$$\text{Effort} \times \text{Length of plane} = \text{Resistance} \times \text{Height to be raised}$$

$$x \times 4 = 200\text{ lb.} \times 1$$

$$x = \frac{200\text{ lb.} \times 1}{4}$$

$$x = 50\text{ lb.}$$

Note: There are no units of measure after the numbers 1 and 4.

8. **(B)** This question requires an understanding of the relationship involved in the mechanical advantage of the inclined plane and the ability to visualize this relationship, keeping in mind that

$$MA = \frac{\text{Length of plane}}{\text{Height to be raised}}$$

On a small piece of paper, measure off the distance to the ground from the top of the box—the height to be raised. Now use this as a guide to measure how many times this height can fit into the inclined plane. Choice B = 4, choice A = 2, choice C = 2, choice D = 1. The choice with the greatest mechanical advantage requires the least effort.

9. **(D)**

$$\text{Effort} \times \text{Length of plane} = \text{Resistance} \times \text{Height to be raised}$$

$$x \times 16\text{ ft.} = 4{,}000\text{ lb} \times 5\text{ ft.}$$

$$x = \frac{4{,}000\text{ lb.} \times 5\text{ ft.}}{16\text{ ft.}}$$

$$x = \frac{20{,}000\text{ ft.-lb.}}{16\text{ ft.}}$$

$$x = 1{,}250\text{ lb.}$$

10. **(D)** The amount of rope that must be pulled is related to the mechanical advantage. Multiply the height the weight is to be raised by the mechanical advantage to determine how much rope must be pulled:

Height to be raised	×	Mechanical advantage	=	Length of rope
2 ft.	×	2	=	4 ft.

11. **(C)**

$$\text{Effort} \times \text{E.D. (circumference)} = \text{Resistance} \times \text{R.D. (pitch)}$$

$$5\text{ lb.} \times 2\pi r = x \times \frac{1}{5}$$

$$5\text{ lb.} \times 2 \times 3.14 \times 28 = \frac{1}{5} \times x$$

$$\frac{1}{5}x = 880\text{ lb.}$$

$$x = 5 \times 880\text{ lb.}$$

$$x = 4{,}400\text{ lb.}$$

12. **(D)**

$$\text{Effort} \times \text{E.D. (circumference)} = \text{Resistance} \times \text{R.D. (pitch)}$$

$$x \times 2\pi r = 2{,}000\text{ lb.} \times \frac{1}{2}$$

$$x \times 2 \times 3.14 \times 14 = \overset{1000}{\cancel{2{,}000}} \times \frac{1}{\cancel{2}}$$

$$88x = 1{,}000$$

$$x = \frac{1{,}000}{88}$$

$x = 11.36$ (when rounded to the nearest $\frac{1}{2}$, the answer is approximately $11\frac{1}{2}$ lb.)

13. **(C)**

Effort	×	Circumference of large wheel	=	Resistance	×	Circumference of small wheel
60 lb.	×	$2 \times \pi \times r$	=	x	×	$2 \times \pi \times r$
60 lb.	×	$2 \times \pi \times 12$	=	x	×	$2 \times \pi \times 3$

(*Note:* Radius = one-half the diameter.)

$$x = \frac{60 \text{ lb.} \times \cancel{2 \times \pi} \times 12 \text{ in.}}{\cancel{2 \times \pi} \times 3 \text{ in.}}$$

$$x = \frac{60 \text{ lb.} \times 12 \text{ in.}}{3 \text{ in.}}$$

$$x = \frac{720}{3} \text{ lb.}$$

$$x = 240 \text{ lb.}$$

14. **(B)**

Effort × Circumference of large wheel = Resistance × Circumference of small wheel

$$x \times 2\pi r = 300 \text{ lb.} \times 2 r \pi$$

$$x = \frac{300 \text{ lb.} \times \cancel{2 \times \pi} \times 4 \text{ in.}}{\cancel{2 \times \pi} \times 10 \text{ in.}}$$

$$x = \frac{300 \text{ lb.} \times 4}{10}$$

$$x = 120 \text{ lb.}$$

15. **(B)** As the wheels move closer to each other, the belt will become loose and will not drive the other wheel. The other statements are correct. *Note:* With a belt drive system, the distance apart has nothing to do with the relative speeds of the wheels.

16. **(D)** The belt from drive wheel A is connected to a smaller wheel (B), which will therefore turn faster. The belt connecting the outer part of wheel B to wheel C is twisted, causing a change in direction.

17. **(A)** Class A fires burn in ordinary combustible materials such as wood, paper, and cloth. The distinguishing characteristic of this class of fire is that it leaves an ash.

18. **(C)** This is the type of current available at the ordinary electric outlet; it differs from direct current in that the flow of electricity reverses direction at regular intervals.

19. **(C)** Direct current is produced by a flow of electrons from one plate in a battery to another. It flows in one direction and can be obstructed by a resistor.

20. **(C)** All metals expand when heated; however, they do not expand at the same rate. The piece of metal shown in the illustration is known as a bimetallic strip and is used in thermostats.

21. **(C)** Friction is the resistance created between two surfaces that are in contact with each other. Choice A—inertia is the tendency of a body at rest to remain at rest or of a body in motion to remain in motion. In either case the body will remain as is until acted upon by an outside force. Choice B—gravity is the force of mutual attraction between

bodies, such as the earth and the moon. Choice D—ebullition is the boiling or bubbling up of a substance.

22. **(B)** The pressure in a closed system (no fluid flowing) is undiminished throughout the system.

23. **(C)** An insulator is a material that serves as a nonconductor. Choice D—you might reason that a poor conductor should act as a fire retardant. However, consider a piece of wood; it is a poor conductor of heat but burns readily.

24. **(C)** As a substance absorbs heat, its molecules are activated; this activation of the molecules results in ice (solid) changing state to water (liquid) and then expanding still further to become steam (gas). Choice A—it does not absorb air, but does displace it. Choice B—volume is space in three dimensions, and usually is expressed as cubic feet, cubic inches, etc. Choice D—density is a measure of the compactness of the parts of a substance.

25. **(A)** Water is a unique substance in that it expands as it approaches the freezing point; other materials contract.

26. **(C)** The heat will cause the CO_2 to expand, thereby leading to cylinder failure. When this happens, parts of the cylinder may fly in all directions, and the cylinder may fly off as a rocket.

27. **(D)** The cold causes the oil to thicken; the thick oil will take longer to circulate throughout the engine. Until this is accomplished, there is a good chance that metal will rub against metal, causing damage to the engine.

28. **(C)** In most cases the system is blown apart and the water cannot reach the fire.

29. **(C)** Water can conduct electricity back to the firefighter through the stream. For this reason special care must be exercised.

30. **(C)** Iron is a good *conductor;* choices A, B, and D are good *insulators.*

31. **(B)** When the acid in the battery is heated, it breaks down and gives off hydrogen gas. Hydrogen gas is very flammable and has led to many accidents and fires.

32. **(B)** Gasoline is a volatile flammable liquid that gives off vapors at very low temperatures. Its vapors are heavier than air; they travel long distances and are easily ignited by a remote ignition source. There are appropriate solvents for cleaning automotive parts, and only these solvents should be used. Gasoline should not be used.

33. **(D)** Spontaneous combustion occurs from the decay of materials by chemical or biological reaction. Choice B—nothing in the question relates to extinguishment; this is purely a distractor. Choice C—spontaneous combustion is an act of nature; arson is a deliberately set fire.

34. **(B)** The cover excludes air, which contains 21 percent oxygen, and allows the smoke to fill up the area under the cover.

35. **(B)** When the valve is opened, the lower atmospheric pressure outside the container allows the compressed air in the extinguisher to expand and push out the water.

36. **(A)** The information on page 191 indicates that water weighs approximately $8\frac{1}{2}$ pounds per gallon.

$$x = 400 \text{ gal.} \times 8\frac{1}{2} \text{ lb.}$$

$$x = \overset{200}{\cancel{400}} \text{ gal.} \times \frac{17}{\cancel{2}} \text{ lb.}$$

$$x = 200 \text{ gal.} \times 17 \text{ lb.}$$

$$x = 3{,}400 \text{ lb.}$$

37. **(C)**

$$x = 8\frac{1}{2} \text{ lb./gal.} \times 5 \text{ gal.}$$

$$x = \frac{17}{2} \text{ lb.} \times 5 \text{ gal.}$$

$$x = \frac{85 \text{ lb.}}{2}$$

$x = 42.5$ lb., which is most nearly 42 (choice C)

38. **(A)**

Volume	=	Length	×	Width	×	Height
V	=	10 ft.	×	10 ft.	×	10 ft.
	=	1,000 ft.^{3}				

If the water weighs 62.4 lb./ft.^{3}, and we have 1,000 ft.^{3}, a full tank would weigh

$$\frac{1{,}000 \text{ ft.}^3 \times 62.4 \text{ lb.}}{1 \text{ ft.}^3} = 62{,}400 \text{ lb.}$$

Since the tank in this problem is only one-half full, we must divide 62,400 lb. by 2; this gives 31,200 lb.

39. **(C)**

Volume	=	Length	×	Width	×	Height
V	=	5 ft.	×	7 ft.	×	3 ft.
V	=	105 ft.^{3}				

105 ft.^{3} × $7\frac{1}{2}$ gal./1 ft.^{3} = number of gallons

787.5 = number of total gallons

40. **(A)** This is a multiple-step problem.

(1) Find the volume.

Volume	=	Length	×	Width	×	Height
V	=	20 ft.	×	20 ft.	×	1 ft.
V	=	400 ft.^{3}				

(2) Compute the number of gallons in 400 ft.^{3}

400 ft.^{3} × $7\frac{1}{2}$ gal/ft.^{3} = 3,000 gal.

(3) Add the three hose streams.

Flow rate = 250 gal./min. + 250 gal./min.+ 250 gal./min. = 750 gal./min.

(4) Divide the total water (3,000 gal.) by the flow rate (750 gal./min.).

$$\frac{3{,}000 \text{ gal.}}{750 \text{ gal./min.}} = 4 \text{ min.}$$

41. **(D)** The length of the ladder is 35 feet. Using the formula given:

$$\frac{\text{Length}}{5} + 2 = \text{distance from the wall}$$

we obtain

$$\frac{35}{2} + 2 = 9$$

Note: Multiplication and division should be done before addition and subtraction.

42. **(A)** We can immediately eliminate choice C; it cannot cover the table since it has a side of only 5 ft. We can also eliminate choice D, because choices A and B are both smaller than D but large enough to cover the table. To determine which is smaller, A or B, we must calculate their areas. It is not necessary to compute the area of the table.

Area	=	Length	×	Width	
Area of A	=	6 ft.	×	8 ft.	= 48 ft.^{2}
Area of B	=	7 ft.	×	7 ft.	= 49 ft.^{2}

The 6 ft. × 8 ft. salvage cover is the best choice.

Note: In this problem we are concerned with only the top of the table, not the overhang.

43. **(C)** The volume of the compartment will determine the amount of hose that can be stored.

Volume	=	Length	×	Width	×	Height	
Volume of A	=	16	×	3	×	4	= 192 ft.^{2}
Volume of B	=	12	×	4	×	4	= 192 ft.^{2}

44. **(A)** If the tank is $\frac{2}{3}$ full of water, then $\frac{1}{2}$ of $\frac{2}{3} = \frac{1}{3}$, and $\frac{2}{3}$ water + $\frac{1}{3}$ air = a full tank.

Choice (B) is incorrect because, if the tank is only $\frac{1}{2}$ filled with water, then $\frac{1}{2}$ of $\frac{1}{2} = \frac{1}{4}$;

adding the air and water we get: $\frac{1}{2}$ water + $\frac{1}{4}$ air = $\frac{3}{4}$ of a tank.

45. **(D)** To determine cubic feet, multiply all three dimensions: length (8 ft.), width (4 ft.), and height (6 ft.) = 192 ft.^{3}

46. **(D)** This follows the pattern established in the reading; it omits steps but keeps the correct order. Choice A is incorrect because the chocks should be placed before the tormentors. Choice B is incorrect because the ladder should be rotated before the fly ladder is raised. Choice C is incorrect because the driver would use the street guide below the window, not the fifth-floor window.

47. **(B)** This would be the most correct sequence as outlined in the passage. Choice A is incorrect because before raising the ladder or engaging the tormentors the driver would need to engage the power take-off. Choice D is incorrect because the driver would stabilize the apparatus before elevating the bed ladder. Choice C is incorrect because the driver must engage the power take-off before engaging the tormentors.

48. **(B)** This follows the pattern established in the passage. Choices A and C are incorrect; the passage implies the location of the fire is unknown and not easily determined from the exterior of the building. The building may need venting, but before this occurs, the firefighters will have to locate the fire, so this will happen at some future point after their arrival. Choice C is incorrect because before the driver can determine if venting is needed, the location of the fire must be found. The fire will be found at some time in the future.

49. **(D)** This follows the intent of the passage: Protect the property most severely exposed and extinguish the fire. Choices A, B, and C are incorrect because the sequences would result in an incorrect hose line placement. Choices A and B are positions for the third hose line, and choice C is a position for the second hose line.

50. **(C)** The priority role of the second hose line is to back up the first hose line. Choice A is incorrect because the second line would be used on the floor above only after it was determined it was not needed as a back-up for the first line. Choices B and D are incorrect because the firefighter would call for a second line before requesting a third line.

10 Mechanical Reasoning

Mechanical Reasoning measures your knowledge of straightforward mechanical and physical concepts. It may be part of an entrance examination for firefighting. Mechanical reasoning does not measure mechanical aptitude.

You may have encountered levers, pulleys, gears, springs, and simple circuits in elementary science classes. Questions about them were pretty straightforward. If you need to refresh your memory about these items, go online and type "Mechanical Reasoning" into your search engine.

Since you are taking a firefighter entrance exam, you should expect some math problems. These questions will test your ability to estimate costs, friction loss, hose pressures, gallons per minute, pounds per square inch, length of hoses, heights of buildings, and what lunch will cost. Even though you don't need knowledge in firefighting to answer them, some of these questions may be in firefighter terms or address other areas of mechanics.

The question is important, not the scenario.

BEFORE PRACTICE

Go back and review Chapters 4, 5, 6, 7, 8, and 9. When you begin the exam, follow all of the instructions, read each question carefully (don't assume anything), and answer only what is asked. Select the answer that is the best choice, and record your selection on the answer sheet. The answer explanations appear at the end of this chapter.

ANSWER SHEET
Practice Exercises

1. Ⓐ Ⓑ Ⓒ Ⓓ
2. Ⓐ Ⓑ Ⓒ Ⓓ
3. Ⓐ Ⓑ Ⓒ Ⓓ
4. Ⓐ Ⓑ Ⓒ Ⓓ
5. Ⓐ Ⓑ Ⓒ Ⓓ
6. Ⓐ Ⓑ Ⓒ Ⓓ
7. Ⓐ Ⓑ Ⓒ Ⓓ
8. Ⓐ Ⓑ Ⓒ Ⓓ
9. Ⓐ Ⓑ Ⓒ Ⓓ
10. Ⓐ Ⓑ Ⓒ Ⓓ
11. Ⓐ Ⓑ Ⓒ Ⓓ
12. Ⓐ Ⓑ Ⓒ Ⓓ
13. Ⓐ Ⓑ Ⓒ Ⓓ
14. Ⓐ Ⓑ Ⓒ Ⓓ
15. Ⓐ Ⓑ Ⓒ Ⓓ
16. Ⓐ Ⓑ Ⓒ Ⓓ
17. Ⓐ Ⓑ Ⓒ Ⓓ
18. Ⓐ Ⓑ Ⓒ Ⓓ
19. Ⓐ Ⓑ Ⓒ Ⓓ
20. Ⓐ Ⓑ Ⓒ Ⓓ
21. Ⓐ Ⓑ Ⓒ Ⓓ
22. Ⓐ Ⓑ Ⓒ Ⓓ
23. Ⓐ Ⓑ Ⓒ Ⓓ
24. Ⓐ Ⓑ Ⓒ Ⓓ
25. Ⓐ Ⓑ Ⓒ Ⓓ

PRACTICE EXERCISES

Directions: For each question choose the best answer—(A), (B), (C), or (D)—and darken in the corresponding letter on your answer sheet next to the number of the question. There are 25 questions in this practice exercise.

1. In the illustration below the mechanical advantage of the inclined plane is

    (A) $2\frac{1}{2}$.
    (B) 4.
    (C) 10.
    (D) 25.

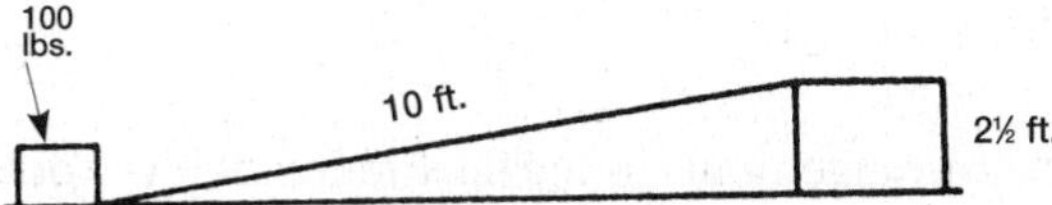

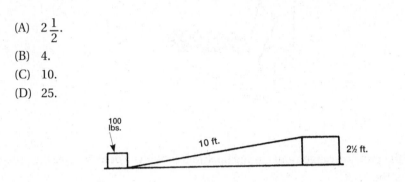

2. In the accompanying drawing a weight of 360 pounds is being raised with the help of a single and movable pulley system. How much effort is required to lift this weight?

    (A) 360 pounds
    (B) 180 pounds
    (C) 120 pounds
    (D) 85 pounds

3. If the weight being lifted by the firefighters in the illustration is 2,000 pounds, how many pounds of effort must the firefighters exert?

(A) 250
(B) 500
(C) 1,000
(D) 2,000

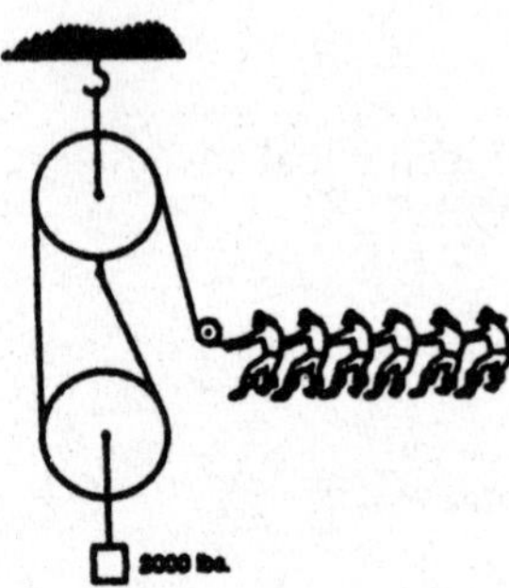

4. Which of the pulley arrangements in the illustration below would require the greatest effort to lift the can?

(A) 1
(B) 2
(C) 3
(D) 4

5. What is the maximum weight that a pulling force of 100 pounds applied to rope A in arrangement 4 would be able to lift?

(A) 100 pounds
(B) 600 pounds
(C) 1,200 pounds
(D) 1,800 pounds

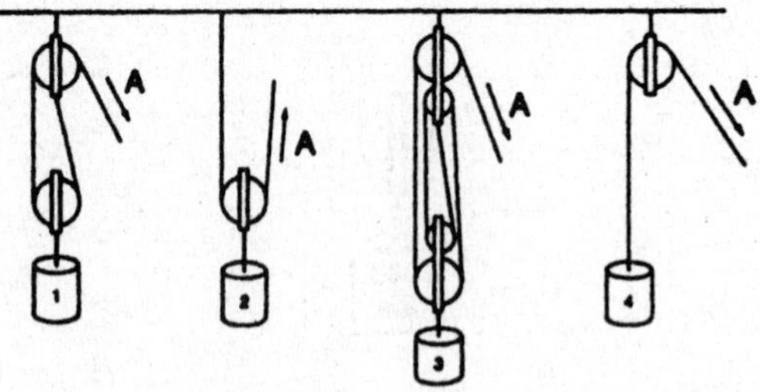

6. If a pull equal to 300 pounds is applied to line A, how much weight can be lifted?

(A) 600 pounds
(B) 900 pounds
(C) 1,500 pounds
(D) 1,800 pounds

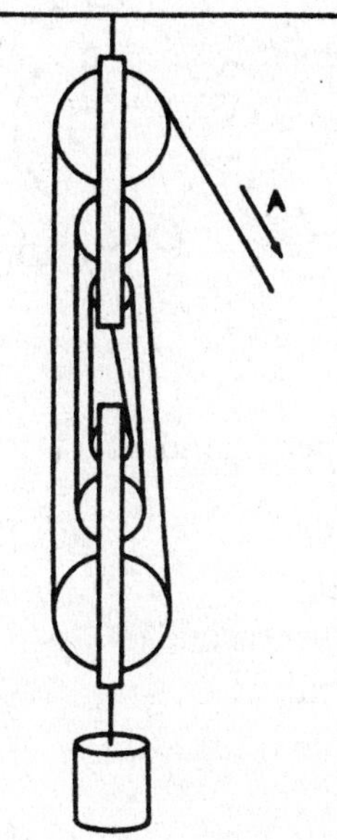

7. If gear A turns clockwise, gear D will

(A) also turn clockwise.
(B) be unable to turn.
(C) turn counterclockwise.
(D) turn in the same direction as gear C.

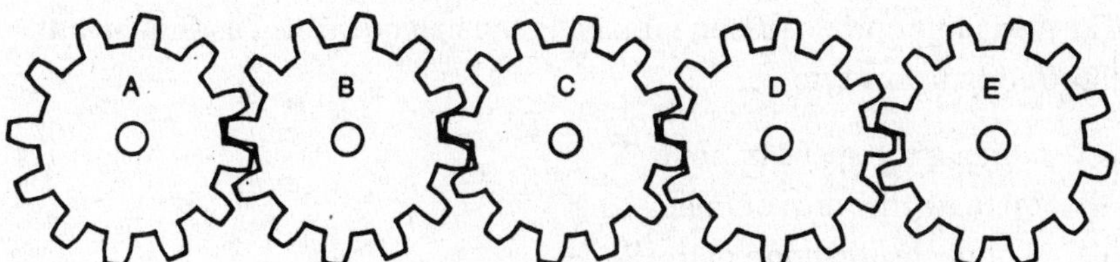

8. It would be correct to state about the gears shown below that

(A) if gear B turns once, gear A will turn twice.
(B) if gear A turns clockwise, gear B will turn clockwise.
(C) if gear B turns twice, gear A will turn once.
(D) if gear B turns counterclockwise, gear A will turn clockwise.

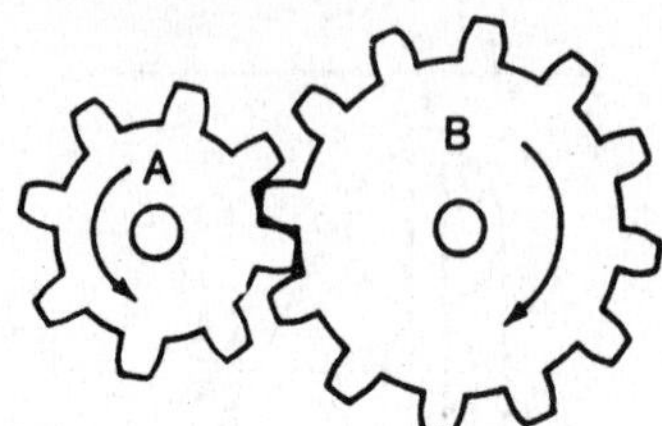

9. If gear A turns one revolution per second, gear D will turn

(A) one revolution per second.
(B) six revolutions per second.
(C) one-sixth of a revolution per second.
(D) sixty revolutions per second.

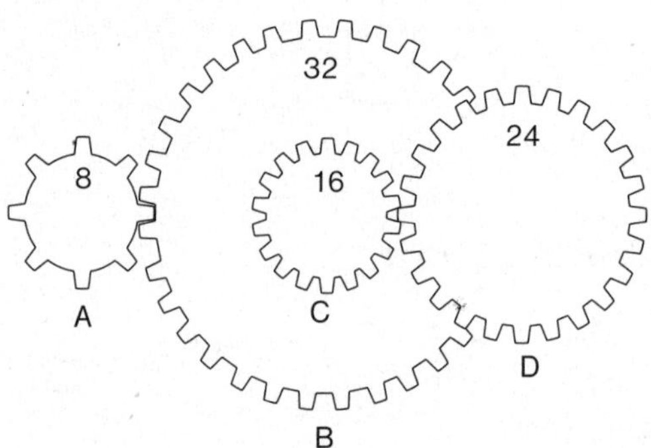

10. The most appropriate reason for having the belt cross over as shown in the illustration below is to

(A) increase the speed of pulley Y.
(B) decrease the force of pulley Y.
(C) change the direction of the force.
(D) increase the safety of the drive system.

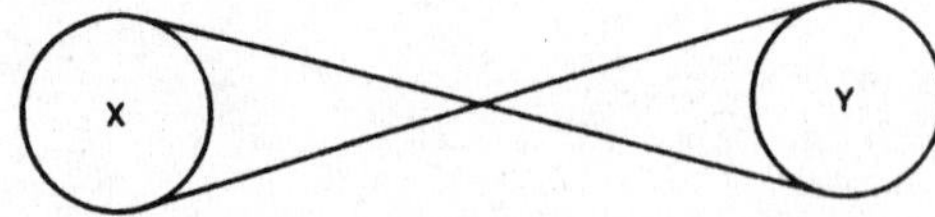

11. According to the National Fire Codes, every building with a standpipe system must be equipped with sufficient stations so that all portions of each story of the building are within 30 feet of a nozzle attached to not more than 100 feet of hose. Which of the following illustrations best shows this concept?

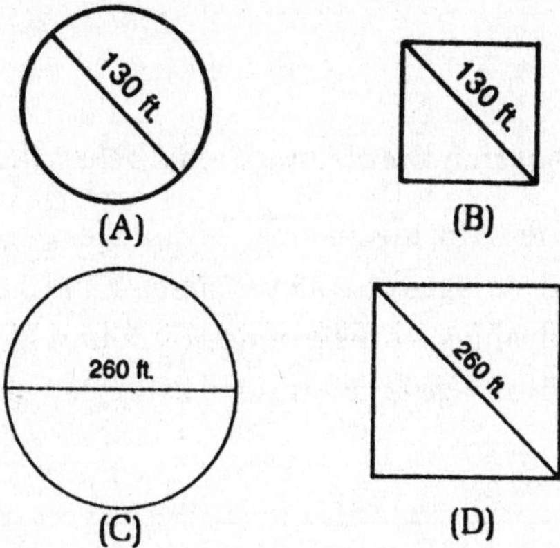

12. If gear A turns in the direction indicated, in what direction will gear C turn?

(A) The same direction as gear A
(B) The same direction as gear B
(C) Toward gear C from direction X
(D) Toward gear A from direction X

13. In the illustration below, if the amount of weight on each pulley system is equal, the pulley system that requires the greatest effort to lift the weight is

(A) 1.
(B) 2.
(C) 3.
(D) 4.

14. It would be correct to say that the pulley systems below show that

(A) all of them have the same mechanical advantage.
(B) the mechanical advantages of pulley systems 2 and 3 are equivalent.
(C) the mechanical advantage is determined by counting the number of pulleys.
(D) the mechanical advantage is determined by the length of the rope.

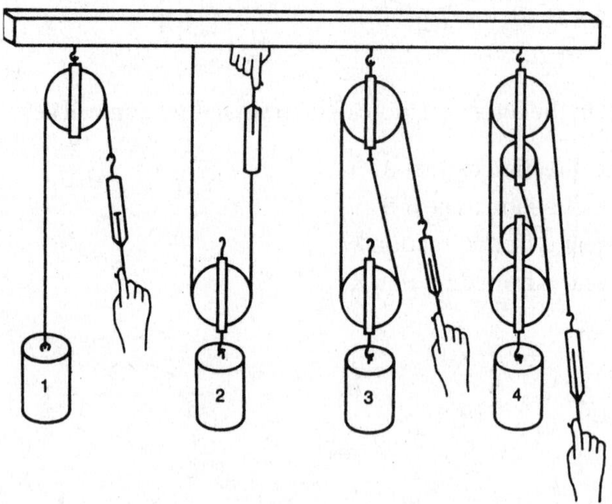

15. If a firefighter pulls 4 feet of rope down, how high will the weight rise?

(A) 1 foot
(B) 2 feet
(C) 3 feet
(D) 4 feet

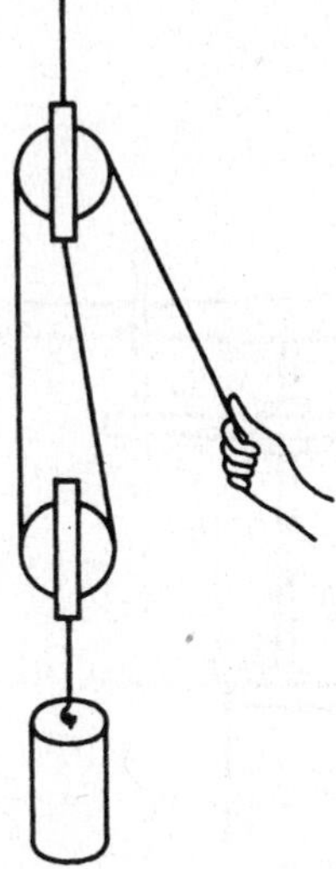

16. Lifting the box in the illustration would be easier if the weight was

(A) closer to the firefighter.
(B) hanging from the bar.
(C) closer to the fulcrum.
(D) lifted without the bar.

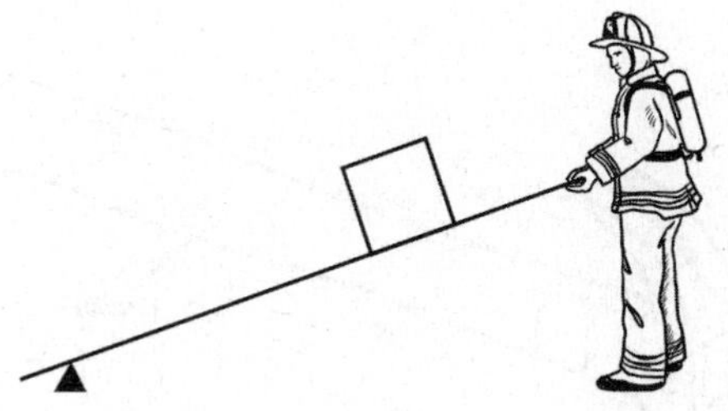

17. The illustration shows a simple lever system used as a safety device on some steam boilers. The pressure at which the steam escapes to the outer air is controlled by moving the weight. To reduce the pressure at which the valve works, how should the weight be moved?

(A) Toward the valve
(B) To the top of the lever
(C) Away from the valve
(D) So that it swings

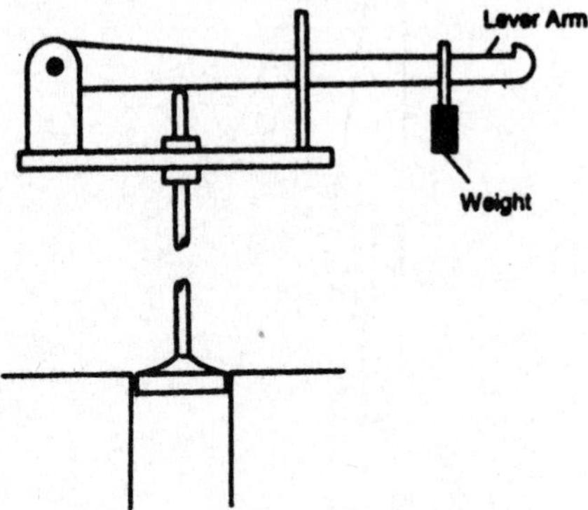

18. If the distance from the claw to the fulcrum is 3 inches and the handle measures 12 inches, how much force will be needed to pull out a nail with a resistance equal to 120 pounds?

(A) 30 pounds
(B) 90 pounds
(C) 360 pounds
(D) 480 pounds

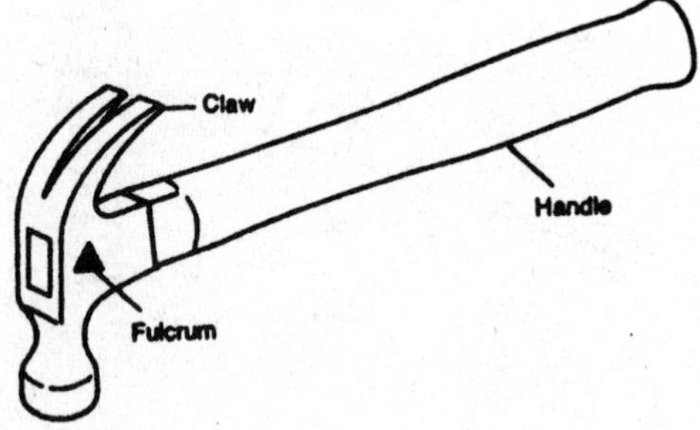

19. The illustration shows two firefighters, one under a ladder and one at the base of the ladder. As the firefighter under the ladder approaches the butt of the ladder,

(A) more force must be exerted.
(B) the tip of the ladder will bend downward.
(C) the firefighter at the base can let go.
(D) the ladder becomes lighter.

20. An axe gains its mechanical advantage by making use of the principle of the

(A) lever.
(B) wedge.
(C) screw.
(D) axle.

21. If the mechanical advantage gained in using the ramp in the illustration below is 5 and the drum weighs 250 lb., how much force must the firefighter use to push the drum up the ramp?

(A) 25 pounds
(B) 50 pounds
(C) 100 pounds
(D) 250 pounds

22. Which of the following would be correct to say about what is shown below?

(A) A greater force would be obtained by the firefighter if he moved his hand close to the lock.
(B) Less effort would be required if the firefighter moved his hand farther from the lock.
(C) A greater force could be obtained by squeezing the vise grips tighter.
(D) The amount of effort required to remove this lock would remain the same regardless of hand position or pressure.

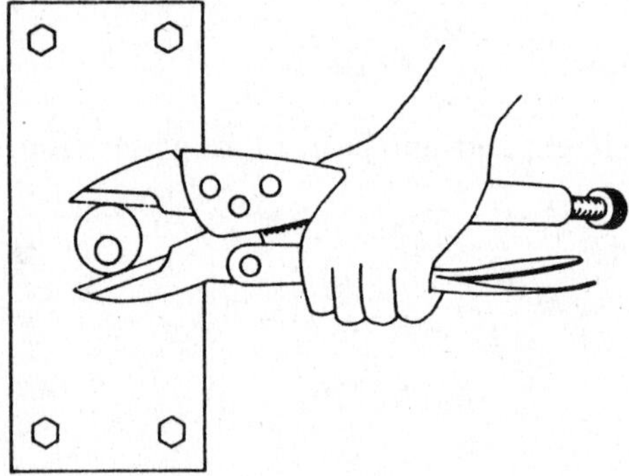

23. You are instructed to build a shed $12' \times 12' \times 8'$ using a 16 oz hammer. To get the greatest amount of driving force, how do you hold the handle?

(A) Near the end
(B) In the middle
(C) Close to the head
(D) It doesn't make any difference

24. Your grandmother calls and says she can't get the outside faucet turned on so she can water her flowers. Which way should she turn the handle?

(A) Counterclockwise
(B) Clockwise
(C) Push down and turn
(D) Pull up and turn

25. The illustration below shows five gears of varying sizes. How many gears are turning clockwise?

(A) 5
(B) 4
(C) 2
(D) 3

ANSWER KEY AND EXPLANATIONS

Answer Key

1. **(B)**	6. **(D)**	11. **(C)**	16. **(C)**	21. **(B)**
2. **(B)**	7. **(C)**	12. **(A)**	17. **(A)**	22. **(B)**
3. **(C)**	8. **(D)**	13. **(A)**	18. **(A)**	23. **(A)**
4. **(D)**	9. **(C)**	14. **(B)**	19. **(A)**	24. **(A)**
5. **(A)**	10. **(C)**	15. **(B)**	20. **(B)**	25. **(D)**

Answer Explanations

1. **(B)** The mechanical advantage (MA) of the inclined plane is equal to the length of the plane divided by the height to be raised. MA = 10 feet divided by 2½ feet = 4.

2. **(B)** A single movable pulley has two ropes that share the load equally. To determine the mechanical advantage (MA), count the number of ropes that carry the load, in this case 2, and then divide the load by the MA. Effort = 360 pounds divided by 2 = 180 pounds

3. **(C)** The mechanical advantage (MA) of this pulley system is 2. Dividing the weight to be lifted (2,000 lb.) by the MA (2) equals 1,000 lb. The small block near the first firefighter is known as a snatch block and has no MA. It serves to change the direction of the pull. The number of firefighters does not affect the MA of the pulley system. Instead, it distributes the load that each firefighter must exert but does not change the total force required.

4. **(D)** This pulley serves only to change direction and does not provide any mechanical advantage (MA). The MA in Choice A equals 2, in choice B equals 2, and in choice C equals 4.

5. **(A)** As stated in question 4, the mechanical advantage (MA) of this system is 1. In other words there is no mechanical advantage, only a change of direction of the pull. 1 times 100 pounds = 100 pounds.

6. **(D)** The mechanical advantage (MA) is 6. Multiplying the MA by the force to be exerted (300 lb. × 6) gives the total weight that can be lifted.

7. **(C)** When two gears mesh together, the second gear turns in the opposite direction. Each successive gear turns the next adjacent gear in the opposite direction.

8. **(D)** When two gears mesh together, the second gear turns in the opposite direction. The number of times a gear will turn is related to the number of sprockets. In illustration 8, gear A has 8 sprockets, and gear B has 12 sprockets. If gear B turns once (choice A), gear A will turn 1½ times. If gear B turns twice (choice C), gear A will turn 3 times. In choice (B), the gears will turn in opposite directions.

9. **(C)** To find the speed of gear A, multiply the number of sprockets of gear A by the number of sprockets of gear C. Then multiply the number of sprockets of gear B by the number of sprockets of gear D. Then divide the total of A and C by the total of B and D. A is 8, and C is 16. Then B is 32, and D is 24. A times C = 128. B times D = 768. 128 divided by 768 = 1/6 of a revolution per second.

10. **(C)** By having the belt take a single twist, the direction of the turn can be reversed. A second twist will return it to the same direction.

11. **(C)** From the standpipe outlet, it is possible to go 130 feet in any direction. Think of the standpipe as the center of a circle and the hose (100 feet) plus 30 feet as the radius. The diameter is 260 feet.

12. **(A)** You must follow the direction of each turning gear. As each gear turns, it will turn the adjoining gear in the opposite direction. Gear A is turning in direction y, gear B is turning in direction x, gear C is turning in direction y, and gear D is turning in direction x.

13. **(A)** This simple pulley serves only to change the direction of motion. It does not give any mechanical advantage.

14. **(B)** To determine the mechanical advantage (MA), count all the ropes except the rope that is being pulled downward and therefore is not counted. Choices (A), (C), and (D) are incorrect.

15. **(B)** Divide the length of rope pulled, 4 feet, by the mechanical advantage, 2. Because there are two ropes, this will give you the height the weight can be raised.

16. **(C)** By moving the weight closer to the fulcrum, it is possible to increase the length of the effort arm and reduce the force needed by the firefighter.

17. **(A)** By moving the weight closer to the valve, we are moving it closer to the fulcrum. Therefore, it will be easier for the valve to lift.

18. **(A)** 3 inches = the distance of the hammer claw from its fulcrum. 12 inches = the distance of the handle from the fulcrum. x = force (effort). The resistance = 120 pounds. $x \times 12 = 120 \times 3$. $12x = 360$ or 30 pounds of force.

19. **(A)** Keep in mind the principle of the lever. The firefighter at the base is at the fulcrum. The firefighter raising the ladder will require more force as the distance from the fulcrum is reduced.

20. **(B)** The edges of the axe form a double inclined plane or wedge that, when inserted into or between two objects, exerts a great force, spreading the two objects apart. A wedge is used when splitting wood or prying a door open.

21. **(B)** Divide the mechanical advantage into the weight of the drum. This will tell you how much force the firefighter must exert to roll the drum up the ramp.

22. **(B)** This would take advantage of the principle of the lever.

23. **(A)** To gain the advantage of the weight of the hammer, hold it at the end of the handle.

24. **(A)** If it is a screw-type valve, you would typically open the valve by turning it counterclockwise. You would close the same valve by turning it clockwise.

25. **(D)** Follow the direction of each turning gear. As each gear turns, it will turn the adjoining gear in the opposite direction. Gear F turns counterclockwise. This turns gear E clockwise. This turns gear D counterclockwise. This turns gear C clockwise. This turns gear B counterclockwise. This turns gear A clockwise. Now count the gears turning clockwise for the answer.

Tools and Definitions

11

TOOLS AND DEFINITIONS

This section discusses various tools and how to use them safely. It is followed by a practice test about recognizing various tools and their uses.

Proper Tool Safety

SAFETY RULES FOR HAND TOOLS

- Use sharp, clean tools. Know the correct way to use them.
- Wear appropriate clothing, hand, and eye protection.
- Clean the area where you will be working before you begin.
- Select the correct tool for the job.
- Plan cutting operations before you begin. Know what you will do and in what order.
- Look behind and around before you swing a tool.
- Don't overreach.
- Put away tools in their place when you are finished.

SAFETY RULES FOR POWER TOOLS

- Know how to shut off a tool before you begin using it.
- Keep tools sharp and clean.
- Study the operating and safety manual before using the tool.
- Clean the area where you will be working before you begin.
- Plan cutting operations before you begin. Know what you will do and in what order.
- Clamp the work before you cut.
- Use protective guards.
- Be sure electrical tools are properly grounded.
- If possible, keep both hands on the tool.
- Avoid wearing loose clothing.
- Pay attention to what you are doing. Don't be distracted.
- Don't be overconfident and careless.
- Never approach a person from the back who is using an electrical tool.
- Never clean scraps or debris from the operating area of the tool with your hands or feet.

Safety Equipment

This equipment is designed to protect the user from injury when using hand or power tools.

hand protection: various types of gloves are made of cotton, leather, and rubberized materials; they are designed to protect the hands against burns, abrasions, and cuts.

head protection: a variety of head protectors are available; Firefighter helmets and construction workers' hard hats are examples

eye protection: eyeglasses, full face shields, wraparound goggles, and many different types of eye protection are available; purchase eye protection suitable for the job and that fits comfortably

foot protection: steel-tipped, steel-soled safety shoes can be purchased at most shoe stores

hearing protection: earplugs or ear muffs should fit comfortably and be worn anytime power tools are in use.

At times, full protective equipment should be worn. Each situation must be assessed individually. If in doubt, always put on more equipment than you need.

Glossary of Tools

Allen wrench (hex key or set screw wrench): a hexagonal bar with a 90-degree bend for extracting or tightening hex head (six-sided) screws or nuts

axes: can have a flat head or a pick opposite the blade; used for ventilating roofs, chopping floors or doors, and where forcible entry may be needed

ball peen hammer: a lightweight hammer used to shape and forge metals, set rivets, and drive chisels

bench grinder: used to hone the cutting edges of tools square and sharp and to remove burrs; when fitted with a wire wheel or a buffing wheel, the grinder can be used to clean and polish surfaces

bionic wrench: squeezing the handle adjusts the wrench to fit any size nut or bolt; it has a ratcheting action so the wrench doesn't have to be removed during the tightening or loosening process

bolt cutter: comes in various handle lengths and sizes; used to cut steel rods, bolts, and locks

caulking hammer: used to drive star drills in masonry, with a wedge to split logs and with a chisel to cut rivets

chain saw: the blade looks like a chain with a series of small cutting tips; it is used for heavy-duty cutting of large beams or trees

channel locks: can be adjusted to allow a larger gripping area; used on pipes and other round objects

circular saw: an electric appliance to cut lumber and plywood to size

claw or nail hammer: used to pound in nails and also to remove them

combination open end wrench: typically the same size on each end, but one end is open and the other is closed

concrete chisel: used with a caulking hammer or sledge hammer to put holes in concrete or to break up concrete

coping saw: used to cut curves, angles, and circles in wood; used for decorative applications

crescent wrench: an adjustable wrench used to tighten or loosen nuts and bolts; an appropriate tool for turning off gas meter valves

crow bar: used as a lever to move or lift heavy objects

diagonal cutting pliers: used to cut and strip wire during electrical installations

drill bits: high speed bit used to drill into metal; masonry bit used to drill into concrete; wood or auger bit used to drill into wood, plastic, and composite products; any of these bits can be used with a hand brace drill or an electric drill

duck bill snips: used to cut light sheet metal

electric drill: can be corded or cordless and can be adapted to perform a number of tasks, such as sanding, buffing, cutting, and drilling; many are reversible and multispeed

electrician's multipurpose tool: used to strip wire and crimp fitting onto wire, also able to cut small bolts to length

electrician's pliers: used to cut and strip wires, similar to diagonal cutting pliers

Flat blade screwdriver: come in long and stubby sizes, used on standard straight-cut screws

forcible entry tool: consists of a roof hook on one end with a sledge and pry end on the other; it is used for removing locks, prying, striking, and forcible entry into buildings

gasoline power saw: may be known by many different names; it is portable and used for cutting through roofs, floors, and walls for gaining access to a fire or people

grease gun: used to force grease into grease fittings to lubricate a moving part

hack saw: a fine-tooth saw with a frame to house the blade; used to cut metal and plastic

halligan bar: has a flat blade on one end that can be inserted between the jamb and the lock and then driven in with a sledge hammer to pry open a door; also used for bending sheet metal in car doors for gaining access to victims

hand saw: used to cut wood, such as 2 × 4s and 4 × 4s

hole saw: comes in various sizes and used to cut a round hole in wood, metal, plastic, drywall, or gypsum board; the hole saw is used mainly to make a perfectly round hole to install dead bolt locks and mechanisms in doors

hydrant wrench: an adjustable wrench placed on the nut at the top of a fire hydrant to open or close a fire hydrant

hydrometer: used to measure the density of the fluid in a wet-cell battery

keyhole saw: a long-bladed saw with a curved handle used for making small holes larger in drywall or plywood; a small hole is drilled first, and then the saw is inserted to make the desired size hole bigger, whether round or oval

K-tool: the function of the K-tool is to pull lock cylinders; by placing the K-tool at the top of the dead bolt lock and hitting it with a flat head ax or hammer, the edges of the tool are forced behind the face of the cylinder; a pry bar is inserted into the back of the tool and by prying downward, the cylinder is pulled from the lock

miter saw: a handsaw used with a miter box to cut precision angles for narrow baseboards and trim; a reciprocal electric miter saw can be used for any size boards and is adjustable to accommodate any cuts or products

monkey wrench: similar to a pipe wrench but without serrated teeth in the jaws; it can be used to tighten or loosen nuts and bolts

needle- or long-nose pliers: used to bend and strip wire; because of the tapered nose, is able to reach inside objects

nut driver: looks similar to a screwdriver and is used on small nuts and bolts; some have a ratcheting handle

offset box wrench: has a 45-degree angle at each end of the wrench to access hidden nuts or bolts

oil can: used to lubricate moving parts or free up stuck parts

open-end wrench: may have a different size at each end

Phillips screwdriver: this screwdriver has different-size tips for various size screws with cross cuts in them; they come in long handle or stubby handle depending on the application.

pipe cutter: used to cut different sizes of steel pipe and tubing; it leaves a smooth edge so little filing or reaming of the pipe is necessary

pipe wrench: an adjustable wrench with serrated teeth in the jaws, used to tighten or loosen pipes and related fittings; it comes in various lengths to provide more leverage if needed.

pitchfork: used to break up earth for easy removal; usually has four pointed tines or blades and is about four feet long with an enclosed handle

plane: either an electric or a hand plane can be used to finish a cabinet or other wood item

propane torch: used for soldering "sweating" copper pipes and fittings

pry axe: a universal tool with an adjustable handle for more leverage; has a blade and a pick used to cut open a laminated windshield with its serrated blade; the pick can be used to make a hole for a purchase point for a larger tool to be inserted during an extrication operation

ratchet and socket wrench: provides a variety of sizes for rapid removal or tightening of nuts and bolts

round file: after drilling a hole in metal or cutting off a pipe, the file can be used to smooth the opening or make it larger

saws all: a universal reciprocating saw used to cut at angles or straight where space may be a problem

shovel: round or flat, long or short handled, used for digging holes and moving materials or debris

sledge hammer: used for heavy-duty pounding or breaking; it is used to drive a K-tool onto a dead bolt lock in a door

slip joint pliers: used to grip almost anything because of the serration on the blades; typically this tool has only two adjustments

soldering gun: an electric appliance used to solder small parts, printed circuits, and reattach wires

spanner wrench: used to tighten and loosen hose couplings on small-diameter hoses

spring-loaded center punch: can be used to make a mark in wood or metal to start a twist drill; the center punch has a strong spring inside and when pressed against a cars side window pane, can shatter the glass; by breaking out the glass and clearing the window, a rescuer can gain access to a person involved in a vehicle accident

star drill: a chisel used for making small or large holes in concrete to insert lead or expansion anchors; screws or bolts are inserted into the anchors and objects may be bolted to them

strap or band wrench: used to remove cannisters, such as oil and fuel filters, where surfaces should not be damaged

storz wrench: used to tighten and loosen large-diameter hose couplings

tin snips: normally used to cut a straight line in sheet metal.

Torx wrench: has a four- or six-sided tip and resembles a screwdriver; comes in various sizes and is used to tighten or loosen special screw heads

tree saw: a tubular frame saw with a serrated blade used to trim tree limbs

trowel: used for finishing cement and laying bricks and blocks

tubing cutter: used to cut rigid and semirigid tubing, such as copper, conduit, and some plastics

turn buckle: a device used on a cable or threaded rod to adjust, increase, or release tension.

vise: usually mounted on a bench or stand, used to hold an item for drilling, sawing, cutting, planing, and shaping

vise grips: by squeezing the handles, the wrench will lock onto an object or bolt and obtain a firm grip without having to apply a great amount of force, and will hold the object firmly, even after letting go of the wrench; could be used as a portable vise

wire stripper: used to strip insulation and cut most wires

wood chisel: used to cut an edge or groove in wood; often used with a wooden mallet

Glossary of Emergency Medical Equipment

automated external defibrillator (AED): used when a patient is having a heart attack to restart the heart into a normal rhythm again

backboard: made of heavy-duty polyethylene plastic or wood and used to immobilize or secure a patient for transport to a medical facility

bag valve mask: used to administer oxygen to a nonbreathing patient

blood pressure cuff: used to measure the pressure being exerted against the walls of the arteries

cervical collar: a semirigid device used to immobilize the neck

oxygen cylinder and regulator: contains oxygen regulated for use on a patient who is having difficulty breathing

oxygen mask: device used to deliver oxygen from a cylinder directly to the mouth and nose of a patient

scoop stretcher: this stretcher can be taken apart into halves and then slid under the patient when the patient cannot be moved in the normal manner and put onto a backboard

stair chair: used to carry people up and down stairs safely

stethoscope: a listening device used to listen to the heart and lungs; it is used with a blood pressure cuff to take a blood pressure

stretcher: a collapsible cot used to transport a patient from the incident to an ambulance or emergency area

ANSWER SHEET
Practice Exercises

1. Ⓐ Ⓑ Ⓒ Ⓓ	16. Ⓐ Ⓑ Ⓒ Ⓓ	31. Ⓐ Ⓑ Ⓒ Ⓓ	46. Ⓐ Ⓑ Ⓒ Ⓓ
2. Ⓐ Ⓑ Ⓒ Ⓓ	17. Ⓐ Ⓑ Ⓒ Ⓓ	32. Ⓐ Ⓑ Ⓒ Ⓓ	47. Ⓐ Ⓑ Ⓒ Ⓓ
3. Ⓐ Ⓑ Ⓒ Ⓓ	18. Ⓐ Ⓑ Ⓒ Ⓓ	33. Ⓐ Ⓑ Ⓒ Ⓓ	48. Ⓐ Ⓑ Ⓒ Ⓓ
4. Ⓐ Ⓑ Ⓒ Ⓓ	19. Ⓐ Ⓑ Ⓒ Ⓓ	34. Ⓐ Ⓑ Ⓒ Ⓓ	49. Ⓐ Ⓑ Ⓒ Ⓓ
5. Ⓐ Ⓑ Ⓒ Ⓓ	20. Ⓐ Ⓑ Ⓒ Ⓓ	35. Ⓐ Ⓑ Ⓒ Ⓓ	50. Ⓐ Ⓑ Ⓒ Ⓓ
6. Ⓐ Ⓑ Ⓒ Ⓓ	21. Ⓐ Ⓑ Ⓒ Ⓓ	36. Ⓐ Ⓑ Ⓒ Ⓓ	
7. Ⓐ Ⓑ Ⓒ Ⓓ	22. Ⓐ Ⓑ Ⓒ Ⓓ	37. Ⓐ Ⓑ Ⓒ Ⓓ	
8. Ⓐ Ⓑ Ⓒ Ⓓ	23. Ⓐ Ⓑ Ⓒ Ⓓ	38. Ⓐ Ⓑ Ⓒ Ⓓ	
9. Ⓐ Ⓑ Ⓒ Ⓓ	24. Ⓐ Ⓑ Ⓒ Ⓓ	39. Ⓐ Ⓑ Ⓒ Ⓓ	
10. Ⓐ Ⓑ Ⓒ Ⓓ	25. Ⓐ Ⓑ Ⓒ Ⓓ	40. Ⓐ Ⓑ Ⓒ Ⓓ	
11. Ⓐ Ⓑ Ⓒ Ⓓ	26. Ⓐ Ⓑ Ⓒ Ⓓ	41. Ⓐ Ⓑ Ⓒ Ⓓ	
12. Ⓐ Ⓑ Ⓒ Ⓓ	27. Ⓐ Ⓑ Ⓒ Ⓓ	42. Ⓐ Ⓑ Ⓒ Ⓓ	
13. Ⓐ Ⓑ Ⓒ Ⓓ	28. Ⓐ Ⓑ Ⓒ Ⓓ	43. Ⓐ Ⓑ Ⓒ Ⓓ	
14. Ⓐ Ⓑ Ⓒ Ⓓ	29. Ⓐ Ⓑ Ⓒ Ⓓ	44. Ⓐ Ⓑ Ⓒ Ⓓ	
15. Ⓐ Ⓑ Ⓒ Ⓓ	30. Ⓐ Ⓑ Ⓒ Ⓓ	45. Ⓐ Ⓑ Ⓒ Ⓓ	

PRACTICE EXERCISES

Directions: Select the item, appliance, or tool that is related to the each of the following statements or questions. Choose the best answer, and enter it on your answer sheet. You should be able to relate tools and equipment with their functions.

1. A ball peen hammer

   (A) a crochet mallet.
   (B) drive a chisel.
   (C) remove a nail.
   (D) break up concrete.

2. A miter saw

   (A) cuts an angle on a board.
   (B) is a hat worn by a British soldier.
   (C) cuts a round hole.
   (D) is used to cut a bolt.

3. Coping saws

   (A) cut a 2×4.
   (B) cut decorative pieces.
   (C) cut an angle on a board.
   (D) cut a round hole.

4. A drill bit

   (A) makes a round hole.
   (B) uses a small amount.
   (C) de-burrs a hole.
   (D) is a dental tool.

5. A pipe cutter is used to

   (A) loosen a pipe.
   (B) make a pipe shorter.
   (C) sever a pipe.
   (D) remove a fitting.

6. A Phillips screwdriver

   (A) loosens a special screw.
   (B) is a drink with orange juice.
   (C) was invented by Mr. Phillips.
   (D) tightens a bolt.

7. Hacksaws

(A) cut a hole in a board.
(B) cut a decorative piece of wood.
(C) cut a piece of metal conduit.
(D) loosen bolts.

8. Crow bars can be

(A) a place to get a drink.
(B) used for leverage.
(C) is slang for crow's feet.
(D) used as a hammer.

9. Tin snips are used to

(A) cut a piece of light sheet metal.
(B) cut the Tin Man's hair.
(C) cut steel pipe.
(D) cut copper tubing.

10. Open-end wrenches

(A) loosen pipe fittings.
(B) loosen bolts.
(C) loosen screws.
(D) loosen clamps.

11. Pipe wrenches help to

(A) tighten screws.
(B) tighten clamps.
(C) tighten pipe fittings.
(D) tighten bolts.

12. A keyhole saw is used to

(A) cut a key.
(B) cut a dead bolt.
(C) enlarge a hole in dry wall.
(D) cut a hinge on a door.

13. An electrician's multipurpose tool usually helps to

(A) strip wires and crimp fittings.
(B) gain entrance through a door.
(C) cut only phone wire.
(D) fix your cable t.v.

14. A grease gun
   (A) 1950s hair gel
   (B) lubricates fittings.
   (C) used for caulking
   (D) submachine gun

15. Use a strap wrench to
   (A) remove a small canister.
   (B) tighten a belt.
   (C) adjust a motor.
   (D) tighten a bolt.

16. A spanner wrench
   (A) is used to connect large-diameter hose.
   (B) is used to connect small-diameter hose.
   (C) attaches to large-diameter hose.
   (D) attaches to small-diameter hose.

17. Vise grips
   (A) are a firm handshake.
   (B) can be used as a portable vise.
   (C) hold a vise in place.
   (D) are slip pliers.

18. A garden fork
   (A) softens dirt.
   (B) shovels dirt.
   (C) Joe Dirt's favorite toy
   (D) moves material.

19. Needle-nose pliers
   (A) are used for sewing.
   (B) get in narrow spaces.
   (C) are adjustable.
   (D) are used to grip pipes.

20. A tubing cutter
   (A) is a small ship.
   (B) removes a ring from a finger.
   (C) cuts copper pipe.
   (D) cuts cast iron pipe.

21. Backboards

(A) add strength to a wall.
(B) transport a patient.
(C) help a spinal column.
(D) are neck braces.

22. A stethoscope helps to

(A) listen to heart and lung sounds.
(B) listen to an iPod.
(C) play a game system.
(D) use an X-ray machine.

23. Cervical collar

(A) a neck brace
(B) transport a patient
(C) administer oxygen
(D) stop bleeding

24. AED

(A) Alaska Emergency Department
(B) automated external defibrillator
(C) automatic electric district
(D) Alabama Education Department

25. Claw hammers

(A) flatten claws.
(B) remove claws.
(C) remove nails.
(D) remove screws.

26. A handsaw

(A) cuts boards.
(B) cuts hands.
(C) cuts a hole in a wall.
(D) cuts limbs off a tree.

27. A crescent wrench is used to

(A) tighten a screw.
(B) tighten a bolt.
(C) hammer a nail.
(D) tighten a pipe.

28. Bench grinders

(A) buff and polish things.
(B) grind down concrete.
(C) remove locks from doors.
(D) are used with a monkey and a music box.

29. A gasoline-powered saw helps to

(A) ventilate a roof.
(B) cut a wall.
(C) cut concrete.
(D) all of the above.

30. A scoop stretcher can

(A) pick up and run.
(B) make a stretcher longer.
(C) be taken apart.
(D) act as a brace.

31. There are two major categories of tools, all purpose and specialized. The most important reason for using specialized tools is because they are

(A) much more impressive to citizens.
(B) cheaper.
(C) easier to obtain.
(D) more effective.

32. What is the best tool to use for removing insulation from a wire?

(A) Vise grips
(B) Wire stripper
(C) Tin snips
(D) Channel locks

33. Which tool should you use to test your automobile battery?

(A) Hydrometer
(B) Barometer
(C) Thermometer
(D) Dynamometer

34. Which tool could be used to cut carriage bolts on a door plate?

(A) Chisel
(B) Knife
(C) Pipe wrench
(D) Pipe cutter

35. The proper grip for holding a hammer has the thumb and fingers

(A) near the end of the handle.
(B) on top of and in line with the claw.
(C) on the same side of the handle as the fingers.
(D) in any of the above positions; all are correct.

36. The purpose of the third prong on a plug is to

(A) hold the plug securely in the outlet.
(B) ensure that the prongs are in the right holes.
(C) act as a guide and make the plug easier to insert.
(D) ground the appliance or tool.

37. Why is a pipe wrench used?

(A) To tighten screws
(B) To repair dents in a car
(C) To drive nails
(D) To tighten loose fittings

38. Lubricants such as grease and oil are used for all of the following except

(A) reduce friction.
(B) cool.
(C) prevent rust.
(D) reduce speed.

39. The term "Phillips head" would be used with which tool?

(A) Wrench
(B) Screw clamp
(C) Screw driver
(D) Saws

40. A turn buckle is a

(A) general purpose wrench.
(B) valve on a water supply line.
(C) coupling used to adjust the tension between rods or wires.
(D) tool that shows which circuit has been activated.

41. A sweat joint

(A) joins two pieces of copper tubing.
(B) allows small amounts of water to leak.
(C) expands under pressure.
(D) uses sweat to make the joint tight.

42. The most appropriate tool to shut off the gas supply line is

(A) a screwdriver.
(B) needle-nose pliers.
(C) a crescent wrench.
(D) a ratchet wrench.

43. Carrying a power tool by the cord would be

(A) incorrect and could lead to a short circuit
(B) correct because the tool is lighter carried that way.
(C) incorrect because the tool is heavier that way.
(D) correct; this helps stretch the cord.

44. Firefighters investigating a fire are told the fire was in a ballast. What should be checked to determine if this is the cause?

(A) Fluorescent light at the ceiling.
(B) Flushometer in the hallway
(C) Oil burner in the basement
(D) Fuse box in the basement

45. A couple returning from vacation found the water pipes had frozen. What is the safest way for them to thaw the pipes?

(A) Have a plumber remove the frozen pipe and replace it.
(B) Turn on the heat in the house and let the pipes thaw naturally.
(C) Use a propane torch to heat the pipes.
(D) Use a hair dryer.

46. The most appropriate item to assist a person down from the upper floor of a building to the street is a

(A) scoop stretcher
(B) backboard
(C) stair chair
(D) ordinary folding chair

47. When you are treating a nonbreathing patient, you would use all of the following except a

(A) bag valve mask.
(B) cervical collar.
(C) oxygen regulator.
(D) oxygen mask.

48. When would a firefighter remove a lock cylinder?

(A) To make sure the door can't be locked
(B) To gain access to the locking mechanism
(C) To teach the owner a lesson
(D) To make sure the door can't be opened

49. A tool used for fine wood finishing is a

(A) circular saw
(B) plane
(C) router
(D) table jig

50. Which of these is not a power tool?

(A) Circular saw
(B) Band saw
(C) Coping saw
(D) Table saw

ANSWER KEY AND EXPLANATIONS

Answer Key

1. **(B)**	11. **(C)**	21. **(B)**	31. **(D)**	41. **(A)**
2. **(A)**	12. **(C)**	22. **(A)**	32. **(B)**	42. **(C)**
3. **(B)**	13. **(A)**	23. **(A)**	33. **(A)**	43. **(A)**
4. **(A)**	14. **(B)**	24. **(B)**	34. **(A)**	44. **(A)**
5. **(C)**	15. **(A)**	25. **(C)**	35. **(A)**	45. **(B)**
6. **(A)**	16. **(B)**	26. **(A)**	36. **(D)**	46. **(C)**
7. **(C)**	17. **(B)**	27. **(B)**	37. **(D)**	47. **(B)**
8. **(B)**	18. **(A)**	28. **(A)**	38. **(D)**	48. **(B)**
9. **(A)**	19. **(B)**	29. **(D)**	39. **(C)**	49. **(B)**
10. **(B)**	20. **(C)**	30. **(C)**	40. **(C)**	50. **(C)**

Answer Explanations

For 1 through 30, the answers will be found in the tool and medical glossaries. If you missed any of the answers, go over the definitions again.

31. **(D)** Special tools meet special needs whether they are expensive or cheap. They are needed to do specific duties. You don't buy specialized tools to impress the public. Specialized tools are never cheap. Many times, these tools are special order or must be made at a factory.

32. **(B)** The answer wire stripper gives you the clue. Look in the tool glossary.

33. **(B)** *Refer to the tool glossary.*

34. **(A)** *Refer to the tool glossary*

35. **(A)** To get the most power from the hammer, wrap the fingers and thumb firmly around near the end of the handle.

36. **(D)** The third prong grounds the appliance. That is why the third prong should never be cut off to accommodate a two-prong outlet.

37. **(D)** *Refer to the tool glossary.*

38. **(D)** The key word is "except." Choices A, B, and C all help to increase speed and reduce wear and tear.

39. **(C)** *Refer to the tool glossary.*

40. **(C)** *Refer to the tool glossary.*

41. **(A)** *Refer to the tool glossary.*

42. **(C)** *Refer to the tool glossary.*

43. **(A)** You could pull the wires out of their connectors and short circuit or burn out the drill.

44. **(A)** A ballast, which is in a fluorescent light fixture, is used to step up the electric power and charge the molecules of the gas in a fluorescent tube. The ballast will become overheated and begin to melt, causing a very pungent odor. The light will eventually shut off, but the odor usually remains. If you smell this odor you should relay this information to the fire department.

45. **(B)** First try slowly letting the pipes thaw. If this doesn't work, then the pipe should be replaced or, if in doubt, call a plumber. If you heat the pipe using a torch, you could start a fire. A hair dryer could be used but takes a long time to heat the area.

46. **(C)** *Refer to the medical glossary.*

47. **(B)** *Refer to the medical glossary.*

48. **(B)** By removing the cylinder, a firefighter can insert a screwdriver or flat blade and open the door without knocking it down. Choice A is wrong because you want to unlock the door not lock it. Choice C is not a good idea. You want to open the door, so choice D is wrong.

49. **(B)** *Refer to the tool glossary.*

50. **(C)** *Refer to the tool glossary.*

PRACTICE EXAMS

50-Question Practice Exams

12

In this chapter you will find four practice exams. They have been developed to allow you to finish in approximately 1½ hours. Even though these practice tests are shorter than the actual tests you will be taking, the questions are representative of the kind of questions you will be confronted with.

When you take the practice exams, be sure that you allow yourself a 1½-hour uninterrupted time period. Do not try to take the exams in parts; if you do, you defeat its purpose. By taking each in one sitting, you will be training yourself to work under test conditions; you will become familiar with your personal idiosyncrasies about sitting and working at a desk for this period of time. When you have finished the four 50-question tests, you will be better able to work through longer tests.

BEFORE TAKING THE EXAMS

You will need someone to assist you with the first part. He or she will read a short passage to you; then you will begin answering the questions. The person helping you needs to be available only at the time you start the exam for about five minutes. DO NOT READ THE PASSAGE YOURSELF.

Before you begin the exams, go back and review quickly the test-taking strategies outlined in Chapters 2, 6, 7, and 8. When you begin each exam, be sure to read and follow all instructions. Read each question carefully, and answer only what is asked of you. Select the answer that is the one *best* choice of those provided, and then record your selection on the answer sheet.

The answer sheet precedes each exam. The Answer Explanations are given at the end.

ANSWER SHEET
Practice Exam One

1. Ⓐ Ⓑ Ⓒ Ⓓ	16. Ⓐ Ⓑ Ⓒ Ⓓ	31. Ⓐ Ⓑ Ⓒ Ⓓ	46. Ⓐ Ⓑ Ⓒ Ⓓ
2. Ⓐ Ⓑ Ⓒ Ⓓ	17. Ⓐ Ⓑ Ⓒ Ⓓ	32. Ⓐ Ⓑ Ⓒ Ⓓ	47. Ⓐ Ⓑ Ⓒ Ⓓ
3. Ⓐ Ⓑ Ⓒ Ⓓ	18. Ⓐ Ⓑ Ⓒ Ⓓ	33. Ⓐ Ⓑ Ⓒ Ⓓ	48. Ⓐ Ⓑ Ⓒ Ⓓ
4. Ⓐ Ⓑ Ⓒ Ⓓ	19. Ⓐ Ⓑ Ⓒ Ⓓ	34. Ⓐ Ⓑ Ⓒ Ⓓ	49. Ⓐ Ⓑ Ⓒ Ⓓ
5. Ⓐ Ⓑ Ⓒ Ⓓ	20. Ⓐ Ⓑ Ⓒ Ⓓ	35. Ⓐ Ⓑ Ⓒ Ⓓ	50. Ⓐ Ⓑ Ⓒ Ⓓ
6. Ⓐ Ⓑ Ⓒ Ⓓ	21. Ⓐ Ⓑ Ⓒ Ⓓ	36. Ⓐ Ⓑ Ⓒ Ⓓ	
7. Ⓐ Ⓑ Ⓒ Ⓓ	22. Ⓐ Ⓑ Ⓒ Ⓓ	37. Ⓐ Ⓑ Ⓒ Ⓓ	
8. Ⓐ Ⓑ Ⓒ Ⓓ	23. Ⓐ Ⓑ Ⓒ Ⓓ	38. Ⓐ Ⓑ Ⓒ Ⓓ	
9. Ⓐ Ⓑ Ⓒ Ⓓ	24. Ⓐ Ⓑ Ⓒ Ⓓ	39. Ⓐ Ⓑ Ⓒ Ⓓ	
10. Ⓐ Ⓑ Ⓒ Ⓓ	25. Ⓐ Ⓑ Ⓒ Ⓓ	40. Ⓐ Ⓑ Ⓒ Ⓓ	
11. Ⓐ Ⓑ Ⓒ Ⓓ	26. Ⓐ Ⓑ Ⓒ Ⓓ	41. Ⓐ Ⓑ Ⓒ Ⓓ	
12. Ⓐ Ⓑ Ⓒ Ⓓ	27. Ⓐ Ⓑ Ⓒ Ⓓ	42. Ⓐ Ⓑ Ⓒ Ⓓ	
13. Ⓐ Ⓑ Ⓒ Ⓓ	28. Ⓐ Ⓑ Ⓒ Ⓓ	43. Ⓐ Ⓑ Ⓒ Ⓓ	
14. Ⓐ Ⓑ Ⓒ Ⓓ	29. Ⓐ Ⓑ Ⓒ Ⓓ	44. Ⓐ Ⓑ Ⓒ Ⓓ	
15. Ⓐ Ⓑ Ⓒ Ⓓ	30. Ⓐ Ⓑ Ⓒ Ⓓ	45. Ⓐ Ⓑ Ⓒ Ⓓ	

PRACTICE EXAM ONE

Directions: Questions 1 through 5 are an oral or listening part of the examination. They are intended to measure your ability to hear, understand, and apply information.

At the beginning of this examination have someone READ the passage, slowly and carefully, to you. DO NOT READ THIS PASSAGE YOURSELF.

Immediately after the reading, answer questions 1 through 5 on the basis of the information found in the passage.

To the assistant: Please read the following passage aloud. Read slowly and distinctly. Once you start, read through to the end with only normal pauses between paragraphs and punctuation. Do not add additional emphasis or discuss the passage. When you have completed reading the passage, your part of this practice examination is complete. Thank you for your help.

Engine 31 and Advanced Life Support Ambulance (ALS) 31 respond to a reported serious accident on the freeway. When they arrive, they find one car flipped over onto its side. There are 2 children and a woman in the car. An adult male, the driver, is lying on the ground about 20 feet from the car. Captain Dentry orders the car to be stabilized and a hose line stretched to be ready if the leaking fuel should ignite. He also orders the firefighters to examine the patients and treat their wounds. The children are easily removed from the car and are found to be in relatively good condition, with only minor cuts and bruises. The woman, the mother, has a major physical trauma, having been thrown into the steering wheel and now lying on her side with her arm folded behind her back. The male, the husband, is also suffering from major physical trauma and is unconscious and not breathing.

At severe accident scenes such as the one just described, firefighters and paramedics must first do triage, which is a rapid assessment of the problems. It means classifying each of the component problems based on the immediately available information, resources, and their capabilities. There are three components of the accident scene that must be taken into account:

1. Identify the activities that must be done to stabilize the accident scene so the problem does not get worse.
2. Identify the seriousness of the injuries of each person.
3. Evaluate the capabilities of the available resources at the scene and call for proper additional help when needed.

Some of the decision criteria to consider in the sample accident scene include: Does the car need to be stabilized, can this be done quickly and safely, and are there sufficient personnel at the scene to do this? If fuel is leaking that could start a fire, do you have sufficient personnel to stretch and charge a protective hose line? How many people are injured, and are they in immediate danger from the car or potential fire? Can the injured be removed from the car to a safe area? How serious are the injuries and will your efforts and the available equipment be able to save the life of the person? Do you have sufficient personnel to attend to each of the tasks needed to be done and how long will it take to get additional help?

Medical care by the first responders begins with an evaluation of the ABCs (Airway, Breathing, and Circulation), severe bleeding, and other serious injuries such as trauma to the head, neck, and spinal cord. These injuries must be treated as soon as possible or death may occur. Treating each of these injuries will require the services of at least one, possibly two, firefighters. When determining which person to treat first, the number of personnel is critical. When only two or three personnel are available, the people with the most severe life-threatening injury, and a chance of living, should be treated first. Treatment of those with minor cuts and bruises can be delayed until additional help arrives.

1. At severe accident scenes, firefighters and paramedics must first

   (A) do triage.
   (B) put their protective clothing on.
   (C) put the fire out.
   (D) do CPR.

2. If you responded to the accident described in the reading, which of the following injuries might not be treated immediately?

   (A) Severe bleeding.
   (B) Large bruise to right arm.
   (C) Unconscious and not breathing.
   (D) Head and neck injury.

3. The ABCs of emergency medicine refer to

   (A) arterial bleeding control.
   (B) artificial breathing control.
   (C) advanced breathing care.
   (D) airway, breathing, and circulation.

4. Triage is a system to

   (A) describe what firefighters and paramedics do.
   (B) ensure stability of cars and trucks when they are overturned.
   (C) evaluate the performance of the firefighters.
   (D) rapidly assess, classify, and make decisions about problems.

5. One of the three critical components of an accident scene that should not be taken into account is to

   (A) evaluate the abilities and effectiveness of the recruit firefighters.
   (B) identify the seriousness of the injuries.
   (C) evaluate the capabilities of the resources.
   (D) identify the activities that must be done.

Directions: Answer questions 6 through 10 using only the information provided in the following illustration. You may look at the illustration while answering these questions.

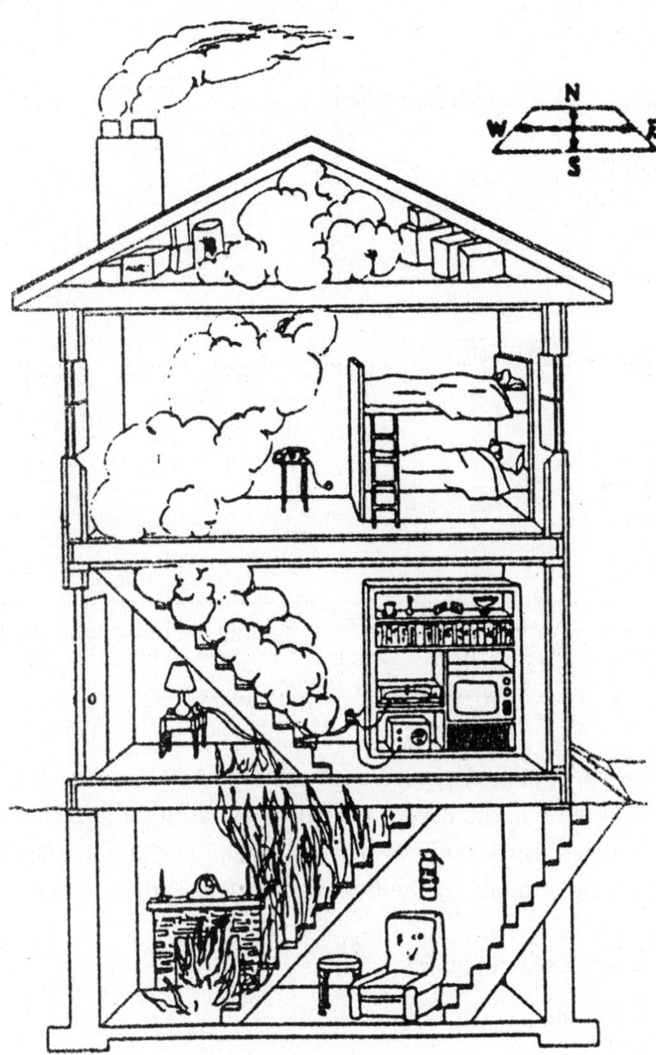

6. How many ways can firefighters enter the house?

   (A) One.
   (B) Two.
   (C) Three.
   (D) Four.

7. The probable cause of the fire was

   (A) sparks from the fireplace.
   (B) the overloaded electrical outlet.
   (C) the combustion of flammable materials in the attic.
   (D) smoking in bed.

8. What would be the most direct entrance for the firefighters to take to save the children?

   (A) East window.
   (B) West window.
   (C) Front window.
   (D) Basement door.

9. In which direction is the wind blowing?

   (A) To the north.
   (B) To the south.
   (C) To the east.
   (D) To the west.

10. The fire extinguisher is in the

   (A) attic.
   (B) bedroom.
   (C) living room.
   (D) basement.

Directions: Answer questions 11 through 14 using only the information in the following passage.

The apparatus hose beds are subdivided and hose is packed into hose beds in accordance with the needs of the fire unit. The deeper hose beds are used for large hose and for longer hose stretches. The smaller, narrower beds are used for small-diameter handheld hose. The needs of the unit are determined by the dominant type of structure and the water supply system in an area.

There are three basic hose load types:

1. The accordion load.
2. The flat load.
3. The horseshoe load.

To load a hose bed using the accordion load, the hose is folded front to rear with the flat side of the hose facing the side wall and working across the hose bed until it is full. A second, third, and fourth layer can then be added. The accordion hose load can be used when hand stretching of the line is required.

The flat load is also a back and forth, front to rear load; however, the flat side of the hose is placed on the base of the hose bed. This load can also be used for hand stretching.

The horseshoe load is started similarly to the accordion load; however, instead of folding it up and down, back on itself, it is wrapped around the outer edge of the hose bed and then in simulated "U"s back around the bed. This type load is effective for laying out line with the apparatus.

For all types of hose loads, the male hose butt is loaded first if the apparatus will stop at the water supply first. This is sometimes called a forward lay. The female hose butt is loaded first if the apparatus will stop at the fire first; this is called a reverse lay.

A hose load that has one end already connected to a discharge outlet on the apparatus is called a "preconnect" and is used for a rapid attack on a fire.

A hose bed that runs across the apparatus, from side to side, and is usually found behind the crew cab, is called a transverse bed or preconnect line.

11. The hose load that is not a basic hose load is the

    (A) preconnect load.
    (B) horseshoe load.
    (C) accordion load.
    (D) flat load.

12. The hose load that is best for laying hose from the water source to the fire building with the apparatus is

    (A) the flat load.
    (B) the horseshoe load.
    (C) the transverse bed load.
    (D) the reverse lay.

13. Hose stored on fire engines is placed in compartments called hose beds. An *inaccurate* statement about hose beds is "Hose beds

    (A) that are deep are used for large-diameter hose."
    (B) are subdivided in accordance with the needs of the fire unit."
    (C) can run across the apparatus or run the length of the apparatus."
    (D) are all small and narrow and used for stretching handheld hose lines."

14. For a rapidfire attack to an interior fire in a single-family dwelling, the firefighter should use

    (A) a preconnect.
    (B) an accordion load.
    (C) a horseshoe load.
    (D) a flatload.

Directions: Answer questions 15 and 16 using only the information in the following passage.

The superintendent of the National Fire Academy is authorized to

1. Train fire service personnel in such skills and knowledge as may be useful to advance their ability to prevent and control fires, including but not limited to
   a. techniques of fire prevention, fire inspection, firefighting, and arson investigation;
   b. tactics and command of firefighting for present and future fire chiefs and commanders;
   c. administration and management of fire services;
   d. tactical training in the specialized field of aircraft fire control and crash rescue;
   e. tactical training in the specialized field of fire control and rescue aboard waterborne vessels; and
   f. the training of present and future instructors in the aforementioned subjects.
2. Develop model training programs or other educational materials suitable for use at other educational institutions, and to make such materials available without charge.
3. Develop and administer a program of correspondence courses to advance the knowledge and skills of fire service personnel.
4. Develop and distribute, to appropriate officials, model questions suitable for use in conducting entrance and promotional examinations for fire service personnel.
5. Encourage the inclusion of fire prevention and detection technology and practices in the education and professional practice of architects, builders, city planners, and others engaged in design and planning affected by fire safety problems.

15. A recruit firefighter wanting to attend a course at the National Fire Academy could expect to be able to register for all of the following courses EXCEPT

    (A) commanding the first response team.
    (B) uniforms, organization, and work rules for his/her local fire department.
    (C) firefighting tactics for ship fires.
    (D) conducting arson investigations.

16. It would be most accurate to state that the intent of the National Fire Academy is to train

    (A) firefighters only.
    (B) firefighters, architects, and builders.
    (C) firefighters, architects, builders, and city planners.
    (D) firefighters, architects, builders, and all private citizens for their own safety.

Directions: Answer questions 17 through 19 using only the information in the following passage.

A firefighter must be concerned with safety when conducting interior search and rescue. A search and escape plan should be in place before conducting the search. It must not be haphazard, uncontrolled, or uncoordinated. Search and rescue is one of the most important and probably one of the most dangerous tasks firefighters perform. Through proper training and conscious preparation, it can be accomplished safely.

Firefighters should be in full firefighting protective clothing, wearing self-contained breathing apparatus (SCBA) and Personal Alert Safety System (PASS) when conducting a search. Each firefighter should have a good working flashlight and a small, strong rope, at least 25 feet long, which can be attached to the doorknob to act as a guideline for an escape route. A 2½- or 3-inch nail can be used between the inside of the door on the hinge side and the door jamb to hold the door open. Press the nail point into the door, then close the door, thus pressing the head against the jamb and keeping the door open.

Another important tool firefighters should carry is a latch strap. This can be purchased from the firefighting supply store or may be homemade. To make your own, cut an inner tire tube into 3-inch-wide strips about 12 to 15 inches long. Cut a small hole about 3 inches from each end. Use the rubber strip and a door with two standard doorknobs to measure where to cut the holes. Make and carry several of them so you can pass through more than one door during the search.

17. During search and rescue, nails are used to

    (A) lay out a trail back to safety.
    (B) prevent a door from opening before the firefighter wants it to.
    (C) prevent a door from closing.
    (D) scratch a mark on the door to tell others the room has already been searched.

18. A latch strap can be used to keep a door open. A firefighter should carry

    (A) a homemade latch strap.
    (B) a commercially made latch strap.
    (C) a latch strap, rope, and flashlight.
    (D) a rope, flashlight, and several latch straps.

19. While conducting a search and rescue mission, firefighters may NOT be

    (A) protected by SCBAs.
    (B) protected by a hose line.
    (C) equipped with a PASS device.
    (D) concerned with safety.

Directions: Answer questions 20 and 21 using only the information in the following passage.

Breaching Walls

Many different types of construction will be encountered in rescue operations. These include walls made of brick with lime mortar, brick with cement mortar, stone, concrete, and concrete block.

When cutting through walls or floors of large buildings, try to locate sections of the structures in which cutting can be done most quickly and safely. When cutting through walls, be sure that support beams and columns are not weakened. After a building has been subjected to a bomb blast, the parts left standing may appear sound, although badly shaken and cracked. Therefore, when cutting away wall sections, especially with air hammers, care must be taken to prevent further collapse.

Openings large enough for rescue purposes usually can be made in brick walls without danger of the masonry falling. The bricks should be removed so that the opening is arch-shaped.

Concrete walls and floors, especially when they are reinforced, are difficult to cut through. Jackhammers or other power tools will be helpful. Squad leaders should call for such equipment from the public works. In all walls and floors except concrete, the best method is to cut a small hole and then enlarge it. With concrete, however, it is better to cut around the edge of the section to be removed. If the concrete is reinforced, the reinforcing bars can then be cut by a hacksaw or torch, and the material removed in one piece. If a torch is used, be sure explosive gases are not present, and that flammable materials are not ignited. A fire extinguisher should be kept nearby.

20. To rescue a person trapped by collapse of a floor may require breaching a wall. When cutting a hole in a wall, a firefighter should

    (A) make the hole as large as possible.
    (B) make the hole round in shape.
    (C) make sure the support beams and columns are not weakened.
    (D) make sure the person to be rescued is alive.

21. When breaking through a reinforced concrete wall, the steel reinforcing rods should be cut with a torch. When this is done, the firefighter should

    (A) remove the material in a number of small pieces.
    (B) cut all the reinforcing rods at the same time.
    (C) make sure any flammable materials are ignited to assist with the cutting.
    (D) have an appropriate portable fire extinguisher nearby.

Directions: Answer questions 22 through 28 using the information provided.

22. Appropriately selected and properly installed fire detection systems can have a major effect in reducing loss of life from fire. A study of the circumstances surrounding 342 dwelling fire deaths indicated that the use of smoke detectors could result in a 41 percent saving of life; the use of thermal detectors could save 8 percent.

    According to this passage,

    (A) heat detectors have consistently proved to be important lifesavers.
    (B) a study found that smoke detectors resulted in the saving of 41 lives.
    (C) life safety can be improved substantially through the installation of smoke detectors.
    (D) a study indicates that 342 dwelling fires resulted in deaths.

23. CPR (cardiopulmonary resuscitation) is a manual technique for keeping the heart pumping blood throughout the body. It is started when someone has a heart attack and, once started, should be done continuously until you are told to stop by medical personnel or you become too exhausted to continue.

    According to the passage,

    (A) CPR and rescue breathing are administered to circulate blood.
    (B) CPR is often done if the person thinks he or she might be having a heart attack.
    (C) rescue breathing is done only if the person is having a heart attack.
    (D) qualified medical help don't give CPR.

24. During Fire Operations, the police assist the firefighters by establishing "fire lines." The fire lines are generally marked off with yellow tape. The most likely reason for setting up fire lines is to

    (A) corral the spectators.
    (B) prevent property damage.
    (C) protect the firefighters and police.
    (D) prevent people from interfering with the firefighters.

25. When a bone is broken, it is classified as a fracture. There are two types of fractures, a closed fracture, where the skin is not broken, and an open fracture, where the bone has penetrated the skin. Initial first aid for a fracture is to prevent motion of the broken parts. While on your way to the firehouse, you see an accident, and the woman is complaining that her arm is hurting very badly.

    There is no blood showing, and the woman is crying; you suspect the arm is broken. You should

    (A) tell the woman to try to move her arm to see if it's broken.
    (B) talk to the woman calmly to try to get her to stop crying.
    (C) tell the woman not to move her arm and that you will call for medical assistance.
    (D) talk to other people at the scene to find out who the injured woman is.

26. As your fire company is leaving the scene of a fire, your lieutenant tells you she needs to know the area of the fire room. She then tells you to go back into the building and find the approximate area of the fire room. You would be most correct if you

(A) multiplied the length, width, and height of the room.
(B) added the length, width, and height of the room.
(C) multiplied the length and width of the room.
(D) added the length and width of the room.

27. If water weighs 62½ pounds per cubic foot, water 1 foot deep covering a floor that is 10 feet × 16 feet will weigh most nearly

(A) 1,000 pounds.
(B) 6,000 pounds.
(C) 10,000 pounds.
(D) 16,000 pounds.

28. In the illustration below, when part *A* revolves in the direction of arrow 1, part *B*

(A) rotates in the direction of arrow 3.
(B) rotates in the direction of arrow 4.
(C) does not rotate.
(D) rotates first in direction 1, then in direction 2.

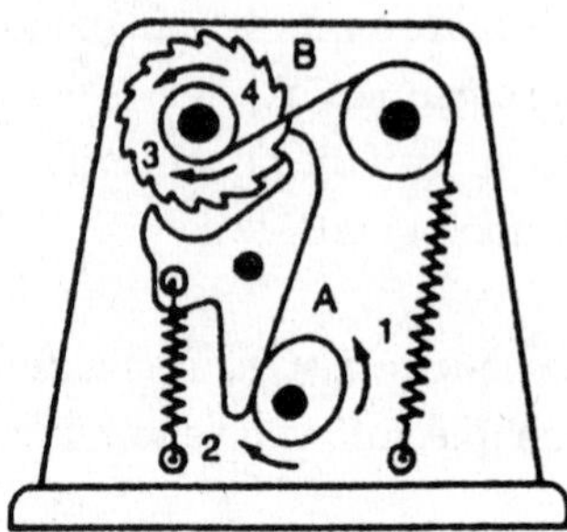

Directions: Answer question 29 using only the information in the following passage.

Handling and using hand tools require an understanding of how the tool works and the proper method for using it. When using a wrench, it is better to pull than push. If you must push, keep your palm open to protect your knuckles from damage. When using a hammer, choose the right type for the job. A carpenter's hammer is used for nails and a maul is used for heavy-duty work. Hammers should not be used for forcing a screw into something hard; use the correct type and size screwdriver.

29. Hand tools usage forces the user to

(A) push, not pull the tool.
(B) make use of the maul for forcing screws into hard objects.
(C) work intelligently.
(D) understand only the purpose of the tool.

Directions: Answer question 30 using only the information in the following passage.

Siamese connections for building fire protection systems are protected by covers. The covers of these systems are painted different colors to let the firefighters know what type of system each is. Covers painted red indicate a "wet standpipe system," green indicates a "wet sprinkler system," silver is used to indicate a "dry sprinkler system," and yellow indicates a combination "wet standpipe and sprinkler system."

30. The driver of Engine Company 21 arriving at a fire in a building equipped with a standpipe system would expect to find a siamese with a

(A) red or green cover.
(B) yellow or silver cover.
(C) green or yellow cover.
(D) red or yellow cover.

Directions: Answer questions 31 and 32 using the information provided.

31. The tool that would be most appropriate to cut a chain securing a gate on a fence would be

(A) an axe.
(B) a bolt cutter.
(C) a pry bar.
(D) a tin snip.

32. A tool that is used to loosen or tighten a set screw is sometimes called a hex key or set-screw wrench. This tool is also known as

(A) a crocodile wrench.
(B) a Stillson wrench.
(C) an Allen wrench.
(D) a crescent wrench.

Directions: Questions 33 through 37 describe a starting point and a destination. Assume you are driving in the area shown on the map accompanying the questions. Use the map as a basis for choosing the shortest way of getting from one point to another without breaking any traffic laws.

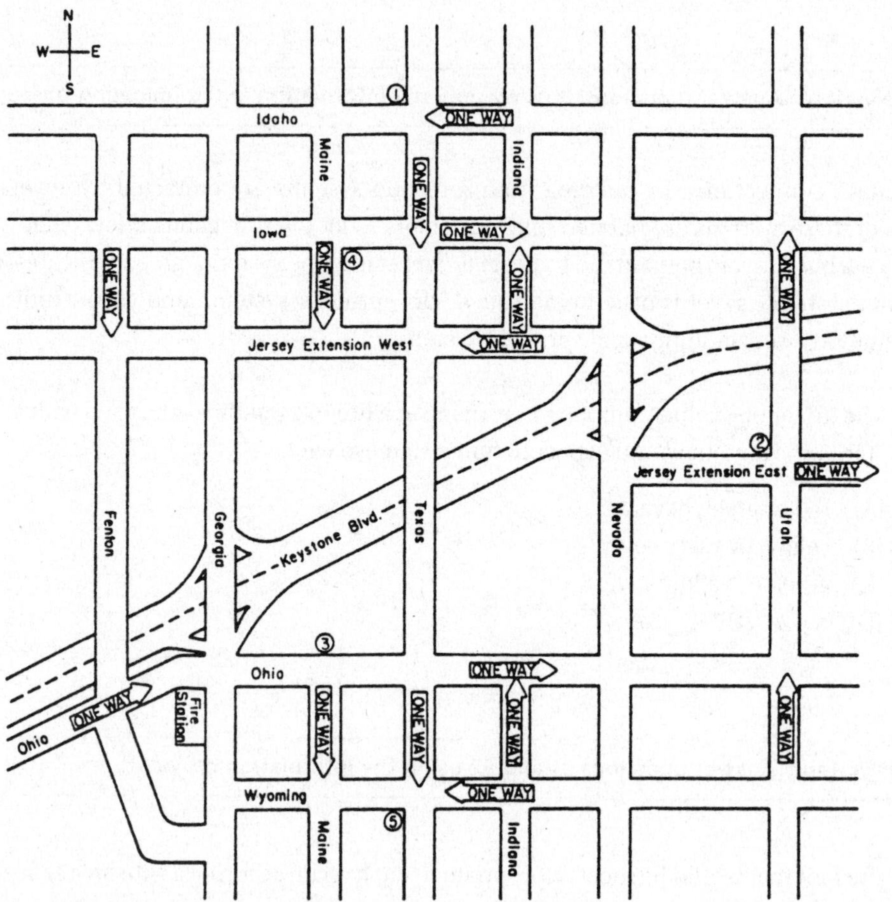

A street marked "One Way" is one way for the full length, even when there are breaks or jogs in the street. *Exception:* a street that does not have the same name over the full length.

33. From the fire station at the corner of Ohio and Georgia, you are to proceed to the northwest corner of Texas and Idaho. Without breaking any traffic laws, what is the shortest route to the corner?

    (A) East on Ohio to Utah, north to Idaho, west to the corner of Texas.
    (B) East on Ohio to Nevada, north to Idaho, west to the corner of Texas.
    (C) North on Georgia to Iowa, east to Indiana, north to Idaho, west to the corner of Texas.

34. From the corner of Idaho and Texas, you are to proceed to the northwest corner of Utah and Jersey Extension East. Without breaking any traffic laws, what is the shortest route to the corner?

(A) South on Texas to Ohio, east to Utah, north to the corner of Jersey Extension East.
(B) South on Texas to Ohio, east to Nevada, north to Jersey Extension East, east to the corner of Utah.
(C) South on Texas to Iowa, east to Nevada, south to Jersey Extension East, east to the corner of Utah.

35. From the corner of Jersey Extension East and Utah, you are to proceed to the intersection of Ohio and Maine. Without breaking any traffic laws, what is the shortest route to the corner?

(A) North on Utah to Idaho, west to Texas, south to Wyoming, west to Georgia, north to Ohio, east to the corner of Maine.
(B) North on Utah to Idaho, west to Nevada, south to Keystone Boulevard, southwest to Georgia exit, south to Ohio, east to the corner of Maine.
(C) North on Utah to Idaho, west to Nevada, south to Ohio, east to the corner of Maine.

36. From the corner of Ohio and Maine, you are to proceed to the southeast corner of Iowa and Maine. Without breaking any traffic laws, what is the shortest route to the corner?

(A) South on Maine to Wyoming, west to Georgia, north to Iowa, east to the corner of Maine.
(B) East on Ohio to Texas, north to Jersey Extension West, west to Maine, north to the corner of Iowa.
(C) East on Ohio to Nevada, north to Idaho, west to Maine, south to the corner of Iowa.

37. From the corner of Iowa and Maine, you are to proceed to the southwest corner of Wyoming and Texas. Without breaking any traffic laws, what is the shortest route to the corner?

(A) South on Maine to Jersey Extension West, west to Georgia, south to Wyoming, east to the corner of Texas.
(B) East on Iowa to Texas, south to the corner of Wyoming.
(C) East on Iowa to Nevada, south to Wyoming, west to the corner of Texas.

Directions: This part of the test measures your ability to understand directions. Each sample question describes a fire scene. You are to choose the drawing that best represents that scene.

In questions 38 through 40, symbols are used to represent vehicles, objects, and equipment. Study the symbols before you answer the questions. The symbols and their meanings in the following box will be repeated in the test.

SYMBOLS

The following symbols are used in the diagrams for questions 38 through 40.

Fire truck; pumper

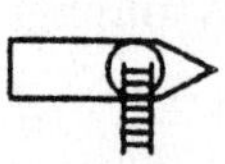

Fire truck

Other vehicles: cars, etc.

Hydrant

Hose Line (attached to hydrant)

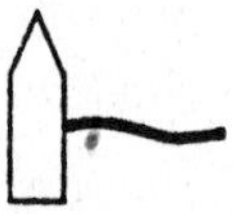

Hose line (attached to pumper)

Ladder

Building

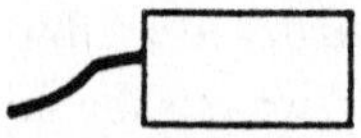

Hose line entering at ground level

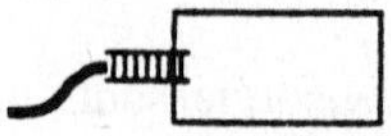

Hose line entering at upper levels

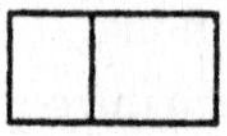

Building with a two-level roof

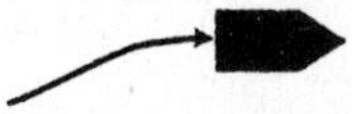

Path of vehicle before an accident is shown with solid line and arrow

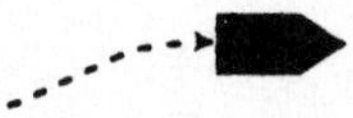

Path of vehicle after an accident is shown with dotted line and arrow

38. A fire truck facing south on a one-way street has to connect to a fire hydrant on the west side of the street to put out a fire in a building on the east side of the street.

(A)

(B)

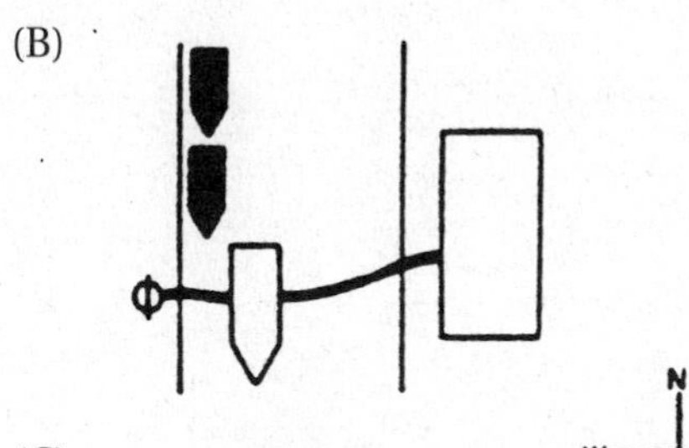

(C)

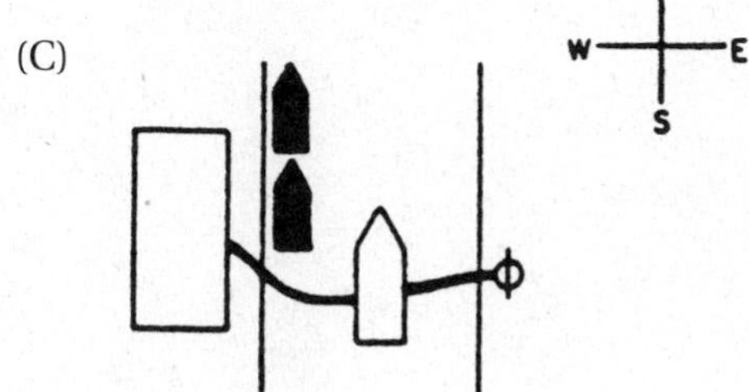

(D)

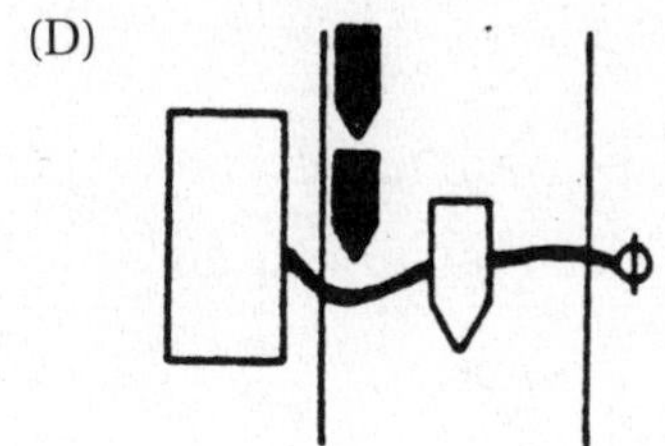

39. Two ladder trucks and one pumper arrive at a burning building. One hose from each truck is taken to the second floor.

(A)

(B)

(C)

(D)

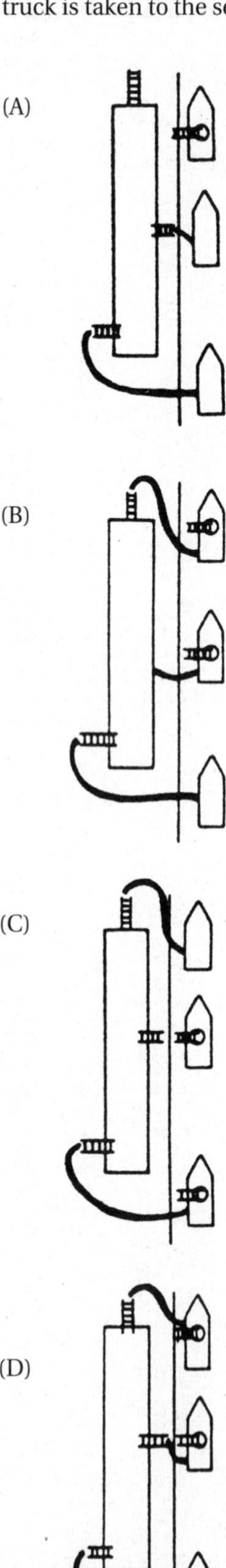

40. A pumper heading east to the intersection at Block and Rahn skids into a ladder truck parked in the opposite direction.

(A)

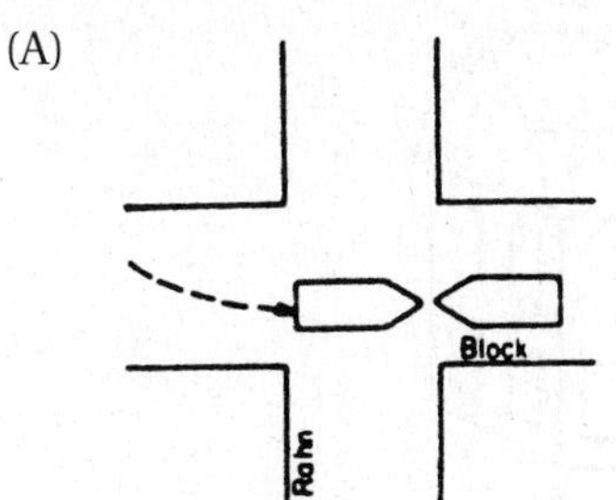

(B)

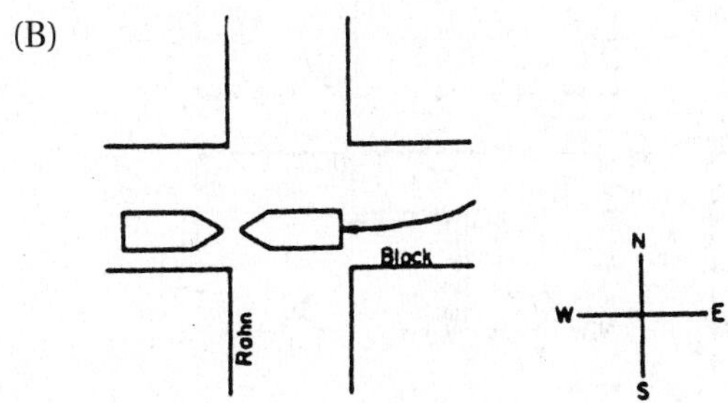

(C)

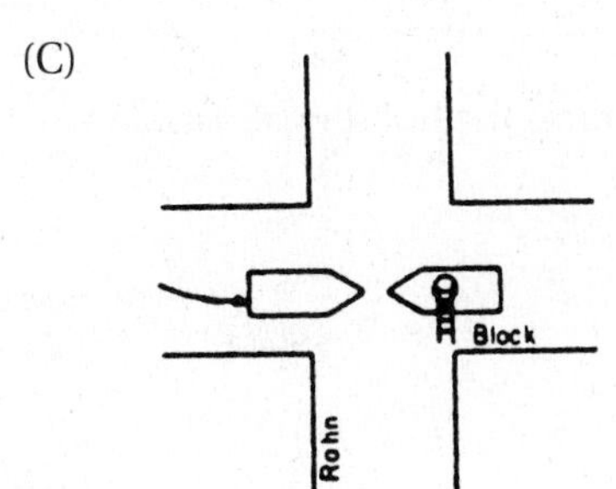

(D)

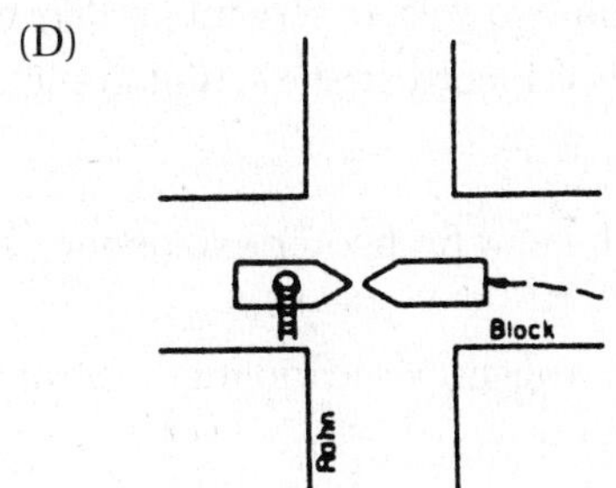

Directions: Answer question 41 using only the information in the illustration.

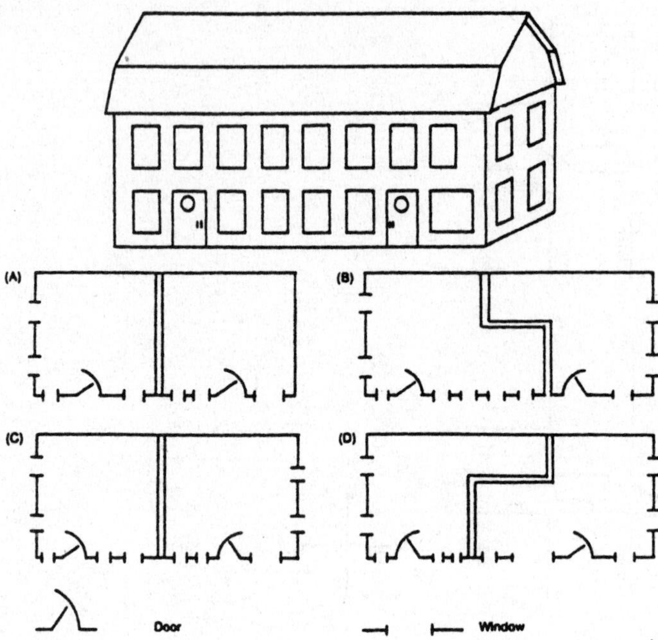

41. Choose the floor plan that most closely demonstrates the building illustrated.

    (A) Floor plan A.
    (B) Floor plan B.
    (C) Floor plan C.
    (D) Floor plan D.

42. A senior firefighter hears a newly appointed firefighter tell a group of schoolchildren that, if their clothing begins to burn, the proper thing to do is to scream for help and beat the flames out with their hands. Knowing this is incorrect, the senior firefighter should

    (A) disagree immediately but cour-teously with the new firefighter's statement, and explain the stop, drop, and roll method.
    (B) agree with the new firefighter's statement but suggest a second method, the stop, drop, and roll method.
    (C) disagree immediately with the new firefighter, and scold him for giving inaccurate information that could seriously endanger someone.
    (D) agree with the new firefighter since he has recently finished school and is probably up to date on all the new techniques.

43. A fire may be burning a block away from a fire station without the firefighters knowing it. This shows that

(A) more fire inspections are needed.
(B) the firefighters are not doing their job.
(C) firefighters should always watch hazardous locations.
(D) an alarm system should be installed.

44. If a person's clothes catch fire, one way to put the fire out is quickly to wrap a blanket around him or her. This method is effective mainly because

(A) it cuts off the supply of air to the fire.
(B) most blankets are fireproof.
(C) blankets are made of material that is a good heat insulator.
(D) the blanket has a cooling effect.

45. You are fighting a fire with a hose in a large storeroom and find that the situation is too dangerous for you to remain there any longer. The room is dark and filled with thick smoke. You cannot see even a short distance. Your best exit would be

(A) light a match to see your way out.
(B) using your recollection of where the door is located.
(C) following the hose back from the nozzle.
(D) spraying water in different directions to locate an exit by sound.

46. A firefighter working at a scene where a high-tension wire connected to a pole transformer is down should

(A) climb the pole and cut the wire close to the transformer.
(B) move the wire to a position where it will not interfere with the flow of traffic.
(C) use a rope to tie off an area around the danger zone.
(D) go to the nearest manhole or transformer vault and disconnect the power.

Directions: Answer questions 47 through 49 using only the information in the following passage.

Firefighters, EMT's, and Paramedics use the Rule of Nines to rapidly assess and classify the severity of a victim's burns. This system divides the body skin into sections and assigns a value to each portion of the body. The firefighter, EMT, or Paramedic examining the burned patient determines the areas that have been burned and then adds the values for each burned portion to determine the total amount of burned area. This information, and the person's age, is used to classify the severity of the burns.

Rule of Nines

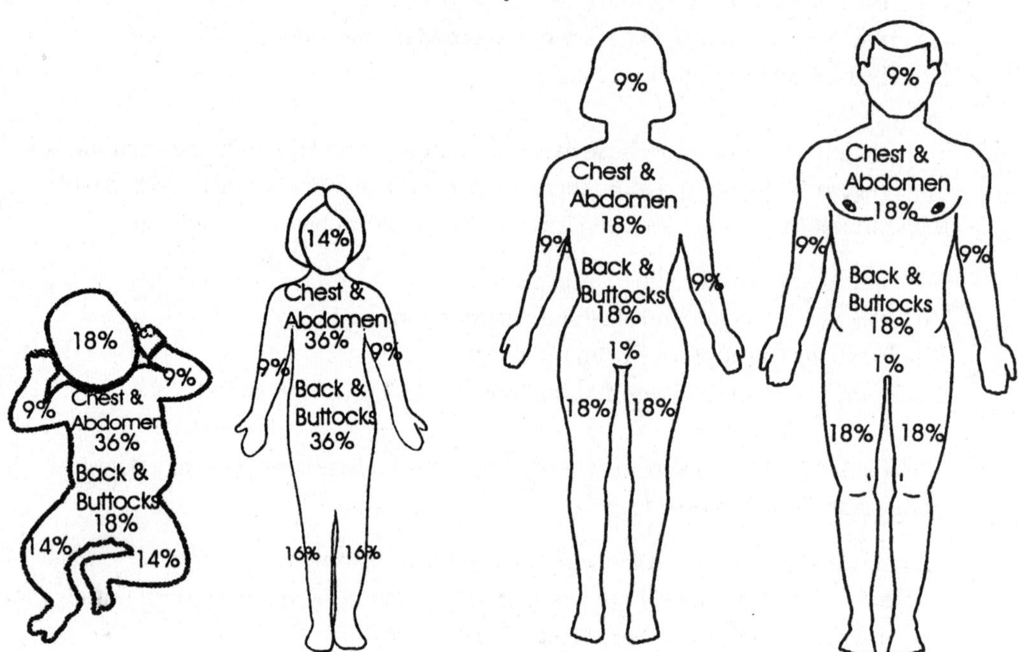

47. A seven-year-old girl spilled boiling water on her left arm, chest, and abdomen. Using the Rule of Nines, the burns account for approximately what portion of the girl's total skin surface?

    (A) 75 percent.
    (B) 65 percent.
    (C) 45 percent.
    (D) 35 percent.

48. A male adult is burned on the back, buttocks, and right arm. The total percent of burns is approximately

    (A) 25 percent.
    (B) 35 percent.
    (C) 45 percent.
    (D) 60 percent.

49. A senior citizen, while lighting a stove, is caught in the initial flash of fire. Only her hair goes on fire. You would be most correct if you predicted the burns to be not more than

(A) 9 percent.
(B) 14 percent.
(C) 18 percent.
(D) 36 percent.

Directions: Answer question 50 using only the information in the following passage.

Engine 1 responds to a reported house fire. Upon arrival, the firefighters find a distraught woman holding her baby. She tells them that a 4-inch water pipe, which supplies water to her home, broke and water is rapidly filling up her basement. The officer tells you the water is flowing at 500 gallons per minute (GPM) and that the flow will have to be stopped at the street valve. A dewatering operation is immediately started and two 250-GPM pumps are put into operation. The officer orders the water company to respond and to bring additional dewatering pumps to the scene. About ten minutes later, the woman asks a firefighter how the operation is going.

50. The firefighter should

(A) tell her that the water is being removed as fast as it is going in and that more pumps and the water department are on their way.
(B) tell her that only the officer can give out that information.
(C) tell her that everything is OK.
(D) not answer her, just continue with assigned duties.

STOP **IF THERE IS STILL TIME REMAINING, you may review your answers.**

ANSWER KEY AND EXPLANATIONS

Answer Key

1. **(A)**	11. **(A)**	21. **(D)**	31. **(B)**	41. **(C)**
2. **(B)**	12. **(B)**	22. **(C)**	32. **(C)**	42. **(A)**
3. **(D)**	13. **(D)**	23. **(A)**	33. **(C)**	43. **(D)**
4. **(D)**	14. **(A)**	24. **(D)**	34. **(C)**	44. **(A)**
5. **(A)**	15. **(B)**	25. **(C)**	35. **(B)**	45. **(C)**
6. **(D)**	16. **(C)**	26. **(C)**	36. **(A)**	46. **(C)**
7. **(A)**	17. **(C)**	27. **(C)**	37. **(B)**	47. **(C)**
8. **(A)**	18. **(D)**	28. **(B)**	38. **(B)**	48. **(A)**
9. **(C)**	19. **(B)**	29. **(C)**	39. **(D)**	49. **(A)**
10. **(D)**	20. **(C)**	30. **(D)**	40. **(C)**	50. **(A)**

Answer Explanations

1. **(A)** The first sentence of the paragraph following the description of the sample accident states that triage is the first thing that must be done. Choice B is incorrect; they should be prepared to go to work when they arrive and should have their protective clothing on before they arrive. Choice C is incorrect; there is no fire, only a chance one might start. Choice D is incorrect; CPR may be needed but triage, determining what to do, comes first.

2. **(B)** This injury is not life-threatening. Choices A, C, and D are life-threatening.

3. **(D)** This is explained in the last part of the reading.

4. **(D)** Triage is explained in the paragraph following the description of the sample accident. Choice A is incorrect; triage is only a small part of what firefighters do. Choice B is incorrect; ensuring the stability of vehicles is a physical activity done by firefighters, whereas triage is a mental process of determining what to do. Choice C is incorrect. Part of triage is to evaluate the capabilities of firefighters; however, it is not used to evaluate their performance (how well they do).

5. **(A)** The evaluation of the effectiveness (performance evaluation) is done after the work has been completed and is not part of the initial evaluation of what needs to be done.

6. **(D)** There are two windows, a front door, and cellar doors in the rear.

7. **(A)** The main body of fire is from the fireplace and up the stairs. Choice B is incorrect; there is an overloaded electrical outlet on the first floor, but there is no indication of fire near. (*Note:* Fire burns upward, until blocked, then horizontally, until it can find a way to go up again.) Choice C is incorrect; these materials are remote from the fire. Choice D is incorrect; there is no indication of anyone smoking in bed.

8. **(A)** The children are sleeping on the second floor next to the window. Based on the direction indicator at the top of the illustration, this is the east side of the house.

9. **(C)** The direction of the wind is indicated by the bending of the smoke coming out of the chimney.

10. **(D)** The fire extinguisher is hanging on the wall just above the chair in the basement.

11. **(A)** The preconnect load means that it is not one of the three basic loads, with one end of the hose already connected to the pumper. See the seventh paragraph of the passage.

12. **(B)** The horseshoe load is found in the fifth paragraph. Choice A is incorrect; based only on the information given, this load is used for hand stretching. Choice C is not a hose load; it is a hose storage location—a hose bed. Choice D refers to the method for stretching hose from the building to the water source.

13. **(D)** The word *all* makes this an incorrect statement. You should be very careful of choices that use such terms as *all, never, always, must.*

14. **(A)** This information is explained in the last two paragraphs of the passage.

15. **(B)** The emphasis of this passage is on training at the National Fire Academy and refers only to training in the areas of firefighting, command, and future trainers. Local fire department personnel problems and rules are not mentioned.

16. **(C)** This choice is the most accurate of all, although incomplete. Choice D is incorrect; the National Fire Academy is *not* for *all citizens.*

17. **(C)** The second paragraph, third sentence tells us this. Choices A, B, and D are incorrect; they are not mentioned in the passage.

18. **(D)** When answering a progression question, you must select the most correct and most complete answer. Choices A, B, and C are accurate answers but less accurate than Choice D. Therefore, only Choice D is correct.

19. **(B)** There is no mention of a hose line in the passage. Choices A, C, and D are incorrect; firefighters should be protected by these devices and concerned with safety.

20. **(C)** The fourth sentence says, "When cutting through walls, be sure that support beams and columns are not weakened." Choice A—the hole should be made only as large as necessary for rescue purposes. Choice B—the shape of the hole depends on the type of wall; for brick walls the opening is arch-shaped (paragraph 3). Choice D—this is not indicated and would not be practical—the person may be unconscious and unable to respond.

21. **(D)** See the last sentence. Choice A—concrete should be removed "in one piece." Choice B—the torch can cut only one rod at a time. Choice C—"be sure . . . that flammable materials are not ignited" (next to last sentence).

22. **(C)** The second sentence says, ". . . the use of smoke detectors could result in a 41 percent saving of life." Choice A—the passage refers to smoke detectors, not heat detectors. Choice B—smoke detectors could result in a 41 percent saving of lives, not a saving of 41 lives. Choice D—the study involved 342 deaths that occurred in dwellings. The number of dwellings involved is unknown; there could have been more than one death in a single dwelling.

23. **(A)** When only one person is available to give CPR, one person can perform life-saving activities. Choice B is incorrect; CPR is done after the heart attack has occurred. Choice C

is incorrect; rescue breathing is done when the person stops breathing, for example, due to drowning. Choice D is incorrect; qualified medical personnel would give CPR.

24. **(D)** The objective of fire lines is to prevent unnecessary interaction with firefighters and injury to people.

25. **(C)** Choice C is correct. The passage explains that initial first aid for a broken arm is to prevent motion (movement).

26. **(C)** Choice C is correct. To find the area multiply the length and width of the space. Choice A is incorrect; multiplying the length, width, and height will give you the volume.

27. **(C)** First determine the number of cubic feet that will be covered:

    Cubic feet (volume) = L × W × H
    Cubic feet = 10 ft. × 16 ft. × 1 ft.
    Cubic feet = 160 ft.^{3}

    Now multiply the weight of 1 cubic foot of water (62.5 lb.) by the total volume (160 ft.^{3}):

    $$62.5 \text{ lb.} \times 160 \text{ ft.}^3 = \text{Total weight}$$
    $$10{,}000 \text{ lb.} = \text{Total weight}$$

28. **(B)** Part *A* is oval in shape, and as it turns it pushes the pawl, causing it to release the ratchet. The purpose of the pawl is to prevent the ratchet from turning in the direction in which the points of the ratchet are facing. The ratchet can turn freely in the direction opposite the ratchet points. However, it can turn in the direction of the points only when the pawl is disengaged. Therefore, when part *A* pushes the pawl away from the ratchet, the ratchet will turn in the direction of arrow 4.

29. **(C)** The passage tells the reader there are different types in the same class of tools. It also explains that the right tool should be selected for each job. Choice A is incorrect; the tool operator is not obligated to push or pull a tool. The choice depends on the situation. Choice B is incorrect; a maul would not be used for this. The word *only* makes Choice D incorrect.

30. **(D)** The passage tells you that the cover of a standpipe siamese can be red, and a combination standpipe and sprinkler siamese is yellow.

31. **(B)** A bolt cutter has hardened jaws and is designed to cut steel rods, bolts, and locks, as well as chains. Choice A—an axe would not cut the chain, but the chain would damage the axe head. Choice C—a pry bar would not be effective and might result in a strain or other injury to the user. Choice D—a tin snip would not provide the cutting head or leverage needed to sever the chain links.

32. **(C)** An Allen wrench is a hexagonal bar that is inserted into the head of the screw and then worked in the same way as a screwdriver.

33. **(C)** This is two blocks shorter than Choice B and 4 blocks shorter than Choice A. Choices A and B are incorrect because the driver must go beyond Indiana to Nevada or Utah and then return the same distance.

34. **(C)** This is the shortest route. Choices A and B take the driver past Jersey Extension East and then require the driver to come back.

35. **(B)** This is the shortest route. Choice A is incorrect; the driver must go past Ohio to Wyoming and then return the same distance. Choice C is incorrect; the driver cannot go east on a one-way westbound street.

36. **(A)** This is the shortest route. Choice B is incorrect; the driver cannot go north on Maine. Choice C is incorrect; it is several blocks longer.

37. **(B)** This is the shortest route. Choice A would require proceeding against the flow of traffic on Wyoming; Choice C is several blocks longer.

38. **(B)** Only choice B has the hydrant on the west side and the fire truck facing south. Choices A and C are incorrect; the fire truck faces north. Choice D is incorrect; the hydrant is on the east side.

39. **(D)** According to the symbols chart, a hose line entering at an upper level must have a ladder and a hose touching the building. The question tells you that all three fire units took hose to the second floor. Only Illustration D has the lines going to the second floor.

40. **(C)** The pumper is heading east on Block across Rahn and is headed for the ladder truck on Block. Choices A and B are incorrect; both units involved are pumpers. Choice D is incorrect; the pumper is headed west.

41. **(C)** For this illustration, use the first floor as a guide. The first floor shows two entrance doors, one picture window, and a total of seven standard-size windows. Compare the floor plan layout with the three-dimensional representation. Choice C most accurately portrays the floor layout.

42. **(A)** An incorrect statement to a young, impressionable group could result in one of them being seriously injured at some future time. Although normally it is not good practice to correct someone in public, this would be an exception (and should be courteously done) because of the potential danger involved. Choice B—the new firefighter's statement is incorrect, and the senior firefighter has the responsibility to point this out, not to agree. Choice C—the newly appointed firefighter should not be scolded; instead the firefighter should be instructed politely as to the proper action. Choice D—the senior firefighter should not assume that the recommended procedure has been changed.

43. **(D)** A fire alarm system notifies the fire department directly of a fire. It tells firefighters not only that there is a fire but also where the fire is located. The fire alarm extends the communication reach of the firefighter out into the community and transmits a fire alarm.

44. **(A)** Smothering is one of the four methods of extinguishing a fire. In this case the blanket cuts off the oxygen supply and starves the fire. Choices B and D are not true, and Choice C is irrelevant to extinguishing the fire.

45. **(C)** The hose line serves as a guide. The hose would have been hooked up to a water supply before you advanced it into the storeroom. By following it back to the water-supply point, you can safely escape. Choice A—a match will not give off sufficient light.

Choice B—in complete darkness you cannot sense direction even if you think you remember the location of an exit. Choice D—spraying water around would be a waste of time and water. Any sound or the lack of it would be misleading.

46. **(C)** The rope will warn people of the danger and should keep them safely away from it. Choices A and B are unsafe acts. Control of the electrical power on the pole should be left to the utility company (A); the wire should not be moved unless there is an immediate, direct hazard to life (B), in which case the wire should be moved only with great caution. Choice D is wrong because underground and aboveground wiring are generally independent of each other. Shutting off the power to the underground system should not affect the aboveground system.

47. **(C)** The illustration for a child indicates Arm = 9%, Chest and Abdomen = 36%, for a total of 45%.

48. **(A)** The illustration for the adult indicates Back and Buttocks = 18% and Arm = 9% for a total of 27%. The Rule of Nines is an approximation. If the person is burned over one quarter of the body, then Choice A is the closest approximation.

49. **(A)** The person is an adult and suffered burns to the hair; the closest approximation of the burn area is the adult head, which equals 9%.

50. **(A)** Two times 250 GPM equals 500 GPM; the flow in is equal to the flow out; the operations are effective but will require more pumps and the water to be shut down. Giving accurate and proper information at an incident is an important part of a firefighter's role. Choice B is incorrect; if you can help the person, you should. Choice C is incorrect; everything is not "OK," the water has not been stopped and the basement still has water in it—do not give out incorrect information. Choice D is incorrect; do not insult or ignore the person.

ANSWER SHEET
Practice Exam Two

1. Ⓐ Ⓑ Ⓒ Ⓓ	16. Ⓐ Ⓑ Ⓒ Ⓓ	31. Ⓐ Ⓑ Ⓒ Ⓓ	46. Ⓐ Ⓑ Ⓒ Ⓓ
2. Ⓐ Ⓑ Ⓒ Ⓓ	17. Ⓐ Ⓑ Ⓒ Ⓓ	32. Ⓐ Ⓑ Ⓒ Ⓓ	47. Ⓐ Ⓑ Ⓒ Ⓓ
3. Ⓐ Ⓑ Ⓒ Ⓓ	18. Ⓐ Ⓑ Ⓒ Ⓓ	33. Ⓐ Ⓑ Ⓒ Ⓓ	48. Ⓐ Ⓑ Ⓒ Ⓓ
4. Ⓐ Ⓑ Ⓒ Ⓓ	19. Ⓐ Ⓑ Ⓒ Ⓓ	34. Ⓐ Ⓑ Ⓒ Ⓓ	49. Ⓐ Ⓑ Ⓒ Ⓓ
5. Ⓐ Ⓑ Ⓒ Ⓓ	20. Ⓐ Ⓑ Ⓒ Ⓓ	35. Ⓐ Ⓑ Ⓒ Ⓓ	50. Ⓐ Ⓑ Ⓒ Ⓓ
6. Ⓐ Ⓑ Ⓒ Ⓓ	21. Ⓐ Ⓑ Ⓒ Ⓓ	36. Ⓐ Ⓑ Ⓒ Ⓓ	
7. Ⓐ Ⓑ Ⓒ Ⓓ	22. Ⓐ Ⓑ Ⓒ Ⓓ	37. Ⓐ Ⓑ Ⓒ Ⓓ	
8. Ⓐ Ⓑ Ⓒ Ⓓ	23. Ⓐ Ⓑ Ⓒ Ⓓ	38. Ⓐ Ⓑ Ⓒ Ⓓ	
9. Ⓐ Ⓑ Ⓒ Ⓓ	24. Ⓐ Ⓑ Ⓒ Ⓓ	39. Ⓐ Ⓑ Ⓒ Ⓓ	
10. Ⓐ Ⓑ Ⓒ Ⓓ	25. Ⓐ Ⓑ Ⓒ Ⓓ	40. Ⓐ Ⓑ Ⓒ Ⓓ	
11. Ⓐ Ⓑ Ⓒ Ⓓ	26. Ⓐ Ⓑ Ⓒ Ⓓ	41. Ⓐ Ⓑ Ⓒ Ⓓ	
12. Ⓐ Ⓑ Ⓒ Ⓓ	27. Ⓐ Ⓑ Ⓒ Ⓓ	42. Ⓐ Ⓑ Ⓒ Ⓓ	
13. Ⓐ Ⓑ Ⓒ Ⓓ	28. Ⓐ Ⓑ Ⓒ Ⓓ	43. Ⓐ Ⓑ Ⓒ Ⓓ	
14. Ⓐ Ⓑ Ⓒ Ⓓ	29. Ⓐ Ⓑ Ⓒ Ⓓ	44. Ⓐ Ⓑ Ⓒ Ⓓ	
15. Ⓐ Ⓑ Ⓒ Ⓓ	30. Ⓐ Ⓑ Ⓒ Ⓓ	45. Ⓐ Ⓑ Ⓒ Ⓓ	

PRACTICE EXAM TWO

Directions: Questions 1 through 10 are an oral or listening part of the examination. They are intended to measure your ability to hear, understand, and apply information.

At the beginning of this examination have someone READ the passage, slowly and carefully, to you. DO NOT READ THIS PASSAGE YOURSELF.

Immediately after the reading, answer questions 1 through 10 on the basis of the information found in the passage.

To the assistant: Please read the following passage aloud. Read slowly and distinctly. Once you start, read through to the end with only normal pauses between paragraphs and punctuation. Do not add additional emphasis or discuss the passage. When you have completed reading the passage, your part of this practice examination is complete. Thank you for your help.

Welcome to the Fire Department. My name is John Soon; I am the Captain in charge of Recruit Training and will be responsible for your training and development. To my left is our Fire Chief, John Roache and to my right are your platoon leaders, Lieutenants Johnson, Rogers, and Garcia.

You have chosen to become a part of our noble firefighting and service-oriented force. The Fire Service is a team-oriented group; during the next 16 weeks you will learn how you will fit into and become a productive contributor to our team. Even though our nation's culture prides itself on the uniqueness of each individual, we will require you to become a team player. People who use their talents, skills, and abilities to achieve the team's goals are people who accept this as being more important than getting what they want, or doing it "my way."

During the next 16 weeks, you will be taught and shown how to perform a wide variety of new skills. You will be required to perform each of the skills, and you will be tested on your ability to implement and use these skills appropriately. Before you complete this portion of your probationary training, you will be required to have successfully passed all the tests we give you. Your probationary training will last for 52 weeks and may be extended up to 78 weeks. Your recruit reporting time while you are assigned to the Fire Academy will be 0800 and you will work until 1700, Monday through Friday. The firefighting work schedule is 24-hour shifts, and they report at 0900. During your time at the Fire Academy and during your probationary period, you may be given additional medical examinations, and you may be required to partake in drug-screening tests. Upon completion of your Fire Academy testing, you will be assigned to a fire company and to a specific work team. You will continue your education and training under the direct leadership of the unit's Company Commander. Even though your probationary period lasts 52 weeks, your training period lasts 156 weeks. After one year, you will be rotated from your first unit to another unit. Upon completion of your second year of service, you will be rotated to a third unit. Upon completion of your third year of service, you will be given the opportunity to select one of these units to be assigned to;

however, your assignment will ultimately be determined by evaluations of your performance and the needs of the Fire Department.

The Fire Department has a very good compensation plan; your initial biweekly salary will be paid every other Friday by direct deposit. You will receive a 5 percent raise at the completion of each of your rotation years. You are eligible for 18 sick days per year and 11 paid holidays. After completion of your first year of service, you will be eligible for 10 workdays of vacation; this will increase at the rate of 3 vacation days for the completion of each 5 years of service. Firefighters are eligible for retirement after 20 years of service. The opportunity for promotion is good and is based upon your ability to perform well on a civil service promotional examination and on your academic and service performance. You will not be eligible to take the promotional examination until you have completed your full training period of 156 weeks.

While you are at the Fire Academy, you will be given medical coverage; however, this does not cover you when you are off duty or away from the Fire Academy. You will be eligible for full medical care after you successfully complete your 16-week Fire Academy training.

From time to time, firefighters are required to be held on duty to perform critical functions. During this additional duty, they are paid overtime at the rate of time and a half for each hour worked. The rule applies to recruits who may be brought to a fire scene to assist regular firefighters. Near the end of your Fire Academy training period, you will be required to work several Saturdays with a fire unit, but you will not be permitted to enter the fire's hot zone. You will be paid for this additional training at straight time and your medical benefits will be active during these tours.

Now, before we begin your training, Chief Roache will address you:

"Good morning—welcome to our Fire Department. As the Captain has told you, you have joined a unique group, a group of unselfish heros: firefighters who dedicate themselves to keeping our community safe and a great place to live. They accomplish this through teamwork. And now your first lesson in teamwork. I want all of you to stand up and introduce yourselves to each other by reaching out and shaking hands with the person alongside, in front of, and in back of you; this will help you to break some cultural barriers and bond with your fellow recruits in a new way.

"As you do this short exercise, I want you to think 'this firefighter may have to save my life someday.' When you have completed the exercise, I want you to sit back down and think about how important it is for you to make sure that each of your fellow recruits learns everything he or she can about his or her new profession. I know it's important that you learn and pass our examinations, but I want you to understand that it may be even more important to you that the other recruits learn as much or more than you. They will be the ones who will be coming to your rescue when you are trapped in a burning building. Firefighting is a dangerous profession. You must become good at what you do and you must be the team member who helps the other members accomplish their tasks and assignments. This mutual helping is what gives us our strength.

"Now go into your new training with an open mind and with enthusiasm. I look forward to seeing you at your academy graduation. Now let's bring back Captain Soon, who will give you your directions for the next training session."

1. The officer in charge of your Fire Academy training is

(A) Rogers.
(B) Garcia.
(C) Soon.
(D) Roache.

2. Probationary training is for ______ weeks.

(A) 16
(B) 156
(C) 52
(D) 260

3. Reporting time for recruits at the Fire Academy is

(A) 6 A.M.
(B) 7 A.M.
(C) 8 A.M.
(D) 9 A.M.

4. During your stay at the Fire Academy, you will be required to work

(A) Monday through Friday and some Saturdays.
(B) Monday, Friday, and Saturday.
(C) Monday through Friday.
(D) Monday through Saturday.

5. During your stay at the Fire Academy, you can anticipate all of the following EXCEPT

(A) being called to participate in drug-screening tests.
(B) helping to fight fires just as the regular firefighters do.
(C) getting paid every two weeks.
(D) meeting many new people.

6. During the next three years of service, you can expect to work in no less than ______ firefighting units.

(A) four
(B) three
(C) two
(D) one

7. Which of the following statements is least accurate?

(A) You will get a raise every 5 years.
(B) You get 18 sick days.
(C) You get 11 paid holidays.
(D) After one year, you get 10 workdays of vacation.

8. You would be most correct if you told a fellow recruit that

   (A) you can retire after 20 years of service.
   (B) all firefighters can participate in promotional examinations.
   (C) the training period is three years.
   (D) full medical coverage begins the day you start at the Fire Academy.

9. Firefighters receive overtime pay at the rate of time and a half

   (A) when fighting fires in the hot zone.
   (B) while at recruit training.
   (C) when assigned, because of the needs of the Fire Department.
   (D) when called in or held over from time to time.

10. The purpose of introducing yourself and shaking hands with your fellow recruits is to

   (A) make sure they know who you are.
   (B) make sure you know who they are.
   (C) start the next training session.
   (D) start the teamwork process.

Directions: Answer questions 11 through 15 using only the information provided in the following illustration and the following passage. You may look at the illustration while answering these questions.

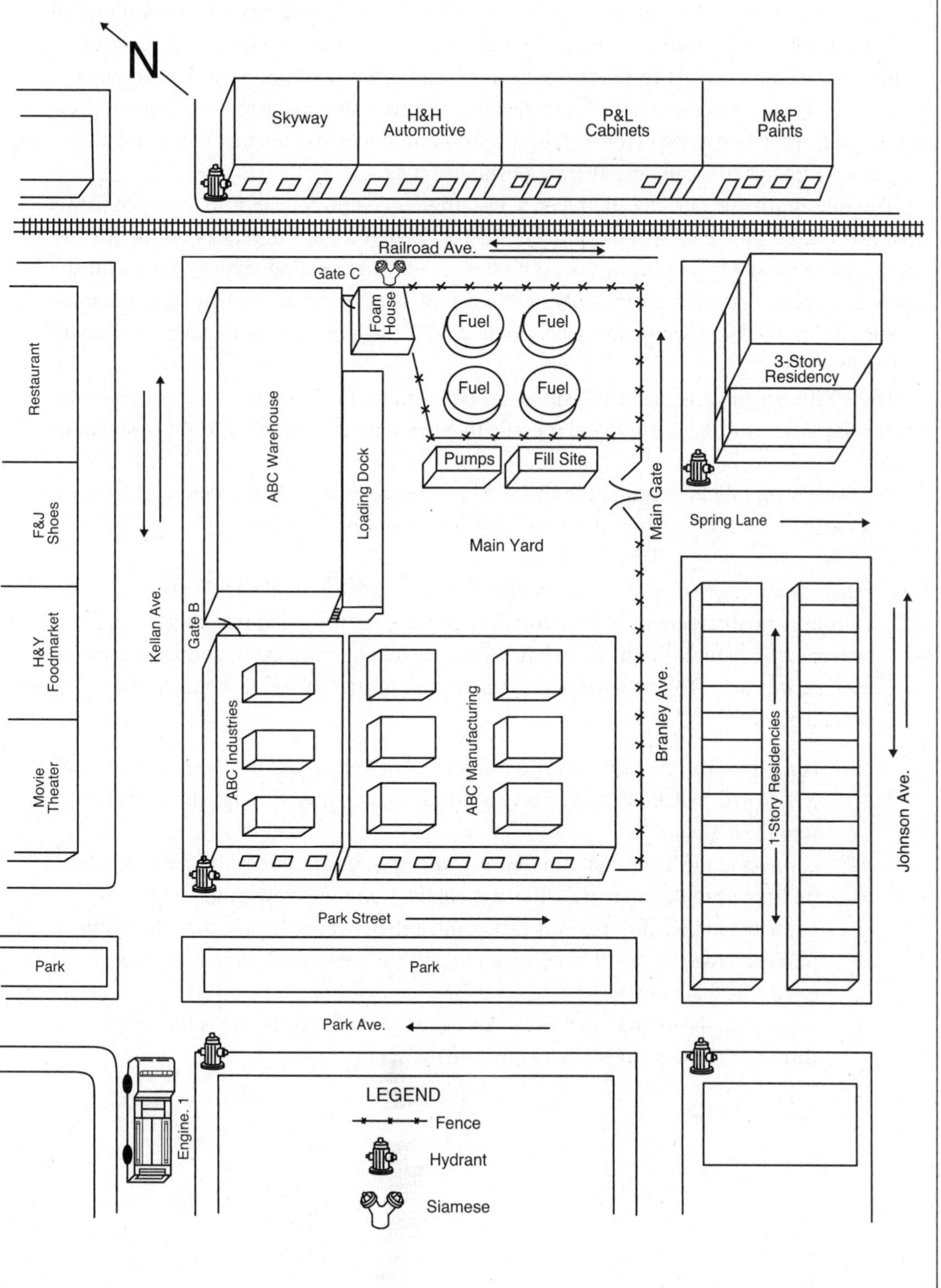

On Thursday at 10:00 hours, you and the other members of your fire unit go with the officer to perform a prefire plan at ABC Industries. The industrial park is located at 423 Kellan Ave. at Park Street. ABC Industries is part of a multi-national corporation that manufactures and distributes numerous products. At the Kellan Ave. site, cabinets and outdoor furniture are produced and stored while waiting for shipment throughout the region. These items are made from plastics and wood. The finished goods are stored in the warehouse and moved onto the loading dock during the night, in preparation for loading onto trucks the next day. During an average day, 30 trucks will pick up a load of finished goods and 12 trucks will deliver raw goods. Raw materials are also delivered by train directly to the raw material storage section at the north end of the warehouse. The warehouse and the manufacturing building have sprinklers that can quickly extinguish most fires.

The ABC industrial site at Kellan Ave. is also the fuel depot for the firm's remote plants that are located on the other side of town. Fuel is delivered from the tanks to the delivery trucks at the fill site by pumps in the pump house. The foam extinguishing system on the site has sufficient capacity to control any predictable-size fire in the fuel tanks. Water must be supplied to the foam house through a siamese on the exterior wall of the foam house facing Railroad Ave.

The entire premises is enclosed within an eight-foot fence. The three access gates are electrically locked at 10 P.M. There is a security force on duty that patrols the entire site once each hour.

You have been told to examine the site and become familiar with its layout and hazards. You have also been told to determine how a fire would be fought at this site.

11. Upon returning to quarters, you are called into the office and asked to make recommendations about which hydrant to connect the fire engine to so it can supply water to the siamese on the foam house. You are told that you cannot bring a hose across the tracks. The closest and most direct way to get water to the foam house would be to

    (A) connect to the hydrant at Park Ave. and Kellan Ave., and bring the hose north on Kellan Ave. to Railroad Ave., then east to Gate C and then through the gate and into the foam house.
    (B) connect to the hydrant at Branley Ave. and Spring Lane and bring the hose north on Branley to Railroad Ave., then west to the siamese on the pump house.
    (C) connect to the hydrant at Park Street and Kellan Ave., then take the hose north on Kellan Ave. to Gate B, then around the warehouse, then north and directly inside the foam house.
    (D) connect to the hydrant at Branley Ave. and Spring Lane, then take the hose through the main gate and directly into the pump house.

12. The lieutenant asks you where the raw materials are stored, and if a fire occurred in this area where could fire companies park their apparatus and use their built-in heavy water streams on the apparatus to extinguish the fire. Your answer should be

(A) in the warehouse at the north end and with a pumper placed on Kellan Ave. or Railroad Ave.
(B) in the warehouse at the south end and a pumper can be placed on Kellan Ave. or in the main yard.
(C) in the manufacturing plant at the north end and a pumper can be placed on Spring Lane or in the main yard.
(D) in the manufacturing plant at the south end and a pumper can be placed on Branley Ave. or Park Street.

13. The lieutenant asks you, "If a fire develops in the fuel tanks and the wind is blowing southwest, what would be in the greatest danger of catching fire?" what should you reply?

(A) ABC warehouse and maybe the restaurant.
(B) Fuel pumps and the ABC manufacturing plant.
(C) Branley Ave. residences.
(D) ABC manufacturing.

14. If a fire occurred in the ABC manufacturing plant, and you were with the first unit to arrive, what would be the first activity you would perform?

(A) Shut down the pumps to the fuel filling site.
(B) Supply water to the sprinkler system in the warehouse.
(C) Supply water to the sprinkler system in the manufacturing plant.
(D) Supply water to the siamese on the foam house.

15. For a fire at the tank truck loading site, it would be best for engine 1 to

(A) proceed north on Kellan Ave., west on Railroad Ave., and south on Branley Ave. to the main gate.
(B) proceed north on Kellan Ave., east on Park Street, north on Branley Ave. to the main gate.
(C) proceed north on Kellan Ave., east on Railroad Ave., and south on Branley Ave. to the main gate.
(D) proceed north on Kellan Ave., east on Park Ave., and north on Branley Ave. to the main gate.

Directions: Answer question 16 using only the information in the illustration.

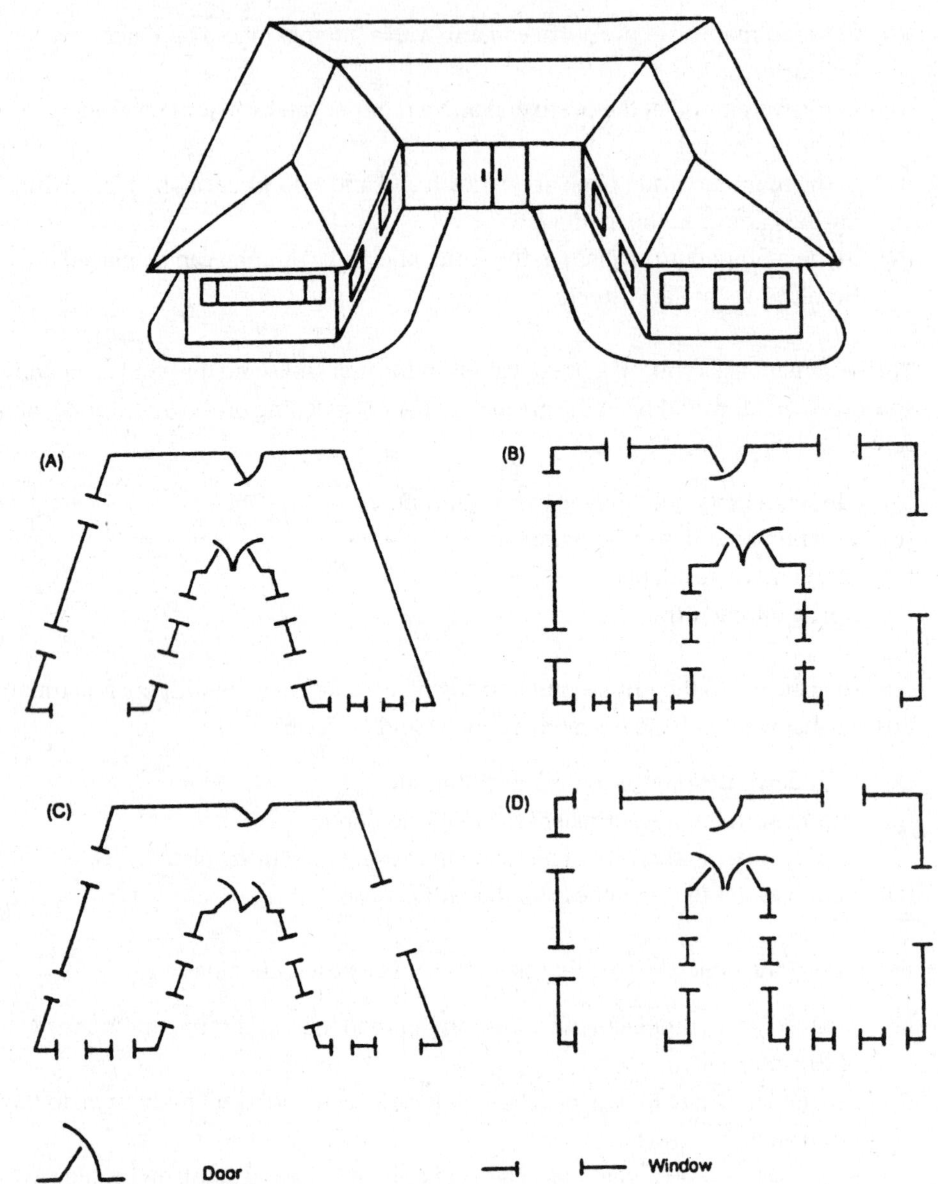

16. Choose the floor plan that most closely demonstrates the building illustrated.

    (A) Floor plan A.
    (B) Floor plan B.
    (C) Floor plan C.
    (D) Floor plan D.

17. When a fire is burning in brush on the side of a hill, the fire generally covers ground fastest

(A) downhill.
(B) uphill.
(C) sideways from the fire.
(D) in the middle of the fire.

18. A sheepshank would be used to

(A) form a noose for hoisting tools.
(B) wrap around fire victims to lower them to the ground.
(C) shorten the effective length of a piece of rope.
(D) lash two ladders together to extend their lengths.

Directions: In questions 19 and 20 you are asked to think like a firefighter. Make your decision based on what is in each paragraph, and select the best answer for each question.

19. While attending a movie at a local theater, a firefighter finds the rear exit doors secured with a chain and lock wrapped through the door handles. The best action for the firefighter to take would be to

(A) pull the interior fire alarm box to summon the local fire company to the scene to enforce the law.
(B) tell the manager to remove the lock immediately because it is unsafe and illegal.
(C) leave the theater because it is unsafe and then report the condition to the local fire company.
(D) take a seat near the open entrance door, tell an usher about the problem, and then watch the movie.

20. Two firefighters on their way to work see a fire in a store on the first floor of a four-story apartment building. What is the best action for these firefighters to take?

(A) Both firefighters enter the building and alert the occupants to the fire.
(B) One firefighter calls the fire department, while the other firefighter alerts the occupants.
(C) One firefighter goes to the fire station to report the fire and let the officer know that the other firefighter will be late in reporting for duty.
(D) One firefighter goes to the nearest fire alarm box and awaits the arrival of the fire company, while the other continues on to the fire station to make sure the company responds and the officer is aware that the second firefighter will be late.

Directions: Answer questions 21 through 24 using only the information in the following passage.

Firefighters have many jobs to do at the scene of a fire. One of the most difficult is the position of roof ventilation. The person assigned to the task of opening up the roof must be an experienced and determined firefighter. The mission of the person assigned to roof ventilation is to open up the top of the building and release the pressure buildup of smoke and heat.

The route taken to the roof is

1. The stairs of the adjoining building, that is, if there is an adjoining building and it is approximately the same height.
2. The aerial ladder, elevating platform, or portable ladder.
3. The fire escape, if there is one. This is the least desirable method.
4. The interior stairs of the fire building should NEVER be used except in a high-rise or a large multiwing building with several enclosed remote stairs.

When arriving at the roof, the firefighters should

1. Let the company officer know that they are at the roof.
2. Immediately open the door leading to the stairs of the fire building.
3. Search for any people who may have tried to use the stairs but were unable to get out. This is particularly important if the entrance door was found securely locked.
4. Remove the skylight over the stairs and hall; this will greatly aid in ventilation.
5. Remove any other skylights that could aid in ventilation.
6. Conduct a visual search of all sides of the building. From the roof, the firefighter can rapidly spot someone in trouble or someone who may have jumped before the Fire Department's arrival.

Let your officer know when the roof has been opened and you have completed your duties at that level. If you leave the roof to attempt a rescue, you must tell your officer or the officer in command of the fire.

21. The least desirable method for getting to the roof of a small four-story residential building is the

    (A) interior stairs of the fire building.
    (B) interior stairs of the adjoining building.
    (C) aerial ladder.
    (D) fire escape.

22. Your objective when assigned to the roof position is to

    (A) open the door to the stairs of the fire building.
    (B) remove the skylight on the fire building.
    (C) release the pressure buildup of smoke and heat.
    (D) rescue a person who may have jumped before the Fire Department's arrival.

23. After completing the roof duties, you should

(A) notify the company officer.
(B) notify the company officer and the officer in command of the fire.
(C) notify the company officer or the officer in command of the fire.
(D) come down the interior stairs to search for people who may be trapped.

24. After arriving safely at the roof, the first action you should take is to

(A) check the perimeter of the building to see if anybody is in trouble.
(B) get the door leading to the interior stairs open.
(C) communicate to the company officer that you are in position on the roof.
(D) open the skylights to relieve the trapped smoke and heat.

Directions: Answer question 25 using only the information in the following passage.

Arson investigation is the responsibility of specially trained personnel. They gather information from the fire scene and make a determination of the point of origin and the cause of the fire. Evidence is circumstantial or physical. At many fires the collection of physical evidence is made difficult because it has been destroyed by the fire. It may also be damaged by the water and overhauling activities of the firefighters. Firefighters can significantly aid in arson investigation by being observant as they respond and by preserving potential evidence at the scene.

25. It would be *most* correct to say that

(A) arson investigators respond to the scene to determine if a crime has been committed and to gather evidence.
(B) firefighters can and do destroy evidence.
(C) arson investigators arrest and prosecute people suspected of arson.
(D) specially trained fire officers are sent to the fire to aid the firefighters in preserving the scene.

Directions: Answer question 26 using only the information in the following passage.

Electricity presents a constant hazard to firefighters. Because of the dangers, firefighters are trained how to react when they respond and find an electrical hazard.

For fire in an underground vault, firefighters should

1. Set up a danger zone around the vault. Request that the power be shut down and that the power company respond.
2. Place the apparatus at a safe point outside the danger zone.
3. Have a team of two firefighters make a determination if any life hazard exists.
4. If a life is in danger, begin rescue operations using the most effective safety and rescue techniques.
5. If no life hazards exist, rope off the area and keep all people safely away.
6. Search the surrounding buildings for signs of a possible fire.
7. Await the arrival of the power company personnel and work with them to control the incident.

26. Firefighters responding to a reported automobile fire find smoke pushing from a manhole cover in the center of the street. They notify the dispatcher to call the power company to shut down the power and respond. They then establish a danger zone, park the apparatus immediately outside the zone, and determine that nobody is in immediate danger. The next thing the firefighters should do is

    (A) search the surrounding buildings for any indication of a possible fire.
    (B) wait for the power company to arrive to shut off the power.
    (C) send in a team of firefighters to see if anyone is in the manhole.
    (D) rope off the area and keep the people away.

Directions: Answer questions 27 through 29 using only the information in the following passage.

One of the most basic and useful tools available to the incident commander is the needed fire flow for a given building. Fire flow is the amount of water needed to extinguish a fire in an occupancy. In most cases, the fire flow calculation exceeds what is really needed to control a fire. This flow is always given in gallons per minute and may be required for a prolonged period.

The needed fire flow allows the incident commander to determine the resources needed, such as staffing, water, and apparatus, before the incident occurs. If a given volume of water is required, one can calculate, rather simply, the number of firefighters required to handle the hose lines.

Consider the following example: If the needed fire flow is 250 GPM, a minimum of three firefighters are needed on each 2½-inch line or two firefighters on each 1½-inch line. Other tactical considerations, such as the degree to which the line must be maneuvered within the building, the effective reach of the 2½-inch line versus the 1½-inch line, the time that will be required to get the line in service, and the ability of the stream to reach its target will be made based on local conditions and can increase the required number of firefighters for each line. When determining the number of personnel needed, the officer must also consider ventilation, search, rescue, command functions, pump operations, and similar activities.

27. The needed fire flow is

    (A) the amount of water three firefighters can handle.
    (B) not considered when figuring out the personnel required to fight a fire.
    (C) the amount of water flowing from a maneuverable effective hose line.
    (D) the amount of water required to extinguish a fire in an occupancy.

28. A minimum of two firefighters are needed

    (A) to operate each 1½-inch hose line.
    (B) to operate a 2½-inch hose line.
    (C) to be sure the needed fire flow is delivered.
    (D) for search and ventilation as well as maneuverability.

29. The needed fire flow is

    (A) determined after the fire is started.
    (B) the amount of water flowing through a 2½-inch hose line.
    (C) a rather simple calculation.
    (D) used to determine the number of firefighters required to handle the hose lines.

Directions: Answer questions 30 and 31 using only the information in the following passage.

At every premises where gasoline, flammable liquids, and/or diesel fuel for motor vehicles are stored in underground storage systems, there shall be posted the name of the owner or person responsible for the testing of such systems and the telephone number where such owner or person can be reached 24 hours a day, 7 days a week in the event of a leak or other emergency. Such sign or notice, in a form acceptable to the Fire Commissioner, shall be posted in such manner that it is easily read from the outside of the premises, and shall include, additionally, the name and phone number of the supplier or distributor who furnishes gasoline or flammable liquid product to the premises.

30. With respect to the sign described in the passage, it is correct to state that

    (A) it shall be easily read from the outside of the premises.
    (B) it shall be posted for all underground storage systems.
    (C) it shall be made of durable materials and be white with red letters.
    (D) it shall indicate the business hours of the occupancy.

31. The sign to be posted shall contain all of the following EXCEPT

    (A) name of owner.
    (B) telephone number where owner can be reached.
    (C) address of owner.
    (D) name and telephone number of supplier or distributor.

Directions: Answer questions 32 and 33 using only the information in the following passage.

Portable ladders are raised at building fires for many reasons. For a fire in a one-story building that has been subdivided into many stores by fire walls, ladders can be used to identify the outer limits of the subdivision. They can be used to gain access to and egress from the roof. Placing ladders remotely located from each other will ensure that firefighters have a safe secondary way to get off the roof rapidly. At fires in multistory residence buildings, ladders can be used to gain entrance to lower floors or as a secondary means of egress for trapped occupants. At a fire located in either the cellar, first, or second floors of a four-story multitenant residence, portable ladders should be raised to areas above and adjacent to the fire area even if the aerial ladder is going to be used. A heavy fire in these areas may make the interior stairs unusable and require the tenants to escape through the windows.

32. At a fire in a one-story shopping complex, portable ladders should be raised for all of the following reasons EXCEPT

    (A) to ensure that occupants can rapidly and safely exit the building.
    (B) to identify the outer subdividing walls of the fire store.
    (C) to give firefighters at least two ways, remote from each other, to get off the roof.
    (D) to gain access to the roof.

33. Arriving at a fire located in the cellar of a small multistory residence building, you are told to put up a portable ladder. You would be correct if you raised the ladder to the

    (A) roof.
    (B) window immediately above the fire.
    (C) window remote from the fire.
    (D) window adjacent to and above the fire.

Directions: Answer questions 34 through 37 using only the information in the following passage.

The use of elevators during fires requires special knowledge and training. To make elevators safer, "firefighter service" has been installed. Firefighter service is activated by the use of a special firefighter's key. The key can be used in the lobby or in the elevator car. The three-position key switch in the lobby will (1) recall the elevators to the lobby, (2) open the car hoistway door after it has closed, and (3) return the system to normal.

To operate the car in firefighter service, insert the key in the switch and

1. Select firefighter service.
2. Press the door-close button.
3. Select a floor.
4. Once the car is moving, test the call-cancel button.
5. If the car stops at the next floor, reselect your floor.
6. When you reach your floor, push and hold the door-open button until the door stops.
7. To move to another floor, begin with step two.
8. When you are on your floor, the car must be returned to the lobby manually.
9. When you are finished with the elevator, the key must be returned to normal.

If water is flowing into the elevator shaft from sprinkler systems or hose lines, do not use the elevator. Water can interfere with the electric circuits and cause the elevator to act erratically. Do not overload the elevator car. Six firefighters are the maximum number of passengers permitted. Any time the elevator acts erratically, leave the elevator, put it out of service, and tell the officer in command of the fire what you have done.

34. Upon entering the lobby of a high-rise office building, you are told by the building manager that there is a fire on the twenty-third floor, and that all the occupants of that floor and the floors immediately above it have been evacuated to a position two floors below the fire. The elevators are on their way up to the twenty-first floor to bring the people down. The first action firefighters should take is to

(A) select firefighter service.
(B) press the door-close button.
(C) use the special key to recall the elevators.
(D) use the special key to open the elevator hoistway door.

35. Firefighters traveling to a fire on the upper floors of a building have activated the firefighter service and are now at the desired floor landing. To exit the elevator, they should

(A) turn and release the special key to normal.
(B) push the door-open button.
(C) push and hold the door-open button.
(D) push the fire emergency release button.

36. While traveling in an elevator, firefighters discover water dripping into the car. After activating the call-cancel button, the firefighters should

(A) activate the door-open button and exit the car.
(B) let the officer in command know the elevator is not working properly.
(C) continue to the destination floor and then put the elevator out of service.
(D) return the car to the lobby manually.

37. A special key is used to activate firefighter service. The key switch in the lobby will NOT

(A) open the doors.
(B) bring the elevators down to the lobby.
(C) put the system in regular operating mode.
(D) close the hoistway entrance to the car.

38. When a fire burns it gives off different types of dangerous products. They are called gases and particulate matter. There are many different dangerous gases in the products of combustion; however, the two most common are carbon monoxide (CO) and carbon dioxide (CO_2). Carbon monoxide is very dangerous to people and can cause death if they are exposed to large quantities for short periods or if they are exposed to small amounts for long periods of time. It would be most correct to say that

(A) CO is dangerous to people if they are exposed to large or small quantities.
(B) CO_2 is not dangerous in small quantities.
(C) particulate matter is not dangerous.
(D) controlled fires produce CO_2 only.

39. While fighting a fire near the ocean, firefighters did not use the salt water from the ocean. The *best* answer for using fresh water instead of salt water is that

(A) salt water is difficult to pump.
(B) fresh water is abundant.
(C) salt water can corrode the fire pumps.
(D) fresh water is a better extinguishing agent.

40. A canvas tarpaulin measures 6 feet by 9 feet. The largest circular area that can be covered completely by this tarpaulin has a diameter of

(A) 9 feet.
(B) 8 feet.
(C) 7 feet.
(D) 6 feet.

41. If the pistons of both pumps in the illustration below go up and down, which of the following statements is true?

(A) In pump 1, water will go out at *A*.
(B) In pump 1, water will go out at *B*.
(C) In pump 2, water will go out at *C*.
(D) In pump 2, water will go out at *D*.

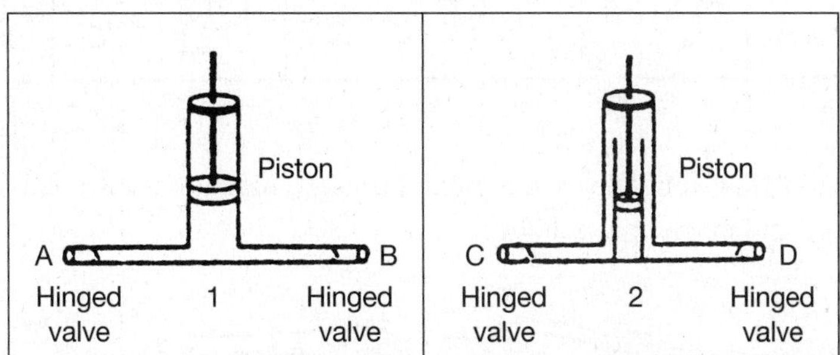

42. As a condition of employment, a firefighter has agreed not to talk about Fire Department activities or operations without first obtaining written approval from the Fire Department.

Evaluate the following: The firefighter rescued a child, who was left alone in a house. While leaving the scene, a woman who claimed to be the mother of the child asked the firefighter what happened to the child and where the child was now. The firefighter would not answer the woman's questions and referred her to the Chief. The firefighter's actions were

(A) correct because it's more important to follow the rules than to help the woman.
(B) incorrect because the mother should be told what happened to the child.
(C) correct because the firefighter did not know the woman to be the mother and the information about the child is sensitive.
(D) incorrect because, in this instance, the firefighter would be permitted to talk about his activities.

43. Choose the tool that best goes with the device in the first illustration.

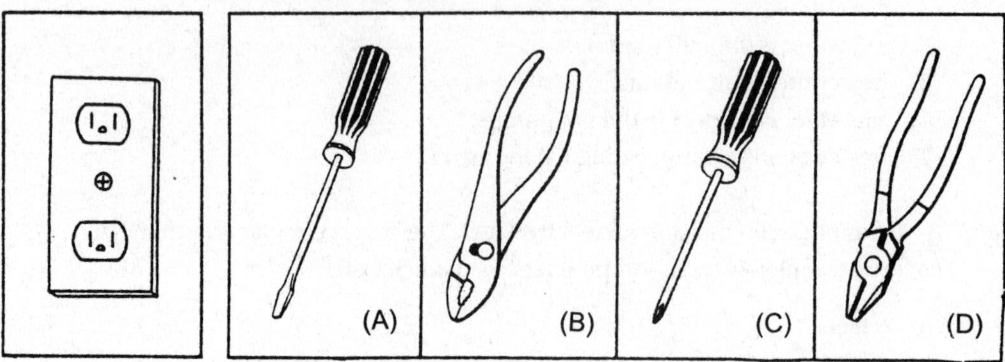

44. Choose the tool that best goes with the device in the first illustration.

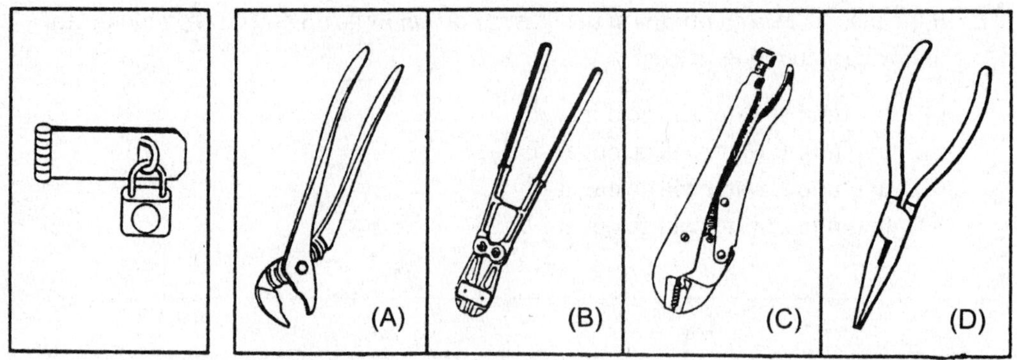

45. The best tool that would be used to hold the clamp together until a bolt and nut could be inserted and made up would be

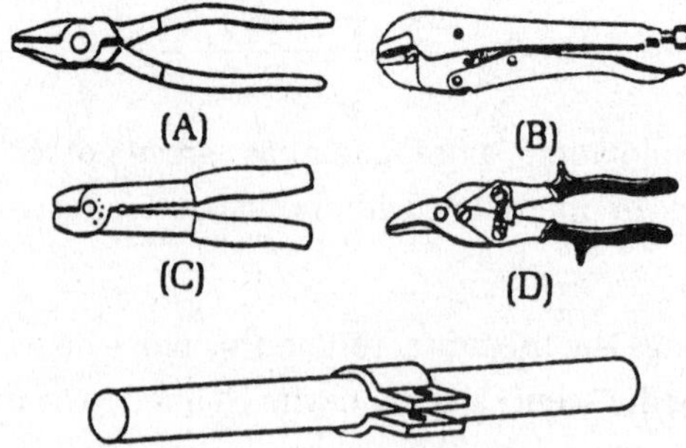

46. The use of power-driven tools can be dangerous. Which of the following would NOT be a safety technique you should observe?

(A) When possible, clamp down the object being worked on.
(B) Use only sharp, clean, well-cared-for tools.
(C) Approach the operator of the tool only from behind.
(D) Plan how you will proceed with the work before you turn the tool on.

Directions: Questions 47 and 48 test your ability to picture how people or objects look from different views or after certain changes have been made in their shape or appearance. In each case, you are to study the picture and then choose the correct answer from one of the four drawings that follow.

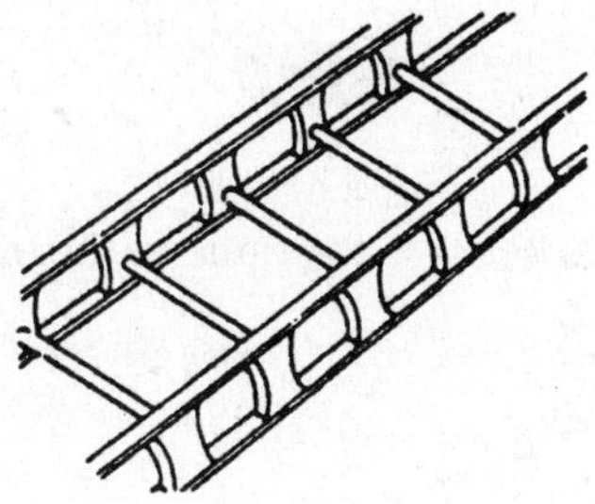

47. Which of the four ladders below is the same as the one above?

(A)

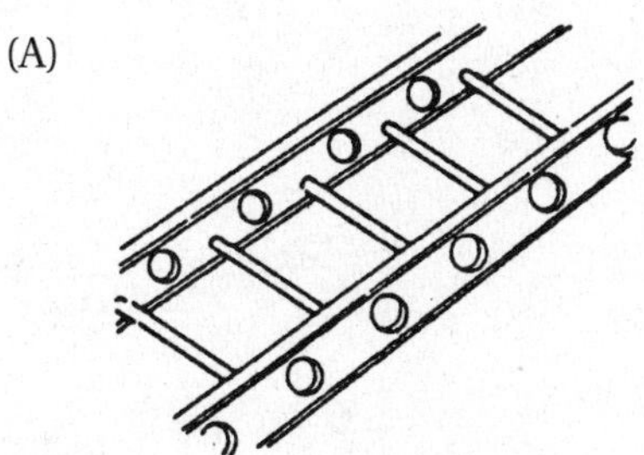

(B)

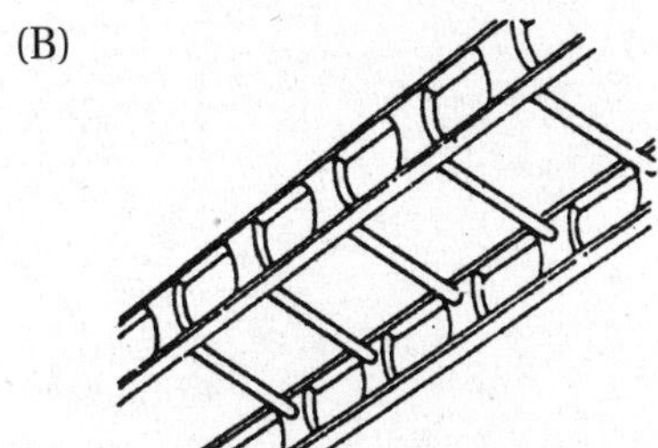

(C)

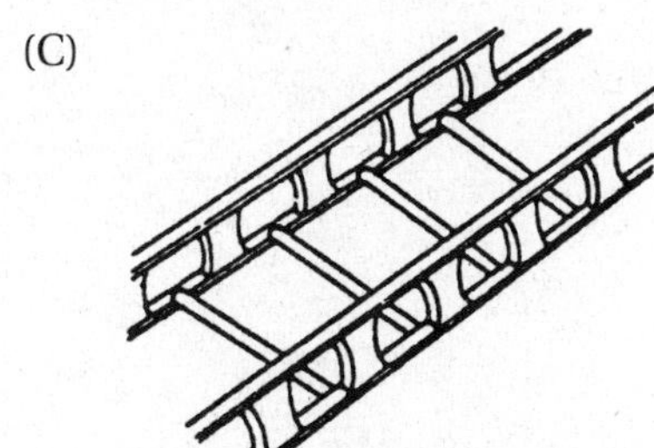

(D)

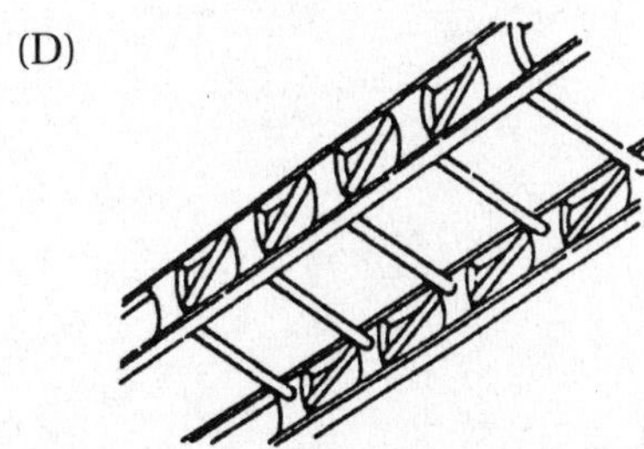

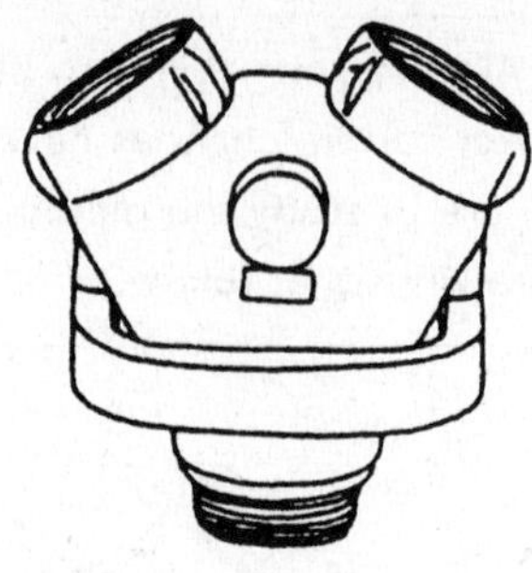

48. Which of the four couplings below is the same as the one above?

(A)

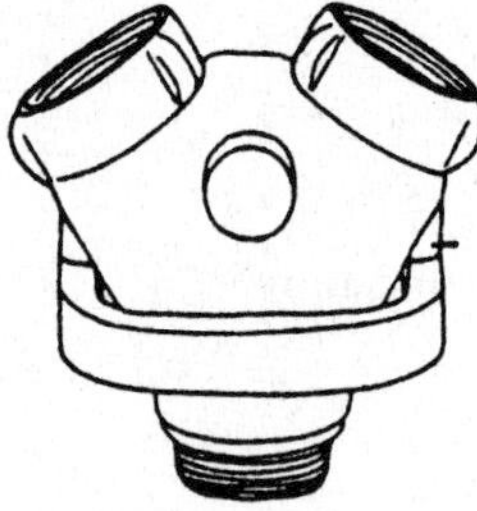

(B)

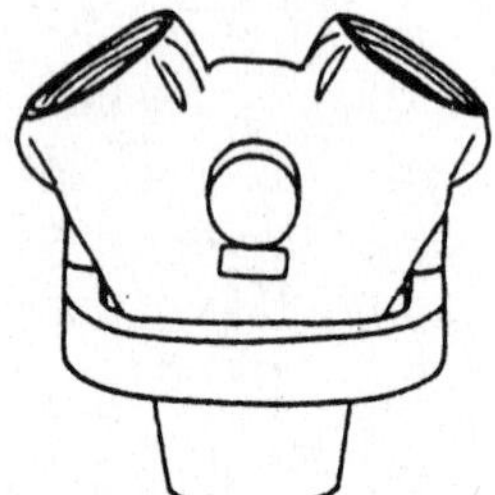

(C)

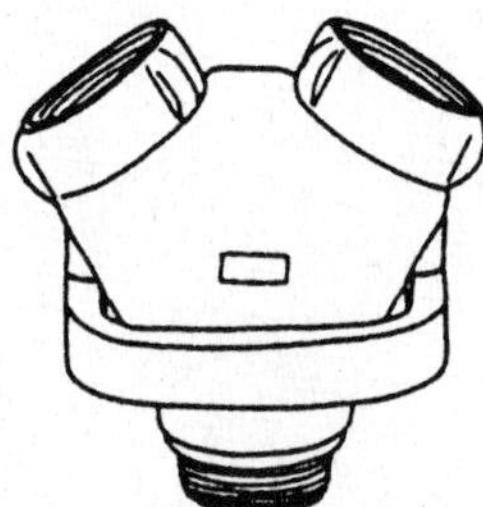

(D)

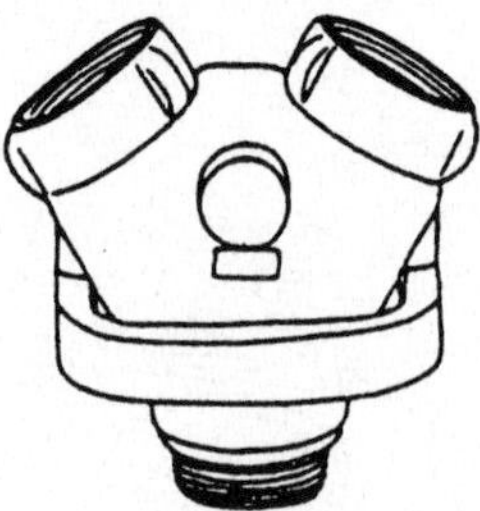

49. After a recent fire, firefighters were distressed to hear that the occupants were irate and complaining that "the firefighters took too long to put the fire out, and had they run into the house like they are supposed to, there would not have been any damage." It would be best to

(A) tell the occupant, "Next time you put the fire out."
(B) try to explain to the occupant why you had to do what you did.
(C) walk away and not say or do anything.
(D) tell the Chief what you heard and ask him to discuss it with the occupant.

50. When your company arrives at a house fire, they find it filled with heavy smoke. The owner of the house tells you that all his family is out and safe. The fire is in the basement in the heating unit and smoke is coming out of everywhere in the house. Your fellow firefighters all begin working, but one is doing something that could be dangerous. What is the potentially dangerous activity?

(A) Smith is having trouble hooking up the hose to the water outlet.
(B) Johnson is breaking the windows in the front.
(C) Abett is pulling a 1¾-inch hose line.
(D) Esiner is entering the house without his mask.

STOP **IF THERE IS STILL TIME REMAINING, you may review your answers.**

ANSWER KEY AND EXPLANATIONS

Answer Key

1. **(C)**	11. **(B)**	21. **(D)**	31. **(C)**	41. **(B)**
2. **(C)**	12. **(A)**	22. **(C)**	32. **(A)**	42. **(C)**
3. **(C)**	13. **(B)**	23. **(A)**	33. **(D)**	43. **(C)**
4. **(A)**	14. **(C)**	24. **(C)**	34. **(C)**	44. **(B)**
5. **(B)**	15. **(B)**	25. **(B)**	35. **(C)**	45. **(B)**
6. **(B)**	16. **(A)**	26. **(D)**	36. **(A)**	46. **(C)**
7. **(A)**	17. **(B)**	27. **(D)**	37. **(D)**	47. **(B)**
8. **(C)**	18. **(C)**	28. **(A)**	38. **(A)**	48. **(D)**
9. **(D)**	19. **(B)**	29. **(D)**	39. **(C)**	49. **(D)**
10. **(D)**	20. **(B)**	30. **(A)**	40. **(D)**	50. **(D)**

Answer Explanations

1. **(C)** Captain Soon is the officer in charge. This is found in the opening sentence. Choice A Rogers and choice B Garcia are instructors. Choice D Roache is the Chief.

2. **(C)** The length of the probationary period is found in the third paragraph. Choice A is incorrect; it refers to the time spent at the Fire Academy. Choice B is incorrect; it refers to the time you will spend in training—3 years or 156 weeks. Choice D is the time until you are eligible for an increase of vacation days.

3. **(C)** Recruit reporting time is 0800, which is 8 A.M.

4. **(A)** The recruit work week is five days, Monday through Friday. Near the end of the Fire Academy training, you will work several Saturday tours. Choice B is incorrect; this is only three days of work. If you selected this choice, it's possible you are rushing or not paying enough attention to the question-answering process. If this is accurate, you should go back and review the test-taking techniques in Chapter 4. Choice C is incorrect; you will be required to work some Saturdays. Choice D is incorrect; you will work only some Saturdays.

5. **(B)** Except is the key word here. You will not be asked to fight fires just like the regular shift would. If you are not sure of the answer, reread the paragraphs on pages 275 and 276.

6. **(B)** You will be assigned to a different unit in each of your first three years.

7. **(A)** Choice A is incorrect; you will get a 5 percent pay raise after the first year of service.

8. **(C)** The training period is 156 weeks or 3 years. Choice A is incorrect; it should read 25 years. Choice B is incorrect; you cannot participate in promotion exams until your training is complete. Thus, firefighters in training cannot take promotion examinations. Choice D is incorrect; full medical coverage begins after you complete your academy training.

9. **(D)** This statement can be found in the sixth paragraph. Choice A is incorrect; overtime pay is based on the hours worked, not on the kind of work done. Choice B is incor-

rect; this should be straight pay. Choice C is incorrect; this is "regular" work; it is at straight pay.

10. **(D)** Chief Roache identified this as your first lesson in teamwork. Choices A and B are incorrect; it is unlikely that you will remember *all* the people you shake hands with and even more unlikely that you will remember their names; however, you and your fellow recruits will create a new bond. Choice C is incorrect; this is one of the lessons. The next lesson starts after Captain Soon assigns you to it.

11. **(B)** The object is to get water, through a hose, from the hydrant to the foam house. You must use the nearest available hydrant with the most direct route. The hydrant at Spring Lane and Branley Ave. is the nearest available hydrant and the directions in Choice B are correct. Choice A is incorrect; this is not the nearest hydrant. Choice C is incorrect; this is not the most direct route. Choice D is incorrect; this is direct but does not take you to the siamese on the foam house; the siamese is outside the foam house on Railroad Ave.

12. **(A)** The passage tells you the raw material storage is in the north end of the warehouse. A look at the map shows that apparatus could be placed on Kellan Ave., Railroad Ave., and in the main yard. Choices B and D are incorrect; raw material is stored at the north end of the warehouse. Choice C is incorrect; the placement of the apparatus on Spring Lane would not be effective.

13. **(B)** When working with a map or floor plan, find the arrow that indicates north. If necessary, turn the page so north is at the top (pointing away from you), east is on your right side, south is pointing toward you, and west is on your left side. For this question you must find southwest—a direction directly between and equidistant from south and west. Choice A is incorrect; this would be in the west direction only. Choice C is incorrect; this would be south. Choice D is incorrect because it omits the first hazard, the fuel pumps.

14. **(C)** The sprinkler is designed to put water directly on the fire automatically. Of the four selections given to you, the best is to supply water to the system where the fire is. Choice A is incorrect; this may need to be done at some later time. However, upon arrival, the danger is in the manufacturing plant, and this is remote from the fuel filling site. Choices B and D are incorrect; these activities would be done after water was supplied to the manufacturing plant.

15. **(B)** This would be the most direct route and would put engine 1 in the best position to gain access to the site and fight the fire.

16. **(A)** The three-dimensional representation shows a U-shaped entrance with two doors, one picture window, and seven standard-size windows. Compare the floor plan layout with the three-dimensional representation. Choice A most accurately portrays the floor layout.

17. **(B)** Heat rises and in doing so preheats the areas above it. As the fire grows, so does the heat output.

18. **(C)** Chapter 2 explains knots commonly used in the fire service. It describes the sheepshank as a knot used to shorten a line or rope. A clove hitch would be used for hoisting

and lowering equipment. A rescue knot or a bowline on a bight would be used to lower victims to the ground. Never lash two ladders together, this is a dangerous practice. So Choices A, B, and D are incorrect.

19. **(B)** The manager should have the lock and chain removed at once, thus taking care of the immediate hazard. The firefighter would follow up by telephoning the fire department and notifying it of the extremely dangerous condition that had been found. Choice A—this action would activate the interior fire alarm bells and could cause distress to patrons in the theater. It would also result in the fire apparatus responding in an unnecessarily fast and hazardous manner. Choice C—the firefighter should stay at the theater until the lock and chain are removed or the local fire company arrives. Should a fire occur meanwhile, the firefighter could probably direct the people to safety. Choice D—this would not be adequate action on the part of the firefighter.

20. **(B)** This makes the best use of the skills of the two firefighters. The one who calls in the fire alarm will direct the arriving units rapidly to the fire, while the second firefighter makes the necessary notification in the apartment building. Choice A—since there are two priorities, both firefighters should not do the same thing. Choices C and D—the important function of alerting the occupants—is ignored.

21. **(D)** This information is in item 3 under "route taken to the roof." Choice A is incorrect; item 4 tells you this NEVER should be done. Choice B is incorrect; this is the most acceptable method. Choice C is incorrect; it is the second most acceptable method.

22. **(C)** This information is found in the last sentence of the first paragraph. Choices A and B are incorrect; these are methods for accomplishing Choice C. Choice D is incorrect; one of the roof person's duties is to act as a spotter and to locate any jumper.

23. **(A)** This information is found in the first sentence of the last paragraph. Choices B and C are incorrect; the officer in command does not need to be notified that you have completed your duties. Choice D is incorrect; this is one of the duties of the roof person and should be completed before notifying the company officer.

24. **(C)** This is found in item 1 under "When arriving at the roof."

25. **(B)** You will find this information in the fifth sentence. The destruction of evidence is not done with malicious intent or to cover up, but does occur during the process of fire extinguishment. Choice A is incorrect; arson investigators respond to determine the point of origin and to gather evidence. Choices C and D are incorrect; this may be true in real life, but the passage does not provide this information and you are told to use only the information in the passage.

26. **(D)** This is item 5 in the passage. You have been told that items 1 through 4 already have been complied with. Choice A is incorrect; this is done after the area has been roped off. Choice B is incorrect; there are actions that have not been done but should be while waiting for the power company's arrival. Choice C is incorrect; there is no need to do this. The cover is still on the manhole and the firefighters have determined no life hazard exists.

27. **(D)** This information is the central theme of the paragraph and is found in the second sentence. Choice A is incorrect; three firefighters can handle a 2½-inch line. However,

more than one 2½-inch line may be required to extinguish the fire. Choice B is incorrect; the needed fire flow is considered. Choice C is incorrect; the amount of water flowing from one hose line is not necessarily the amount of water required to put the fire out.

28. **(A)** This information is found in the beginning of the third paragraph. Choice B is incorrect; three firefighters are needed for this size line. Choices C and D are incorrect; the passage does not tell us how many firefighters are required for these activities.

29. **(D)** This information is found in the second paragraph. By knowing the amount of water required, we can quickly determine a minimum number of firefighters required. Choice A is incorrect; resource needs are determined *before* the fire. Choice B is incorrect; 250 is the fire flow for one 2½-inch hose line. Choice C is incorrect; the staffing calculation is simple, not the needed fire flow. We are not told in the passage how difficult it is.

30. **(A)** The second sentence says that the sign ". . . shall be posted in such a manner that it is easily read from the outside of the premises. . . ." Choice B—not all underground systems, only those storing gasoline, flammable liquids, and/or diesel oil for motor vehicles require signs. Choices C and D—although these ideas may be good, they are not mentioned in the passage and hence cannot be considered.

31. **(C)** The owner's address is not necessary and is not mentioned in the passage. Choices A, B, and D are all specifically required.

32. **(A)** At a one-story shopping complex, the occupants will not be found on the roof.

33. **(D)** This information is found in the sixth sentence of the passage.

34. **(C)** This information is found in the opening paragraph of the passage. You have been told the elevators are traveling to the upper floors. To use the elevators, you must recall them. You are also told the people are now safe two floors below the fire.

35. **(C)** This information is item 6. Choice A is incorrect; this would disable the special safety features. Choice B is incorrect; the button must be pushed until the door is open and stopped. Choice D is incorrect; there is no mention of a fire emergency release button in the reading. It is a plausible answer created by the test maker to distract you.

36. **(A)** This requires knowledge from two different parts of the passage. The last paragraph directs you to leave the car immediately; to do this you must push the door open button.

37. **(D)** You are looking for an incorrect action. Choices A, B, and C are correct actions as explained in the first paragraph of the passage. There is no mention of how the hoist doors are closed.

38. **(A)** This is found in the second sentence of the paragraph. Choice B is incorrect; it is dangerous. Choice C is incorrect; particulate matter is dangerous. Choice D is incorrect; the control of the fire is not related to the products of combustion.

39. **(C)** Salt water reacts with the metal in the pump and corrodes the fire pump. Choice A is incorrect; it is approximately the same as fresh water. Choice B is incorrect; salt

water is more abundant. Choice D is incorrect; they have approximately equal capacity to extinguish fires.

40. **(D)** The diameter of a circle is a straight line that passes through the center of the circle from one side to the other. Since the tarpaulin's smallest dimension is 6 feet, this is the largest circular area that can be covered.

41. **(B)** The hinge valves at points *A* and *B* are known as check valves. They are put into the pipe to restrict the flow of water to one direction only. On the top is the swinging check valve; below it is a projection (stop) that keeps the valve from swinging in the opposite direction. The actual flow of water is in the direction in which the check valve appears to be pointing. If the flow is reversed, the check valve will be forced back against the stop and will restrict the flow in that direction. When the piston in illustration 1 is pushed down, the water in the system is pushed against the check valve at point *A*, closing it, and against the check valve at point *B*, opening it. By raising the piston and reducing the pressure, a new supply of water will enter at point *A* and the water at point *B* will be prevented from returning into the pump. In illustration 2, on an upward stroke water will enter from points *C* and *D*, and on a downward stroke both valve *C* and valve *D* would close, preventing any discharge.

42. **(C)** This is correct for two reasons. One, it would be a violation of the firefighters' agreement with the Fire Department, and two, there is a possibility of a crime having been committed—leaving the children alone. The firefighter does not know the woman and has no proof the woman claiming to be the mother of the child is in fact the person she claims to be. Choice A is incorrect; the firefighter should attempt to help the woman; however, in this instance, the best help is to refer her to the Chief. Choice B is incorrect; because of the nature and seriousness of the fire, only the Incident Commander or his designated representative should release any information about the fire.

43. **(C)** The Phillips head screwdriver would be the most effective tool to remove the screw.

44. **(B)** The bolt cutter is the most effective tool for cutting the hasp or lock.

45. **(B)** This tool is vise grips. It can be used as a small, portable handheld vise. Choice A is a lineman's pliers; choice C, an electrician's multipurpose tool; choice D, duck-bill snips.

46. **(C)** Do not approach the operator from the rear. The operator may not see or hear you and may react in such a way as to cause an accident.

47. **(B)** When working with this type of question, try to eliminate the wrong choices first. After eliminating the choices, prove to yourself that the remaining choice is correct. Choice A has round holes in the beams of the ladder. Choice C has the rungs of the ladder attached to the cutout portion of the beams. Choice D shows an additional rod in the cutout of the beams. Choice B is the same construction as the illustration on the top of the page.

48. **(D)** See the first two sentences of Answer 47. Choice A lacks the small rectangle below the round object in the center of the siamese. (*Note:* The object portrayed is a portable siamese.) Choice B lacks the thread on the bottom of the siamese. Choice C lacks the round object above the rectangle in the center. Choice D is the same construction as the illustration on the left.

49. **(D)** The Chief will get someone experienced in handling these matters to speak to the person or give the person a chance to file a complaint and then have it properly investigated. Choice A is incorrect; this is a negative remark and would only make matters worse. Choice B is incorrect; the occupant is very upset at this moment and will be unlikely to accept what you will tell the occupants. Choice C is incorrect; doing nothing will confirm the occupant's belief that you were wrong. Some action should be taken.

50. **(D)** Entering the smoked-filled house alone and without a self-contained breathing mask is very dangerous. Choice A is not dangerous; the fact that Smith is having a problem is not necessarily dangerous. Choice B is not dangerous; it is a normal practice to ventilate windows. It would be preferred to open them; however, sometimes this is not possible from the outside, and they must be broken. Choice C is not dangerous; it is a routine task for firefighters.

ANSWER SHEET
Practice Exam Three

1. Ⓐ Ⓑ Ⓒ Ⓓ
2. Ⓐ Ⓑ Ⓒ Ⓓ
3. Ⓐ Ⓑ Ⓒ Ⓓ
4. Ⓐ Ⓑ Ⓒ Ⓓ
5. Ⓐ Ⓑ Ⓒ Ⓓ
6. Ⓐ Ⓑ Ⓒ Ⓓ
7. Ⓐ Ⓑ Ⓒ Ⓓ
8. Ⓐ Ⓑ Ⓒ Ⓓ
9. Ⓐ Ⓑ Ⓒ Ⓓ
10. Ⓐ Ⓑ Ⓒ Ⓓ
11. Ⓐ Ⓑ Ⓒ Ⓓ
12. Ⓐ Ⓑ Ⓒ Ⓓ
13. Ⓐ Ⓑ Ⓒ Ⓓ
14. Ⓐ Ⓑ Ⓒ Ⓓ
15. Ⓐ Ⓑ Ⓒ Ⓓ
16. Ⓐ Ⓑ Ⓒ Ⓓ
17. Ⓐ Ⓑ Ⓒ Ⓓ
18. Ⓐ Ⓑ Ⓒ Ⓓ
19. Ⓐ Ⓑ Ⓒ Ⓓ
20. Ⓐ Ⓑ Ⓒ Ⓓ
21. Ⓐ Ⓑ Ⓒ Ⓓ
22. Ⓐ Ⓑ Ⓒ Ⓓ
23. Ⓐ Ⓑ Ⓒ Ⓓ
24. Ⓐ Ⓑ Ⓒ Ⓓ
25. Ⓐ Ⓑ Ⓒ Ⓓ
26. Ⓐ Ⓑ Ⓒ Ⓓ
27. Ⓐ Ⓑ Ⓒ Ⓓ
28. Ⓐ Ⓑ Ⓒ Ⓓ
29. Ⓐ Ⓑ Ⓒ Ⓓ
30. Ⓐ Ⓑ Ⓒ Ⓓ
31. Ⓐ Ⓑ Ⓒ Ⓓ
32. Ⓐ Ⓑ Ⓒ Ⓓ
33. Ⓐ Ⓑ Ⓒ Ⓓ
34. Ⓐ Ⓑ Ⓒ Ⓓ
35. Ⓐ Ⓑ Ⓒ Ⓓ
36. Ⓐ Ⓑ Ⓒ Ⓓ
37. Ⓐ Ⓑ Ⓒ Ⓓ
38. Ⓐ Ⓑ Ⓒ Ⓓ
39. Ⓐ Ⓑ Ⓒ Ⓓ
40. Ⓐ Ⓑ Ⓒ Ⓓ
41. Ⓐ Ⓑ Ⓒ Ⓓ
42. Ⓐ Ⓑ Ⓒ Ⓓ
43. Ⓐ Ⓑ Ⓒ Ⓓ
44. Ⓐ Ⓑ Ⓒ Ⓓ
45. Ⓐ Ⓑ Ⓒ Ⓓ
46. Ⓐ Ⓑ Ⓒ Ⓓ
47. Ⓐ Ⓑ Ⓒ Ⓓ
48. Ⓐ Ⓑ Ⓒ Ⓓ
49. Ⓐ Ⓑ Ⓒ Ⓓ
50. Ⓐ Ⓑ Ⓒ Ⓓ

PRACTICE EXAM THREE

Directions: You are given 5 minutes to study the following floor plan and to commit to memory as many details as you can. You are *not* permitted to make any written notes during the 5 minutes you are studying the illustration.

After 5 minutes, stop studying the illustration, turn the page, and answer the questions without referring to the illustration. The next time you are permitted to look at the illustration is when you have completed the test and are verifying your answers.

Now start your 5 minutes on a clock and begin.

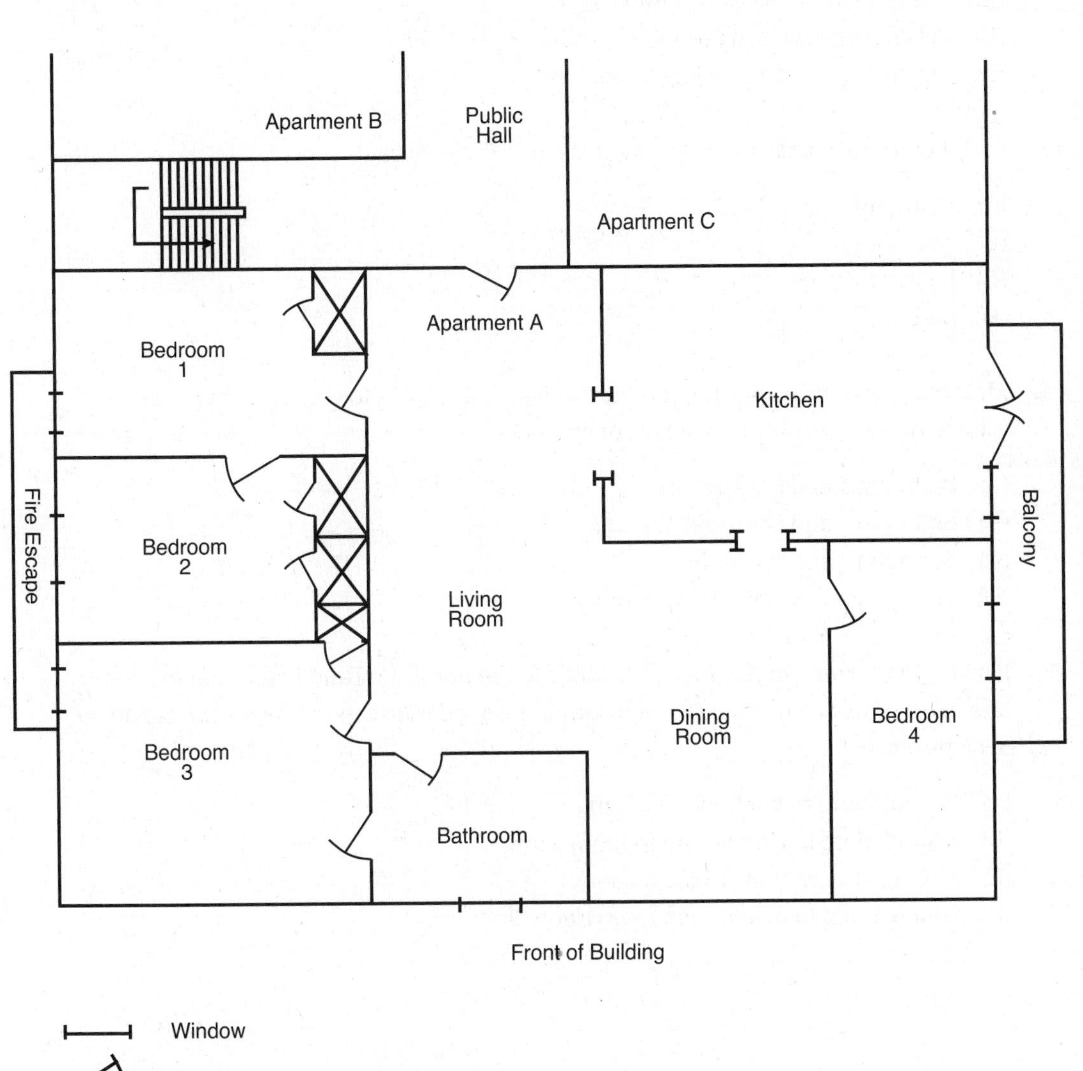

1. The occupants of apartment A could safely escape from the apartment and reach the street by how many means if no fire department ladders were used?

(A) 1
(B) 2
(C) 3
(D) 4

2. To escape from a fire in bedroom 2 of apartment A and exit via the public hall would require passing through

(A) bedroom 1 and the living room.
(B) bedroom 3 and the living room.
(C) the kitchen and living room.
(D) the dining room and living room.

3. Each bedroom in apartment A has at least one closet except

(A) bedroom 1.
(B) bedroom 2.
(C) bedroom 3.
(D) bedroom 4.

4. Most of the rooms in apartment A offer at least three ways to escape from them. Which rooms have only two means of escape?

(A) Bedroom 1 and the kitchen.
(B) Bedroom 2 and bedroom 4.
(C) Bedroom 3 and the bathroom.
(D) The living room and dining room.

5. If a fire was burning in the area of the door to the public hall and beginning to extend into bedroom 1 of apartment A, what would be the best escape route for the occupant of bedroom 4?

(A) Dining room to kitchen to balcony.
(B) Dining room to living room to bathroom.
(C) Through the window to the balcony.
(D) Dining room to living room to bedroom 3.

6. From which room in apartment A are there two ways to get directly to the outside air?

(A) Bedroom 3.
(B) The bathroom.
(C) Bedroom 4.
(D) The kitchen.

7. From which window of apartment A would it be possible for the fire department to make a rescue by using an aerial ladder?

(A) Bedroom 4.
(B) Dining room.
(C) Bathroom.
(D) Bedroom 3.

8. In a very heavy smoke condition the most difficult room in apartment A for firefighters to search and then escape from safely would be

(A) the bathroom because it is farthest from the entrance door.
(B) bedroom 4 because it is the farthest from the entrance door.
(C) bedroom 2 because it is the most complex.
(D) the kitchen because it is wide open.

9. According to the diagram of apartment A, what is the total number of windows in the apartment?

(A) 2
(B) 4
(C) 6
(D) 8

10. According to the diagram of apartment A, how many doors lead into or out of a room?

(A) 5
(B) 6
(C) 7
(D) 8

Directions: Answer questions 11 through 15 using only the information in the following passage.

Dispensing Flammable Liquids

The inherent hazards of flammable liquids are greatest when transferring such liquids from one container to another. Heavy vapors can travel considerable distances to sources of ignition. The following precautions should be taken to ensure maximum safety when refueling the fire apparatus.

1. Prior to refueling, assure the following:
   - (A) Allow no visitors in quarters.
   - (B) Permit no smoking.
   - (C) Safeguard against all sources of ignition, that is,
     - (1) apparatus ignition system
     - (2) battery chargers
     - (3) exposed battery terminals
     - (4) mobile radios
   - (D) Close kitchen and cellar doors if present. Doors and windows on apparatus floor can provide proper ventilation.
2. Whenever possible, transfer fuel from storage directly to vehicle tank.
3. When necessary in lieu of above, use only safety-type cans and observe the following precautions:
   - (A) Avoid overfill or spillage.
   - (B) Never use a device to hold open the spring-loaded cap.
4. Immediately flush away spills with copious amounts of water. Avoid flushing spills into sewer systems. Consideration should also be given, when feasible, to using sand to dike and cover a spill or other appropriate measures.
5. Maintain contact between fuel tank and nozzle, just prior to and during refueling operation. This method of grounding will prevent static sparks.
6. Maintain hose, nozzles, and safety cans in proper condition. Replace as necessary. Mark unserviceable safety cans appropriately and remove them from quarters.
7. Keep suitable extinguishers readily available.

11. Flammable liquids are most dangerous

    (A) when being created.
    (B) when being used.
    (C) when being transferred.
    (D) when being stored.

12. Which of the following would NOT be a viable precaution to take when handling flammable liquids?

    (A) Prevent visitors from entering the refueling area.
    (B) Prohibit smoking in the refueling area.
    (C) When possible, use a safety can to transfer fuel from storage to the vehicle tank.
    (D) Keep appropriate portable fire extinguishers available.

13. When transferring gasoline from a gasoline pump to the fire apparatus tank, the nozzle should be kept inside the tank and in contact with the fill pipe. The main reason for this procedure is

    (A) to prevent the loss of flammable fuel.
    (B) to activate the automatic nozzle shut-off.
    (C) to prevent the nozzle from coming out.
    (D) to prevent static electric sparks.

14. When using a 5-gallon safety can to refuel a fire apparatus, all of the following precautions shall be adhered to EXCEPT

    (A) keeping all doors and windows open.
    (B) avoiding overfill or spillage.
    (C) not using a tool to prop open the spring-loaded cap.
    (D) not permitting any smoking.

15. With respect to the dispensing of flammable liquids, it is correct to state that

    (A) the battery charger may be left plugged in.
    (B) the fire apparatus radio should be turned down.
    (C) spills should be flushed with large quantities of water.
    (D) water should be flushed into the sewer.

Directions: Answer questions 16 through 18 using only the information in the following passage.

All firefighters should be aware of their responsibilities pertaining to fire station safety. Because supervision may not be available at all times, the individual has to accept the responsibility of safety awareness. This information is gained through training and experience. Unfortunately, in many cases the firefighters do not become safety conscious until they have a close call or a friend gets seriously hurt.

To have a good attitude toward safety, it is important to understand the reasons for safety rules. Although we may understand the safety rules, we may not fully appreciate them until they are vividly brought home; ideally this can be accomplished by citing incidents that have occurred in other departments. Concern by all will increase as firefighters become more involved in the safety program. Take charge of your own situation. Often you will be the only one who knows if you operate in an unsafe manner. Communicate with others to let them know of changes in their surroundings. If you must plug a battery charger into an engine, let the rest of the shift know so they will not trip on the wire.

By informing others of the situation, you can make your fire station work area safer. Taking corrective action soon after a situation has changed could save you time and problems later. If you see that someone spilled oil on the apparatus floor, clean it up right away; this will prevent an accident.

Knowing the station conditions and thinking ahead can be a sound way of eliminating problems later. For example, let's consider a condition where the alarm has just sounded and you are getting ready to run down the stairs to the apparatus. However, because you are unaware of the current conditions, you know several other firefighters are going to take the same route. So, you take an alternate route.

Station equipment, such as power saws, drills, and grinders, should be used properly and only with the correct safety devices in place.

16. Firefighting is a hazardous occupation and demands that the firefighter be very aware of the safety features that can and will reduce the chance of serious injury. A firefighter should *NOT*

    (A) wait to become safety conscious until a friend gets hurt.
    (B) be concerned about the department's safety program.
    (C) be thinking ahead and using good common sense to eliminate problems of the future.
    (D) communicate with others that the conditions have changed.

17. An example of a good safety attitude is expressed in which selection?

    (A) Searching the rear bedroom of a smoke-filled house alone because you are only going one room in and you can easily get out.
    (B) Sharpening the axe quickly on the grinder without eye protection because it takes only a couple of seconds.
    (C) Using only a small extension cord to plug in the battery charger, which is hooked up to the apparatus battery, so nobody will trip on it.
    (D) Using different stairs than the other firefighters when responding to an alarm.

18. All firefighters should be constantly aware of their own safety needs and accept the responsibility for implementing them because

    (A) they are supervised at all times.
    (B) it will eliminate problems later.
    (C) information can be gained only through experience.
    (D) we fully appreciate the value of safety.

Directions: Answer questions 19 through 22 using only the information in the following illustration. You may look at the illustration while answering these questions.

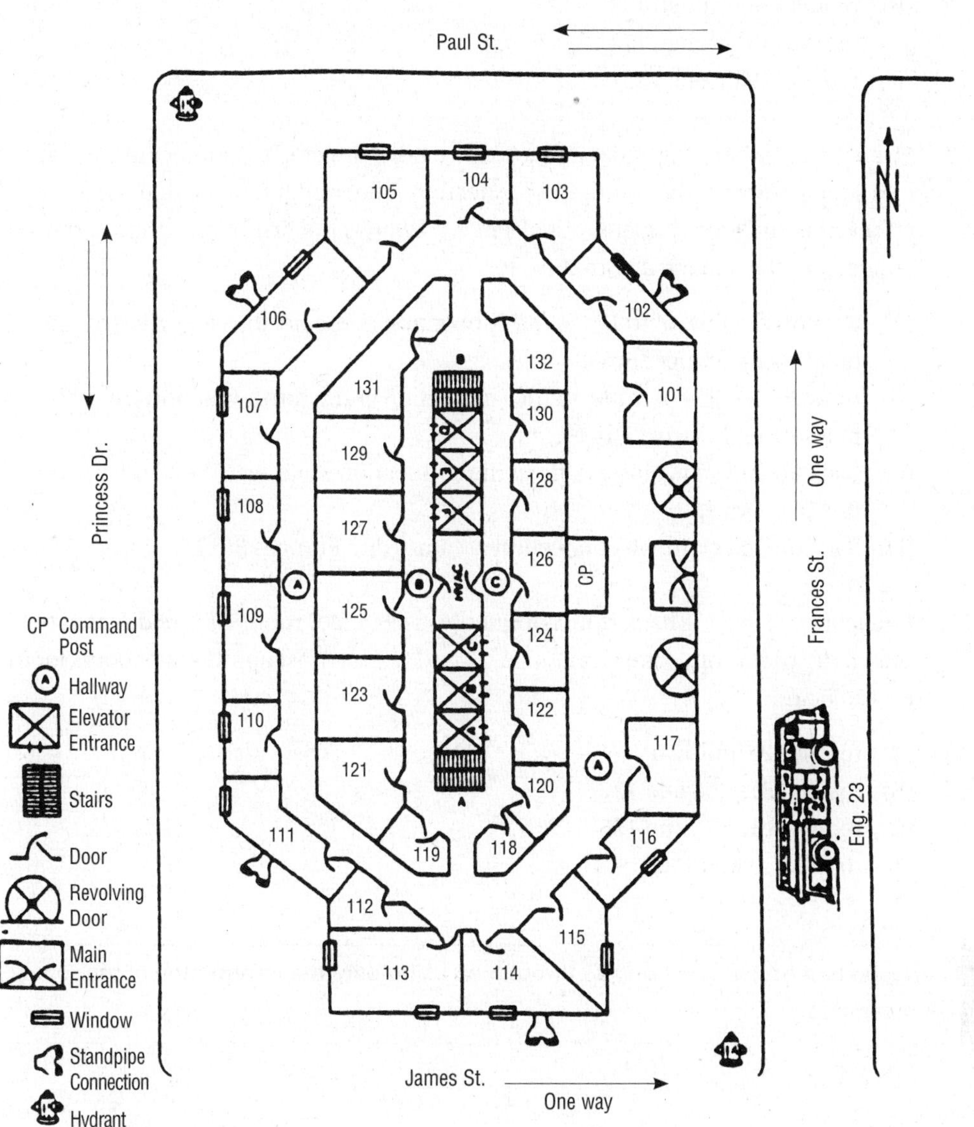

The illustration is of a typical floor of a high-rise building. The numbers designate office spaces, C.P. is the designation of the Command Post, and HVAC is the location of the Heating, Ventilation, and Air-conditioning Control Room.

19. Firefighters reporting into the command post are directed to a smoke condition in room 121. The most direct route to this location is

(A) north in hallway A, then southeast in hallway B.
(B) south in hallway A, then northeast in hallway C.
(C) south in hallway A, then northwest in hallway B.
(D) north in hallway A, then southwest in hallway B.

20. A firefighter directed to search all the offices with access from hallway B will be searching

    (A) rooms 101 through 105.
    (B) rooms 118 through 132.
    (C) rooms 117 through 112.
    (D) rooms 119 through 131.

21. Firefighters responding with engine 23 have been directed to connect to a hydrant and supply water to the standpipe connection. The firefighters see that the connection on James Street is out of service. What is the first hydrant and standpipe connection that engine 23 can drive to?

    (A) Go with the flow of traffic to the connection at the northeast portion of the building on Frances Street.
    (B) Go with the flow of traffic to the connection at the northwest portion of the building on Princess Drive.
    (C) Back up and go against traffic to the connection at James Street and Princess Drive.
    (D) Back up and go to the connection at James and Frances Streets.

22. Firefighters reporting back from conducting a search of room 106 are directed to search the rooms opposite elevators A, B, and C. The most appropriate rooms for them to search are

    (A) rooms 122 and 124.
    (B) rooms 131, 129, and 127.
    (C) rooms 121, 123, and 125.
    (D) rooms 118 and 120.

Directions: Answer questions 23 through 26 using only the information in the following passage.

Fire Detection

The purpose of detection is twofold: It can reduce life loss and it can reduce property loss. Where human lives are at risk, time becomes an important factor. Time is needed to alert the occupants and time is needed for them to reach an area of refuge. Throughout this time period it is essential that an escape route be passable. Where the risk to life is minimal and property loss reduction is the consideration, longer detection times are often tolerated for the sake of minimizing needless alarms. Often the sprinkler system with its water flow alarm doubles as the detection system. Sprinkler systems as presently used are often slow to respond to smoldering fires—those which produce large quantities of toxic products.

23. Sprinkler systems are used to control and extinguish fires. Another use of the sprinkler system is to

(A) act as a fire detection system.
(B) maintain the escape route in passable condition.
(C) reduce the production of toxic chemicals.
(D) limit the flow of water to needless areas of the occupancy.

24. The passage places great emphasis on time. It would be LEAST correct to say that

(A) time becomes important when human life is at stake.
(B) where risk to life is minimal, less time for fire detection is tolerated.
(C) time is needed to alert the occupants.
(D) reaching the area of refuge takes time.

25. The purpose of fire detection is

(A) threefold.
(B) to report a fire to the fire department.
(C) to find and extinguish fires.
(D) to reduce property damage and loss of life.

26. The passage says that sprinkler systems

(A) do not react quickly to smoldering fires.
(B) produce large quantities of toxic products.
(C) will not extinguish large, smoldering fires.
(D) are not presently in use.

Directions: Answer question 27 using only the information in the following passage.

Building and fire prevention laws are designed to ensure life safety in buildings. High-rise office buildings require that doors leading to exits must not be locked. The exceptions are as follows:

1. Doors that lead from the stairs to the street and open directly out to the street may be locked on the street side but must be openable from inside.
2. If the building is less than 100 feet in height, then all doors in a stairway may be locked to prevent access onto a floor.
3. If the building is 200 feet or more in height, then doors on every fourth floor must be openable from the stairs side. All other doors may be locked.
4. In case of fire, all doors leading from any floor onto the stairs must be openable.

27. Exit doors in stairways of high-rise buildings that are less than 100 feet in height may be locked

(A) on all floors, including the street level.
(B) on all floors above the street floor.
(C) on all floors except the fourth floor.
(D) on all floors except the roof.

Directions: Answer questions 28 through 33 using the information provided.

28. During a serious fire a firefighter searching an apartment house is confronted by a large and apparently ferocious dog preventing access to the apartment above the fire. The most appropriate action for this firefighter to take is to

(A) hold the dog at bay with an axe and yell into the apartment, "Is anybody there?"
(B) try to find the dog's owner.
(C) report back to his officer that the apartment cannot be searched because of the dog.
(D) get help from another firefighter to control the dog and then enter and search the apartment.

29. At a fire in a large multi-apartment house the officer instructed one of the firefighters to shut off the gas supply to the entire building. After the fire a resident of an apartment three floors below the fire requested that the gas be turned back on. The firefighter was instructed by the officer not to comply with this request. The best reason for this is:

(A) the pilot lights in unoccupied apartments are out and gas will accumulate.
(B) firefighters are not taught how to turn the gas supply on.
(C) firefighters are permitted to turn the gas on only when requested to do so by the utility company.
(D) the fire is probably not under complete control, and the gas would present a hazard.

30. While directing a hose stream, a firefighter straddles a hose line. This action of the firefighter is

(A) safe, mainly because the firefighter will not be hit if the hose ruptures.
(B) unsafe, because the firefighter may become tangled in the hose if a fast escape is required.
(C) safe, because the firefighter has complete control of the hose and nozzle.
(D) unsafe because the firefighter may be hit if the hose line ruptures.

31. Every fire should be thoroughly investigated to determine how it started. The primary reason for finding out how the fire started is to

(A) evaluate the firefighting units.
(B) collect statistics on the number and types of fires.
(C) reduce the possibilities of future fires.
(D) prove that the fire was arson.

32. Ventilation is the opening of windows, doors, and the roof to allow superheated gases and smoke to escape and let clean air enter the building. This aids the firefighter in rescuing victims and quickly extinguishing most fires. Which of the following would not be a benefit of ventilation?

(A) It extinguishes the fire more quickly.
(B) It increases visibility to aid in rescuing.
(C) It causes less water damage.
(D) It decreases the amount of dangerous gases present.

33. A problem likely to be found in a hotel fire but not usually encountered in fires involving other types of residences, is

(A) obstructions in hallways and other passageways.
(B) large numbers of people in a small number of rooms.
(C) delay in the transmission of the fire alarm.
(D) the presence of many occupants who don't know the location of exits.

Directions: Answer questions 34 and 35 using only the information in the following passage.

A common problem for firefighters is the fact that, as the fire burns, it consumes the wood it is feeding on. This reduces the overall size of the structural member and weakens its ability to carry the weight being loaded on it. Even though steel is not easily consumed by building fires, it does expand and twist. When steel expands, it can push the walls out of alignment and may cause collapse. When steel twists, it may cause structural members resting on it to fall free and collapse. Concrete does not fail under most fire conditions, but it can spall (break away in small pieces) and can expose the steel reinforcing rods. If this happens, the steel will expand and separate from the concrete. Concrete relies on its bond with the steel to keep its strength. If the steel and the concrete separate, the chance of collapse is much greater.

34. During serious fires the wall may be pushed out by

(A) hot expanding gases created by the fire.
(B) the force of the hose streams hitting the wall.
(C) the heating of wooden beams, causing them to twist.
(D) the heating of steel beams, causing them to get larger.

35. Fires in buildings generally consume

(A) the brick facade.
(B) the wooden floor beams.
(C) the steel columns.
(D) the concrete block walls.

Directions: Answer questions 36 through 38 using only the information in the following passage.

A chute called a compactor shaft is often installed in multistory buildings. The compactor or refuse chute is an enclosed shaft inside the building, which transports the occupants' garbage from each floor of the building to the collection point, usually in the basement. Once in the basement, the refuse enters a compacting system where it's pressed tightly and packaged for removal by the janitor. The entire compactor system has many components: the compactor mechanism, the shaft, a fire protection system (usually a sprinkler system), a series of automatic self-closing doors, and a ventilation system.

36. A refuse collection system consists of all components EXCEPT the following:

(A) Sprinkler system.
(B) Ventilation system.
(C) Manual closing door system.
(D) Compactor system.

37. According to the passage, the refuse is pressed tightly

(A) by the occupant.
(B) at each floor.
(C) in the basement.
(D) after it is removed.

38. It would be most accurate to say that a compactor system

(A) has an exterior refuse chute.
(B) services only the needs of the building owner.
(C) transports the occupants' garbage to the basement.
(D) removes the rubbish from the building.

39. Tools can be divided into categories, such as cutting, safety, sports, and hard work. Which of these tools are used for cutting?

(A) Axe, circular saw, utility knife
(B) Cones, helmet, flashlight
(C) Gloves, face mask, net
(D) Shovel, pickaxe, sledgehammer

Directions: Questions 40 and 41 test your ability to picture how people or objects look from different views or after certain changes have been made in their shape or appearance. In each case, you are to study the picture and then choose the correct answer from one of the four drawings that follow.

40. On which of the four hoses below is the rope pattern the same as the one in the illustration above?

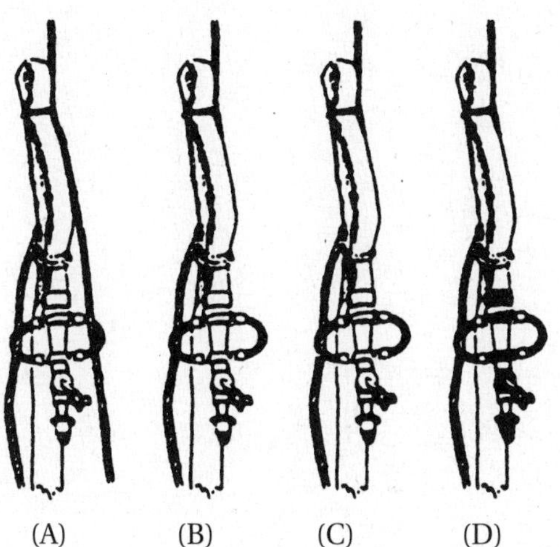

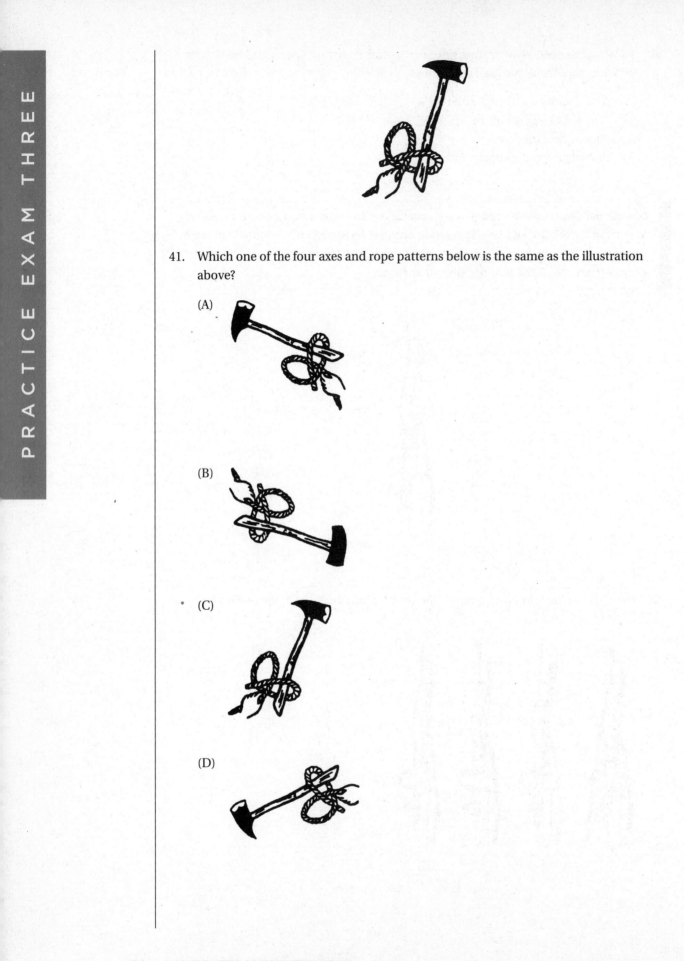

41. Which one of the four axes and rope patterns below is the same as the illustration above?

(A) 

(B) 

(C) 

(D) 

42. Some tools are known as all-purpose tools because they may be used for a great variety of purposes; others are called special-purpose tools because they are suitable only for a particular purpose. Generally, an all-purpose tool, as compared to a special tool for the same purpose, is

(A) cheaper.
(B) less efficient.
(C) safer to use.
(D) simpler to operate.

43. The device indicated in the illustration below would be used to

(A) force open center-closing elevator doors.
(B) open or close the operating valve on a fire hydrant.
(C) hold several wide boards together.
(D) jack up the bumper of an automobile.

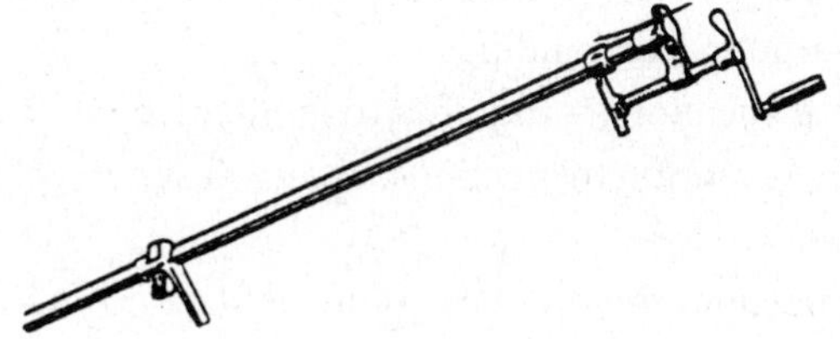

44. If sections of fire hose are never more than 50 feet long and never less than 40 feet long, how many sections are needed to ensure that, when connected together, they will reach at least 300 feet?

(A) 9
(B) 8
(C) 7
(D) 6

45. If the sliding shaft on gear *A* in the illustration below is pushed to the left, what will happen to drum *B*?

(A) It will turn in direction 1.
(B) It will turn in direction 2.
(C) It will move to the right and will not turn.
(D) It will move to the left and will not turn.

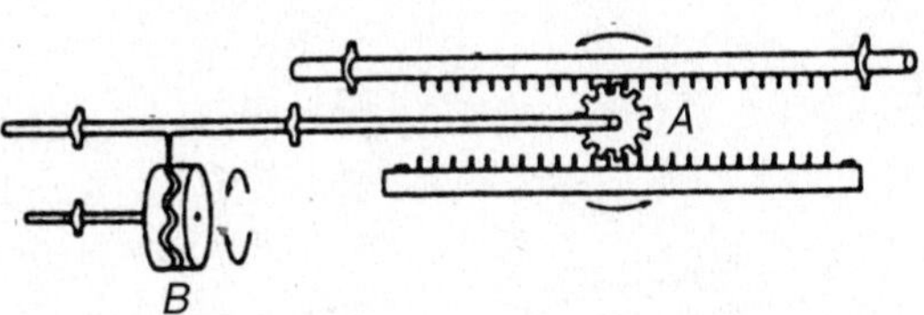

Directions: Questions 46 through 50 are an oral or listening part of the examination. They are intended to measure your ability to hear, understand, and apply information.

At the beginning of this examination, have someone READ the passage, slowly and carefully, to you. DO NOT READ THIS PASSAGE YOURSELF.

Answer questions 46 through 50 on the basis of the information found in the passage.

To the assistant: Please read the following passage aloud. Read slowly and distinctly. Once you start, read through to the end with only normal pauses between paragraphs and punctuation. Do not add additional emphasis or discuss the passage. When you have completed reading the passage, your part of this practice examination is complete. Thank you for your help.

At a recruit training session, the trainees are told they will be assigned to a building inspection team that will go into the field on Thursday. The lieutenant supervising the team is William Holt, a veteran fire officer. The team will work in the downtown area, and will be expected to visit a minimum of five buildings.

Participation in these inspections is required to familiarize the trainees with proper practices for conducting Fire Prevention Inspections. They will show typical fire hazards that may be found in each occupancy.

On the day of the inspection, the trainees are introduced to firefighter Bill Hartman and the other members of the team—John Grasso, George Carrol, and Ray Kelly. While en route downtown, Ray tells them they will start at the Tops Hotel and that this is a continuation of the inspection they had been working on yesterday. So far, three minor violations have been found: accumulation of rubbish in the rear, a nonfunctional exit light on the fourth floor, and a recently outdated permit for the storage of fuel oil.

During the inspection, a fellow trainee finds a locked exit door and says that "this is very serious" and calls for the "immediate issuing of a summons." You are asked to act as a witness, and the lieutenant orders the other trainee to fill out and serve the summons.

The next inspection takes place in a small restaurant that is well run and in proper order. The third occupancy inspected is a retail drugstore using its basement for the storage of its combustible goods. The inspection reveals that it has sprinklers throughout the basement. The lieutenant explains, "The requirement for a sprinkler system is a recent change in the building laws designed to improve fire safety throughout the city. The law also requires the owner to have several spare sprinkler heads stored at the control valve so a quick replacement can be made if a fire occurs." A further inspection finds no spare sprinkler heads on the premises.

46. The trainees were assigned to go out into the field and to participate in inspection activities on

(A) Monday.
(B) Tuesday.
(C) Wednesday.
(D) Thursday.

47. The officer in command of your inspection team was

(A) William Holt.
(B) Ray Kelly.
(C) John Grasso.
(D) Bill Hartman.

48. Which of the following occupancies was NOT inspected?

(A) hotel
(B) retail store
(C) cold storage warehouse
(D) restaurant

49. A summons was issued by

(A) you.
(B) a fellow trainee.
(C) the supervising lieutenant.
(D) you, a fellow trainee, and the lieutenant.

50. During the inspection of the drugstore, which of the following violations of law was found?

(A) An accumulation of rubbish.
(B) A locked exit.
(C) An out-of-date permit.
(D) Missing spare sprinkler heads.

STOP **IF THERE IS STILL TIME REMAINING, you may review your answers.**

ANSWER KEY AND EXPLANATIONS

Answer Key

1. **(D)**	11. **(C)**	21. **(B)**	31. **(C)**	41. **(D)**
2. **(A)**	12. **(C)**	22. **(A)**	32. **(C)**	42. **(B)**
3. **(D)**	13. **(D)**	23. **(A)**	33. **(D)**	43. **(C)**
4. **(B)**	14. **(A)**	24. **(B)**	34. **(D)**	44. **(B)**
5. **(D)**	15. **(C)**	25. **(D)**	35. **(B)**	45. **(D)**
6. **(D)**	16. **(A)**	26. **(A)**	36. **(C)**	46. **(D)**
7. **(C)**	17. **(D)**	27. **(B)**	37. **(C)**	47. **(A)**
8. **(C)**	18. **(B)**	28. **(D)**	38. **(A)**	48. **(C)**
9. **(C)**	19. **(C)**	29. **(A)**	39. **(A)**	49. **(B)**
10. **(D)**	20. **(D)**	30. **(D)**	40. **(D)**	50. **(D)**

Answer Explanations

1. **(D)** There are four ways to escape without using ladders: the interior public stairs and three bedroom windows to the fire escape. The balcony cannot be used to go from one level to another without the aid of a ladder.

2. **(A)** The door from bedroom 2 opens into bedroom 1 only. Therefore escape through the apartment door would require passing through bedroom 1 and the living room.

3. **(D)** Bedroom 4 has no closet. There are two closets in bedroom 2, and one closet in each of bedrooms 1 and 3.

4. **(B)** From bedroom 2 a person can go either out to the fire escape or into bedroom 1. From bedroom 4 a person can go into the dining room or out to the balcony and then in through the kitchen to the front door.

5. **(D)** This route would allow the occupants to go down the fire escape and to safety. Choices A and C result in stranding the occupant on the balcony to await help from the fire department. Choice B is incomplete and unwise. The occupant of bedroom 4 must still go through bedroom 3 to escape, and going via the bathroom would take extra time and effort.

6. **(D)** The kitchen has both a door and a window that open onto the balcony.

7. **(C)** This is the only room with a window that opens on the front of the building and is not obscured by the balcony or fire escape. Note that the dining room (B) does not have a window.

8. **(C)** To reach bedroom 2 requires going through one of two doors; searching involves the room and two closets. The possibility of becoming disoriented is high in this type of situation. Choices A and B (bathroom and bedroom 4) are incorrect because the distances are not excessive in this relatively small apartment. Choice D (the kitchen) would be relatively easy to search.

9. **(C)** There is one window in each of the four bedrooms, one in the bathroom, and one in the kitchen.

10. **(D)** The kitchen and each of the four bedrooms have one door apiece; there are also two doors in the bathroom and a door out to the public hall.

11. **(C)** The first sentence of the passage gives this information.

12. **(C)** Not "whenever possible," but *only* when direct transfer is not possible, should a portable can be used (see items 2 and 3 of the passage).

13. **(D)** See the last sentence of item 5. Placing the nozzle against the fill pipe grounds the pipe to the pump and reduces the chance of a static spark.

14. **(A)** Not all doors should be kept open; kitchen doors and cellar doors should be closed (item 1D) to reduce the chance of the vapors reaching the pilot light on the kitchen stove or the firehouse heating unit. The vapors of gasoline are heavier than air.

15. **(C)** "Large quantities" of water and "copious amounts" of water (see item 4) have the same meaning. Choice A—the battery charger should be disconnected from the apparatus and the outlet. Choice B—the radio should be turned off, not down. Choice D—spills should not be flushed into the sewer.

16. **(A)** This information is found in the last sentence of the first paragraph. Choices B, C, and D are incorrect; you *should* do these activities.

17. **(D)** This example is found in the fourth paragraph. Choice A is incorrect; because the house is smoke filled, you may not be able to see your way out, and because you are alone, you will have no one to help you. Choice B is incorrect; safety eye protection should always be worn when working with power tools. Choice C is incorrect; use the proper size cord and tell the other firefighters of the hazard.

18. **(B)** This is the central theme of the passage and is stated in the first sentence of paragraph four. Choice A is incorrect; it should read "not supervised." Choice C is incorrect; information can also be learned through education and training. Choice D is incorrect; as indicated in the last sentence of the first paragraph, we often do not appreciate safety until something goes wrong.

19. **(C)** This is the most direct route. Choices A and D are incorrect; they are significantly longer. Choice B takes the firefighter in the wrong direction.

20. **(D)** Odd-numbered rooms 119 through 131 open onto hallway B.

21. **(B)** Going with the flow of traffic is the best method; the nearest hydrant would be at the northwest corner of Princess Street.

22. **(A)** Rooms 122 and 124 are directly opposite Elevator A.

23. **(A)** The next to last sentence tells us that a sprinkler system often doubles as a detection system. Choice B—while this function is possible, the passage does not say so. The passage says that the escape route must be passable but does not tell us how to achieve this. Choice C—sprinkler systems do not control the production of chemicals; there is no mention of this in the passage. Choice D—the passage addresses the subject of needless alarms (sentence 5), but not needless water or needless areas of the occupancy.

24. **(B)** The fifth sentence states that "... longer detection times are tolerated ..." where there is minimal risk to life, not less time.

25. **(D)** This information is given in the first sentence. Choice A—the purpose is twofold, not threefold (sentence 1). Choice B—this is not indicated in the passage. Choice C—in a broad, general sense this is true, but it is not specifically supported by the passage, as is Choice A.

26. **(A)** See the last sentence. Choice B—smoldering fires, not sprinklers, can produce large quantities of toxic products (last sentence). Choice C—this is not indicated in the passage and is not correct; responses to smoldering fires are slow but do occur. Choice D—sprinkler systems are very much in use (note "as presently used" in the last sentence).

27. **(B)** Item 1 in the passage tells the reader that the street-level door must be openable from the inside. Item 2 tells the reader that in a building less than 100 feet in height, doors opening onto a floor of the building may be locked. This means that all floors above the street floor may be locked in buildings less than 100 feet high.

28. **(D)** The apartment immediately above the fire is one of the most seriously exposed areas and presents an extreme life hazard for the occupants. The firefighter must get into the apartment and search for overcome victims. Normally a dog can be controlled by one or more firefighters, thus allowing another firefighter to conduct the search. Choice A—yelling will not be effective if the victim is unable to hear the firefighter or has been overcome and cannot answer. Choice B—this will result in delay, and the dog's owner may meanwhile be overcome in the apartment. Choice C—this statement is untrue because, with the aid of one or more other firefighters, search is possible.

29. **(A)** When the main gas supply is shut down, all the gas to the building is turned off. Even though the valves on each gas stove may be shut off, there is normally a pilot light which is supposed to burn a small amount of gas continuously. If the pilot light is out and the gas goes on, an accumulation of unburned gas can develop and can be ignited and explode. Once the gas main is shut down, only the utility company should turn it back on. Choice B—firefighters are taught how the entire system functions. Choice C—firefighters are generally not permitted to turn on the gas supply. Choice D—this contradicts the stem of the question and is incorrect.

30. **(D)** The fire hose under pressure can whip around when the nozzle is opened or closed and will whip violently if the line bursts or is ruptured. This can cause and has caused many serious injuries. Straddling the line puts the firefighter in a position where an injury is almost a certainty. Choices A and C are incorrect—straddling the hose line is not safe. Choice B is correct in calling this practice unsafe but gives the wrong reason.

31. **(C)** By determining how fires started, unsafe practices and faulty equipment can be identified and such causes can be changed, corrected, or removed. Choice A—identifying the cause of a fire would in no way help to evaluate the actions of the firefighters. Choice B—statistics are a tool used to prove that the cause of the fire, once identified, is or is not a continuing problem. Choice D—the question refers to every fire, not just arsonous ones.

32. **(C)** Nothing in the paragraph is about water damage. Ventilation aids in quicker extinguishment of fires. Ventilation increases visibility because the smoke rises. It also releases the dangerous gases associated with a fire..

33. **(D)** A person checking into a hotel for a short stay may not take the time to locate an exit other than the one by which he entered the building. Choices A and C are problems common to all residence occupancies. Choice B is incorrect because hotels have large numbers of people but also have large numbers of rooms; also, the average hotel room is occupied by only one or two people.

34. **(D)** The passage tells us that when steel heats, it expands (gets larger) and can push out the walls. Choice A is incorrect; hot gases expand and do exert a pressure but they generally do not blow out walls. Choice C is incorrect; wooden beams are consumed by the fire.

35. **(B)** This is found in the beginning of the passage.

36. **(C)** The door system is an automatic self-closing one.

37. **(C)** Refuse is collected and compacted in the basement.

38. **(A)** The chute drops the refuse in the basement. Choice A is incorrect; the chute is on the interior. Choice B is incorrect; it serves the needs of the tenants and the owner. Choice D is incorrect; the compacted rubbish is removed by the janitor.

39. **(A)** These three tools are all used to cut.

40. **(D)** When working with this type of question, try to eliminate the wrong choices first. After eliminating the incorrect choices, prove to yourself that the remaining choice is correct. Choice A has an extra rope. Choices B and C have the hose butts and nozzle clear. (In the illustration on the left, these parts are blackened in.) Choice D is the same pattern as the illustration on the left.

41. **(D)** See the first two sentences of Answer 40. Choice A shows the rope behind the loop passing around the axe; the illustration at the top of the page shows it going through this loop. Choice B shows the outside of the rope loop. Choice C shows the rope passing over the loop beyond the axe; the illustration shows it passing through the loop. Choice D is the same as the illustration. *Hint:* Rotate the paper to get the object into the same viewing position.

42. **(B)** A multipurpose tool is often more convenient because it offers many different functions in one package. It replaces several special-purpose tools but is often made with a lesser degree of tolerance and hence is less efficient. Choice A—generally, all-purpose tools are more, not less, expensive than single-purpose tools. Choice C—because all-purpose tools are not specifically designed for a single, selected task, they must be adjusted to meet the needs of a particular application, thus making them more complicated to operate.

43. **(C)** The tool shown in illustration 43 is a pipe clamp, used to hold wide boards together.

44. **(B)** If we assume the worst case, each length is 40 feet. We divide the total length needed (300 feet) by a single length (40 feet) to get the number of lengths:

Total length ÷ Single length = Number of lengths

$$300 \text{ feet} \div 40 \text{ feet} = x$$
$$7.5 = x$$

Round to the next highest whole number: $x = 8$.

45. **(D)** As the shaft attached to gear *A* is moved, the projection from the sliding shaft into drum *B* will push the sliding shaft attached to drum *B* in the direction of the push, in this case to the left. Choices A and B are incorrect; the drum will turn only if the sliding shaft attached to it is turned. Choice C is incorrect because the drum will move in the direction of the push, *not* in the opposite direction.

46. **(D)** This information is found in the first sentence: "At a recruit training session, the trainees are told they will be assigned to a building inspection team that will go into the field on Thursday."

47. **(A)** The name of the officer is found in the second sentence: "The lieutenant supervising the team is William Holt, a veteran fire officer."

48. **(C)** During the inspection, you viewed a hotel, a small restaurant, and a (retail) drugstore. You did not inspect the storage warehouse. A cold storage warehouse is a building without heat, used exclusively for the long-term storage of people's goods.

49. **(B)** This information is found in the second sentence of the fourth paragraph: "You are asked to act as a witness, and the lieutenant orders the other trainee to fill out and serve the summons."

50. **(D)** This is explained in the last sentence of the passage: "A further inspection finds no spare sprinkler heads on the premises."

ANSWER SHEET
Practice Exam Four

1. Ⓐ Ⓑ Ⓒ Ⓓ	16. Ⓐ Ⓑ Ⓒ Ⓓ	31. Ⓐ Ⓑ Ⓒ Ⓓ	46. Ⓐ Ⓑ Ⓒ Ⓓ
2. Ⓐ Ⓑ Ⓒ Ⓓ	17. Ⓐ Ⓑ Ⓒ Ⓓ	32. Ⓐ Ⓑ Ⓒ Ⓓ	47. Ⓐ Ⓑ Ⓒ Ⓓ
3. Ⓐ Ⓑ Ⓒ Ⓓ	18. Ⓐ Ⓑ Ⓒ Ⓓ	33. Ⓐ Ⓑ Ⓒ Ⓓ	48. Ⓐ Ⓑ Ⓒ Ⓓ
4. Ⓐ Ⓑ Ⓒ Ⓓ	19. Ⓐ Ⓑ Ⓒ Ⓓ	34. Ⓐ Ⓑ Ⓒ Ⓓ	49. Ⓐ Ⓑ Ⓒ Ⓓ
5. Ⓐ Ⓑ Ⓒ Ⓓ	20. Ⓐ Ⓑ Ⓒ Ⓓ	35. Ⓐ Ⓑ Ⓒ Ⓓ	50. Ⓐ Ⓑ Ⓒ Ⓓ
6. Ⓐ Ⓑ Ⓒ Ⓓ	21. Ⓐ Ⓑ Ⓒ Ⓓ	36. Ⓐ Ⓑ Ⓒ Ⓓ	
7. Ⓐ Ⓑ Ⓒ Ⓓ	22. Ⓐ Ⓑ Ⓒ Ⓓ	37. Ⓐ Ⓑ Ⓒ Ⓓ	
8. Ⓐ Ⓑ Ⓒ Ⓓ	23. Ⓐ Ⓑ Ⓒ Ⓓ	38. Ⓐ Ⓑ Ⓒ Ⓓ	
9. Ⓐ Ⓑ Ⓒ Ⓓ	24. Ⓐ Ⓑ Ⓒ Ⓓ	39. Ⓐ Ⓑ Ⓒ Ⓓ	
10. Ⓐ Ⓑ Ⓒ Ⓓ	25. Ⓐ Ⓑ Ⓒ Ⓓ	40. Ⓐ Ⓑ Ⓒ Ⓓ	
11. Ⓐ Ⓑ Ⓒ Ⓓ	26. Ⓐ Ⓑ Ⓒ Ⓓ	41. Ⓐ Ⓑ Ⓒ Ⓓ	
12. Ⓐ Ⓑ Ⓒ Ⓓ	27. Ⓐ Ⓑ Ⓒ Ⓓ	42. Ⓐ Ⓑ Ⓒ Ⓓ	
13. Ⓐ Ⓑ Ⓒ Ⓓ	28. Ⓐ Ⓑ Ⓒ Ⓓ	43. Ⓐ Ⓑ Ⓒ Ⓓ	
14. Ⓐ Ⓑ Ⓒ Ⓓ	29. Ⓐ Ⓑ Ⓒ Ⓓ	44. Ⓐ Ⓑ Ⓒ Ⓓ	
15. Ⓐ Ⓑ Ⓒ Ⓓ	30. Ⓐ Ⓑ Ⓒ Ⓓ	45. Ⓐ Ⓑ Ⓒ Ⓓ	

PRACTICE EXAM FOUR

Directions: Questions 1 through 4 are an oral or listening part of the examination. They are intended to measure your ability to hear, understand, and apply information.

At the beginning of this examination have someone READ the passage, slowly and carefully, to you. DO NOT READ THIS PASSAGE YOURSELF.

Immediately after the reading, answer questions 1 through 4 on the basis of the information found in the passage.

To the assistant: Please read the following passage aloud. Read slowly and distinctly. Once you start, read through to the end with only normal pauses between paragraphs and punctuation. Do not add additional emphasis or discuss the passage. When you have completed reading the passage, your part of this practice examination is complete. Thank you for your help.

Firefighters respond to a wide range of fire problems. Some are small, requiring only a bucket of water, whereas others may require multiple master streams. Hose streams are classified as hand-held lines and master streams. Handheld hose lines are sized 1″, 1½″, 1¾″, 2″ and 2½″. A 2½″ hose delivers approximately 250 gallons of water per minute (GPM). Master streams deliver 300 GPM or more to the fire. Firefighters also have a system of classifying the order of magnitude of a fire. A light fire condition is one where one handheld line or less is required to extinguish the fire. A medium fire condition is when the use of two handheld lines will extinguish the fire and a heavy fire condition is when three or more handheld lines or a master stream and any combination of handheld lines is needed to extinguish the fire. Handheld lines flowing more than 180 GPM should have no less than two firefighters operating them.

1. Two firefighters are required on hose lines when

   (A) flowing more than 180 gallons per minute.
   (B) flowing water.
   (C) they are handheld lines.
   (D) they are master streams.

2. A master stream is one where more than __________ gallons are being delivered to the fire.

   (A) 200
   (B) 250
   (C) 300
   (D) 350

PRACTICE EXAM FOUR

3. What is considered a medium fire condition?

   (A) 1¾″ hose line is put into operation.
   (B) Two 1¾″ hose lines are put into operation.
   (C) Master stream is put into operation.
   (D) Hose line requiring two firefighters is put into operation.

4. According to the information presented in the reading, firefighters respond to

   (A) master stream fires.
   (B) a wide range of fire problems.
   (C) automobile accidents.
   (D) water leaks flowing more than 180 GPM.

Directions: You are given 5 minutes to study the following floor plan and to commit to memory as many details as you can. You are not permitted to make any written notes during the 5 minutes you are studying the illustration.

After 5 minutes, stop studying the illustration, cover it, and answer the questions without referring to the illustration. The next time you are permitted to look at the illustration is when you have completed the test and are verifying your answers.

Now start your 5 minutes on a clock and begin.

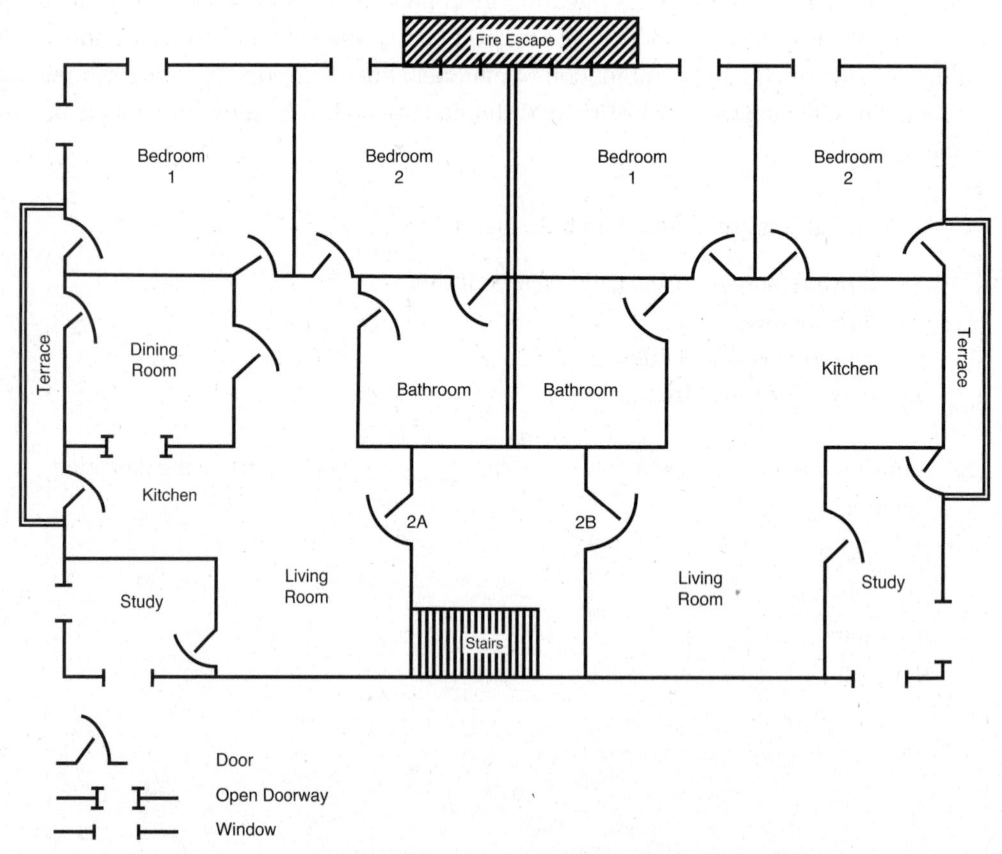

5. In apartment 2B, which room is farthest from the fire escape?

(A) Bedroom 2.
(B) Living room.
(C) Study.
(D) Foyer.

6. Which room has two doors?

(A) Kitchen in apartment 2A.
(B) Bathroom in apartment 2B.
(C) Bedroom 2 in apartment 2B.
(D) Bedroom 1 in apartment 2B.

7. Which room of apartment 2A can firefighters reach directly from the fire escape?

(A) Bedroom 2.
(B) Bedroom 1.
(C) Dining room.
(D) Study.

8. Which room does not have egress to the exterior?

(A) Living room.
(B) Study in apartment 2B.
(C) Bedroom 1 in apartment 2A.
(D) Bedroom 2 in apartment 2B.

9. A firefighter leaving the bathroom in apartment 2B would be in

(A) the dining room.
(B) bedroom 2.
(C) the kitchen.
(D) bedroom 1.

10. Firefighters on the terrace of apartment 2A could not directly enter the

(A) bedroom 1 in apartment 2A.
(B) study in apartment 2A.
(C) kitchen in apartment 2A.
(D) dining room in apartment 2A.

11. Which room has at least one window on two sides of the building?

(A) Living room of apartment 2B.
(B) Bedroom 2 of apartment 2A.
(C) Bedroom 1 of apartment 2B.
(D) Study of apartment 2B.

Directions: Answer questions 12 and 13 using only the information in the following passage.

The "wye" and "siamese" are often confused by the recruit. The wye is a device used to divide a hose stream into two or more streams. The water flows into the large single opening and out two or three smaller openings. The siamese is a tool used by firefighters to collect water from a number of smaller streams into a larger stream. Wyes are often gated to allow the control of the flow of water through each of the smaller outlets. The siamese is fitted with a check valve to prevent the water from flowing out of the system and back into the smaller hose. A siamese will be found on a sprinkler and a standpipe system.

12. To reduce a hose line from 2½ inches to 1½ inch a firefighter could use a

    (A) gated wye.
    (B) gated siamese.
    (C) standpipe wye.
    (D) standpipe siamese.

13. A "check valve" will be found on a

    (A) standpipe siamese.
    (B) standpipe wye.
    (C) standpipe outlet.
    (D) standpipe hose line.

14. In any fire, destruction is present in varying degrees. In addition to the destruction caused directly by the fire, there is also destruction caused in fighting the fire. If the sum of destruction to a building by fire and firefighters is greater for one method of combating the fire than another, the method causing the lower level of destruction should be employed.

    According to this passage, which of the following statements is correct?

    (A) Firefighting methods are responsible for the major destruction in most fires.
    (B) Unavoidable damage by firefighters should be ignored when choosing a firefighting method.
    (C) The aim when choosing a method of attack is to find the one that will cause the least amount of total damage.
    (D) Ways of fighting fires that are not dangerous to firefighters should be chosen.

15. Spray nozzles use considerably less water than straight-stream nozzles to achieve the same results. They are well suited, therefore, for use in situations where the water supply is limited.

According to this passage, spray nozzles

(A) should be used more often than straight-stream nozzles.
(B) achieve better results than straight-stream nozzles.
(C) are not effective when the water supply is large.
(D) can be used where only a small supply of water is available.

16. Fires cannot be fought entirely by rules or set procedures. The successful firefighter studies past fires and applies what he learns to future firefighting action.

According to the above paragraph, which of the following is correct?

(A) Little can be learned about firefighting by studying rules and procedures.
(B) The most successful firefighter is the one with the most fire fighting experience.
(C) Studying past fires helps solve problems that may be met in future fires.
(D) Fires are successfully fought only through experience, but Rules and Procedures are valuable if based on a study of past fires.

Directions: Answer questions 17 through 26 using only the information in the following passage.

Regulations Governing the Use and Storage of Ammunition for Powder-Actuated Tools in the Construction and Alteration of Buildings

1. The following regulations shall apply whether or not a permit for the storage of ammunition is required.
2. Powder-actuated tools using ammunition shall be of an approved type and so labeled.
3. Such tools shall not be used in an explosive atmosphere.
4. a. The main supply of ammunition shall be kept in a locked metal box interlined with ½-inch asbestos or other noncombustible insulating material.
   b. Storage and distribution of ammunition shall be supervised by a competent person who shall have the key to the storage box in his possession.
   c. The ammunition storage box shall be kept away from heat and shall not be stored in the same compartment or shanty in which compressed gases or flammable liquids are kept.
5. The compartment or shanty in which the locked ammunition box is stored shall bear a permanent sign with the words "DANGER—AMMUNITION" in 2-inch white letters on a red background.
6. There shall be provided one 2½-gallon water-type extinguisher or equivalent where ammunition is stored.
7. "No Smoking" signs shall be posted in areas where ammunition is stored.

8. a. Powder-actuated tools utilizing ammunition shall be used only by a person holding a Certificate of Fitness issued by the Fire Department upon submission of evidence that said person has satisfactorily completed a training program in the safe use of such equipment, acceptable to the Fire Department.

b. No powder-actuated tool utilizing ammunition shall be used unless the Certificate of Fitness holder establishes a safe zone behind the work area by the use of ½-inch steel backup plate and/or maintenance of an area clear of all people.

17. Ammunition for powder-activated tools shall be stored

(A) in a special box and in a compartment or shanty.
(B) in a special box at least 5 feet from heat or compressed gases.
(C) in a shanty with a black and white sign reading "DANGER—AMMUNITION."
(D) in a shanty if the special box is not locked.

18. The ammunition storage box must be

(A) made of steel.
(B) lined with asbestos.
(C) not more than ½ inch thick.
(D) equipped with a lock.

19. Regulations governing the use and storage of ammunition for powder-activated tools in the construction and alteration of buildings include all of the following EXCEPT

(A) a permit is always required to store ammunition.
(B) only approved and labeled equipment shall be used.
(C) these tools shall be used only in a nonexplosive atmosphere.
(D) the ammunition storage box shall be kept away from flammable liquids.

20. A Certificate of Fitness issued by the Fire Department is required to operate

(A) all tools.
(B) power-activated tools.
(C) pneumatic-activated tools.
(D) powder-activated tools utilizing ammunition.

21. The storage and distribution of ammunition for use with a powder-activated tool shall be supervised by

(A) a person with a Certificate of Fitness.
(B) a person with a special permit.
(C) a competent person.
(D) any available worker.

22. The shanty where the main supply of ammunition is stored should have all of the following EXCEPT

(A) "No Smoking" signs posted in the area.
(B) two buckets of sand to cover ammunition.
(C) a 2½-gallon water-type portable fire extinguisher.
(D) a "DANGER—AMMUNITION" sign.

23. When a powder-activated tool is going to be used,

(A) a competent person shall establish a safe zone in front of the work area.
(B) a Certificate of Fitness holder shall establish a safe zone in front of the work area.
(C) a competent person shall establish a safe zone behind the work area.
(D) a Certificate of Fitness holder shall establish a safe zone behind the work area.

24. It would be correct to say that a safe zone can be established by using a

(A) ½-inch metal backup plate.
(B) ½-inch asbestos backup plate.
(C) ½-inch P.V.C. (polyvinyl chloride) backup plate.
(D) ½-inch steel backup plate.

25. At a construction site where a powder-activated tool is going to be used, no appropriate backup plate is available. In this situation

(A) the tool may not be used.
(B) any metal backup plate may be used.
(C) no backup plate is required if the front of the work area is maintained clear of all people.
(D) no backup plate is required if the back of the work area is maintained clear of all people.

26. To obtain a Certificate of Fitness as a user of powder-activated tools, a person must

(A) be a high school graduate.
(B) pass a Fire Department examination on the operation of such tools.
(C) submit evidence that he has passed a training program approved by the Fire Department.
(D) attend the Fire Department training program and complete the course satisfactorily.

Directions: Answer questions 27 through 31 using only the information in the following passage.

Ensuring Safety at Intersections

The crossing of intersections, particularly against traffic controls, has consistently produced some of the most severe apparatus accidents.

Many fire departments require department vehicles to stop before entering an intersection against a red light, stop sign, or yield sign to assure that the right-of-way is being yielded by all intersection traffic.

Slowing at an intersection without stopping offers only enough time for a quick glance in each direction. Too often this glance does not identify the vehicle that will fail to yield the right-of-way. The correct procedure, when crossing an intersection against traffic controls, is as follows: (1) Stop. (2) See that the cross traffic is yielding. (3) Proceed.

27. A speeding fire apparatus on the way to a fire should NOT

    (A) stop before entering an intersection against a red light.
    (B) stop for a yield sign at an intersection.
    (C) stop at all intersections.
    (D) stop for a stop sign at an intersection.

28. Slowing at an intersection without stopping

    (A) is permissible if the light is about to change.
    (B) is not permitted.
    (C) doesn't allow sufficient time to avoid a collision.
    (D) is not necessary.

29. The correct procedure for a fire apparatus crossing an intersection against traffic controls includes all of the following EXCEPT

    (A) stop.
    (B) wait for the light to change.
    (C) see the traffic stop.
    (D) proceed when safe.

30. Many severe firefighting apparatus accidents occur because of

    (A) excessive speeding.
    (B) failure to obey department regulations.
    (C) crossing traffic against controls.
    (D) the carelessness of the driver.

31. As a firefighter instructing a class of new recruits, it would be correct for you to say that

(A) all fire departments require their vehicles to stop before entering an intersection.
(B) crossing intersections against traffic controls causes the most accidents.
(C) slowing at an intersection without stopping is sufficient to determine whether other traffic will yield the right-of-way.
(D) stop signs and yield signs at intersections should be treated just like red lights.

Directions: Answer questions 32 and 33 using only the information in the following passage.

When a person is severely injured, immediate care and aid are very important. The loss of body heat can send the person into shock. This is a strong possibility in cases involving serious injuries. An essential and often overlooked action that should be taken when encountering a seriously injured person is properly blanketing the person. Many times a blanket is put over the person; however, little thought is ever given to the loss of body heat from the back of the person. Proper protection for an injured person lying on the street and awaiting transportation to a hospital should be wrapping the individual with blankets. To accomplish this, with minimum movement of the person, take a blanket and place it lengthwise alongside the person. Tuck about two thirds of the blanket snugly against the person. Having completed this, gently roll the person about an eighth of a turn away from the blanket and push the tucked blanket as far under the person as possible. Now roll the person back onto the blanket and then pull the blanket out the other side and wrap it around the top of the body.

32. Arriving at the scene of an automobile accident, you find a seriously injured young woman lying on the street. She is not bleeding, but is in severe pain. It would be best if you put a blanket

(A) over her to keep her warm.
(B) under her to keep her warm.
(C) around her to keep her warm.
(D) around her injury to keep her warm.

33. The first thing to do after pushing the blanket under the person is to

(A) roll the person toward the blanket.
(B) roll the person away from the blanket.
(C) pull the blanket over the person.
(D) pull the blanket under the person.

Directions: Answer question 34 using only the information in the following passage.

When an obstructed airway emergency occurs, there is little time to take the proper actions. If the item caught in the throat cannot be dislodged rapidly, then the abdominal thrust should be used to save the person's life. The abdominal thrust is more commonly known as the Heimlich maneuver. To administer an abdominal thrust, stand behind the person and wrap your arms around the person in trouble. Make a fist and put the thumb side of the fist against the front of the upper body, slightly above the navel but well below the center of the chest bone. Now grasp your fist with the other hand and give a quick inward and upward pull or thrust. This may have to be repeated a number of times to dislodge the object.

34. To execute the Heimlich maneuver, you should

    (A) stand in back of the person, put your fist in the stomach area, and pull up and in quickly.
    (B) face the person, wrap your arms around the person, place your fist slightly above the navel, and thrust up and in rapidly.
    (C) place your fist on the chest cavity and with a quick inward and upward pull force the air out of the lungs to make the object pop out.
    (D) displace the object by giving several abdominal punches in quick succession in an upward and inward direction.

35. A person bitten by a stray dog should

    (A) clean the wound with baking soda if the skin is cut or torn.
    (B) tightly wrap the wound with ice and elevate the limb with the wound.
    (C) apply a hot compress for 10 minutes and raise the wound above the head.
    (D) be taken to see a doctor if the skin is cut or torn.

36. A city official questioned you about the order of arrival at the scene of a recent house fire. You explained that the unit assigned to arrive first arrived about 1 minute after the company assigned to arrive second, and the unit assigned to arrive third arrived third, 7 minutes after the box was transmitted. Of the following, it would be most accurate to say that the:

    (A) third unit arrived 5 minutes after the first unit.
    (B) second unit arrived in one minute.
    (C) first unit arrived as assigned.
    (D) first unit to arrive was the second assigned unit.

37. While doing a fire prevention inspection of a multiple dwelling you find the following:

a. Two boys in the basement cleaning parts for their outboard motor in a bucket filled with gasoline.
b. The owner cleaning the heating unit with a commercial degreaser.
c. A woman on the third floor putting rubbish into the compactor chute.
d. Several small children playing in a chain-link fenced-in area on the roof.

It would be most correct to tell the unit's officer that you found _____ unsafe conditions.

(A) 1
(B) 2
(C) 3
(D) 4

Directions: Answer question 38 using only the information in the following passage.

Good driving rules are essential for your personal safety and the safety of your passengers. As a defensive driver, you should aim high while steering by making repeated glances well ahead of your driving path. Get the big picture; scan the front, sides, and rear. Anticipate and prepare when something unusual is seen. Keep your eyes moving. Do not become fixed on one target. Leave yourself room. You should prepare to stop and have enough room to do it safely. Make sure others can see you; check to see that all the car lights are working and use them to signal when you turn or change lanes.

38. A newly appointed firefighter, you are being taught to drive the fire apparatus and are told to aim high. You should take this to mean

(A) make plans to become a certified apparatus operator.
(B) keep your eyes moving from front to rear and side to side when driving a fire apparatus.
(C) keep in the middle of the road when driving.
(D) glance far ahead down the road to see what is approaching.

Directions: Answer question 39 using only the information provided.

39. Firefighters have just arrived at the scene of a reported fire and are told by the occupants that there has been an explosion. An excited person tells the firefighters that the water pipes in her apartment have all been broken and water is ruining her rugs and furniture. Another person complains that the gas pipe to the meter has been damaged and is leaking. It can be seen that the roof has been damaged but does not look as if it will collapse. There are three people in the street and they report that 12 people live in the building but most of them were not home. Everyone who was in the building is accounted for. The most serious problem facing the firefighters now is

    (A) the destruction of the person's furniture and rugs.
    (B) accounting for the missing people.
    (C) shutting off the gas.
    (D) shoring up the roof.

Directions: Answer questions 40 and 41 using only the information in the following passage.

At times, a portable ladder is needed on an upper floor or on the roof of a building. To raise a portable ladder to the roof, firefighters perform the following in the order given.

1. A team of firefighters equipped with a hose roller, rope, and safety belts goes to the roof.
2. At the roof, a firefighter places the hose roller on the outer wall in a position between the line of windows where the ladder will be raised.
3. The rope is lowered to the street.
4. A firefighter in the street ties a bowline knot and passes it through the first two rungs above the center of the ladder. The ladder should be positioned below and in line with the destination point.
5. Sufficient rope should be drawn through the ladder to allow the loop of the bowline to be slipped over both beams at the butt. The rope is then drawn taut and the ladder turned over so the knot faces the ground.
6. A signal is given to the firefighters to haul up the ladder. The firefighter in the street holds the butt end of the beams to guide it into position.
7. While the ladder is being raised, the firefighter in the street acts as a safety and keeps people away from the area.
8. To lower a ladder use the procedure in Steps 5 and 6, except that the knot should face toward the sky. Once on the roof, the ladder can be used as a bridge between buildings, a safety cover over a large hole, or a tool to climb to higher heights.

40. While operating at a fire in a six-story factory, you are told to help a team of firefighters bring a 20-foot portable ladder up to the roof. Your position is in the street. You would be expected to perform all of the following EXCEPT

(A) tie a bowline knot.
(B) put on a safety belt.
(C) signal the roof to raise the ladder.
(D) keep people away.

41. At a fire, firefighters at the roof lower a rope to raise a portable ladder. The first action that should be taken by the firefighter in the street is to

(A) tie a knot in the rope.
(B) turn the ladder over.
(C) line the ladder up with the windows.
(D) place a ladder roller on the wall.

42. While speaking to a group of schoolchildren, you are asked what number they should dial in an emergency. The best answer is

(A) the number of the local fire station.
(B) the number for fire headquarters.
(C) 911 or (0), The operator.
(D) the international fire number, 1-800-GOT-FIRE.

43. After attending a stimulating talk on public relations, you decide to take an active role in this area. What is the first thing you should do?

(A) Contact the local newspaper's public relations office.
(B) Send a letter to organizations announcing your intent to speak.
(C) Ensure your own duties are conducted professionally and courteously.
(D) Inform others of your decision, and urge them to do the same.

44. If a piece of rope 100 feet long is cut so that one piece is $\frac{2}{3}$ as long as the other piece, the length of the longer piece must be

(A) 60 feet.
(B) $66\frac{2}{3}$ feet.
(C) 70 feet.
(D) 75 feet.

45. Assume that two identical insulated jugs are filled with equal quantities of water from a water tap. A block of ice is placed in one jug, and the same quantity of ice, chopped into small cubes, is placed in the other jug. The water in the jug containing the chopped ice, as compared with the water in the other jug, will be chilled

(A) faster and to a substantially lower temperature.
(B) faster and to approximately the same temperature.
(C) slower but to a substantially lower temperature.
(D) slower and to approximately the same temperature.

46. A woman tells you there is a store by her house that always keeps its exit doors locked and piles cardboard in front of these doors. What is your best action at this point?

(A) Refer her to the fire prevention bureau.
(B) Go to the market and check it out yourself.
(C) Contact the fire prevention bureau yourself.
(D) Tell the woman you will check it out the next time you inspect the building.

Directions: Answer questions 47 and 48 using only the information in the following passage.

The most significant improvements in personnel selection procedures can be expected from a program designed to obtain more precise statements of the requirements for a particular position, to select not just those applicants who are generally best, but those whose abilities and personal characteristics provide the closest fit to the specific job requirements.

47. The most desirable applicant for a position is

(A) the person who has all the necessary training, even though he or she lacks the personal characteristics required.
(B) the one whose abilities and personal characteristics are of the highest order.
(C) the person who has the greatest interest in obtaining the position.
(D) the one whose qualifications are most nearly the same as the job requirement.

48. Better personnel selection procedures will result from

(A) simplifying job descriptions.
(B) instituting better recruiting procedures.
(C) obtaining more detailed experience data from applicants.
(D) obtaining detailed statements of the training and skills required for various positions.

49. An elevator in a large apartment house became stuck between floors, and the fire department was called to remove the trapped passengers. Soon after arriving, the officer in command informed the passengers that the fire department was present and would start rescue operations immediately. The main reason for informing passengers of the firefighters' arrival was to reduce the chance that

(A) another agency would receive credit for the rescue.
(B) the fire department could be criticized for being slow in responding.
(C) the passengers would not cooperate with the rescuers.
(D) the passengers could become panic stricken if they did not know help was at hand.

50. Each year many children die in fires that they started by playing with matches. Which of the following measures would be *most* effective in preventing such tragedies?

(A) Warn children of the dangers involved.
(B) Punish parents who are found guilty of neglecting their children.
(C) Educate adults to keep matches out of the reach of children.
(D) Tell people to use only safety matches.

IF THERE IS STILL TIME REMAINING, you may review your answers.

ANSWER KEY AND EXPLANATIONS

Answer Key

1. **(A)**	11. **(D)**	21. **(C)**	31. **(D)**	41. **(A)**
2. **(C)**	12. **(A)**	22. **(B)**	32. **(C)**	42. **(C)**
3. **(B)**	13. **(A)**	23. **(D)**	33. **(A)**	43. **(C)**
4. **(B)**	14. **(C)**	24. **(D)**	34. **(A)**	44. **(A)**
5. **(C)**	15. **(D)**	25. **(D)**	35. **(D)**	45. **(B)**
6. **(C)**	16. **(C)**	26. **(C)**	36. **(D)**	46. **(C)**
7. **(A)**	17. **(A)**	27. **(C)**	37. **(A)**	47. **(D)**
8. **(A)**	18. **(D)**	28. **(C)**	38. **(D)**	48. **(D)**
9. **(C)**	19. **(A)**	29. **(B)**	39. **(C)**	49. **(D)**
10. **(B)**	20. **(D)**	30. **(C)**	40. **(B)**	50. **(C)**

Answer Explanations

1. **(A)** The last sentence in the passage tells us this information.

2. **(C)** The fifth sentence tells us a master stream delivers 300 GPM.

3. **(B)** This information is found in the eighth sentence of the passage.

4. **(B)** This information is found in the opening sentence of the passage. Choice A is incorrect; master streams may be used at fires but are not a reason for responding. Choice C is incorrect; even though firefighters may respond to automobile accidents, it is not discussed in the passage. The directions tell you to use only the information in the passage. Picking a choice that you know to be an accurate activity of firefighters but not part of the question is a common error and is sometimes called "fighting the question." You must follow the directions; they are a part of the examination process. Choice D is incorrect; this refers to the requirement for two firefighters on the hose line.

5. **(C)** To get from the fire escape to the study, a person would have to pass through bedroom 1, the kitchen, and the living room.

6. **(C)** Of the selections offered, only Choice C has two doors. Choice A is incorrect because the kitchen has a door and a doorway.

7. **(A)** In 2A, bedroom 2 is the only room directly accessible from the fire escape.

8. **(A)** The living room has an access to a hall and stairs, but no direct egress to the exterior.

9. **(C)** In 2B, the bathroom door opens directly into the kitchen space.

10. **(B)** In 2A, there are three doors from the terrace. They lead to the kitchen, dining room, and bedroom. To get to the study from the terrace, you must pass through the kitchen and the living room.

11. **(D)** Of the choices offered, only the study in apartment 2B has access to two sides of the building.

12. **(A)** Sentences two and five in the passage will lead you to this answer. Choices B and D are incorrect; a siamese is used to increase the flow. Choice C is incorrect; there is no mention of the use of a wye on a standpipe.

13. **(A)** The sixth sentence of the passage makes this statement. The check valve would be found on the input side of a device. Choices B, C, and D are discharge devices.

14. **(C)** This information can be found in the last sentence of the passage. Choice A—the destruction done by firefighters can *sometimes* be greater than that caused by the fire. The passage does not indicate that this is true *most* of the time; the numbers of times are not indicated for the two causes of destruction. Choice B—the method that causes the lowest level of destruction should be chosen (last sentence). Choice D—the passage does not address the question of danger to firefighters. The answer must be based on the information in the passage.

15. **(D)** See the second sentence of the passage. Choice A—the passage indicates that the spray stream can achieve the same results as the straight stream (first sentence). We can assume, therefore, that there are situations where a spray stream is preferable and other situations where the straight stream is more effective. No information is given as to which type of situation occurs more often. Choice B—spray nozzles achieve the same, not better, results. Choice C—if spray nozzles are effective with limited water supplies, they will also be effective where adequate or large-volume water supplies are available.

16. **(C)** This means the same as the second sentence of the passage. Choice A—the passage says that not everything can be learned from rules and procedures. However, this does not mean that only a little can be learned. Choice B—the passage tells us that the successful firefighter is the one who studies past fires and applies what is learned; it does not mention on-the-job experience. Choice D—according to the passage, the application of rules, set procedures, and operations at past fires leads to successful firefighting.

17. **(A)** See Sections 4.a and 5: All ammunition must be kept in "a locked metal box" in a "compartment or shanty." Choice B—no special distance is given; the box may not be stored in a shanty with compressed gases or flammable liquids (Section 4.c). Choice C—the sign should be red and white. Choice D—the box should not be left open; it must be kept locked.

18. **(D)** See Sections 4.a, 4.b, and 5. Choice A—the box must be made of metal, but which metal is not stated. Choice B—the box must be lined with asbestos or other noncombustible insulating material (Section 4.a). Choice C—no thickness is specified for the box.

19. **(A)** The regulations apply whether or not a permit is required (see Section 1).

20. **(D)** See Section 8.a. Choice A—the title states specifically that the regulations apply only to "powder-actuated tools." Choices B and C—these refer to other forms of energy used to activate tools; they are not discussed in the passage.

21. **(C)** See Section 4.b. No special requirements are indicated other than competency. Choice A is incorrect; this applies to the person who will be using the ammunition.

22. **(B)** The passage does not mention buckets of sand. Choice A is specified in Section 7; Choice C, in Section 6; Choice D, in Section 5.

23. **(D)** This answer is given in Section 8.b. Choices A, B, and C are all incorrect on the basis of the passage.

24. **(D)** Section 8.b specifies a steel backup plate. Choice A—it is true that steel is metal; however, not all metals are steel. Choice B—asbestos is required in the ammunition box. Choice C—P.V.C. is a plastic and hence not acceptable.

25. **(D)** Section 8.b states the conditions: a safe zone behind the work area, established by means of a ½-inch steel backup plate, or an area clear of all people.

26. **(C)** Refer to Section 8.a. Choice A is not mentioned in the passage. Choice B—the prospective user need not pass a test, but rather must submit evidence of having satisfactorily completed a training program. Choice D—the training program is not given by the Fire Department, but must be acceptable to it.

27. **(C)** The second paragraph tells us specifically what a fire apparatus should stop for. Choices A, B, and D are all required, but Choice C is only a "maybe." It therefore is the best choice as something that would *not* be done.

28. **(C)** The third paragraph explains that slowing without stopping does not provide enough time to recognize what a car or truck is going to do. There is no justification in the passage for Choices A, B, and D.

29. **(B)** It is not necessary to wait for the light to change, but only to ensure that other vehicles have yielded the right-of-way.

30. **(C)** This is stated in the opening sentence in the passage. Choices A, B, and D are possible causes of severe accidents but are not mentioned in the passage and therefore cannot be considered.

31. **(D)** The second paragraph says that the apparatus should stop for all three traffic control devices. Choice A—according to the passage, many, but not all, fire departments have this regulation. Choice B—not the *most* accidents, but some of the *most severe* accidents, occur when intersections are crossed against controls. Choice C—slowing is not sufficient (see paragraph 3).

32. **(C)** This is the theme of the passage. Choices A, B, and D are incorrect; these are examples of incomplete blanketing.

33. **(A)** This information is found in the ninth sentence of the passage. Choice B is incorrect; this should be done before you push the blanket under the person. Choices C and D are incorrect; these are done after Choice A.

34. **(A)** Choice B is incorrect; stand in back of the person. Choice C is incorrect; place the fist in the abdominal area. Choice D is incorrect; you would not punch the person.

35. **(D)** The injury may be more serious than it appears to the untrained person. Stray dogs can carry potentially infectious bacteria. Choice A is incorrect; baking soda is not correct. The answer selection should recommend covering with a sterile bandage. Choice B is incorrect; if the wound is tightly wrapped, it could cut off the blood circulation. Choice

C is incorrect; it should recommend a cold compress and elevation higher than the level of the heart.

36. **(D)** The second sentence tells us the first unit did not arrive until 1 minute after the second unit arrived. Choice A is incorrect; we are not told what time the alarm was transmitted or the time that the first or second units arrived. Because we do not have the necessary information, we cannot tell what time the third unit arrived. We could only say with confidence that the third unit arrived in 7 minutes and that all three units arrived in 7 minutes or less. Choice B is incorrect; the logic is similar to explanation for answer A. Choice C is incorrect; the second unit arrived first, and the first assigned unit arrived second.

37. **(A)** Gasoline vaporizes naturally at very low temperatures and is highly flammable. A spark or a pilot light could ignite the vapors; this condition is very dangerous. Action b. is not dangerous; commercial degreasers are used to remove dirt. Action c. is incorrect; the chute is designed for this activity. Action d. is incorrect; roof activities are generally permitted if appropriate safety precautions are taken. The chain-link fence is one of the precautions.

38. **(D)** This is explained in the second sentence. Choice A is incorrect; it is a bogus statement. Choice B is incorrect; this is "getting the big picture." Choice C is incorrect; it is not mentioned in the passage. Driving safely requires that you stay in the center of your lane, not in the center of the road.

39. **(C)** Gas leaking from a pipe in an apartment house creates a very dangerous condition. If it should ignite, an explosion and fire will occur. Choices A and D are incorrect; they require attention, but not until after the gas leak has been corrected. Choice B is incorrect; you were told all the people are accounted for.

40. **(B)** There would be no need for a safety belt in the street. Choices A, C, and D are required actions.

41. **(A)** This is item 4. Choice B is incorrect; the ladder is turned over after the knot has been tied and the rope is secured to the ladder. Choice C is incorrect; the roller is lined up between the windows. Choice D is incorrect; the roller is put into position on the roof before the rope is lowered.

42. **(C)** 911 is the universal emergency number for contacting police or fire throughout the United States. Teaching this number to schoolchildren early helps them in case of an emergency. Choices A and B are incorrect because the companies may be out of the building and won't be able to answer the phone. Choice D is also incorrect.

43. **(C)** You should conduct your duties professionally and courteously. By implementing these actions immediately, you can start making a positive impression on others. Unless you have a degree in public relations, local newspapers may not want to talk to you. So Choice A is incorrect. Choice B is incorrect because it is not the first action you should take. Although you can encourage your peers to enter this field, urging them to do so is too forceful. So Choice D is incorrect.

44. **(A)** If the smaller of the two pieces is $\frac{2}{3}$ of the larger, then the size of the larger piece must be $\frac{3}{3}$. The total length of the rope is then equal to the sum of the two parts ($\frac{3}{3} + \frac{2}{3}$), or $\frac{5}{3}$. If we divide the length of the original rope (100 feet) into 5 equal parts, we get 20 feet. Now we multiply this by the length of each rope: $3 \times 20 = 60$, and $2 \times 20 = 40$. The longer rope is 60 feet long.

45. **(B)** When water changes from a solid to a liquid, it takes on heat energy. The rate of energy absorbed depends on the amount of surface area available to absorb it. When a block of ice is chopped up, more surface area becomes available to absorb heat; therefore the ice will melt faster, eliminating choices C and D. The amount of heat required to melt a given volume of ice is the same, regardless of whether the ice is in block or chopped form; therefore choice A is incorrect.

46. **(C)** Contacting the fire prevention bureau yourself will ensure that they are notified of a potentially dangerous situation immediately. Since the woman may get lost going to another station, choice A is not correct. Choice B is incorrect because you may not be able to leave immediately and check out the market. Choice D is definitely not a professional response.

47. **(D)** This is another way of saying "... those whose abilities and personal characteristics provide the closest fit to the specific job requirements." Choice A—training is not mentioned in the passage, whereas the importance of personal characteristics is stressed. Choice B—abilities and characteristics need not be of the highest order, but should provide the best fit to the specific job requirements. Choice C—interest is an admirable quality; however, it is the person's abilities and personal characteristics that the passage stresses.

48. **(D)** The passage says that selection procedures can be improved by obtaining "... more precise statements of the requirements for a particular position." Choice A—job descriptions should be made more precise, not simplified. Choice B—"recruiting" means getting people to apply; the passage refers to choosing the best applicants from those that have already applied. Choice C—this is not mentioned or implied in the passage.

49. **(D)** When confined in a small space with no apparent way out and faced with the possibility of serious danger, many people will undertake irrational acts in an attempt to save themselves. Letting the people know that help is at hand and that something is being done will tend to reduce their fears.

50. **(C)** If matches are kept out of the reach of children, they cannot play with them and cannot get burned by them. Choice A—a warning serves to inform the child but does not remove the temptation to play with the matches; also, some children are too young to understand the danger. Choice B—punishing parents may not prevent the child from playing with matches again. Choice D—safety matches are more difficult to light and may self-extinguish, but a child can still play with them and light them.

100-Question Practice Exams

13

This chapter includes two 100-question practice exams. The practice exams do not have time limits. However, you should try to take each in an uninterrupted sitting. This will give you an idea of the amount of time an exam of this kind will take under actual exam conditions. After you complete Exam Five, note which questions you answered incorrectly. Before looking up the correct answers, go back over the exam and try to correct your mistakes. If you are puzzled by a question, review the Answer Explanations. By trying to correct the answer before looking it up, you will get an idea about why and how you are making mistakes.

BEFORE TAKING THE EXAMS

Go back and review the test-taking strategies outlined in Chapters 4, 6, 7, and 8. When you begin the exams, be sure to read and follow all instructions. Read each question carefully, and answer only what is asked of you. Select the answer that is the *best* choice of those provided, and then record your selection on the answer sheet.

Use the answer sheet that precedes the exam to record your answers. The Answer Explanations are given at the end of each exam.

ANSWER SHEET
Practice Exam Five

1. Ⓐ Ⓑ Ⓒ Ⓓ
2. Ⓐ Ⓑ Ⓒ Ⓓ
3. Ⓐ Ⓑ Ⓒ Ⓓ
4. Ⓐ Ⓑ Ⓒ Ⓓ
5. Ⓐ Ⓑ Ⓒ Ⓓ
6. Ⓐ Ⓑ Ⓒ Ⓓ
7. Ⓐ Ⓑ Ⓒ Ⓓ
8. Ⓐ Ⓑ Ⓒ Ⓓ
9. Ⓐ Ⓑ Ⓒ Ⓓ
10. Ⓐ Ⓑ Ⓒ Ⓓ
11. Ⓐ Ⓑ Ⓒ Ⓓ
12. Ⓐ Ⓑ Ⓒ Ⓓ
13. Ⓐ Ⓑ Ⓒ Ⓓ
14. Ⓐ Ⓑ Ⓒ Ⓓ
15. Ⓐ Ⓑ Ⓒ Ⓓ
16. Ⓐ Ⓑ Ⓒ Ⓓ
17. Ⓐ Ⓑ Ⓒ Ⓓ
18. Ⓐ Ⓑ Ⓒ Ⓓ
19. Ⓐ Ⓑ Ⓒ Ⓓ
20. Ⓐ Ⓑ Ⓒ Ⓓ
21. Ⓐ Ⓑ Ⓒ Ⓓ
22. Ⓐ Ⓑ Ⓒ Ⓓ
23. Ⓐ Ⓑ Ⓒ Ⓓ
24. Ⓐ Ⓑ Ⓒ Ⓓ
25. Ⓐ Ⓑ Ⓒ Ⓓ
26. Ⓐ Ⓑ Ⓒ Ⓓ
27. Ⓐ Ⓑ Ⓒ Ⓓ
28. Ⓐ Ⓑ Ⓒ Ⓓ
29. Ⓐ Ⓑ Ⓒ Ⓓ
30. Ⓐ Ⓑ Ⓒ Ⓓ
31. Ⓐ Ⓑ Ⓒ Ⓓ
32. Ⓐ Ⓑ Ⓒ Ⓓ
33. Ⓐ Ⓑ Ⓒ Ⓓ
34. Ⓐ Ⓑ Ⓒ Ⓓ
35. Ⓐ Ⓑ Ⓒ Ⓓ
36. Ⓐ Ⓑ Ⓒ Ⓓ
37. Ⓐ Ⓑ Ⓒ Ⓓ
38. Ⓐ Ⓑ Ⓒ Ⓓ
39. Ⓐ Ⓑ Ⓒ Ⓓ
40. Ⓐ Ⓑ Ⓒ Ⓓ
41. Ⓐ Ⓑ Ⓒ Ⓓ
42. Ⓐ Ⓑ Ⓒ Ⓓ
43. Ⓐ Ⓑ Ⓒ Ⓓ
44. Ⓐ Ⓑ Ⓒ Ⓓ
45. Ⓐ Ⓑ Ⓒ Ⓓ
46. Ⓐ Ⓑ Ⓒ Ⓓ
47. Ⓐ Ⓑ Ⓒ Ⓓ
48. Ⓐ Ⓑ Ⓒ Ⓓ
49. Ⓐ Ⓑ Ⓒ Ⓓ
50. Ⓐ Ⓑ Ⓒ Ⓓ
51. Ⓐ Ⓑ Ⓒ Ⓓ
52. Ⓐ Ⓑ Ⓒ Ⓓ
53. Ⓐ Ⓑ Ⓒ Ⓓ
54. Ⓐ Ⓑ Ⓒ Ⓓ
55. Ⓐ Ⓑ Ⓒ Ⓓ
56. Ⓐ Ⓑ Ⓒ Ⓓ
57. Ⓐ Ⓑ Ⓒ Ⓓ
58. Ⓐ Ⓑ Ⓒ Ⓓ
59. Ⓐ Ⓑ Ⓒ Ⓓ
60. Ⓐ Ⓑ Ⓒ Ⓓ
61. Ⓐ Ⓑ Ⓒ Ⓓ
62. Ⓐ Ⓑ Ⓒ Ⓓ
63. Ⓐ Ⓑ Ⓒ Ⓓ
64. Ⓐ Ⓑ Ⓒ Ⓓ
65. Ⓐ Ⓑ Ⓒ Ⓓ
66. Ⓐ Ⓑ Ⓒ Ⓓ
67. Ⓐ Ⓑ Ⓒ Ⓓ
68. Ⓐ Ⓑ Ⓒ Ⓓ
69. Ⓐ Ⓑ Ⓒ Ⓓ
70. Ⓐ Ⓑ Ⓒ Ⓓ
71. Ⓐ Ⓑ Ⓒ Ⓓ
72. Ⓐ Ⓑ Ⓒ Ⓓ
73. Ⓐ Ⓑ Ⓒ Ⓓ
74. Ⓐ Ⓑ Ⓒ Ⓓ
75. Ⓐ Ⓑ Ⓒ Ⓓ
76. Ⓐ Ⓑ Ⓒ Ⓓ
77. Ⓐ Ⓑ Ⓒ Ⓓ
78. Ⓐ Ⓑ Ⓒ Ⓓ
79. Ⓐ Ⓑ Ⓒ Ⓓ
80. Ⓐ Ⓑ Ⓒ Ⓓ
81. Ⓐ Ⓑ Ⓒ Ⓓ
82. Ⓐ Ⓑ Ⓒ Ⓓ
83. Ⓐ Ⓑ Ⓒ Ⓓ
84. Ⓐ Ⓑ Ⓒ Ⓓ
85. Ⓐ Ⓑ Ⓒ Ⓓ
86. Ⓐ Ⓑ Ⓒ Ⓓ
87. Ⓐ Ⓑ Ⓒ Ⓓ
88. Ⓐ Ⓑ Ⓒ Ⓓ
89. Ⓐ Ⓑ Ⓒ Ⓓ
90. Ⓐ Ⓑ Ⓒ Ⓓ
91. Ⓐ Ⓑ Ⓒ Ⓓ
92. Ⓐ Ⓑ Ⓒ Ⓓ
93. Ⓐ Ⓑ Ⓒ Ⓓ
94. Ⓐ Ⓑ Ⓒ Ⓓ
95. Ⓐ Ⓑ Ⓒ Ⓓ
96. Ⓐ Ⓑ Ⓒ Ⓓ
97. Ⓐ Ⓑ Ⓒ Ⓓ
98. Ⓐ Ⓑ Ⓒ Ⓓ
99. Ⓐ Ⓑ Ⓒ Ⓓ
100. Ⓐ Ⓑ Ⓒ Ⓓ

Directions: Memorize this floor plan. Then you will answer some questions about it without looking at it.

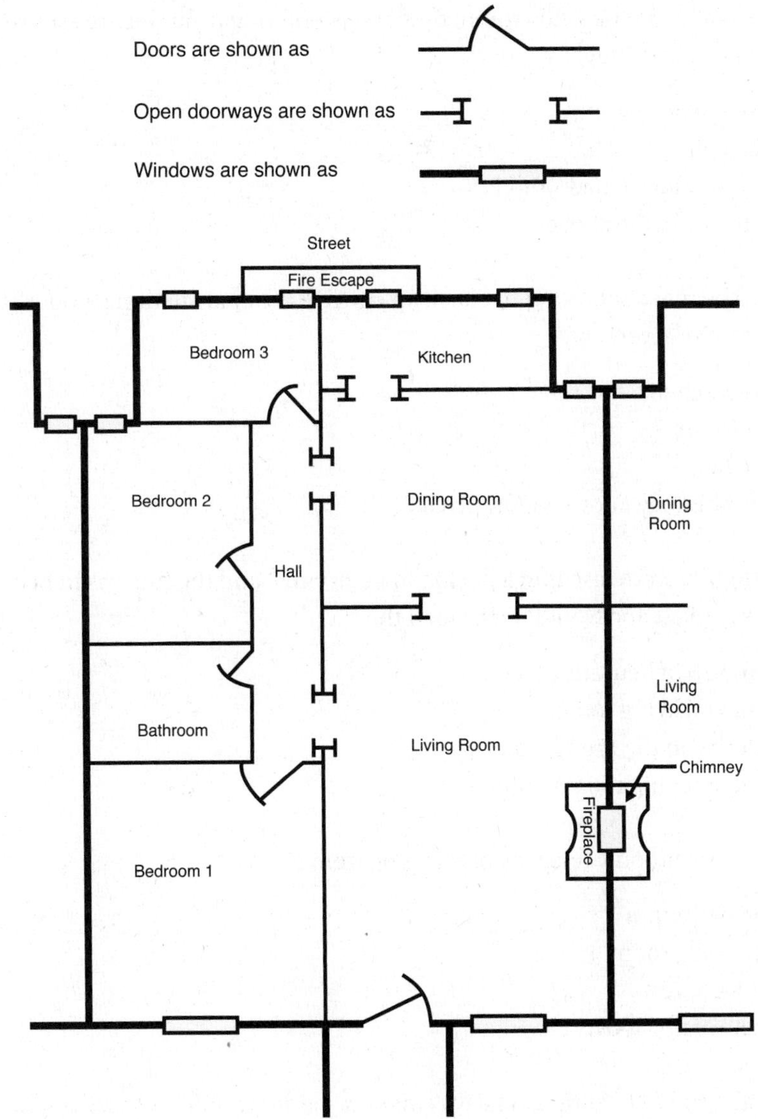

1. Which room has no doors that can be closed?

   (A) bedroom 1
   (B) living room
   (C) dining room
   (D) none of these

2. Which room is farthest from the bathroom?

   (A) bedroom 3
   (B) living room
   (C) dining room
   (D) kitchen

3. If there is a fire in the living room, firefighters entering from the fire escape should bring a hose in through

   (A) the kitchen window.
   (B) the hall.
   (C) the window of bedroom 2.
   (D) any one of the above.

4. It would be most important to check for a fire in the apartment next door if a fire in this apartment were in

   (A) the kitchen.
   (B) bedroom 3.
   (C) the hall.
   (D) the chimney above the fireplace.

5. If a firefighter were rescuing a person in bedroom 2 and the fire was in bedroom 3, the safest way of escape would be through the

   (A) window of bedroom 2.
   (B) hall and living room.
   (C) kitchen to the fire escape.
   (D) hall to dining room window.

6. Which room has only one way of escaping from it?

   (A) the bathroom
   (B) the living room
   (C) bedroom 3
   (D) none of the above

7. If the hall were full of fire and heavy smoke, a ladder would be necessary to remove a person trapped in

   (A) the dining room.
   (B) the kitchen.
   (C) the living room.
   (D) bedroom 2.

8. Which room has four ways of escape?

   (A) bedroom 1
   (B) dining room
   (C) kitchen
   (D) none of them

9. Which room does *not* have a door or doorway leading directly into the hall?

   (A) the bathroom
   (B) the living room
   (C) the kitchen
   (D) bedroom 1

10. Of the following, the shortest way from the fire escape to the kitchen is through

   (A) bedroom 3, hall, and dining room.
   (B) bedroom 2, hall, and dining room.
   (C) bedroom 1, living room, and dining room.
   (D) the living room and dining room.

Directions: Answer questions 11 through 15 on the basis of the passage below.

Arsonists are people who set fires deliberately. They don't look like criminals, but they cost the nation millions of dollars in property loss, and sometimes loss of life. Arsonists set fires for many different reasons. Sometimes a shopkeeper sees no way out of losing his business, and sets fire to it so he can collect the insurance. Another type of arsonist wants revenge, and sets fire to the home or shop of someone he feels has treated him unfairly. Some arsonists just like the excitement of seeing the fire burn and watching the firefighters at work; arsonists of this type have even been known to help fight the fire.

11. The writer of the passage feels that arsonists

   (A) usually return to the scene of the crime.
   (B) work at night.
   (C) don't look like criminals.
   (D) never leave their fingerprints.

12. An arsonist is a person who

   (A) intentionally sets a fire.
   (B) enjoys watching fires.
   (C) wants revenge.
   (D) needs money.

13. Arsonists have been known to help fight fires because they

(A) felt guilty.
(B) enjoyed the excitement.
(C) wanted to earn money.
(D) didn't want anyone hurt.

14. Shopkeepers sometimes become arsonists in order to

(A) commit suicide.
(B) collect insurance money.
(C) hide a crime.
(D) raise their prices.

15. The point of this passage is that arsonists

(A) would make good firefighters.
(B) are not criminals.
(C) are mentally ill.
(D) are not all alike.

Directions: Answer questions 16 through 21 on the basis of the passage below.

Water and ventilation are the keys to fire fighting. Firefighters put out most fires by hosing water on the burning material, and by letting the smoke and gases out. When burning material is soaked with cooling water it can no longer produce gases that burn. In a closed room, hot gases can raise the temperature enough for the room to burst into flame. This can happen even though the room is far away from the fire itself. Therefore, firefighters chop holes in roofs and smash windows in order to empty the house of gases quickly. This is called ventilation.

16. Burning material will stop giving off hot gases when it is

(A) allowed to burn freely.
(B) exposed to fresh air.
(C) cooled with water.
(D) sprayed with chemicals.

17. Hot gases cause a room to burn by

(A) creating a draft.
(B) exploding.
(C) giving off sparks.
(D) raising the room temperature.

18. A room can burst into flames even though it is

(A) far from the fire.
(B) soaked with water.
(C) well ventilated.
(D) cold and damp.

19. Firefighters sometimes smash windows and chop holes in roofs in order to

(A) reach trapped victims.
(B) remove burning materials.
(C) ventilate a building.
(D) escape from a fire.

20. Ventilation is important in firefighting because it

(A) releases trapped smoke and gases.
(B) puts out flames by cooling them.
(C) makes it easier for firefighters to breathe.
(D) makes the flames easier to see and reach with a hose.

21. Hot gases are most dangerous when they are in a room that is

(A) large.
(B) closed.
(C) damp.
(D) cool.

Directions: Answer questions 22 through 25 on the basis of the passage below.

When there is a large fire in an occupied apartment or tenement, the fire escapes often become overcrowded. To relieve this overcrowding, a portable ladder is often raised to the first level of the fire escape and put opposite to the drop ladder. For added help, an additional ladder can be raised from the ground to the second level. If the fire escape is located in the rear of the building, a "gooseneck" ladder that hooks over the roof can also be used. Then firefighters can help some occupants from the fire escape to the roof instead of to the ground.

22. Portable ladders are raised to fire escapes so that

(A) firefighters can reach the roof from outside.
(B) occupants can reach a higher level of the fire escape.
(C) firefighters can enter windows more easily.
(D) occupants can leave fire escapes more rapidly.

23. If all the ladders described in the passage are used, how many ways can the occupants reach the ground directly by ladder from the fire escape at the first level?

(A) 1
(B) 2
(C) 3
(D) 4

24. A "gooseneck" ladder is sometimes used

(A) opposite the drop ladder.
(B) from the top level.
(C) from the first level.
(D) from the second level.

25. The main topic of the paragraph is

(A) relieving overcrowding on fire escapes.
(B) setting up and using portable ladders.
(C) rescuing occupants from apartments.
(D) using the roof to escape from fires.

Directions: Answer questions 26 through 31 on the basis of the passage below.

During search operations the first step is usually to rescue victims who can be seen and heard, or those whose exact locations are known. Disorganized or careless search must be avoided since victims may be underneath rubble. Disorganized movement could cause injury or death. The best method is to start from the outer edge and work toward the center of an area. Sometimes a trapped or buried victim may be located by calling out or by tapping on pipes. Rescue workers should first call out, then have a period of silence to listen for tapping sounds from a victim.

26. The main point of the paragraph is that

(A) firefighters should call and listen often.
(B) trapped victims can usually be heard.
(C) searching should be an organized procedure.
(D) many victims are buried in fires.

27. Normally the first victims to be rescued during a search are those who are

(A) unconscious.
(B) trapped under rubble.
(C) easy to see and hear.
(D) injured.

28. When searching for buried victims it is very important for firefighters to

(A) have periods of silence.
(B) keep moving constantly.
(C) search rubble piles quickly.
(D) stay away from rubble piles.

29. The best way to search an area is

(A) around the edges.
(B) from center to edge.
(C) from corner to corner.
(D) from edge to center.

30. Disorganized movement by a rescue worker can cause

(A) panic and confusion.
(B) property destruction.
(C) wasted time.
(D) death or injury.

31. Tapping on pipes is a good way to locate victims because

(A) firefighters can use Morse code.
(B) sound travels through a pipe.
(C) firefighters can signal each other this way.
(D) pipes usually aren't covered by rubble.

Directions: Answer questions 32 through 36 on the basis of the passage below.

Fire often travels inside the partitions of a burning building. Many partitions contain wooden studs that support the partitions. The studs leave a space for the fire to travel along. Flames may spread from the bottom to the upper floors through the partitions. Sparks from a fire in the upper part of a partition may fall and start a fire at the bottom. Some signs that a fire is spreading inside a partition are: (1) blistering paint, (2) discolored paint or wallpaper, or (3) partitions that feel hot to the touch. If any of these signs are present, the partition must be opened up to look for the fire. Finding cobwebs inside the partition is one sign that fire has not spread through the partition.

32. Fires can spread inside partitions because

(A) there are spaces between studs inside of partitions.
(B) fires can burn anywhere.
(C) partitions are made out of materials that burn easily.
(D) partitions are usually painted or wallpapered.

33. Cobwebs inside a partition are a sign that the fire has not spread inside the partition because

(A) cobwebs are fire resistant.
(B) fire destroys cobwebs easily.
(C) spiders don't build cobwebs near fires.
(D) cobwebs fill up the spaces between studs.

34. If a firefighter sees the paint on a partition beginning to blister, he should first

(A) wet down the partition.
(B) check the partitions in other rooms.
(C) chop a hole in the partition.
(D) close windows and doors and leave the room.

35. One way to tell if fire is spreading within a partition is the

(A) temperature of the partition.
(B) color of the smoke.
(C) age of the plaster.
(D) spacing of the studs.

36. The main point of the passage is

(A) how fire spreads inside partitions.
(B) how cobwebs help firefighters.
(C) how partitions are built.
(D) how to keep fires from spreading.

Directions: Answer questions 37 through 40 on the basis of the passage below.

When backing a fire truck into the firehouse, all firefighters should remain outside the building. Firefighters assigned to stop traffic should face traffic so they can alert the driver in case of an emergency. Additional firefighters should stand on the sidewalk in front of the firehouse to guide the driver. The truck should be slowly backed into the firehouse and immediately stopped upon orders of any firefighter. When the truck is completely in the firehouse, then and only then should the officer contact central headquarters for the placement of the company in service. Following this, the officer orders the entrance doors closed.

Use this diagram to help answer questions *37* through *39.* The letters indicate where fire-fighters are standing.

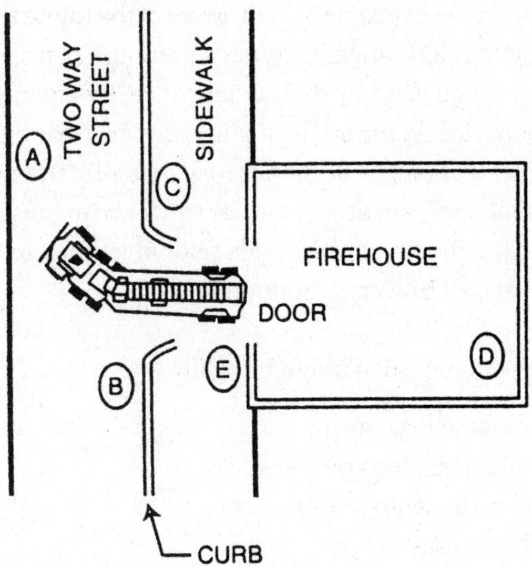

37. The truck is backing into the firehouse. Which firefighter is *not* needed according to the regulations?

    (A) firefighter A
    (B) firefighter B
    (C) firefighter C
    (D) firefighter D

38. Which firefighters are responsible for stopping cars?

    (A) firefighters A and C
    (B) firefighters C and E
    (C) firefighters A and B
    (D) firefighters B and E

39. Which firefighters can order the truck to stop?

    (A) firefighters A and B only
    (B) firefighters C and E only
    (C) firefighter D only
    (D) any of them

40. When is central headquarters notified that the company is ready to be put in service?

    (A) when the truck is returning from a fire
    (B) after the truck is parked in the firehouse
    (C) after the firehouse doors are closed
    (D) when all of the firefighters have entered the firehouse

Directions: Answer questions 41 through 45 on the basis of the passage below.

Unless they have had a fire, most people are not aware of the things firefighters do. Too often the public thinks of firefighters as lounging around a firehouse between fires. Firefighters can help change this image in small ways by their appearance, by greeting visitors who come to the firehouse, by their behavior on the street at a fire, and by treating the public in a courteous manner. For example, 90 percent of the rescues made by the average fire department take place at relatively small fires, not at spectacular extra-alarm fires. The public rarely hears about many rescues because the fire departments seldom let the press know about firefighters who have performed acts of bravery at routine fires.

41. What are firefighters doing when not fighting fires?

    (A) lounging around the firehouse
    (B) working on public relations projects
    (C) making repairs to the equipment
    (D) the passage doesn't say.

42. The passage places responsibility for improving the fire department's image on the

    (A) fire department itself.
    (B) press.
    (C) public.
    (D) people rescued by firefighters.

43. Most of the rescues made by firefighters take place at

    (A) extra-alarm fires.
    (B) special emergencies where no fire is involved.
    (C) relatively small fires.
    (D) spectacularly large fires.

44. The public rarely hears about rescues made by firefighters at routine fires because

    (A) information about fires must be kept confidential.
    (B) fire departments seldom report these rescues to the press.
    (C) most of these rescues take place late at night.
    (D) reporters aren't interested in covering routine fires.

45. What would be the best title for this passage?

    (A) An Inside Look at the Fire Department
    (B) Making the Most of Fire Prevention Week
    (C) Improving the Fire Department's Public Image
    (D) Brave Acts Performed by Firefighters

Directions: Questions 46 through 70 test your general knowledge. These questions are based on information you should know about politics, government, history, spelling, sentence structure, and judgment. Each question or statement is followed by four choices. For each question, choose the *best* answer. On your answer sheet, use a No. 2 pencil to blacken the oval containing the same letter as your answer.

46. In what year did the United States declare its freedom from England?

    (A) 1767
    (B) 1776
    (C) 1777
    (D) 1876

47. The Second Continental Congress approved the Declaration of __________.

    (A) Incontinence
    (B) Equality
    (C) Freedom
    (D) Independence

48. What are the three branches of government?

    (A) Legal, judging, executor
    (B) Legislative, judgmental, executional
    (C) Executive, legislative, judicial
    (D) Congressional, republican, democratic

49. Who was the first president of the United States?

    (A) John Adams
    (B) George Washington
    (C) George Washington Carver
    (D) James Madison

50. The American flag has how many stripes?

    (A) 11
    (B) 12
    (C) 13
    (D) 14

51. The United States consists of __________ states.

    (A) 57
    (B) 50
    (C) 49
    (D) 48

52. How long did the War of 1812 last?

(A) 2 years
(B) 5 years
(C) 1 year
(D) 3 years

53. Columbus sailed to the New World in what year?

(A) 1492
(B) 1592
(C) 1620
(D) 1812

54. The first colonies in the United States were settled along the east coast. How many colonies comprised the first settlement?

(A) 11
(B) 12
(C) 13
(D) 15

55. Pet dogs sometimes save their masters' lives by waking them up when there is a fire in the house. The most probable reason that dogs detect fire before their masters is that

(A) dogs are more used to fires than their masters are.
(B) dogs are more sensitive to smoke than their masters.
(C) dogs always sense danger.
(D) fires make dogs thirsty.

56. Where was President Lincoln assassinated by John Wilkes Booth?

(A) Chevrolet's Theatre
(B) Chrysler's Theatre
(C) Dodge's Theatre
(D) Ford's Theatre

57. What is the name of the election where people compete for their party's nomination?

(A) Republican
(B) Primary
(C) Democrat
(D) Secondary

58. Where is the North Pole is located?

(A) Canada
(B) Antarctica
(C) The Arctic
(D) Greenland

59. During the mid-1800s, the Underground Railroad was created. What does this refer to?

(A) Tunnels underground
(B) Secret subway society
(C) Intercontinental railroad
(D) Escape route for slaves

60. Who invented the cotton gin?

(A) Thomas Edison
(B) Eli Whitney
(C) Stephen Douglas
(D) J. C. Whitney

61. Which of these items would firefighters be *least* likely to need when putting out a fire at the scene of an automobile accident on a city street?

(A) a portable ladder
(B) a portable fire extinguisher
(C) a stretcher
(D) a hose

62. What was the Gettysburg Address?

(A) The address of the White House
(B) Lincoln's home address
(C) A speech given at the dedication of a cemetery
(D) None of the above

63. What did Alexander Graham Bell invent?

(A) The locomotive
(B) The electric lightbulb
(C) The automobile
(D) The telephone

64. In 1849, a mineral was discovered in California, and thousands of people went west. What was that mineral?

(A) Silver
(B) Gold
(C) Copper
(D) Coal

65. The United States has six time zones. If it is 7 P.M. in Maryland, what time is it in Hawaii?

(A) 1 P.M.
(B) 2 P.M.
(C) 3 P.M.
(D) 4 P.M.

66. A labor union is a group of workers that help to improve working conditions. What do the initials AFL stand for?

(A) American Federation of Leaders
(B) American Freedom of Labor
(C) American Federation of Labor
(D) American Federation of Long Shoremen

67. In the late 1800s immigrants from Europe first arrived at

(A) Easter Island.
(B) Faeroe Island.
(C) Staten Island.
(D) Ellis Island.

68. Immigrants can become citizens through a process called ________.

(A) naturalization
(B) immigration
(C) migration
(D) discrimination

69. On May 20, 1927, Charles Lindbergh became the first aviator to fly solo across what ocean?

(A) Pacific
(B) Indian
(C) Arctic
(D) Atlantic

70. What caused the stock market to crash in 1929?

(A) People were selling off stocks for cash.
(B) People were not buying enough stocks.
(C) People were reinvesting in other commodities.
(D) People were buying too many stocks.

Directions: Questions 71 through 74 test your knowledge of mechanical reasoning. Read each question carefully, and insert the *best* answer on your answer sheet.

71. The reason for crossing the belt connecting these wheels is to

(A) make the wheels turn in opposite directions.
(B) make wheel 2 turn faster than wheel 1.
(C) save wear on the belt.
(D) take up slack in the belt.

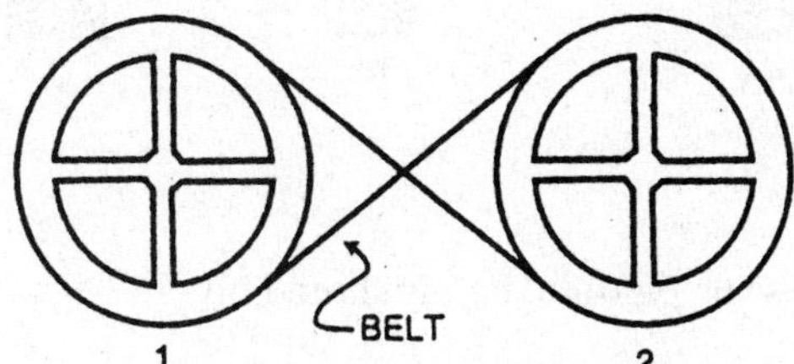

72. The purpose of the small gear between the two large gears in the illustration below is to

(A) increase the speed of the larger gears.
(B) allow the larger gears to turn in different directions.
(C) decrease the speed of the larger gears.
(D) make the larger gears turn in the same direction.

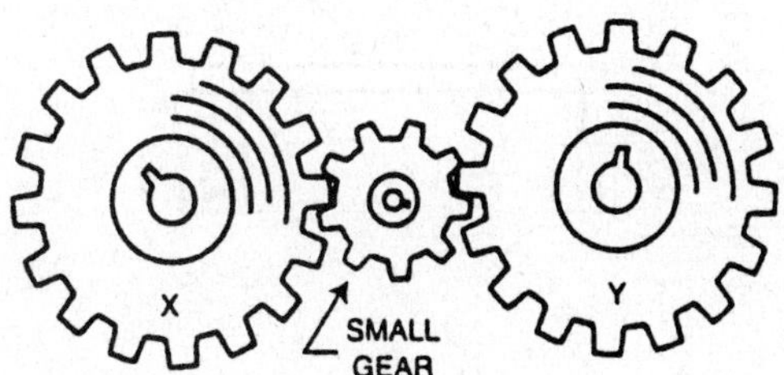

73. Each of the three-foot-high water cans below has a bottom with an area of one square foot. The pressure on the bottom of the cans is

(A) least in A.
(B) least in B.
(C) least in C.
(D) the same in all.

74. The reading on the scale pictured below should be

(A) zero.
(B) 10 pounds.
(C) 13 pounds.
(D) 26 pounds.

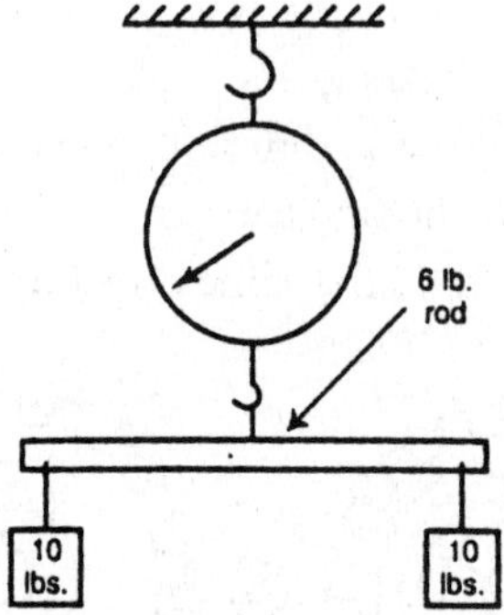

Directions: Select the item, appliance, or tool that is related to each in questions 75 through 80. Answer A, B, C, or D on the answer sheet. You should be able to relate tools with their functions just by recognizing the name of the tool.

75. A twist drill

    (A) staple gun
    (B) hand drill
    (C) sander
    (D) caulking gun

76. Jumper cables

    (A) light socket
    (B) battery
    (C) paint brush
    (D) p-trap

77. Crowbar

    (A) grate
    (B) p-trap
    (C) battery
    (D) table

78. A wood chisel

    (A) tin snips
    (B) mallet
    (C) pipe wrench
    (D) paint brush

79. A piece of wood

    (A) vise
    (B) bench grinder
    (C) torch
    (D) plane

80. A brick wall

    (A) file
    (B) trowel
    (C) claw hammer
    (D) awl

Directions: Questions 81 through 100 test you on dealing with people, general knowledge, history, and politics. Choose the *best* answer for each question, and blacken the correct circle on your answer sheet.

81. When a firefighter arrives at a fire, an angry woman screams at the firefighter for not coming sooner. She says it has been nearly half an hour since she called and all her things will be burned up before the firefighter gets the fire out. The firefighter knows it has been only 6 minutes since the alarm came in. What should the firefighter do?

    (A) Ask her exactly what time she called and show her it was only 6 minutes ago.
    (B) Explain to her how firefighters respond to a fire and go on fighting the fire.
    (C) Tell her that times seems longer when people are worried and she is wrong.
    (D) Refer the woman to an officer.

82. When inspecting a store, a firefighter sees some trash piled on a stair landing. This is a dangerous fire condition which violates the law. The owner says that the last inspector said it was okay because the people can use the elevator instead of the stairs. What should the firefighter do *first?*

    (A) Ignore the violation since firefighters should back each other up in dealing with the public.
    (B) Insist that the owner remove the trash since it is a violation of the law.
    (C) Ask the owner for the name of the previous inspector.
    (D) Try to find out why the owner wants to store trash on the stair landing.

83. While on house watch, you receive a phone call from a lady stating she thought she saw smoke coming from a house about a block away from the station. What would be the best thing for you to do?

    (A) Run up the block and do a quick investigation
    (B) Notify the officer in charge
    (C) Send a police officer to investigate
    (D) Disregard the call; if there is a fire, someone else will call it in too

84. On a globe or chart are lines of longitude and latitude. Longitude lines run

    (A) north to south.
    (B) east and west.
    (C) east to west.
    (D) north and south.

85. Some people buy shares of a business in the hope of making money. What is this called?

(A) Digesting
(B) Investing
(C) Ingesting
(D) Divesting

86. The transcontinental railroad used a special spike at its dedication in the 1800s. What was it made of?

(A) Silver
(B) Copper
(C) Gold
(D) Steel

87. General George Armstrong Custer fought the Battle of ______________.

(A) North Dakota
(B) the Sioux Reservation
(C) the Battle of Bull Run
(D) the Little Bighorn

88. A ______________ searches for gold, silver, or other mineral resources.

(A) prospector
(B) predictor
(C) projector
(D) protractor

89. What does the acronym NATO stand for?

(A) North Atlantic Tea Organization
(B) North American Testing Organization
(C) North Atlantic Treaty Organization
(D) North Amsterdam Treaty Opponent

90. The right of citizens to equal treatment is called

(A) civil obedience.
(B) civil religion.
(C) civil rights.
(D) civil regions.

91. Keeping natural resources from being wasted or destroyed is called

(A) conservation.
(B) concentration.
(C) preservation.
(D) consternation.

92. There are 7 continents: Africa, Asia, Europe, Antarctica, North America, South America, and

(A) Canada.
(B) Arctic.
(C) Australia.
(D) China.

93. A Scout troop visits a firehouse to see the equipment. The firefighters show them around the firehouse. Letting scouts visit the firehouse is

(A) good, because firefighters should be kept busy at all times.
(B) bad, because firefighters should rest when not fighting fires.
(C) good, because it gives the firefighters a chance to teach the Scouts about fire safety.
(D) bad, because the Scouts can cause damage to the equipment in the firehouse.

94. During an inspection, a building manager becomes angry and tells a firefighter that the fire department does a rotten job and inspections are a waste of time. The firefighter should

(A) tell the building manager to clean up his own place first before complaining about the fire department.
(B) suggest that they trade jobs for a few hours.
(C) try to find out why he feels this way.
(D) inform the building manager that the real problem is his bad attitude.

95. While putting firefighting equipment back on the fire truck after an apartment fire, a firefighter is falsely accused by a woman of stealing ten dollars she had kept hidden in a sugar bowl in her apartment. The firefighter should

(A) ask her why firefighters would risk their lives for ten dollars.
(B) give her ten dollars to get her out of the way.
(C) tell her she had no business keeping money in a sugar bowl.
(D) tell her she should report it to an officer.

96. After firefighters had put out a fire in a store, the owner yelled to a firefighter that another firefighter had chopped a hole in the roof and had caused more damage than the fire. What should the firefighter do *first?*

(A) Tell the owner insurance pays for the damage.
(B) Tell the owner to talk to the firefighter who chopped the hole.
(C) Explain that it was necessary to make a hole to ventilate the fire.
(D) Suggest to the owner that he put his complaint in writing to the Fire Commissioner.

97. After giving a talk on fire prevention to a group of schoolchildren, a firefighter finds that the children have more questions than can be answered in the time allowed. The firefighter should

(A) answer as many questions as possible and try to arrange another visit.
(B) let only the teacher ask questions.
(C) stay with the children and answer all their questions.
(D) refuse to answer any questions.

98. Some neighborhood children have been coming to the firehouse several times a day. They mean to be friendly, but they are keeping the firefighters from doing their work. The firefighters should

(A) tell them not to come back to the firehouse anymore.
(B) call their parents and ask them to keep the children away.
(C) suggest that they start visiting the neighborhood police station.
(D) ask them to leave but explain that firefighters have work to do.

99. After a fire has been put out, you see a firefighter pulling down loose plaster from the ceiling, without wearing a helmet. You should

(A) report the firefighter to the officer in charge.
(B) say nothing about what happened.
(C) tell the firefighter to put the helmet on because falling plaster can be dangerous.
(D) use force, if necessary, to make the firefighter wear the helmet.

100. While on duty, firefighters usually prepare their meals in the firehouse. Most of the firefighters in a certain firehouse like to take turns cooking. However, one of them offers to clean up the dishes rather than having to cook. The other firefighters should

(A) tell the firefighter that cooking can be fun.
(B) agree to the firefighter's offer.
(C) let the firefighter make sandwiches instead of meals for dinner.
(D) excuse the firefighter from cooking and doing the dishes.

IF THERE IS STILL TIME REMAINING, you may review your answers.

ANSWER KEY AND EXPLANATIONS

Answer Key

1. **(C)**	21. **(B)**	41. **(D)**	61. **(A)**	81. **(D)**
2. **(D)**	22. **(D)**	42. **(A)**	62. **(C)**	82. **(B)**
3. **(A)**	23. **(B)**	43. **(C)**	63. **(D)**	83. **(B)**
4. **(D)**	24. **(B)**	44. **(B)**	64. **(B)**	84. **(D)**
5. **(B)**	25. **(A)**	45. **(C)**	65. **(B)**	85. **(B)**
6. **(A)**	26. **(C)**	46. **(B)**	66. **(C)**	86. **(C)**
7. **(D)**	27. **(C)**	47. **(D)**	67. **(D)**	87. **(D)**
8. **(B)**	28. **(A)**	48. **(C)**	68. **(A)**	88. **(A)**
9. **(C)**	29. **(D)**	49. **(B)**	69. **(D)**	89. **(C)**
10. **(A)**	30. **(D)**	50. **(C)**	70. **(A)**	90. **(C)**
11. **(C)**	31. **(B)**	51. **(B)**	71. **(A)**	91. **(A)**
12. **(A)**	32. **(A)**	52. **(D)**	72. **(D)**	92. **(C)**
13. **(B)**	33. **(B)**	53. **(A)**	73. **(D)**	93. **(C)**
14. **(B)**	34. **(C)**	54. **(C)**	74. **(D)**	94. **(C)**
15. **(D)**	35. **(A)**	55. **(B)**	75. **(B)**	95. **(D)**
16. **(C)**	36. **(A)**	56. **(D)**	76. **(B)**	96. **(C)**
17. **(D)**	37. **(D)**	57. **(B)**	77. **(A)**	97. **(A)**
18. **(A)**	38. **(C)**	58. **(C)**	78. **(B)**	98. **(D)**
19. **(C)**	39. **(D)**	59. **(D)**	79. **(D)**	99. **(C)**
20. **(A)**	40. **(B)**	60. **(B)**	80. **(B)**	100. **(B)**

Answer Explanations

1. **(C)** The dining room has three doorways but no doors. The kitchen has a doorway but no door; however, it is not included as an answer choice.

2. **(D)** This question is based on travel distance, and the room that requires a person leaving the bathroom to travel the greatest distance is the kitchen.

3. **(A)** Of the choices offered, the kitchen is the only room with a window from the fire escape. Bedroom 3 also has a window from the fire escape, but it is not given as a choice.

4. **(D)** Because the chimney is shared by both apartments, a possibility of fire extension exists.

5. **(B)** This is the safest route, leading away from the fire and toward the main entrance of the apartment. Choice C would put the persons in close proximity to the fire and increase the risk of injury. Choices A and D are secondary means of escape. The best choice is the door that leads to a known safe area.

6. **(A)** The only way out of the bathroom is through the door and into the hall; from the hall there are two ways of escape.

7. **(D)** The fire and smoke in the hall would not permit escape via that route. In this case the only way out of bedroom 2 would be through the window and down a ladder. People

in the dining room (A), kitchen (B), and living room (C) can get access to the living room door or the fire escape without passing through the hall.

8. **(B)** The four ways are (1) through the kitchen, (2) through the hall, (3) through the living room, and (4) through the window.

9. **(C)** The kitchen is an isolated room leading only to the dining room and the fire escape.

10. **(A)** This kind of question can be confusing; it asks you to enter the apartment from the fire escape and then go to the kitchen. The obvious way is the direct route—fire escape to kitchen, but this is not offered as a choice. At this point you must fight the temptation to say that the question is wrong. You have to look at it closely. It is possible to enter the apartment from the fire escape through the window of bedroom 3 and go through the hall into the dining room and then the kitchen. This is the route spelled out in choice A.

11. **(C)** The second sentence makes this statement. Choices A and B may be true but are not stated directly in the passage. You must always choose the best answer on the basis of what you have just read.

12. **(A)** An arsonist is defined in the opening sentence as one who deliberately sets fires. Choices B, C, and D may be correct for some arsonists but not for all. The best choice is the one that fits all occurrences.

13. **(B)** This is clearly stated in the last sentence. Choices A, C, and D are not mentioned.

14. **(B)** This information is found in the fourth sentence.

15. **(D)** This choice is derived from looking at the several sentences that show who the arsonist may be.

16. **(C)** This information is found in the third sentence.

17. **(D)** The fourth sentence says that hot gases can raise room temperature sufficiently for flames to appear.

18. **(A)** The fifth sentence tells us that this can occur. Choice B—this is incorrect; soaking with water will prevent the generation of gases that will burn. Choice C—the last two sentences state that ventilation removes the hot gases. Choice D—there is no mention of the effect of cold on a fire; damp objects will not give off gases readily.

19. **(C)** This information is found in the last two sentences. Choices A, B, and D may have some degree of truth, but you must base your answer only on the material presented to you.

20. **(A)** This is the thrust of the last two sentences. Choice B—ventilation does not extinguish the fire; water does. Choices C and D—these may be true but are not mentioned in the passage.

21. **(B)** This information is found in the fourth sentence; it tells us that in a closed room the temperature can rise enough for the room to burst into flame.

22. **(D)** This is the theme of this passage. By providing rapid escape routes, firefighters relieve overcrowding of fire escapes.

23. **(B)** The correct answer is found in the second sentence. The two ladders are the portable ladder and the drop ladder. Four ladders are mentioned, but only two are used from the first level of the fire escape.

24. **(B)** This requires some deductive reasoning to find the one best answer. The passage tells us that the "gooseneck" ladder hooks over the roof. We know that the roof may or may not be above the first or above the second floor, but it is always above the top floor (level). Choice A is incorrect; a portable ladder is placed opposite the drop ladder (see the second sentence).

25. **(A)** This is a repetition of question 22 in a different form. The thrust of the passage, overcrowded fire escapes, is given in the first sentence, as is often the case.

26. **(C)** In this passage the author leads us to the correct answer by the use of such terms as "disorganized," "the first step," "start," and "first call out." All of these indicate a strong need for organization. The other selections are mentioned in the passage only once. Keep in mind that the main point or theme is the recurring thought.

27. **(C)** This information is found in the opening sentence; these victims may or may not be unconscious (Choice A), trapped under rubble (Choice B), or injured (Choice D). However, since they are easily seen and heard, they can be immediately rescued.

28. **(A)** The need for periods of silence is stated in the last sentence.

29. **(D)** The fourth sentence tells us to start from the outer edge and work toward the center. Don't be misled by the dropping of the word "outer." In this case "edge" and "outer edge" mean the same thing.

30. **(D)** This is stated in the third sentence.

31. **(B)** The fifth sentence tells us that victims are sometimes located by calling out or tapping on pipes, that is, through the use of sound. Choice D is incorrect; pipes normally are covered at least partially by rubble. Choice C may be true, but the purpose of the calling out or tapping is to locate the victim, not to signal other firefighters. Choice A is similar to choice C in that this is a method for sending messages to other firefighters and is not appropriate for locating a victim. Choice B states that sound travels, and it is possible for both a victim and firefighters to hear it.

32. **(A)** This is clearly stated in the third sentence.

33. **(B)** Since there is no clear-cut answer to this question, you must eliminate the poor choices first. Choice A—cobwebs are organic material and are destroyed easily. Choice C—spiders have no idea when or where a fire will occur. Choice D—cobwebs are lacy and open and will not fill a void. By elimination choice B is the best choice.

34. **(C)** The seventh sentence tells us that if there is blistering paint, one sign of spreading fire, the partition must be opened. This would be done by chopping a hole; a small hole is often sufficient.

35. **(A)** In the sixth sentence, item 3, we are told that a hot partition is identified by touch.

36. **(A)** How a fire spreads is the recurring idea of the passage.

37. **(D)** This firefighter is inside the fire station, where a guide is *not* needed, and therefore is in violation of the directive found in the first sentence.

38. **(C)** Firefighters A and B are clearly in the street and hence are responsible for the stopping of cars. Firefighters C and E are responsible for stopping pedestrian traffic.

39. **(D)** This information is found at the end of sentence 4.

40. **(B)** Sentence 5 gives this information.

41. **(D)** This passage tells us that many do not know what firefighters do between fires and that firefighters could do something about this lack of knowledge; however, it does not tell us what they do. If you chose A, B, or C, you probably were using information or impressions you already had, not information contained in the passage.

42. **(A)** The third sentence says very clearly: "Firefighters can help change this image . . . ," and the fifth sentence reinforces this by saying that "fire departments seldom let the press know . . . ."

43. **(C)** The fourth sentence tells us that 90 percent of the rescues occur at small fires. There is no justification in the passage for any other choice.

44. **(B)** The fifth sentence says that fire departments seldom let the press know about firefighters who have performed acts of bravery at routine fires.

45. **(C)** The title should clearly state the theme of the passage—in this case, the need to correct the public perception of what firefighters do. The title that best fits this concept is choice C—Improving the Fire Department's Public Image.

46. **(B)** The United States declared its freedom from England in 1776.

47. **(D)** The Second Continental Congress approved the Declaration of Independence. Choice A is incorrect because *incontinence* means lack of bladder control. Choices B and C are incorrect because they don't correctly complete the name of the document.

48. **(C)** The three branches of government are executive (the president), the legislative (the Congress), and the judicial (the Supreme Court). Choices A, B, and D are included to confuse you.

49. **(B)** George Washington was the first president of the United States. Choice A, John Adams, was the second president. George Washington Carver, choice C, was an African-American scientist who researched better and more efficient agricultural methods. Choice D, James Madison, was the fourth president of the United States.

50. **(C)** Count the number of stripes on an American flag. There are 13, which stand for the original 13 colonies.

51. **(B)** The United States consists of 50 states. An immigrant needs to know this information to pass the naturalization test.

52. **(D)** The War of 1812 was fought from 1812 to 1815, so choice D, three years, is correct.

53. **(A)** Christopher Columbus sailed across the Atlantic Ocean and landed in the New World in 1492. Choice B, 1592, is just a detractor. In 1620, choice C, the Pilgrims landed on Plymouth Rock. The War of 1812 was fought in 1812, which is choice D.

54. **(C)** Before becoming a country, the United States originally consisted of 13 colonies. This is why the American flag has 13 stripes.

55. **(B)** This question asks you to select the "most probable" answer; knowing the exact reason is not necessary. For each selection, ask, "Is this probable?" If the answer is yes, then ask, "Is it more or less probable than the preceding choice?" Then select the best choice—B, in this case.

56. **(D)** John Wilkes Booth assassinated President Abraham Lincoln at Ford's Theater in 1865.

57. **(B)** A primary is an election where people compete for their party's nomination. Choices A and C are incorrect because they are the names of the two major political parties. Choice D is a detractor.

58. **(C)** The North Pole is located in the Arctic. Although part of Canada is in the Arctic, the North Pole is not part of Canada. So choice A is incorrect. The South Pole is in Antarctica, so choice B is incorrect. Most of Greenland is in the Arctic, but the North Pole is not part of Greenland. Therefore choice D is not correct.

59. **(D)** The Underground Railroad was neither underground nor a railroad. It was a system of escape routes leading to freedom for escaped slaves. The people who helped the slaves were called conductors, which is how the railroad got its name.

60. **(B)** Eli Whitney invented the cotton gin in 1793. This machine cleaned cotton and prepared it for market faster than a human could. Thomas Edison, choice A, invented many things but not the cotton gin. Choice C, Stephen Douglas, was a politician who debated Abraham Lincoln. J. C. Whitney, choice D, is a car parts warehouse.

61. **(A)** An automobile is a low object, and a ladder would have very limited or no use. Choices B and D may be used to extinguish a fire or wash away spilled flammable liquids. Choice C, "stretcher," may be used to transport an injured person.

62. **(C)** The Gettysburg Address is the very well-known and very short (just about 2 minutes long) speech that Abraham Lincoln gave to dedicate the Soldiers' National Cemetery in Gettysburg, Pennsylvania, honoring soldiers who had died in battle.

63. **(D)** Alexander Graham Bell invented the telephone. The first words he successfully transmitted by telephone were "Mr. Watson, come here. I want to see you."

64. **(B)** In 1849, gold was discovered at Sutter's Mill in California. The substances listed in the other choices were discovered at different times in other areas of the country.

65. **(B)** Maryland is on the east coast, which means it is in the Eastern Time Zone. When it is 7 P.M. in the Eastern Time Zone, it is 6 P.M. in the Central Time Zone (Louisiana), 5 P.M. in the Mountain Time Zone (Colorado), 4 P.M. in the Pacific Time Zone (California), and 3 P.M. in the Alaska Time Zone. So in the Hawaii Time Zone, it is 2 P.M.

66. **(C)** The American Federation of Labor (AFL) was organized in 1886 by Samuel Gompers with the goal of improving working conditions in factories and other businesses.

67. **(D)** Immigrants from Europe arrived at Ellis Island, New York, and were processed before they were allowed to enter the United States. Ellis Island is no longer used for immigration purposes. The main building now houses the Immigration Museum. Choice A is incorrect because Easter Island is located in the South Pacific. The Faeroe Islands are an island group and archipelago located between Iceland, Norway, and the British Isles. Staten Island, choice C, is located at the entrance to New York Harbor and was not used for immigration purposes.

68. **(A)** Immigrants can become U.S. citizens through the process of naturalization. They must live in the United States for several years and pass a test before being granted citizenship. Immigration, choice B, is when citizens of one country enter another country in order to live there. Choice C is incorrect because migration is the act of moving from one country to another. Discrimination is treating someone or something with partiality.

69. **(D)** Charles Lindbergh left New York in a small airplane called the *Spirit of St. Louis* and made a solo flight across the Atlantic. After 34 hours, he landed in Paris, France. If he had left California and flown west, choice A would be the correct answer. Choice B, the Indian Ocean, is too far south and too far west. The Arctic Ocean, choice C, is too cold and too far north.

70. **(A)** People didn't trust anyone and were selling stocks for cash. Then on October 29, 1929, prices on the stock market fell sharply. Nearly everyone who owned stocks lost money. Many lost everything they owned. This was the beginning of the Great Depression.

71. **(A)** Crossing the belts allows the wheels to transmit power in opposite directions. When the belt is straight, power goes in the same direction.

72. **(D)** When two sprocket gears mesh, a change in the direction of one produces an opposite change in the other. When you draw an arrow to indicate the direction, make sure the arrow goes at least halfway around the gear. This will give you a much clearer picture of what is happening.

73. **(D)** Pressure from fluid is independent of the shape of the container. It depends on the height of the fluid and the density of the fluid. In this question all the cans are the same height (3 ft.), and water would have the same density in each can.

74. **(D)** To determine the weight you must add all the weights attached to the scale. The rod weighs 6 lb., and each of the two weights attached to the rod weighs 10 lb.: 10 lb. + 10 lb. + 6 lb. = 26 lb.

75. **(B)** A drill bit would be related to a hand drill; (A), (C), and (D) are listed in the tool glossary.

76. **(B)** Booster cables would be related to a battery especially if you wanted to jump start an automobile; (A), (C), and (D) are listed in the tool glossary.

77. **(A)** If you had to remove a floor or wall grate the appropriate tool would be a crow bar or pry bar; (B), (C), and (D) are listed in the tool glossary.

78. **(B)** A mallet can be used to drive a wooden chisel; (A), (C), and (D) are listed in the tool glossary.

79. **(D)** A plane is used to trim a piece of wood; (A), (B), and (C) are listed in the tool glossary.

80. **(B)** A trowel is used to strike mortar from the seams of a brick and to lay cement in between each layer of brick; (A), (C), and (D) are listed in the tool glossary.

81. **(D)** Firefighters must set priorities. Explaining to the woman the time sequence of the response to the fire is important but must be postponed until the fire has been extinguished. After the fire is under control, a fire officer should tell the woman the actual response time and explain why she perceived the passing of time so differently.

82. **(B)** Ensuring that fire hazards are removed and fire safety laws are obeyed is the primary task of every firefighter while on fire-prevention inspection.

83. **(B)** You should always notify an officer of any emergency. Since you are on house watch, you can't leave. Whenever there is a fire or a medical emergency, the police should be notified after the officer and the fire department have been dispatched. Choice D is an improper act and may lead to disciplinary action.

84. **(D)** Lines of longitude denote distance east and west of the prime meridian but run north and south around the world. Latitude lines run around the world east and west, designating north and south distances. These lines are used to determine a location anywhere in the world. This is how a Global Positioning System (GPS) works in your car.

85. **(B)** When you buy stock or shares in a business or enterprise, you are investing in the business. Digesting happens after you eat. Ingesting is when you take in food. Divesting is when you are getting rid of something.

86. **(C)** A gold spike was used.

87. **(D)** The Battle of Little Bighorn was won by the Sioux and Cheyenne tribes. General George Armstrong Custer was outnumbered by 2,500 Native Americans and was killed along with all of his troops.

88. **(A)** A prospector searches for gold, silver, or other mineral resources. A predictor, choice B, is someone or something that claims to know the future. Choice C, a projector, shows movies or slides. A protractor is a tool used in math classes to measure angles.

89. **(C)** The North Atlantic Treaty Organization (NATO) was established after World War II as a way to make sure Europe would remain at peace.

90. **(C)** Civil Rights are equal rights and equal treatment for everyone under the law.

91. **(A)** Conservation protects the environment by keeping natural resources from being wasted or destroyed. Concentration means the amount of substance in a volume

or means thinking intensely about a subject. Preservation is protecting something. Consternation means amazement or confusion.

92. **(C)** Australia is the continent missing from the list.

93. **(C)** Teaching fire safety is one of the many roles of a firefighter.

94. **(C)** Often people misinterpret or do not completely understand the role of the fire service. By finding out why the manager is so hostile, the firefighter will be better equipped to explain why the laws and the fire service are important and in place.

95. **(D)** Accusations of theft and other wrongdoing should be directed to superiors for investigation. In this case we know from the question that the accusation is false, and the superior officer would have the duty and responsibility of defending the firefighter's innocence.

96. **(C)** This is a common problem. After the fire has been extinguished and the smoke has lifted, there may appear to have been no need for the hole. However, during the fire, conditions warranted chopping a hole in the roof to vent the smoke and heat. Explaining to the store owner that this action reduces the *overall* damage will most likely decrease his anger.

97. **(A)** Talking to schoolchildren is an important and pleasant part of a firefighter's duties. By offering to set up another visit, the firefighter shows a willingness to answer additional questions at another time.

98. **(D)** When the firefighters explain the need to do their work, the children understand the problem and do not feel offended by the request to leave.

99. **(C)** There is a time to tell a supervisor and a time to approach a fellow firefighter directly. The general rule is as follows: If the improper act is immediately dangerous, you should let the person know about it without going through the chain of command. If the action is an infraction that is not immediately dangerous, you generally should notify the firefighter's supervisor.

100. **(B)** Preparing meals and cleaning up are voluntary activities in fire stations. Within a group, individuals must be allowed to contribute according to their own strengths and capabilities. A firefighter who cannot cook but is willing to clean up is still contributing.

ANSWER SHEET
Practice Exam Six

1. Ⓐ Ⓑ Ⓒ Ⓓ	26. Ⓐ Ⓑ Ⓒ Ⓓ	51. Ⓐ Ⓑ Ⓒ Ⓓ	76. Ⓐ Ⓑ Ⓒ Ⓓ
2. Ⓐ Ⓑ Ⓒ Ⓓ	27. Ⓐ Ⓑ Ⓒ Ⓓ	52. Ⓐ Ⓑ Ⓒ Ⓓ	77. Ⓐ Ⓑ Ⓒ Ⓓ
3. Ⓐ Ⓑ Ⓒ Ⓓ	28. Ⓐ Ⓑ Ⓒ Ⓓ	53. Ⓐ Ⓑ Ⓒ Ⓓ	78. Ⓐ Ⓑ Ⓒ Ⓓ
4. Ⓐ Ⓑ Ⓒ Ⓓ	29. Ⓐ Ⓑ Ⓒ Ⓓ	54. Ⓐ Ⓑ Ⓒ Ⓓ	79. Ⓐ Ⓑ Ⓒ Ⓓ
5. Ⓐ Ⓑ Ⓒ Ⓓ	30. Ⓐ Ⓑ Ⓒ Ⓓ	55. Ⓐ Ⓑ Ⓒ Ⓓ	80. Ⓐ Ⓑ Ⓒ Ⓓ
6. Ⓐ Ⓑ Ⓒ Ⓓ	31. Ⓐ Ⓑ Ⓒ Ⓓ	56. Ⓐ Ⓑ Ⓒ Ⓓ	81. Ⓐ Ⓑ Ⓒ Ⓓ
7. Ⓐ Ⓑ Ⓒ Ⓓ	32. Ⓐ Ⓑ Ⓒ Ⓓ	57. Ⓐ Ⓑ Ⓒ Ⓓ	82. Ⓐ Ⓑ Ⓒ Ⓓ
8. Ⓐ Ⓑ Ⓒ Ⓓ	33. Ⓐ Ⓑ Ⓒ Ⓓ	58. Ⓐ Ⓑ Ⓒ Ⓓ	83. Ⓐ Ⓑ Ⓒ Ⓓ
9. Ⓐ Ⓑ Ⓒ Ⓓ	34. Ⓐ Ⓑ Ⓒ Ⓓ	59. Ⓐ Ⓑ Ⓒ Ⓓ	84. Ⓐ Ⓑ Ⓒ Ⓓ
10. Ⓐ Ⓑ Ⓒ Ⓓ	35. Ⓐ Ⓑ Ⓒ Ⓓ	60. Ⓐ Ⓑ Ⓒ Ⓓ	85. Ⓐ Ⓑ Ⓒ Ⓓ
11. Ⓐ Ⓑ Ⓒ Ⓓ	36. Ⓐ Ⓑ Ⓒ Ⓓ	61. Ⓐ Ⓑ Ⓒ Ⓓ	86. Ⓐ Ⓑ Ⓒ Ⓓ
12. Ⓐ Ⓑ Ⓒ Ⓓ	37. Ⓐ Ⓑ Ⓒ Ⓓ	62. Ⓐ Ⓑ Ⓒ Ⓓ	87. Ⓐ Ⓑ Ⓒ Ⓓ
13. Ⓐ Ⓑ Ⓒ Ⓓ	38. Ⓐ Ⓑ Ⓒ Ⓓ	63. Ⓐ Ⓑ Ⓒ Ⓓ	88. Ⓐ Ⓑ Ⓒ Ⓓ
14. Ⓐ Ⓑ Ⓒ Ⓓ	39. Ⓐ Ⓑ Ⓒ Ⓓ	64. Ⓐ Ⓑ Ⓒ Ⓓ	89. Ⓐ Ⓑ Ⓒ Ⓓ
15. Ⓐ Ⓑ Ⓒ Ⓓ	40. Ⓐ Ⓑ Ⓒ Ⓓ	65. Ⓐ Ⓑ Ⓒ Ⓓ	90. Ⓐ Ⓑ Ⓒ Ⓓ
16. Ⓐ Ⓑ Ⓒ Ⓓ	41. Ⓐ Ⓑ Ⓒ Ⓓ	66. Ⓐ Ⓑ Ⓒ Ⓓ	91. Ⓐ Ⓑ Ⓒ Ⓓ
17. Ⓐ Ⓑ Ⓒ Ⓓ	42. Ⓐ Ⓑ Ⓒ Ⓓ	67. Ⓐ Ⓑ Ⓒ Ⓓ	92. Ⓐ Ⓑ Ⓒ Ⓓ
18. Ⓐ Ⓑ Ⓒ Ⓓ	43. Ⓐ Ⓑ Ⓒ Ⓓ	68. Ⓐ Ⓑ Ⓒ Ⓓ	93. Ⓐ Ⓑ Ⓒ Ⓓ
19. Ⓐ Ⓑ Ⓒ Ⓓ	44. Ⓐ Ⓑ Ⓒ Ⓓ	69. Ⓐ Ⓑ Ⓒ Ⓓ	94. Ⓐ Ⓑ Ⓒ Ⓓ
20. Ⓐ Ⓑ Ⓒ Ⓓ	45. Ⓐ Ⓑ Ⓒ Ⓓ	70. Ⓐ Ⓑ Ⓒ Ⓓ	95. Ⓐ Ⓑ Ⓒ Ⓓ
21. Ⓐ Ⓑ Ⓒ Ⓓ	46. Ⓐ Ⓑ Ⓒ Ⓓ	71. Ⓐ Ⓑ Ⓒ Ⓓ	96. Ⓐ Ⓑ Ⓒ Ⓓ
22. Ⓐ Ⓑ Ⓒ Ⓓ	47. Ⓐ Ⓑ Ⓒ Ⓓ	72. Ⓐ Ⓑ Ⓒ Ⓓ	97. Ⓐ Ⓑ Ⓒ Ⓓ
23. Ⓐ Ⓑ Ⓒ Ⓓ	48. Ⓐ Ⓑ Ⓒ Ⓓ	73. Ⓐ Ⓑ Ⓒ Ⓓ	98. Ⓐ Ⓑ Ⓒ Ⓓ
24. Ⓐ Ⓑ Ⓒ Ⓓ	49. Ⓐ Ⓑ Ⓒ Ⓓ	74. Ⓐ Ⓑ Ⓒ Ⓓ	99. Ⓐ Ⓑ Ⓒ Ⓓ
25. Ⓐ Ⓑ Ⓒ Ⓓ	50. Ⓐ Ⓑ Ⓒ Ⓓ	75. Ⓐ Ⓑ Ⓒ Ⓓ	100. Ⓐ Ⓑ Ⓒ Ⓓ

PRACTICE EXAM SIX

Directions: Look at this floor plan of an apartment, then answer questions 1 through 10.

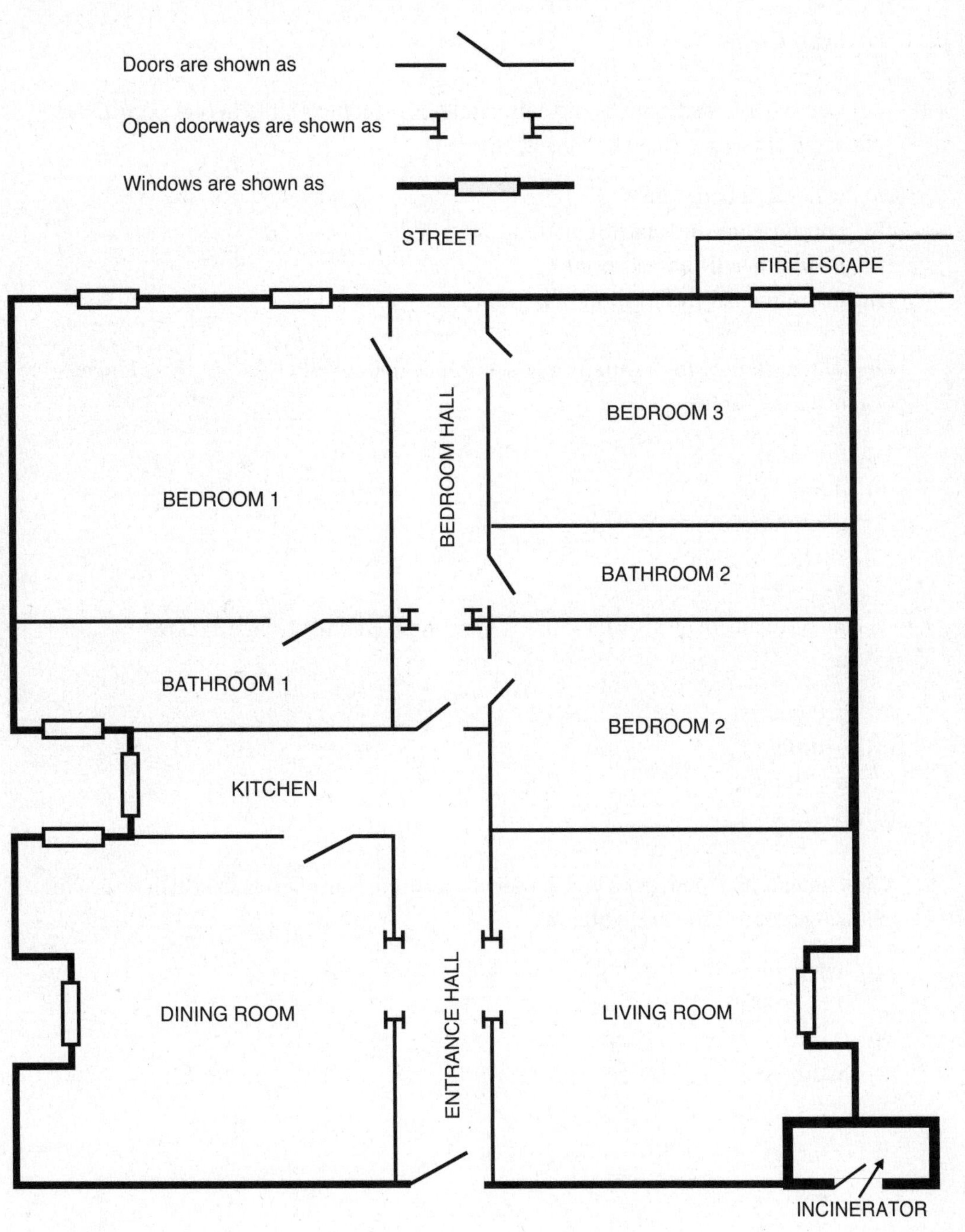

1. A person escaping a fire in the apartment can get on the fire escape by going through the window of

(A) bedroom 1.
(B) bedroom 2.
(C) bedroom 3.
(D) living room.

2. If there is a fire in bedroom 3, and a firefighter is rescuing a child in bedroom 2, the safest way of escape would be through the

(A) window of bedroom 2.
(B) entrance hall and apartment door.
(C) bedroom hall and bedroom 1.
(D) bedroom hall and window of bathroom 2.

3. Firefighters coming in the apartment's entrance door would have to go the longest distance to get to the

(A) fire escape.
(B) dining room.
(C) door of bathroom 2.
(D) kitchen window.

4. Which one of the following rooms in the apartment *cannot* be closed off by a door?

(A) living room
(B) bedroom 1
(C) bathroom 1
(D) bedroom 2

5. A firefighter is in a room from which there is only one way of escape. Which one of the following rooms is the firefighter in?

(A) living room
(B) dining room
(C) kitchen
(D) bedroom 2

6. There is a fire in the apartment and the ladder of the fire truck in the street cannot be placed against the fire escape. The ladder should be raised from the street to reach a window in

(A) bedroom 1.
(B) bedroom 2.
(C) bedroom 3.
(D) bedroom hall.

7. A door from the kitchen leads directly into

(A) the dining room.
(B) the living room.
(C) bathroom 1.
(D) the entrance hall.

8. If a fire breaks through the walls of the incinerator, the people in the apartment nearest to the fire are those in

(A) bedroom 2.
(B) bathroom 1.
(C) the kitchen.
(D) the living room.

9. Which one of the following choices lists two rooms which have *no* windows?

(A) bedroom 1 and bathroom 1
(B) bedroom 2 and bathroom 2
(C) kitchen and bathroom 2
(D) living room and dining room

10. The door that can be closed to separate the bedrooms from the rest of the apartment is the door between the

(A) entrance hall and the bedroom hall.
(B) living room and the entrance hall.
(C) kitchen and the living room.
(D) dining room and the living room.

Directions: Questions 11 through 13 should be answered solely on the basis of the passage below.

Automatic sprinkler systems are installed in many buildings. They extinguish or keep from spreading 96 percent of all fires in areas they protect. Sprinkler systems are made up of pipes which hang below the ceiling of each protected area and sprinkler heads which are placed along the pipes. The pipes are usually filled with water and each sprinkler head has a heat sensitive part. When the heat from the fire reaches the sensitive part of the sprinkler head, the head opens and showers water upon the fire in the form of spray. The heads are spaced so that the fire is covered by overlapping showers of water from the open heads.

11. Automatic sprinkler systems are installed in buildings to

    (A) prevent the buildup of dangerous gases.
    (B) eliminate the need for fire insurance.
    (C) extinguish fires or keep them from spreading.
    (D) protect 96 percent of the floor space.

12. If more than one sprinkler head opens, the area sprayed will be

    (A) flooded with hot water.
    (B) overlapped by showers of water.
    (C) subject to less water damage.
    (D) about 1 foot per sprinkler head.

13. A sprinkler head will open and shower water when

    (A) it is reached by heat from a fire.
    (B) water pressure in the pipes gets too high.
    (C) it is reached by sounds from a fire alarm.
    (D) water temperature in the pipes gets too low.

Directions: Some of questions 14 through 28 test your general knowledge.

14. Between fires, firefighters clean and check their equipment and vehicles. They probably do this because they want to

    (A) look busy when the public visits.
    (B) have more free time to watch TV or play cards
    (C) make the neighborhood proud of the appearance of the equipment and vehicles.
    (D) make sure the equipment and vehicles are in good working order.

15. Storekeepers are most likely to follow fire safety rules if they

    (A) have just opened up a new store.
    (B) have plenty of time.
    (C) are ordered to follow them.
    (D) understand the reasons for them.

16. Flammable liquids are generally heavier than air and tend to

    (A) accumulate at the ceiling.
    (B) seek out low points when spilled.
    (C) spread out very slowly.
    (D) decompose rapidly.

17. Which of the following is true about electric fuses?

    (A) They often blow and can be replaced by putting a penny behind them.
    (B) They are a safety device and blow when there is an overload of electricity.
    (C) They often blow and should be replaced by a larger size.
    (D) They are a safety device and should be handled only by a licensed electrician.

18. Hydrogen produced by charging a storage battery has been found to diffuse rapidly in the air above the battery. What does this indicate?

    (A) The gas is dangerous and needs ventilation.
    (B) The battery is fully charged.
    (C) You need to supply oxygen to the area.
    (D) The battery is rapidly deteriorating.

19. If a length of fire hose does not exceed 50′ and is no less than 40′, what is the minimum amount of hose needed to reach a fire 350′ away?

(A) 7 lengths
(B) 9 lengths
(C) 11 lengths
(D) 15 lengths

20. A fire engine has a tank with 1,000 gallons of water and pumps it at the rate of 150 gallons per minute. About how long will the water supply last?

(A) 10 minutes
(B) 8½ minutes
(C) 6½ minutes
(D) 5 minutes

21. Minimum wage means

(A) you work for little or no money.
(B) the least amount of hourly pay you can receive.
(C) you earn as much as you want.
(D) you earn only a small amount.

22. A German leader named Adolf Hitler ruled as a ____________.

(A) director
(B) dictator
(C) derelict
(D) degenerate

23. When did the Japanese attack Pearl Harbor?

(A) June 5, 1941
(B) December 17, 1941
(C) December 7, 1941
(D) June 5, 1945

24. The *Enola Gay* dropped a bomb on Hiroshima, Japan. What type of bomb was it?

(A) Atomic
(B) Hydrogen
(C) Aerial
(D) TNT

25. The Democratic and Republican Parties each have a symbol. The Democratic Party's symbol is a donkey. What is the symbol of the Republican Party?

(A) Goat
(B) Elephant
(C) Horse
(D) Burro

26. The bringing together of all races in education, jobs, and housing is

(A) interacting.
(B) inflammation.
(C) interracial.
(D) integration.

27. Everyone is entitled to a trial by a panel of their peers. A _______ is a group of citizens who decide your case.

(A) jury
(B) journey
(C) supreme court
(D) appellate court

28. The first ten amendments to the Constitution are called

(A) the Premise.
(B) the Preamble.
(C) the Bill of Rights.
(D) the Promise.

Directions: Questions 29 through 32 should be answered solely on the basis of the passage below.

About 48 percent of all reported fires are false alarms. False alarms add more risk of danger to firefighters, citizens, and property, as well as waste the money and time of the fire department. When the first firefighters are called to a reported fire, they do not know if the alarm is for a real fire or is a false alarm. Until they have made sure that the alarm is false, they must not respond to a new alarm even if a real fire is burning and people's lives and property are in danger. If they do not find a fire or an emergency at the original location, then the firefighters radio the fire department that they have been called to a false alarm. The fire department radios back and tells the firefighters that they are in active service again and tells them where to respond for the next alarm. If that location is far from that of the false alarm, then the distance and the time it takes to get to the new location are increased. This means that firefighters will arrive later to help in fighting the real fire and the fire will have more time to burn. The fire will be bigger and more dangerous just because someone called the firefighters to a false alarm. In addition, each time the firefighters ride to the location of a false alarm, there is additional risk of unnecessary accidents and injuries to them and to citizens.

29. The main point of the passage is that false alarms

    (A) seldom interrupt other activities in the firehouse.
    (B) occur more often during the winter.
    (C) are rarely turned in by children.
    (D) add more risk of danger to life and property.

30. When firefighters are called to a false alarm, they must not respond to other alarms until they

    (A) turn in a written report to the fire department.
    (B) take a vote and all agree to go.
    (C) are put back into active service by the fire department.
    (D) decide on the quickest route.

31. Before firefighters get to the location of a reported fire, they

    (A) finish eating their lunch at the firehouse.
    (B) do not know if the alarm is real or false.
    (C) search the neighborhood for the person who made the report.
    (D) do not know if the alarm is from an alarm box or telephone.

32. The passage states that false alarms

    (A) shorten travel time to real fires.
    (B) give firefighters needed driving practice.
    (C) save money on fuel for the fire department.
    (D) account for about 48 percent of reported fires.

Directions: Answer questions 33 through 35 using the information provided.

33. An elderly man staggers into the firehouse and tells the firefighters on duty that he is having trouble breathing. Of the following, it would be best for the firefighters to

    (A) send the elderly man away as his staggering shows that he has been drinking too much.
    (B) place the elderly man in a chair and quickly call for assistance.
    (C) tell the elderly man to go to the hospital and see a doctor.
    (D) help the elderly man leave the firehouse as this is not a problem that firefighters should handle.

34. When firefighters travel to and from their firehouse they usually look around the neighborhood in order to spot dangerous conditions. If they spot a dangerous condition, firefighters will take action to correct it. They do this because they want to prevent fires. While on the way to work overtime at a nearby firehouse, a firefighter passes a local gas station and spots a leaking gasoline pump. Which one of the following is the most appropriate course of action for the firefighter to take?

    (A) Stop at the gas station and make sure that the leak is actually gasoline by lighting a match to it.
    (B) Continue on to work because the gas station attendant will take care of the leak.
    (C) Stop at the gas station and tell the gas station attendant to make sure the leak is repaired.
    (D) Call the Mayor's Office to complain that the leaking gasoline is polluting the area.

35. A newly appointed firefighter is assigned to go with an experienced firefighter to inspect a paint store. The paint store owner refuses to allow the inspection, saying that she is closing the store early that day and going on vacation. The new firefighter demands rudely that the inspection be allowed, even though it would be permissible to delay it. Of the following, it would be best for the experienced firefighter to

    (A) repeat the demand that the inspection be allowed and quote the law to the store owner.
    (B) tell the new firefighter that it would be best to schedule the inspection after the store owner's vacation.
    (C) tell the store owner to step aside, and instruct the new firefighter to enter the store and begin the inspection.
    (D) tell the new firefighter to forget about the inspection because the store owner is uncooperative.

Directions: Questions 36 through 43 are to be answered by referring to the items pictured below. The sizes of the items shown are not drawn to scale. Each item is identified by a number. For each question, select the answer which gives the identifying number of the item that best answers the question.

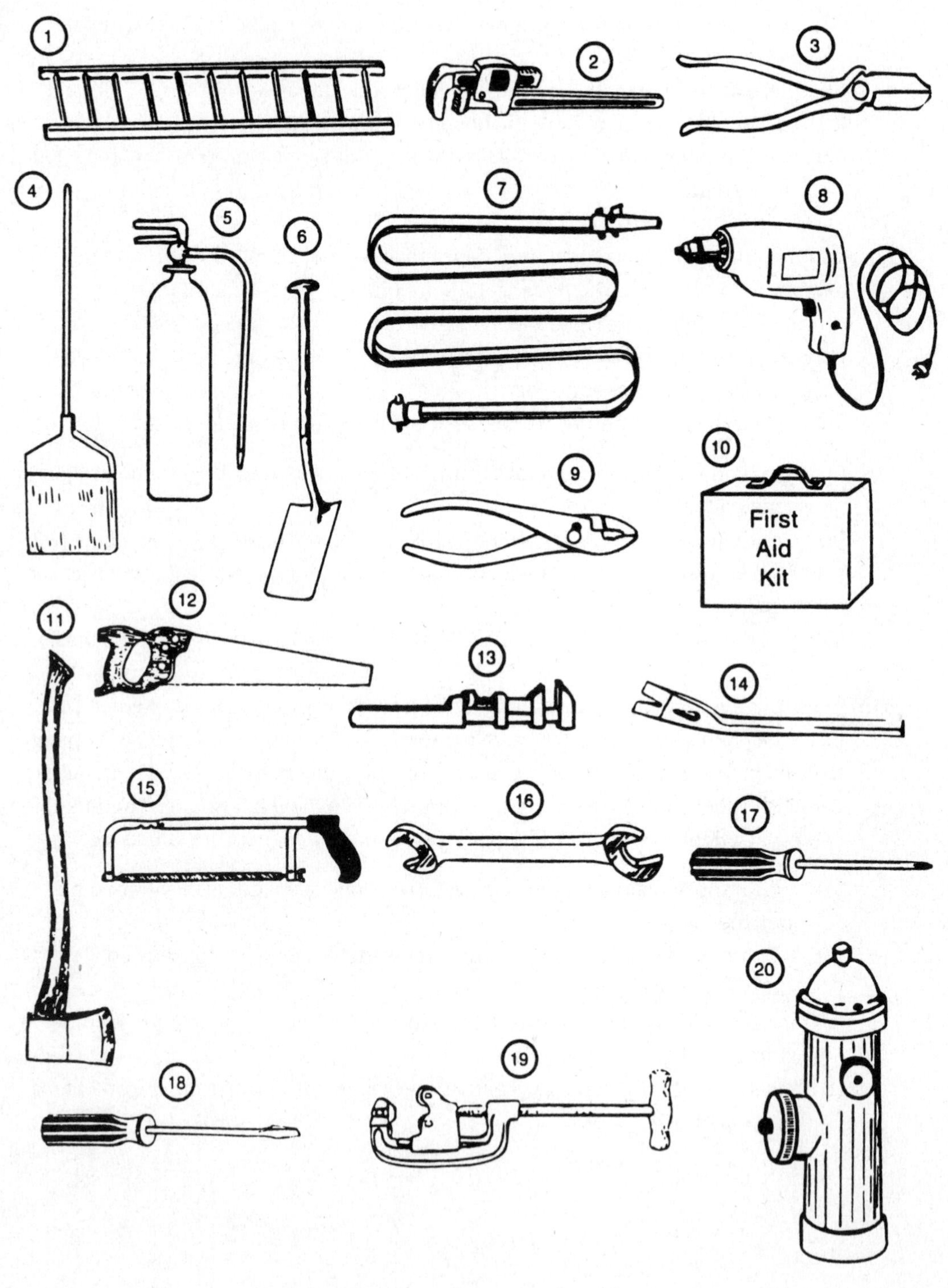

36. Which item should be connected to a hydrant and used to put out a fire?

(A) 5
(B) 7
(C) 8
(D) 17

37. Which pair of items could be used after a fire to clean a floor covered with small pieces of burned materials?

(A) 1 and 14
(B) 4 and 6
(C) 10 and 12
(D) 11 and 13

38. Which pair of items could be used for cutting a branch from a tree?

(A) 2 and 3
(B) 8 and 9
(C) 11 and 12
(D) 14 and 15

39. Which item should be used to rescue a victim from a second-floor window?

(A) 1
(B) 10
(C) 15
(D) 20

40. Which pair of items should be used to tighten a nut on a screw?

(A) 2 and 3
(B) 8 and 19
(C) 9 and 14
(D) 16 and 18

41. Which item should be used to repair a leaky faucet?

(A) 4
(B) 5
(C) 12
(D) 13

42. Which item should be used as a source of water at a fire?

(A) 2
(B) 6
(C) 9
(D) 20

43. Which item should be used for cutting metal?

(A) 6
(B) 13
(C) 15
(D) 18

Directions: Answer questions 44 and 45 using the illustration.

44. The illustration below shows a firefighter standing on a ladder. The firefighter should notice that a dangerous condition exists. Which of the following choices corresponds to the letter in the diagram showing the dangerous condition?

(A) The firefighter's coat is too long for safe climbing of the ladder.
(B) A helmet keeps the firefighter from seeing what is going on.
(C) The firefighter's feet are on the ladder rung.
(D) The ladder rung is missing.

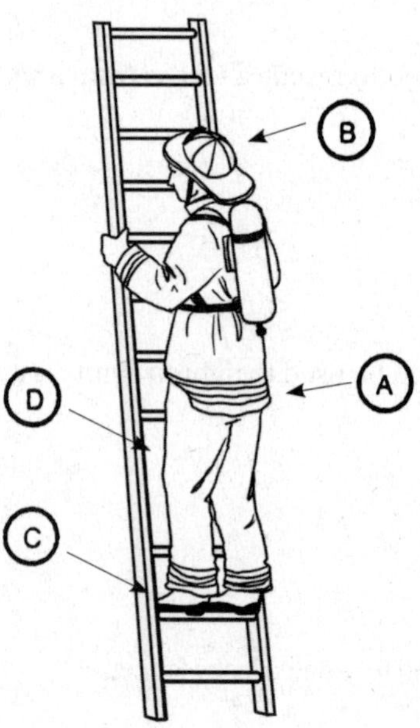

45. A firefighter is ordered to set up a hose on the street outside a building in which the second floor is on fire. The hose should be located about 30 feet from the building and should be aimed directly at the fire. Which one of the following diagrams shows how the firefighter should position the hose to aim it at the fire?

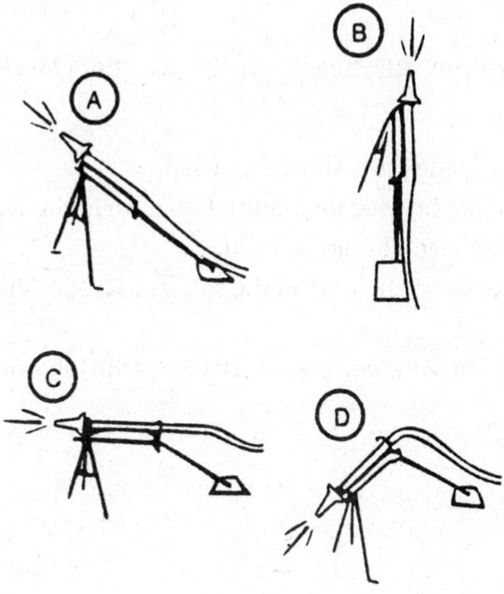

Directions: Questions 46 through 52 are to be answered solely on the basis of the following information.

The portable power saw lets the firefighter cut through various materials so that a fire can be reached. It can be dangerous, however, if it is not properly used or if it has not been inspected and tested to insure that it is in serviceable condition. The parts of the saw should be clean and free of foreign material, especially the exhaust port and spark arrestor, the carburetor enclosure, the cooling fins, the spark plugs, and the V-belt pulley if the saw has one.

The saw should be checked to make sure it has both air and fuel filters. It should never be run without an air filter. The V-belt pulley, if present, must be checked to make sure it is not too tight or too loose. If too loose, it could cause slipping. If too tight, the blade might turn when the engine idles, there might be damage to the clutch bearing, or the motor might stall when the blade is stopped. All nuts, bolts, and screws should be checked for tightness.

The saw may use carbide-tipped blades, aluminum oxide blades, or silicon carbide blades. Carbide-tipped blades should be returned for replacement when two or more tips are broken or missing or when the tips are worn down to the circumference of the blade. Aluminum oxide and silicon carbide blades should be replaced when they are cracked, badly nicked, or when worn down to an eight-inch diameter or less.

46. The principal reason for inspecting power saws is to make sure that

(A) they are clean.
(B) they are in serviceable condition.
(C) the pulley is not too tight or too loose.
(D) the blades are replaced.

47. What does the passage mean when it says the saw should be kept free of foreign material?

(A) Only American-made parts should be used.
(B) The saw should not be used on material that might damage it.
(C) Both air and fuel filters should be used.
(D) Anything that does not belong on the saw or in it should be removed.

48. Some saws are made to work *without* which one of the following items?

(A) an air filter
(B) a fuel filter
(C) a V-belt pulley
(D) blades

49. If the V-belt pulley on a power saw is too loose, it is most likely to cause

(A) the blade to turn when the engine idles.
(B) damage to the clutch bearing.
(C) the motor to stall when the blade is stopped.
(D) slipping.

50. The passage says that a power saw should *never* be run without

(A) an air filter.
(B) a fuel filter.
(C) a V-belt pulley.
(D) a blade.

51. Which of the following blades should be replaced when two or more tips are missing?

(A) Both aluminum oxide and carbide-tipped blades
(B) Carbide-tipped blades only
(C) Both silicon carbide and aluminum oxide blades
(D) Silicon carbide blades only

52. Which of the following blades would not be replaced when worn down to an eight-inch diameter or less?

(A) Both aluminum oxide and carbide-tipped blades
(B) Carbide-tipped blades only
(C) Both silicon carbide and aluminum oxide blades
(D) Silicon carbide blades only

Directions: Answer questions 53 and 54 using the information provided in the question.

53. Fire engines use diesel motors to make them run. Diesel motors have devices called air cleaners, which keep dirt from the inside of the motor. To make sure that the air cleaners are cleaned or replaced when necessary, an indicator on the fire engine will display a red color if the air cleaner has become too dirty. Each time the lubricating oil in the motor is changed, or whenever the indicator shows red, the air cleaners must be inspected and cleaned or replaced.

Of the following, the most accurate statement concerning air cleaners on fire engine diesel motors is that they should be

(A) cleaned every day.
(B) replaced only when the oil is changed.
(C) inspected and cleaned only when the oil is changed.
(D) inspected and cleaned or replaced when the indicator shows red.

54. Firefighter Green must check the supply of air tank cylinders at the beginning of each tour of duty. There must be ten air tank cylinders always full of air and ready to be exchanged for used, empty air tank cylinders. At the start of a new tour of duty, Firefighter Green finds that out of twenty cylinders present, only five cylinders are full and ready to be exchanged. What is the minimum number of used empty cylinders that Firefighter Green must replace with full cylinders?

(A) 5
(B) 10
(C) 15
(D) 20

Directions: Questions 55 through 58 should be answered solely on the basis of the passage below.

Fires in vacant buildings are a major problem for firefighters. People enter vacant buildings to remove building material or they damage stairs, floors, doors and other parts of the building. The buildings are turned into dangerous structures with stairs missing, holes in the floors, weakened walls and loose bricks. Children and arsonists find large amounts of wood, paper and other combustible materials in the buildings and start fires which damage and weaken the buildings even more. Firefighters have been injured putting out fires in these buildings due to these dangerous conditions. Most injuries caused while putting out fires in vacant buildings could be eliminated if all of these buildings were repaired. All such injuries could be eliminated if the buildings were demolished. Until then, firefighters should take extra care while putting out fires in vacant buildings.

55. The problem of fires in vacant buildings could be solved by

(A) repairing buildings.
(B) closing up the cellar door and windows with bricks and cement.
(C) arresting suspicious persons before they start the fires.
(D) demolishing the buildings.

56. Firefighters are injured putting out fires in vacant buildings because

(A) there are no tenants to help fight the fires.
(B) conditions are dangerous in these buildings.
(C) they are not as careful when nobody lives in the buildings.
(D) the water in the buildings has been turned off.

57. Vacant buildings often have

(A) occupied buildings on either side of them.
(B) safe empty spaces where neighborhood children can play.
(C) combustible materials inside them.
(D) strong walls and floors that cannot burn.

58. While firefighters are putting out fires in vacant buildings, they should

(A) be extra careful of missing stairs.
(B) arrest the arsonists who start the fires.
(C) learn the reasons why the fires are set.
(D) help to repair the buildings.

Directions: Answer questions 59 through 63 solely on the basis of the following information and map.

A firefighter may be required to assist civilians who seek travel directions or referral to city agencies and facilities.

The following is a map of part of a city, where several public offices and other institutions are located. Each of the squares represents one city block. Street names are as shown. If there is an arrow next to the street name, it means the street is one way only in the direction of the arrow. If there is no arrow next to the street name, two-way traffic is allowed.

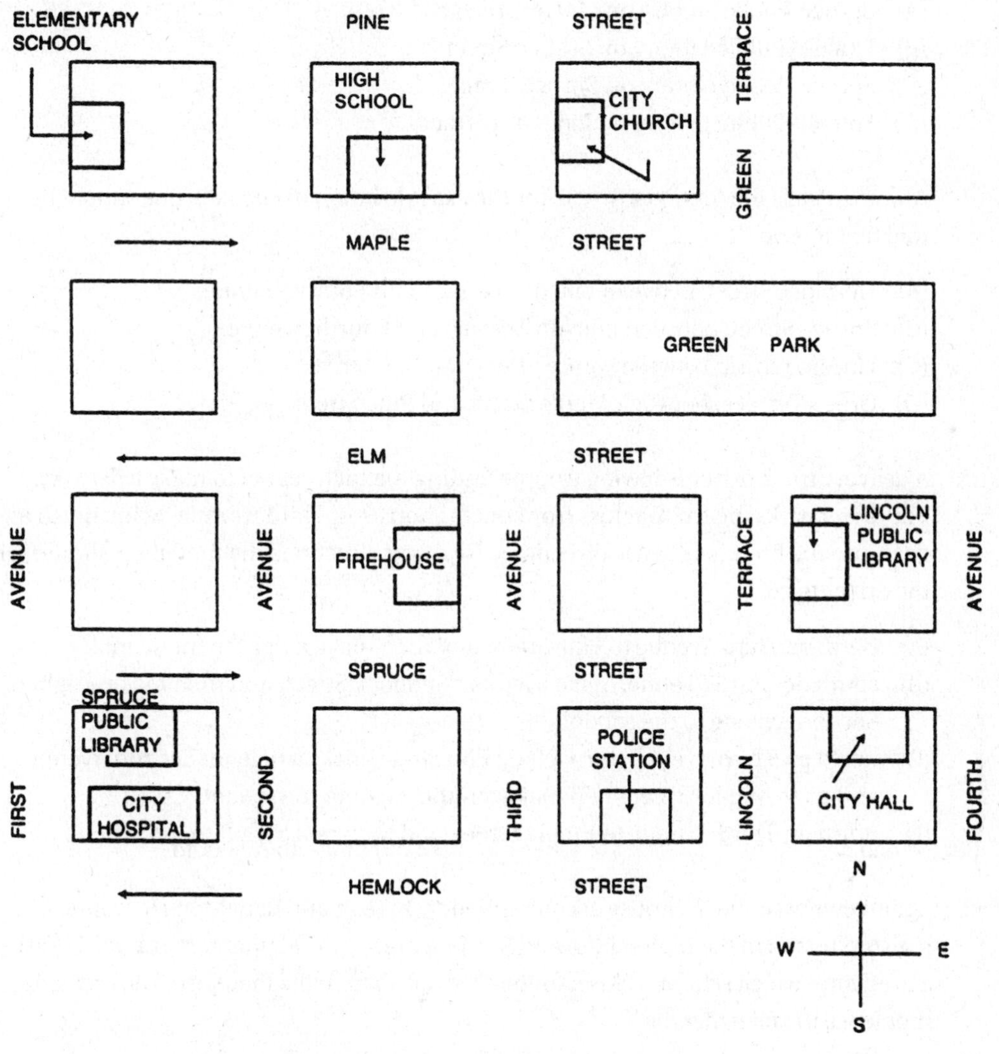

59. A woman whose handbag was stolen from her in Green Park asks a firefighter at the firehouse where to go to report the crime. The firefighter should tell the woman to go to the

(A) police station on Spruce St.
(B) police station on Hemlock St.
(C) city hall on Spruce St.
(D) city hall on Hemlock St.

60. A disabled senior citizen who lives on Green Terrace telephones the firehouse to ask which library is closest to her home. The firefighter should tell the senior citizen it is the

(A) Spruce Public Library on Lincoln Terrace.
(B) Lincoln Public Library on Spruce Street.
(C) Spruce Public Library on Spruce Street.
(D) Lincoln Public Library on Lincoln Terrace.

61. A woman calls the firehouse to ask for the exact location of city hall. She should be told that it is on

(A) Hemlock Street, between Lincoln Terrace and Fourth Avenue.
(B) Spruce Street, between Lincoln Terrace and Fourth Avenue.
(C) Lincoln Terrace, between Spruce Street and Elm Street.
(D) Green Terrace, between Maple Street and Pine Street.

62. A delivery truck driver is having trouble finding the high school to make a delivery. The driver parks the truck across from the firehouse on Third Avenue facing north and goes into the firehouse to ask directions. In giving directions the firefighter should tell the driver to go

(A) north on Third Avenue to Pine Street and then make a right to the school.
(B) south on Third Avenue, make a left on Hemlock Street, and then make a right on Second Avenue to the school.
(C) north on Third Avenue, turn left on Elm Street, make a right on Second Avenue and go to Maple Street, then make another right to the school.
(D) north on Third Avenue to Maple Street, and then make a left to the school.

63. A man comes to the firehouse accompanied by his son and daughter. He wants to register his son in the high school and his daughter in the elementary school. He asks a firefighter which school is closer for him to walk to from the firehouse. The firefighter should tell the man that the

(A) high school is closer than the elementary school.
(B) elementary school is closer than the high school.
(C) elementary school and high school are the same distance away.
(D) elementary school and the high school are in opposite directions.

Directions: Questions 64 through 68 should be answered solely on the basis of the passage below.

Sometimes a fire engine leaving the scene of a fire must back out of a street because other fire engines have blocked the path in front of it. When the fire engine is backing up, each firefighter is given a duty to perform to help control automobile traffic and protect people walking nearby. Before the driver starts to slowly back up the fire engine, all the other firefighters are told the route he will take. They walk alongside and toward the rear of the slowly moving fire engine, guiding the driver, keeping traffic out of the street, and warning people away from the path of the vehicle. As the fire engine, in reverse gear, approaches the intersection, the driver brings it to a full stop and waits for his supervisor to give the order to start moving again. If traffic is blocking the intersection, two firefighters enter the intersection to direct traffic. They clear the cars and people out of the intersection, making way for the fire engine to back into it. The driver then goes forward, turning into the intersection. Two other firefighters keep cars and people away from the front of the fire engine as it moves. Because of the extra care needed to control cars and protect people in the streets when a fire engine is backing up, it is better to drive a fire engine forward whenever possible.

64. A fire engine is leaving the scene of a fire. The street in front of it is blocked by people and other fire engines. Of the following, it would be best for the driver to

(A) put on the siren to clear a path.
(B) back out of the street slowly.
(C) drive on the sidewalk around the other fire engines.
(D) move the other fire engines out of the way.

65. Firefighters walk alongside and behind the fire engine when it is backing up in order to

(A) strengthen their legs and stay physically fit.
(B) look around the neighborhood for fires.
(C) ensure that the engine moves slowly.
(D) control traffic, protect people, and assist the driver.

66. A fire engine going in reverse approaches an intersection blocked with cars and trucks. The driver should

(A) go forward, and then try to back into the intersection at a different angle.
(B) slowly enter the intersection as the firefighters guiding the driver give the signal to move.
(C) back up through the intersection without stopping.
(D) stop, then enter the intersection only when the supervisor gives the signal to move.

67. The passage states that the two firefighters who first enter the intersection

(A) clear the intersection of cars and people.
(B) direct the cars past the fire engine when the engine is in forward gear.
(C) see if the traffic signal is working properly.
(D) set up barriers to block any traffic.

68. The diagram to the right shows a fire engine backing slowly out of Jones Street. The letters indicate where firefighters are standing. Which firefighter is *not* in the correct position?

(A) Firefighter D
(B) Firefighter E
(C) Firefighter A
(D) Firefighter C

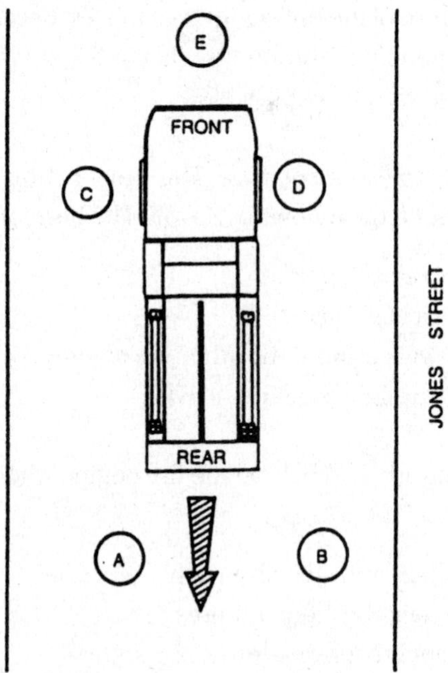

Directions: Questions 69 through 74 are to be answered solely on the basis of the following information.

In order to extinguish fires, firefighters must pull enough hose from the fire engine to reach the fire. Each length of hose is 50 feet long. The lengths of hose are attached together so that the water can go from the pump on the fire engine to a position where it will extinguish the fire.

69. If the total distance to reach the fire is 50 feet, what is the minimum number of lengths of hose needed?

(A) 1
(B) 2
(C) 3
(D) 4

70. If the total distance to reach the fire is 250 feet, what is the minimum number of lengths of hose needed?

(A) 3
(B) 4
(C) 5
(D) 6

71. If the total distance to reach the fire is 175 feet, what is the minimum number of lengths of hose needed?

(A) 2
(B) 3
(C) 4
(D) 5

72. If the total distance to reach the fire is 125 feet, what is the minimum number of lengths of hose needed?

(A) 2
(B) 3
(C) 4
(D) 5

73. If the total distance to reach the fire is 315 feet, what is the minimum number of lengths of hose needed?

(A) 3
(B) 5
(C) 6
(D) 7

74. If the total distance to reach the fire is 230 feet, what is the minimum number of lengths of hose needed?

(A) 4
(B) 5
(C) 6
(D) 7

Directions: Questions 75 through 79 concern various forms, reports, or other documents that must be filed according to topic. Listed below are four topics numbered 1 through 4 under which forms, reports and documents may be filed. In each question choose the topic under which the form, report or document concerned should be filed.

1. Equipment and supplies
2. Fire Prevention
3. Personnel
4. Training

75. Under which topic would it be most appropriate to file a letter on a heroic act performed by a member of the fire company?

    (A) 1
    (B) 2
    (C) 3
    (D) 4

76. Under which topic should a firefighter look for information about the fire company's new portable ladder?

    (A) 1
    (B) 2
    (C) 3
    (D) 4

77. Under which topic should a firefighter locate a copy of the fire company's fire prevention building inspection schedule for the current year?

    (A) 1
    (B) 2
    (C) 3
    (D) 4

78. Under which topic should a firefighter file a copy of a report on company property which has been damaged?

    (A) 1
    (B) 2
    (C) 3
    (D) 4

79. Under which topic should a firefighter be able to locate a roster of firefighters assigned to the company?

(A) 1
(B) 2
(C) 3
(D) 4

Directions: Questions 80 and 81 should be answered solely on the basis of the passage below.

Firefighters inspect many different kinds of places to find fire hazards and have them removed. During these inspections the firefighters try to learn as much as possible about the place. This knowledge is useful should the firefighters have to fight a fire at some later date at that location. When inspecting subways, firefighters are much concerned with the effects a fire might have on the passengers because, unless they have been trapped in a subway car during a fire, most subway riders do not think about the dangers involved in a fire in the subway. During a fire, the air in cars crowded with passengers may become intensely hot. The cars may fill with dense smoke. Lights may dim or go out altogether, leaving the passengers in darkness. Ventilation from fans and air conditioning may stop. The train may be stuck and unable to be moved through the tunnel to a station. Fear may send the trapped passengers into a panic. Firefighters must protect the passengers from the fire, heat and smoke, calm them down, get them out quickly to a safe area, and put out the fire. To do this firefighters may have to climb from street level down into the subway tunnel to reach a train stopped inside the tunnel. Before actually going on the tracks, they must be sure that the 600 volts of live electricity carried by the third rail is shut off. They may have to stretch fire hose a long distance down subway stairs, on platforms, and along the subway tracks to get the water to the fire and put it out. Subway fires are difficult to fight because of these special problems, but preparing for them in advance can help save the lives of both firefighters and passengers.

80. During a subway fire a train is stuck in a tunnel. Firefighters have been ordered into the tunnel. Before firefighters actually step down on the tracks they must be sure that

(A) all the passengers have been removed from the burning subway cars to a safe place.
(B) they have stretched their fire hose a long distance to put water on the fire.
(C) live electricity carried by the third rail is shut off.
(D) the train is moved from the tunnel to the nearest station.

81. According to the above passage, fire in the subway may leave passengers in subway cars in darkness. This occurs mainly because

(A) the lights may go out.
(B) air in the cars may become very hot.
(C) ventilation may stop.
(D) people may panic.

Directions: Answer question 82 using the information and illustraitons provided.

82. Firefighters must check gauges on fire engines so that defects are discovered and corrected. Some fire engines are equipped with gauges called "voltmeters" which indicate whether or not the electrical system is operating properly. When the fire engine's motor is running, the voltmeter of a properly operating electrical system will show a reading of 13.5 to 14.2 volts on the scale.

Which one of the following gauges shows a properly operating electrical system?

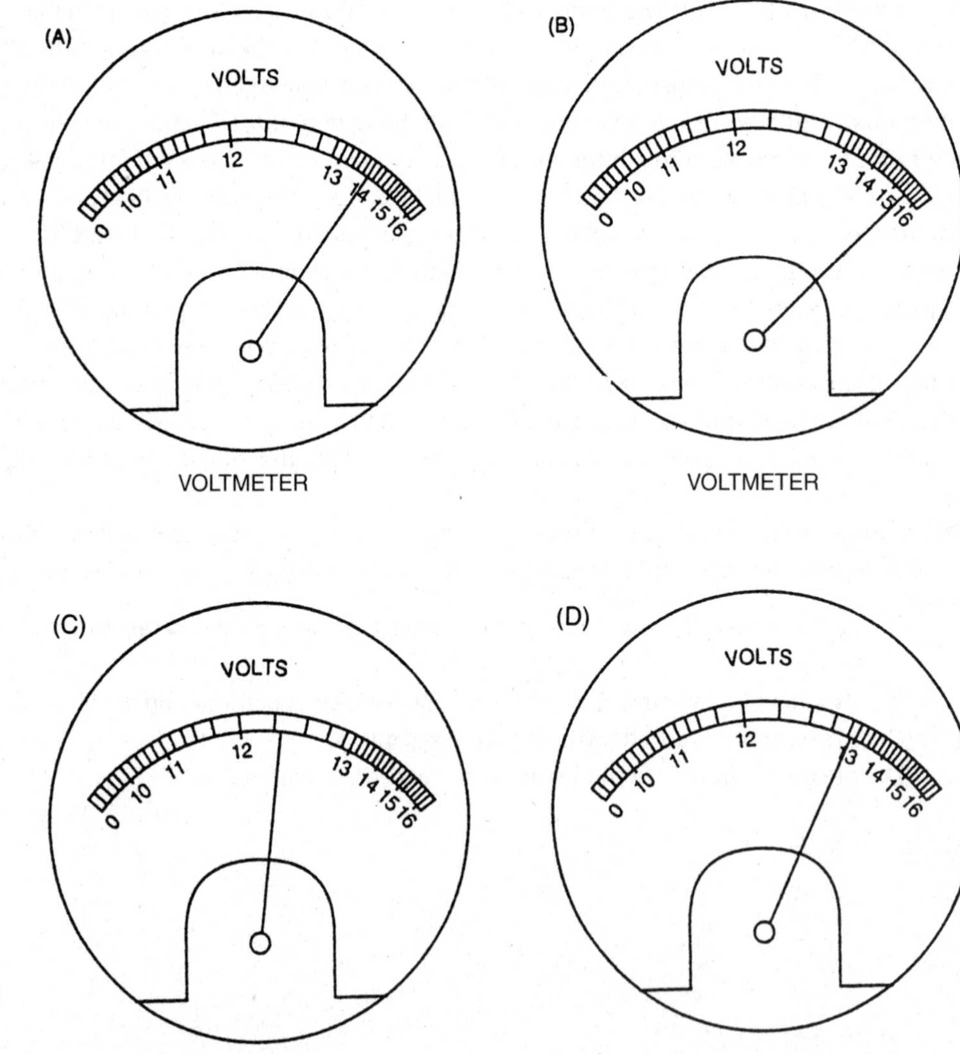

Directions: Answer questions 83 and 84 using the diagrams and information provided.

Firefighters breathe through an air mask to protect their lungs from dangerous smoke when fighting fires. The air for the mask comes from a cylinder which the firefighter wears. A full cylinder contains 45 cubic feet of air when pressurized to 4,500 pounds per square inch.

83. A gauge that firefighters read to tell how much air is left in the cylinder is pictured in the diagram below. The gauge indicates that the cylinder is

    (A) full.
    (B) empty.
    (C) more than ¾ full.
    (D) less than ½ full.

84. A gauge which is part of the cylinder shows the pressure of the air in the cylinder in hundreds of pounds per square inch. Which of the following diagrams shows a cylinder which is more than half full?

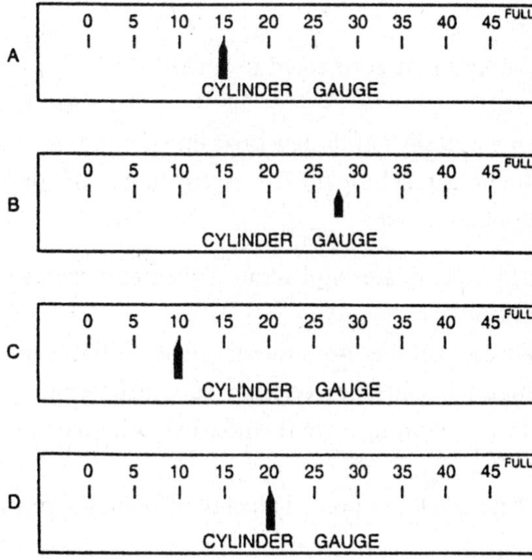

PRACTICE EXAM SIX

Directions: Questions 85 and 86 should be answered solely on the basis of the passage below.

The Fire Department uses a firehose nozzle with an automatically adjusting tip. The automatically adjusting nozzle tip keeps the water pressure at the tip constant even though the amount of water being pumped through the hose from the fire engine may vary. A partial loss of water in the hose line does not result in the stream of water from the nozzle falling short of the target. A partial loss of water is caused by a kink in the hose somewhere between the fire engine pumping the water and the nozzle or by insufficient pressure being supplied by the fire engine pumping water into the hose line.

The danger of this automatic nozzle is that as the nozzle tip adjusts to maintain constant water pressure, the number of gallons of water per minute flowing out of the nozzle is reduced. When the number of gallons of water per minute flowing from the nozzle is reduced, the nozzle is easier to handle and the stream of water coming from the nozzle appears to be adequate. However, since the number of gallons of flow is reduced, the cooling power of the hose stream will probably not be enough to fight the fire. If a firefighter can physically handle the hose line alone, the nozzle is not discharging enough water, even though the stream coming out of the nozzle appears adequate. An adequate fire stream requires two firefighters to handle the hose line.

85. An officer tells a firefighter to find out why enough water is not coming out of a hose line equipped with an automatic nozzle. The firefighter follows the hose line from the nozzle back to the fire engine pumping the water into the hose, but finds no kinks in the hose. The firefighter should inform the officer that the inadequate flow of water is probably due to

    (A) a defective automatic nozzle.
    (B) the nozzle stream being aimed in the wrong direction.
    (C) insufficient pressure being supplied by the fire engine pumping water into the hose line.
    (D) the fire engine not being connected to a hydrant.

86. One firefighter alone is easily handling a hose line equipped with an automatic nozzle. The hose line's stream is reaching the fire. According to the passage, the firefighter should probably conclude that

    (A) being able to handle the hoseline alone indicates extreme strength and excellent physical condition.
    (B) the stream of water coming from the nozzle is probably not an acceptable firefighting stream because not enough water is flowing.
    (C) the stream of water coming from the nozzle is adequate and is helping to save water.
    (D) the automatic nozzle has adjusted itself to provide the proper amount of water to fight the fire.

Directions: Answer questions 87 through 90 solely on the basis of the following facts and diagrams below.

The gauges shown below in Diagrams I and II represent gauges on a fire engine's pump control panel at the scene of a fire. Diagram I gives the readings at 10 A.M. and Diagram II gives the readings at 10:15 A.M. Each diagram has one gauge labeled "Intake" and one gauge marked "Discharge." The "Intake" gauges show the pressure in pounds per square inch (psi) of the water coming into the pumps on the fire engine from a hydrant. The "Discharge" gauges show the pressure in pounds per square inch (psi) of the water leaving the pumps on the fire engine. The pumps on the fire engine raise the pressure of the water coming from the hydrant to the higher pressures needed in the fire hoses.

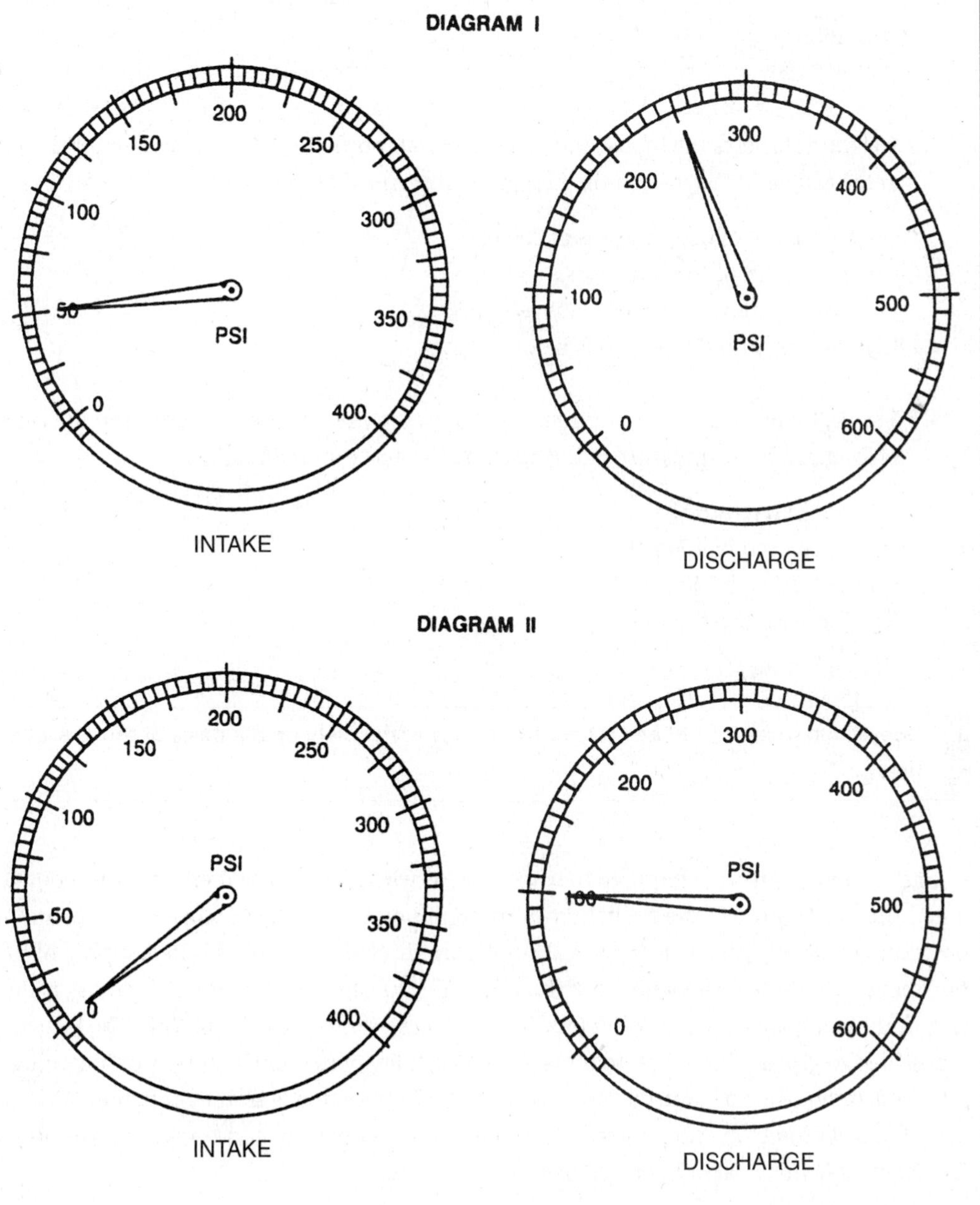

PRACTICE EXAM SIX

87. The firefighter looks at the gauges as shown in Diagram I and observes that the pressure in pounds per square inch (psi) of the water coming into the pumps is most nearly

(A) 50.
(B) 250.
(C) 300.
(D) 500.

88. The firefighter looks at the gauges shown in Diagram I and observes that the pressure in pounds per square inch (psi) of the water going out of the pumps is most nearly

(A) 25.
(B) 50.
(C) 250.
(D) 500.

89. Diagram II shows the intake and discharge water pressure 15 minutes later. By looking at the gauges in Diagram II, the firefighter observes that the water

(A) going out of the pumps is at 200 psi.
(B) going out of the pumps is at 5 psi.
(C) coming into the pumps is above 10 psi.
(D) coming into the pumps is below 10 psi.

90. The firefighter is able to determine that, between the time of Diagram I and the time of Diagram II, the pressure of the discharge water from the pumps

(A) increased by 50 psi.
(B) decreased by 150 psi.
(C) decreased by 45 psi.
(D) increased by 145 psi.

Directions: Questions 91 and 92 are to be answered solely on the basis of the passage below.

Firefighters at times are required to work in areas where the atmosphere contains contaminated smoke. To protect the firefighter from breathing the harmful smoke, a self-contained breathing mask is worn. The mask will supply the firefighter with a limited supply of pure breathing air. This will allow the firefighter to enter the smoke-filled area. The mask is lightweight and compact which makes it less tiring and easier to move around with. The face mask is designed to give the firefighter that maximum visibility possible. The supply of breathing air is limited and the rate of air used depends upon the exertion made by the firefighter. Although the mask will protect the firefighter from some types of contaminated smoke, it gives no protection from flame, heat or heat exhaustion.

91. The rate at which the firefighter breathes the air from the mask will depend upon the

(A) amount of energy used by the firefighter.
(B) amount of smoke the firefighter will breathe.
(C) color of the flames that the firefighter will enter.
(D) color of the heat that the firefighter will enter.

92. According to the passage, the mask will protect the firefighter from some types of

(A) flames.
(B) smoke.
(C) heat.
(D) heat exhaustion.

Directions: Questions 93 through 96 should be answered solely on the basis of the passage below.

In each firehouse one firefighter is always on Housewatch duty. Each 24-hour Housewatch tour begins at 9 A.M. each day, and is divided into eight 3-hour periods. The firefighter on Housewatch is responsible for the correct receipt, acknowledgment, and report of every alarm signal from any source. Firefighters on Housewatch are required to enter in the Company Journal the receipt of all alarms as well as other matters required by Department Regulations. All entries by the firefighter on Housewatch should be written in blue or black ink. Any entries made by firefighters not on Housewatch are made in red ink. Most entries, including receipt of alarms, are recorded in order, starting in the front of the Company Journal on page 1. Certain types of entries are recorded in special places in the Journal. When high level officers visit the company, those visits are recorded on page 500. Company training drills and instruction periods are recorded on page 497. The monthly meter readings of the utility companies which serve the firehouse are recorded on page 493.

93. A firefighter is asked by the company officer to find out what alarms were received the previous day, August 25, between 1 A.M. and 2 A.M. Where in the Company Journal should the firefighter look to obtain this information?

(A) on page 493.
(B) between page 1 and page 492, on the page for August 25.
(C) on page 500.
(D) between page 497 and page 500, on the page for August 25.

94. A firefighter on Housewatch is asked to find out how much electricity was used in the firehouse between the last two meter readings taken by Con Edison. On which one of the following pages of the Company Journal should the firefighter look to find the last two electrical meter readings entered?

(A) 253
(B) 493
(C) 497
(D) 500

95. A firefighter on Housewatch duty is notified by a passing civilian of a rubbish fire around the block. The company responds, extinguishes the rubbish fire and returns to the firehouse. The firefighter on Housewatch should

(A) make no entry in the Company Journal of the receipt of the alarm because it was received orally from the civilian.
(B) record the alarm in red ink in the Company Journal.
(C) record the alarm in blue ink in the Company Journal.
(D) ask the civilian to record the alarm in red ink in the Company Journal.

96. The company officer asks the firefighter on Housewatch to find out the last date on which the company had a training drill on high-rise building fire operations. On which one of the following pages of the Company Journal should the firefighter on Housewatch look to find the date of the training drill?

(A) 36
(B) 493
(C) 497
(D) 500

Directions: Answer questions 97 and 98 solely on the basis of the following passage.

Fire Department Regulations require that upon receiving an alarm while in the firehouse, the officer of the fire company directs the firefighters to take positions in front of the firehouse. The firefighters warn pedestrians and vehicles that the fire engine is leaving the firehouse. The officer directs the driver of the fire engine to move the fire engine to the front of the firehouse, then stop to check for vehicles and pedestrian traffic. While the fire engine is stopped, the firefighters will get on and the officer will signal the driver to go to the alarm location.

97. When do the firefighters who were sent to the front of the firehouse actually get on the fire engine?

(A) as the fire engine turns into the street leaving the firehouse
(B) as the fire engine slows down while leaving the firehouse
(C) inside the firehouse, before the fire engine is moved
(D) after the fire engine has been moved to the front of the firehouse and stopped

98. When responding to an alarm, why are the firefighters sent out of the firehouse before the fire engine?

(A) to make sure that the firehouse doors are fully opened
(B) to go to the nearest corner to change the traffic signal
(C) to warn pedestrians and vehicles that the fire engine is coming out of the firehouse
(D) to give the firefighters time to put on their helmets and boots

Directions: Answer questions 99 and 100 using the information provided.

99. When the engine oil drum in the firehouse is nearly empty, it must be replaced by a new drum full of oil. A firefighter gives the drum a kick. It sounds empty. The firefighter then checks the written log to see how many gallons of oil have been taken out of the drum so far. Checking the written log is

(A) unnecessary, since the oil drum sounded empty when the firefighter kicked it.
(B) necessary, since the log should tell the firefighter exactly how much oil is left.
(C) unnecessary, since the firefighter should avoid paperwork whenever possible.
(D) necessary, since the firefighter should always try to keep busy with useful activity.

100. The Fire Department provides each firehouse with such basic necessities as electric lightbulbs. As the items are used up, new supplies are ordered before the old ones are all gone. Of the following, the best reason for ordering more electric lightbulbs before the old ones are all gone is to

(A) decrease the amount of paperwork a firehouse company must complete.
(B) be sure that there are always enough lightbulbs on hand to replace those that burn out.
(C) make sure that the firehouse has enough electric lightbulbs to supply nearby firehouses.
(D) decrease the cost of providing electricity to the firehouse.

IF THERE IS STILL TIME REMAINING, you may review your answers.

ANSWER KEY AND EXPLANATIONS

Answer Key

1. **(C)**	21. **(B)**	41. **(D)**	61. **(B)**	81. **(A)**
2. **(B)**	22. **(B)**	42. **(D)**	62. **(C)**	82. **(A)**
3. **(A)**	23. **(C)**	43. **(C)**	63. **(A)**	83. **(D)**
4. **(A)**	24. **(A)**	44. **(D)**	64. **(B)**	84. **(B)**
5. **(D)**	25. **(B)**	45. **(A)**	65. **(D)**	85. **(C)**
6. **(A)**	26. **(D)**	46. **(B)**	66. **(D)**	86. **(B)**
7. **(A)**	27. **(A)**	47. **(D)**	67. **(A)**	87. **(A)**
8. **(D)**	28. **(C)**	48. **(C)**	68. **(B)**	88. **(C)**
9. **(B)**	29. **(D)**	49. **(D)**	69. **(A)**	89. **(D)**
10. **(A)**	30. **(C)**	50. **(A)**	70. **(C)**	90. **(B)**
11. **(C)**	31. **(B)**	51. **(B)**	71. **(C)**	91. **(A)**
12. **(B)**	32. **(D)**	52. **(B)**	72. **(B)**	92. **(B)**
13. **(A)**	33. **(B)**	53. **(D)**	73. **(D)**	93. **(B)**
14. **(D)**	34. **(C)**	54. **(A)**	74. **(B)**	94. **(B)**
15. **(D)**	35. **(B)**	55. **(D)**	75. **(C)**	95. **(C)**
16. **(B)**	36. **(B)**	56. **(B)**	76. **(A)**	96. **(C)**
17. **(B)**	37. **(B)**	57. **(C)**	77. **(B)**	97. **(D)**
18. **(A)**	38. **(C)**	58. **(A)**	78. **(A)**	98. **(C)**
19. **(A)**	39. **(A)**	59. **(B)**	79. **(C)**	99. **(B)**
20. **(C)**	40. **(D)**	60. **(D)**	80. **(C)**	100. **(B)**

Answer Explanations

1. **(C)** There is only one fire escape and only one window leading to it, the window in bedroom 3.

2. **(B)** The two exits from this apartment are the fire escape outside bedroom 3 and the apartment entrance door. Since the fire is in bedroom 3, the best exit route would be through the entrance hall and apartment door.

3. **(A)** To get to the fire escape a firefighter must pass through both halls and bedroom 3.

4. **(A)** The living room, the kitchen, and the dining room cannot be closed off, but only the living room is offered as a choice.

5. **(D)** Every room except bedroom 2 and bathroom 2 has a window and also either a door or a doorway.

6. **(A)** This would permit access to the adjacent room and would provide the occupants with an escape route. Bedroom 2 (B) and the bedroom hall (D) have no windows, and the window in bedroom 3 (C) opens on the fire escape.

7. **(A)** The kitchen has three exits: a window, a doorway, and a door. The question asks you to select the room into which the door leads.

8. **(D)** The incinerator adjoins only the living room.

9. **(B)** Rooms that have only one means of entrance and exit should be identified and remembered when you study the plan.

10. **(A)** The door between the two halls divides the apartment into two parts and is the only interior entrance to the bedroom area.

11. **(C)** This information is found in the second sentence of the passage. Note that this statement does not say that sprinkler systems extinguish all fires or keep all fires from spreading. Choices A and B are not mentioned or implied in the passage. Choice D is incorrect; 96 percent refers to the rate of effectiveness.

12. **(B)** This information is found in the last sentence of the passage.

13. **(A)** The fifth sentence of the passage states this directly.

14. **(D)** Having clean equipment in good working order is essential for effectively responding to fires.

15. **(D)** When storekeepers understand the reasons behind the rules, they can better appreciate how the rules help to protect their property.

16. **(B)** Most flammable liquids are heavier than air so they collect in low areas. They became close to the ground with the air above them.

17. **(B)** The electric fuse contains a wire that conducts electric current. The wire melts when a certain temperature is reached because the capacity of the wire has been exceeded. Choices A and C are dangerous techniques for bypassing the blown fuse. Choice D is incorrect because most adults should be able to change a fuse. An electrician is rarely needed.

18. **(A)** Hydrogen is a highly flammable gas that mixes with air and can cause an explosion if exposed to an open flame. Adequate ventilation allows the gas to escape harmlessly.

19. **(A)** Divide 350 feet by 50 feet to get the minimum amount—7 lengths.

20. **(C)** Divide 1,000 gallons (the volume of the tank) by 150 gallons (the discharge rate).

21. **(B)** The government establishes a minimum wage for every worker. It is the least amount per hour someone can earn.

22. **(B)** During World War II Adolf Hitler ruled as a dictator.

23. **(B)** The surprise attack on Pearl Harbor occurred on December 7, 1941.

24. **(A)** On August 6, 1945, the American bomber *Enola Gay* flew over the industrial city of Hiroshima, Japan. It dropped a single atomic bomb.

25. **(B)** The Republican Party symbol is an elephant.

26. **(D)** Integration is the bringing together of all races. During the Civil Rights Movement, people argued for integration.

27. **(A)** The Constitution says that every person charged with a crime shall be judged by a jury of his or her peers.

28. **(C)** The Bill of Rights is the first ten amendments to the Constitution. It specifies certain rights, such as freedom of religion, freedom of speech, and due process. Choice B, the Preamble, is a brief introduction to the Constitution. Choices A and D are distractors.

29. **(D)** The passage indicates that false alarms cause delays in response to actual fires and present unnecessary and additional risks to the firefighters and citizens.

30. **(C)** This is stated in sentences 5 and 6.

31. **(B)** Sentence 3 states that "... the first firefighters ... do not know. ..." There is no mention of any of the other choices.

32. **(D)** See the opening statement.

33. **(B)** Providing necessary first aid and summoning professional help is a primary function of firefighters. Choices A, B, and C would all be forms of neglect of duty and might cause the elderly man to suffer serious ill effects.

34. **(C)** Gasoline is a volatile, flammable liquid, and all leaks must be taken care of immediately. Otherwise, a spark, a hot catalytic converter on a car, or a carelessly discarded match or cigarette may cause a violent fire. Choice A—this action would lead directly to a fire and probably serious injury to the firefighter. Choice B—this situation is serious and must be handled immediately; leaving to chance the possibility that the attendant is aware of it is foolish and unsafe. Choice D—this would result in extreme delay and would not remove the immediate hazard.

35. **(B)** The question does not indicate an unusual hazard. The purpose of a fire-prevention inspection is to reduce fire hazards, and a major goal of this activity is to get the owner to maintain a fire-safe environment even when the fire department is not there to inspect. In this case the occupant has given the firefighters a reasonable explanation of why the inspection is inconvenient at this time. The new firefighter should *not* have been rude; the inspection should be rescheduled for the next available date. Choice A—this type of attitude does not build good rapport between the firefighter and the owner and tends to defeat the purpose of the fire-prevention program. Choice C—this is incorrect procedure; the store is private property and if the owner refuses admittance, the firefighter must obtain a search warrant in order to have the legal right to inspect. Note, however, that this is not required where a fire condition exists. Choice D—this would represent neglect of duty.

36. **(B)** Illustration 7 shows a hose line and nozzle. Choice A is a portable fire extinguisher. Choice C is a portable electrical drill. Choice D is a Phillips head screwdriver.

37. **(B)** Illustrations 4 and 6 show a broom and a shovel. The items in Choice A are a portable straight ladder and a pry bar; in Choice C, a first-aid kit and a hand saw; in Choice D, an axe and a monkey wrench.

38. **(C)** Illustrations 11 and 12 show an axe and a hand saw. The items in Choice A are a pipe or Stillson wrench and an engineer's pliers; in Choice B, a hand drill and a slip joint pliers; in Choice D, a pry bar and a hacksaw.

39. **(A)** Illustration 1 shows a portable straight ladder. Choice B is a first-aid kit. Choice C is a hacksaw. Choice D is a fire hydrant.

40. **(D)** A nut requires the use of a wrench, and the screw requires a screwdriver. Illustrations 16 and 18 show a double open-end wrench and a standard square-blade screwdriver. The items in Choice A are a pipe wrench and engineer's pliers; in Choice B, a portable electric drill and a pipe cutter; in Choice C, slip-joint pliers and a pry bar.

41. **(D)** Illustration 13 shows a monkey or adjustable wrench. Choice A is a broom. Choice B is a portable fire extinguisher. Choice C is a hand saw.

42. **(D)** Illustration 20 shows a fire hydrant, which is a primary source of water. Choices A (a pipe wrench), B (a fire extinguisher), and C (pliers) could not serve this purpose.

43. **(C)** Illustration 15 shows a hacksaw, which has fine teeth and is designed for cutting metal. Choices A (a shovel), B (a monkey wrench), and D (a screwdriver) are not used for cutting.

44. **(D)** The illustration indicates that the fourth rung from the bottom is missing. This can cause the firefighter to slip from the ladder and be injured. Choice A—the coat is the proper length. Choice B—the firefighter has a clear line of vision. Choice C—the firefighter's feet belong on the rung.

45. **(A)** In this illustration the hose is at about a 45-degree angle. This allows the water to be projected upward and outward at the same time. Choice B projects the water upward only. Choice C projects the water outward but not upward. Choice D projects the water downward.

46. **(B)** First paragraph, second sentence states that "It [the power saw] can be dangerous . . . if it has not been inspected and tested to insure that it is in serviceable condition."

47. **(D)** The use of the word *foreign* in this context means "having little or no relationship to" the tool. For example, wood chips, gravel, and plaster would be foreign materials in this sense.

48. **(C)** The second paragraph, sentence 3, says, "The V-belt pulley, if present, must be checked . . ."; the words *if present* indicate that the item named may be lacking. Therefore some saws will work without a V-belt pulley.

49. **(D)** See the second paragraph, sentence 4. Choices A, B, and C occur if the belt is too tight.

50. **(A)** The second paragraph, sentence 2, states clearly the need for an air filter.

51. **(B)** Carbide-tip blades must be replaced when two or more tips are broken or missing or the tips are worn down (see paragraph 3). The other blades should be changed when cracked, badly nicked, or worn down to an 8-inch diameter or less.

52. **(B)** This information is given in paragraph 3, in the last two sentences. Choice B is correct, the carbide tip blade would not be changed unless it is worn down to the circumference of the blade. Answers A, C, and D are incorrect because at least one of the blades would need to be changed if they were worn down to an eight-inch diameter or less.

53. **(D)** To some examinees this type of question can be confusing. The best way to approach such a question is to eliminate each choice as you read it. Choice A—changed *not* every

day, but *only* when the indicator shows red. Choice B—replaced *not only* when the oil is changed, *but also* when the indicator shows red. Choice C—inspected *not only* when the oil is changed, *but also* each time the indicator shows red. With A, B, and C eliminated, D must be the best choice. Going back to the passage, you find that the last sentence verifies your selection.

54. **(A)** Firefighter Green *needs* 10 full air cylinders. Firefighter Green *has* 20 air cylinders, 5 of which are full and 15 of which are empty. Since only 10 full air cylinders are needed, and 5 are already on hand, only 5 air cylinders need to be replaced.

55. **(D)** The next to last sentence states, "All such injuries could be eliminated if the buildings were demolished." Repairing the buildings (A) would represent only a partial solution.

56. **(B)** The third and fourth sentences support choice B. There is no mention of choices A, C, and D in the passage.

57. **(C)** See sentence 4. Choices A, B, and D are not mentioned in the passage.

58. **(A)** The danger of missing stairs is mentioned in the third sentence. There is no mention of choices B, C, and D.

59. **(B)** The appropriate place to report a crime is a police station. There is only one police station, and it is located on Hemlock Street between Third Avenue and Lincoln Terrace.

60. **(D)** There are two public libraries. First locate Green Terrace; then trace with your fingertip the route to each library. The closest library is on Lincoln Terrace and is the Lincoln Public Library. When you have identified the correct location, go back to the question and locate the choice that agrees with what you found. This will be the correct answer.

61. **(B)** Locate city hall, write down the street it faces, and then note the cross streets. Now go to the answer choices and find the selection that agrees with what you found.

62. **(C)** Locate the firehouse and the high school. Using your fingertip, trace the various routes to the school until you find the most direct one. Remember to watch for one-way streets. Finally, locate the choice that agrees with the route you have selected.

63. **(A)** Follow the same procedure as in question 62. However, in this case (the man and his children are on foot) there is no need to consider one-way streets.

64. **(B)** The correct answer is found in the first sentence: ". . . must back out of a street because other fire engines have blocked the path in front of it." Choices A, C, and D are not practicable and are not mentioned in the passage.

65. **(D)** The fourth sentence provides the information for this answer. Choices A, B, and C are not mentioned in the passage.

66. **(D)** This information is found in the fifth sentence of the passage. Choices A, B, and C would be unsafe acts; they are not mentioned in the passage.

67. **(A)** The sixth and seventh sentences state that " . . . two firefighters enter the intersection to direct traffic. They clear the cars and people out of the intersection. . . ."

68. **(B)** See the fourth sentence: "They [firefighters] walk alongside and to the rear of the slowly moving fire engine. . . ." Firefighter E is in front of the apparatus, the wrong position.

69. **(A)** Each length is 50 feet (sentence 2); therefore only one length is required.

70. **(C)** Each length is 50 feet.

$$\frac{\text{Distance to fire}}{\text{Single length of hose}} = \text{Number of lengths}$$

$$\frac{250 \text{ ft}}{50 \text{ ft}} = 5 \text{ lengths}$$

71. **(C)** Each length is 50 feet.

$$\frac{\text{Distance to fire}}{\text{Single length of hose}} = \text{Number of lengths}$$

$$\frac{175 \text{ ft}}{50 \text{ ft}} = 3\frac{1}{2} \text{ lengths}$$

Since you cannot use $\frac{1}{2}$ length, you must round your answer to the next highest whole number. In this case 4 = Number of lengths.

72. **(B)** Each length is 50 feet.

$$\frac{\text{Distance to fire}}{\text{Single length of hose}} = \text{Number of lengths}$$

$$\frac{125 \text{ ft}}{50 \text{ ft}} = 2\frac{1}{2} \text{ lengths}$$

Rounding to the next highest whole number gives 3 lengths.

73. **(D)** Each length is 50 feet.

$$\frac{\text{Distance to fire}}{\text{Single length of hose}} = \text{Number of lengths}$$

$$\frac{315 \text{ ft}}{50 \text{ ft}} = 6\frac{3}{10} \text{ lengths}$$

Rounding to the next highest whole number gives 7 lengths.

74. **(B)** Each length is 50 feet.

$$\frac{\text{Distance to fire}}{\text{Single length of hose}} = \text{Number of lengths}$$

$$\frac{230 \text{ ft}}{50 \text{ ft}} = 4\frac{3}{5} \text{ lengths}$$

Rounding to the next highest whole number gives 5 lengths.

75. **(C)** A letter regarding a heroic act is unique to the individual and would show that the firefighter had performed outstandingly. This information should be saved and reviewed when assignments or promotions are considered. It would be kept in the individual's Personnel file.

76. **(A)** A ladder is a piece of equipment; therefore any information about it should be kept in the Equipment and Supplies file.

77. **(B)** The fire prevention schedule would be kept in the Fire Prevention file.

78. **(A)** As used in this passage, "property" is considered "equipment and supplies." The report should be filed under Equipment and Supplies.

79. **(C)** The assignment of firefighters to units is controlled by the organization's Personnel department. The roster would be kept in the Personnel file.

80. **(C)** Sentence 13 states, "Before actually going on the tracks, they [firefighters] must be sure that the 600 volts of live electricity carried by the third rail is shut off." Choices A, B, and D are not mentioned or implied anywhere in the passage. Answers must be based solely on information found in the passage.

81. **(A)** The question could be rephrased as follows: "Why are passengers in subway cars in darkness?" Of the choices offered, the only one that will answer this question is A. Now refer to the passage to verify this choice; sentence 7 shows that you have selected the correct answer.

82. **(A)** To determine the correct illustration you should first mark off the outer boundaries of a "properly operating electrical system." The question states that these boundaries are 13.5 and 14.2. Mark lines through these points on each of the illustrations. Then select the illustration in which the indicating needle is within the boundaries you have marked off. Choice B is above the range, and C and D are below it.

83. **(D)** The indicator arrow is pointing toward a position between $\frac{1}{4}$ full and $\frac{1}{2}$ full. This would tell the firefighter that the cylinder is less than $\frac{1}{2}$ full of air.

84. **(B)** According to the passage preceding questions 83 and 84, a full cylinder contains air at 4,500 pounds per square inch. Question 84 asks you to select the gauge that indicates a cylinder that is more than $\frac{1}{2}$ full. Therefore: $4{,}500 \times \frac{1}{2} = 2{,}250$ lb. The gauge is divided in air pressure increments of 500 pounds per square inch. A reading above 22.5 would indicate a cylinder that is more than $\frac{1}{2}$ full. Choice B indicates a reading above 25; it is therefore more than $\frac{1}{2}$ full. Choice A indicates 1,500 psi. Choice C indicates 1,000 psi. Choice D indicates 2,000 psi. Each of these (A, C, and D) is below $\frac{1}{2}$ full.

85. **(C)** Paragraph 1, fourth sentence, states that there are two causes for a partial loss of water at the nozzle: a kink in the hose, and insufficient pressure from the fire engine pump. In question 85 the firefighter found no kinks in the hose; therefore the cause must be insufficient pressure being supplied by the fire pump. Choices A, B, and D are not mentioned in the passage, thereby eliminating them from consideration.

86. **(B)** The second paragraph, next to last sentence, states, "If a firefighter can physically handle the hose line alone, the nozzle is not discharging enough water . . ."; in other words, the firefighting stream is probably not acceptable.

87. **(A)** The gauge marked "Intake" in Diagram I shows the indicator pointing to 50. This tells the firefighter that water is entering the pumps at a pressure of 50 psi.

88. **(C)** The gauge marked "Discharge" in Diagram I shows the indicator pointing halfway between 200 and 300 psi. This tells the firefighter that the pressure of the water leaving the pumps is 250 psi.

89. **(D)** The gauge marked "Intake" in Diagram II shows the indicator pointing just above zero and below the first indicator line. This tells the firefighter that water is entering the pumps at a pressure less than 5 psi—therefore less than 10 psi.

90. **(B)** In the gauge marked "Discharge" in Diagram II the indicator points to a pressure of 100 psi. In the corresponding gauge of Diagram I the pressure is 250 psi.

250 psi (original pressure) – 100 psi (current pressure) = 150 psi (decrease)

91. **(A)** The seventh sentence tells you that ". . . air used depends upon the exertion made by the firefighter"—in other words, the amount of energy used by the firefighter. Choice B is wrong because the mask protects against breathing any smoke. Choices C and D have no relationship to the mask or breathable air.

92. **(B)** This information is found in the second sentence.

93. **(B)** According to the passage, all alarms are entered in the Company Journal. If pages 493 to 500 are reserved for special purposes, then alarms must be recorded on pages 1 through 492. Choice A—page 493 is for utility meter readings. Choice C—page 500 is for visits by high-level officers. Choice D—page 497 is for company drill records.

94. **(B)** Con Edison is a utility company, and meter readings taken by a utility company employee should be recorded on page 493 (see the last sentence).

95. **(C)** According to the passage, all alarms are recorded from any source, and entries by the firefighter on Housewatch should be written in blue or black ink. Choice C is the only one that meets these specifications. Choice A is incorrect; an entry must be made in the Journal. Choice B is incorrect; the entry should be made in blue or black ink. Choice D is incorrect; the entry must be made by the firefighter.

96. **(C)** According to the next to last sentence of the passage, company drills are recorded on page 497.

97. **(D)** The passage tells you that when an alarm is received the firefighters are directed to take positions in front of the firehouse, and the apparatus is driven out and stopped. Then the firefighters board the apparatus. Choice D best agrees with this procedure. Choices A, B, and C are contrary to the regulations as explained in the passage.

98. **(C)** Sentence 2 of the passage indicates that the purpose of assigning firefighters to the front of the firehouse is to caution pedestrians and vehicles.

99. **(B)** Kicking the drum will indicate only that the drum is empty or nearly empty. To know for sure how much oil is in the drum, the firefighter must know how much oil the full drum can hold and how much oil has been removed from the drum. Each time oil is taken from the drum, it is recorded in the log; a running total of how much oil has been used is also recorded. If the firefighter subtracts the total oil used from the original amount of oil that was in the drum, the firefighter will know whether any oil remains and, if so, how much.

100. **(B)** One of the strong attributes of firefighters is that they are always prepared. If the firefighters waited until the last lightbulb was used, they would then be faced with the possibility that other bulbs could burn out, thereby interfering with their fast, safe response to an alarm. Obtaining replacement bulbs, parts, tools, etc. takes time and often is impossible at night. These items must be immediately available when needed.

A FINAL WORD

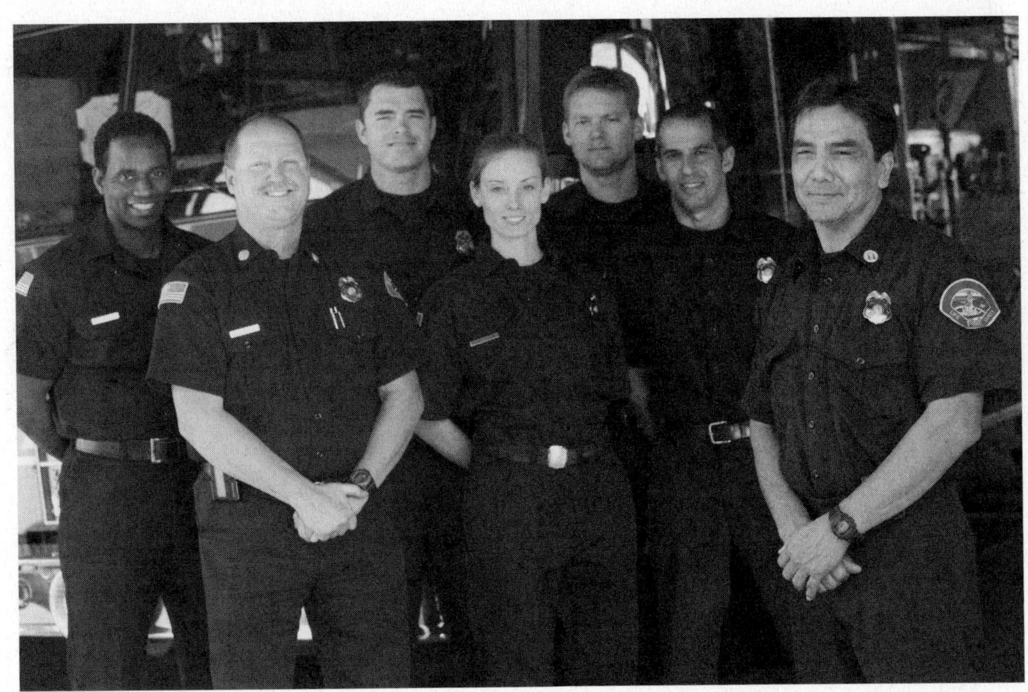

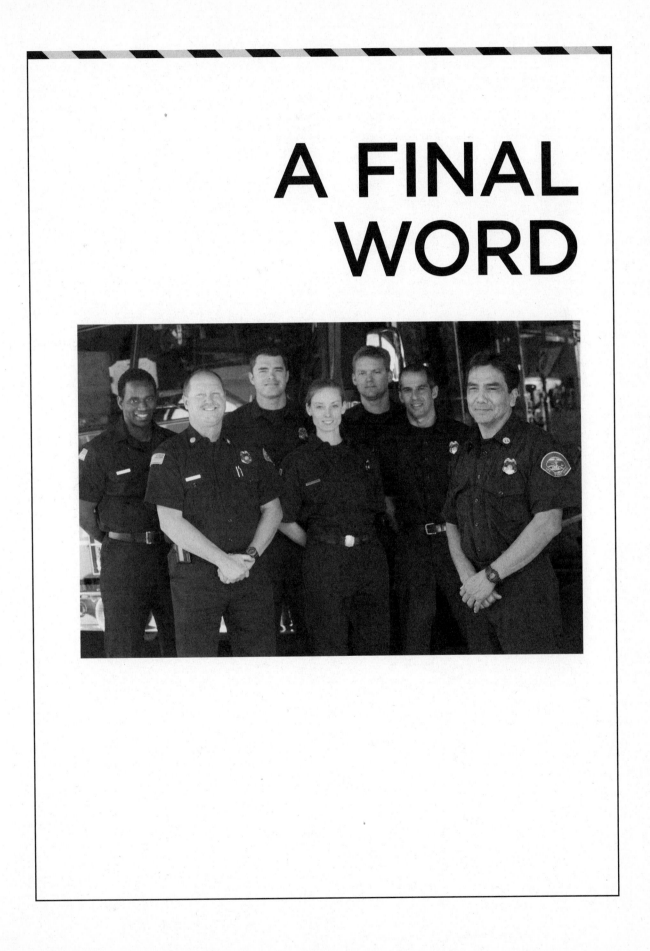

What to Do Immediately Before, During, and After the Exam

14

THE WEEK BEFORE THE EXAM

The time draws near. What should be done in the days immediately before the examination?

Do not be fearful. If you have prepared well, you should do well. Remember that you have helped yourself pass the examination every time you worked with this text. In a sense, therefore, you will be collecting your reward when you take the examination.

But what actions should be taken on the days just before the examination?

Seven Days Before

Keep exercising but take care not to injure or overexert yourself; you must ensure that you are healthy on the day of the test.

Review Chapters 4, 5, 7, 8, 9, 10, 11, and 15. Identify again the areas in which you have the greatest difficulty.

Some time during this week, you should ensure that you know the exact location of the exam site and the best way to get there. If you are going on public transportation, take a "dry run." Note exactly where the bus or train stops.

Chances are that the exam may be given on a weekend, so ask about the transportation schedule for that day. Do not be left waiting for a bus or train that does not run on the weekend. You have greatly increased your chances of successfully competing in the exam by following the instruction given in this book, but you have to be there to take the test.

Always make sure you know the exact date, the day of the week, the location, and the time for the orientation, written exam, physical ability test, oral interview, and any other tests that may be required.

Remember each test will have its own date, time, and location. Although a lot of tests are administered on weekends, the trend now is to offer them during the week. You should have enough time to adjust your schedule to accommodate the testing. If you really want to become a firefighter, you will need to make some sacrifices to meet the testing schedule.

Arrive at each test site at least one half-hour before the actual starting time. This will give you additional time to compose yourself before going into the test or interview.

The same applies if you are driving. Make sure the car you are using is in mechanical order. It is not a bad idea to have someone drive you, if you can. In this way, should any difficulties with the vehicle arise, you can continue on your own. If you are going to drive yourself, leave sufficient time to overcome traffic delays. It's a good idea to have a backup plan for how you will get there if your car does not work properly or some other obstacle blocks your prompt arrival at the test site. Be certain that you know the route to the examination and a safe, legal parking area. Taking the examination while you are preoccupied about your car is not a good idea. Give yourself every advantage.

SIX AND FIVE DAYS BEFORE

Zero in on the chapter or chapters that deal with your greatest weakness. Although studying what you don't know is always good, don't forget about studying what you do know. Don't dwell on one subject for too long or you will remember only that subject. Most of the questions you will be asked on the test will be general knowledge, so memorizing everything is not necessary. Scanning provides insight into what the material is about. However, it does not provide in-depth understanding or patient evaluation of questions and answers. The practice of scanning and skimming may lead to poor test-taking skills and can be a hindrance to you on the day of the exam. When reading, the scanning and skimming process is the search process. In contrast, reading carefully is the evaluation process.

FOUR, THREE, AND TWO DAYS BEFORE

On each of these days, review one of the sample exams given in Chapters 5 through 13. This will reacquaint you with what to expect when you take the actual examination. Review the tests under simulated exam conditions, as follows.

Sit in a room at a desk or table. Time yourself, making sure that you stay within the time allotted. You will then be less uneasy about this during the actual examination. If you are a smoker, do not smoke; the chances are that you will not be able to do so during the actual exam. Use the test techniques explained in Chapters 4, 6, 7, and 8.

Use the same kind of pencil you will use on exam day. Usually, you will be asked to bring a No. 2 lead pencil. The idea is to duplicate conditions as closely as possible those you will be experiencing on examination day. Eat healthy foods, stay hydrated (drink plenty of water), and take a two-day rest period from heavy exercise.

ONE DAY BEFORE

Reread Chapter 5, which deals with test taking, and Chapter 3, the subsection on What to Do on the Day of the Physical Abilities Test. That's it—by now you should be prepared. Do not try to cram on this last day. Your test preparation is over. Begin to relax.

Eat a normal dinner on the evening before the exam. Get your regular amount of sleep the night before. Although you do not need more rest, you should not get less. Be careful of taking sedatives to help you sleep. You may feel drowsy the next day. This is generally not a good night to go to a party.

The theme is to keep yourself as you would at any other time. Remember: Tomorrow is just another day. You have prepared well for the exam; nothing more need be done.

THE DAY OF THE EXAM

On the day of the exam, wake up with enough time to dress, have a good breakfast, and check over whatever test-taking equipment you will be taking with you. Although an alarm clock may get you up, a call from a friend is sometimes helpful.

In regard to test-taking equipment, follow whatever instructions you have received from the testing agency (for example, about pencils or a watch). Bring an extra sweater. If it's not needed to keep warm, you can always take it off. (You may want to sit on it; a desk seat can become very uncomfortable after an hour or so.)

What else? Well, a pencil sharpener is helpful, as are a good eraser and a working pen to sign in ink if required. A photo identification card may be required; you should have this with you.

Some candidates have found that a chocolate bar is a source of quick energy during the examination. If you wear glasses, make sure you have an extra pair, if possible, and something with which to clean them.

Before you arrive at the examination, charge up your brain and body with a little stretching exercise. Do just enough to stimulate your heart and breathing; avoid overdoing it and becoming tired. Refer to Chapter 4.

When you reach the test site, go to your assigned room and follow the instructions of the proctors. Inspect your seat and report any problems to your proctor immediately. Follow instructions to the letter.

Dealing with Anxiety and Panic

During the exam you may begin to experience sweating palms, heart palpitations, queasiness, inability to concentrate, or a general feeling of discomfort. These common signs of stress, anxiety, and fear can be overcome. Stop taking the examination for a few moments. During this short break use a predampened handkerchief to refresh your face, hands, and the back of your neck. This technique helps to reduce tension and relax you while you take the exam. As a result, you will be better prepared for the next section of the test. Breathe slowly and deeply, and concentrate on something positive, such as a previous success that you have had.

Believe in your ability. Many others just like you have passed firefighter candidate exams. You can too!

AFTER YOU HAVE FINISHED THE EXAM

You must prepare for the end of the examination; you cannot just get up and walk out. You must have a plan for what you will do during the last 15 minutes, and you must know what to do after the exam is over.

The Last 15 Minutes

The last 15 minutes of the exam is the time to double-check that you have recorded all your selections properly. This is your last chance to check for recording errors during the test. You may have made a simple error of marking the wrong box or line for a question. Now is the time to uncover that error and correct it. Record, on the test booklet or the answer sheet, the number of your test booklet and any other identifying symbols that are available. If you have been following the procedures taught in this guide, you will have ample time at the end of the examination to do this.

The End of the Exam

The end of the exam will be signaled by some type of notification. You must stop working at that point; if you don't, you may be disqualified. Remain seated, and follow the directions of the proctor. Finally, make sure that all parts of your test are properly collected and checked.

You must turn in all the testing materials to the proctors before you leave the test site, including the exam, scratch paper, and other items associated with the test. There may be a sign-out sheet at the proctor table. Make sure that you sign out or your name is checked off, and that all of your current information is correct. If you move, get married, change names, change phone numbers, or change e-mail addresses at any time during the testing process, you must notify the fire department and the testing agency so they can contact you for the next step in the testing process.

A WORD ABOUT THE FUTURE

Once you have become a firefighter, you must direct your efforts toward professionalism and advancement. Many fire science programs are offered in our nation's colleges, and the National Fire Academy makes available excellent courses that can be taken either on or off campus. In addition, there is an abundant supply of job-related texts and guides for you to study.

You'll be back to the beginning, striving to master new material and reaching new goals with new rewards.

Welcome to the fire service!

Fire Service Terminology

15

IMPORTANT TERMINOLOGY

This list of terminology was assembled from many different sources. It is a guide to help you learn some of the language of the fire service. It is not meant to be a complete or definitive list.

The following terms will help you understand those words and phrases that might be found on the exam.

A

ability the capacity to perform a task

abrasion the act of wearing away by rubbing, as the rubbing of hose against the curb

academy the educational institution where firefighters receive their initial training and subsequent formal retraining

accelerant a substance used to start a fire and/or make it spread rapidly

accordion load arrangement of fire hose in a hose bed or compartment in which the hose lies on edge with the folds adjacent to each other

ADA—Americans with Disabilities Act of 1990 Public Law 101-336 a federal statute intended to remove barriers—physical and otherwise—that limit access by individuals with disabilities

adapter a device for connecting, joining, or fitting one object to another; *example:* the mechanism that changes a two-prong electrical outlet so that it will accept a three-prong plug

Advanced Firefighter sometimes referred to as Firefighter II or Firefighter III; when inquiring about state certification programs always check with the state fire marshal for the appropriate title and what requirements are needed

Advanced Life Support (ALS) an advanced level of prehospital and interhospital emergency care and nonemergency medical care that includes basic life support care, cardiac monitoring, cardiac defibrillation, electrocardiography, intravenous therapy, administration of medications, drugs, and solutions, use of adjunctive medical devices, trauma care, and other authorized techniques and procedures as outlined in the Advanced Life Support National Curriculum of the United States Department of Transportation and any modifications to that curriculum specified

aerial ladder power-operated turntable ladder attached to a ladder truck; also known as an aerial apparatus or aerial device

Affirmative Action administrative law adopted by the Equal Employment Opportunity Commission (EEOC) to implement the requirements of Title VII of the Civil Rights Act of 1964

air chisel a device that operates on compressed air and is used for cutting sheet metal. The air chisel is commonly used for extrication from autos

air cylinder made of metal or composite material, a cylinder or tank that contains the supply of compressed air for a breathing apparatus, also called an air tank or air bottle

air pack a protective device that uses a face piece, compressed air tank, and air flow regulator to provide compressed air to the wearer (see SCBA)

air regulating valve an adjustable valve used to regulate airflow to the face-piece; a helmet supplied with air through an air hose attached to a compressed air cylinder

alarm an audible or visual signal that indicates the existence of a fire or emergency condition

alleged the word commonly used when the police are not certain of the facts, or when the matter is currently being decided in court; *example:* "an alleged crime," or "the alleged perpetrator"

alternating current electrical current which reverses direction with each cycle

ambulance any publicly or privately owned vehicle that is specifically designed, constructed, or modified, and equipped and intended to be used and maintained for the emergency transportation of people who are sick, injured, wounded, or otherwise incapacitated or helpless; or the nonemergency medical transportation of people who require the presence of medical personnel to monitor their condition or the medical apparatus being used

amperes the practical unit of electric-current strength; such a current as would be given with an electromotive force of one volt through a wire having a resistance of one ohm

antifreeze extinguisher a fire extinguisher that contains a compound or solution that lowers the freezing point below that of water

apartment house a building or structure that contains three or more dwelling units

apparatus fire vehicle tank trucks, ladder trucks, pumpers, crash and rescue trucks, and others

appliance generic term applied to any nozzle, wye, Siamese, deluge monitor, or other piece of hardware used in conjunction with a fire hose for the purpose of delivering water

area to find the area of a square with equal or unequal sides the formula is length times width; to find the area of a circle the formula is diameter times the circumference or radius squared times the circumference

arson willful burning of a building, vehicle, or structure, including one's own

arsonist a person who attempts or commits an act of arson

atmospheric pressure 14.7 lb. per inch square; the pressure exerted by the weight of the air surrounding the earth

atom the building block of all matter composed of electrons, protons, and neutrons

attack actions taken to apply water or some other extinguishing agent to a fire

attic the area between the roof of a building and the ceiling of the top floor

attic ladder a folding ladder used for inside work, especially to gain access to an attic

audiovisual materials educational materials that can be seen as well as heard

Authority Having Jurisdiction (AHJ) a legal entity that has statutory authority to enforce codes

automatic alarm an alarm that is activated by a fire detector or other automatic device

automatic sprinkler a water spray system with spraying nozzle heads, held in a closed position by a low-melting alloy link, breakable bulb, or chemical pellet, installed in a pipe grid, and supplied by a water system

avoidable accident an accident that should have been prevented with proper equipment and behavior

axe a tool with a heavy blade-edged head designed to cut an object when forcibly struck

B

backdraft an explosion caused by a sudden rush of oxygen-rich air into superheated gases in a room or an area

balcony a platform projecting from a wall

Basic Firefighter referred to in some states as Firefighter I or Firefighter II

Basic Life Support (BLS) a basic level of prehospital and interhospital emergency care and nonemergency medical care that includes airway management, cardiopulmonary resuscitation (CPR), control of shock and bleeding, and splinting of fractures, as outlined in a Basic Life Support National Curriculum of the United States Department of Transportation and any modifications to that curriculum specified

battalion a fire department district made up of several fire stations

battery a device consisting of cells for converting energy into electrical current

BLEVE acronym for boiling liquid expanding vapor explosion caused by the failure of a tank of a pressurized product by overheating and overpressurizing the tank to the point of rupture; the vessel explodes when the temperature of the liquid rises above its normal boiling point

booster line, booster reel, or red line a noncollapsible rubber covered hose wound on a reel, mounted on an engine, apparatus, or brush truck, that can be used for initial attack and extinguishment of a fire

British thermal unit (BTU) the amount of heat required to raise 1 pound of water 1 degree Fahrenheit.

building grade the ground level of a building

bunker gear (personal protective equipment [PPE]) term for the protective clothing worn by firefighters

business district an area of a city or town set apart for commercial and business purposes

C

cadet a person between the ages of 16 and 21 working at a fire department as a volunteer, part time, or paid-on-call; these youths come from Scouting organizations and are trainee firefighters

call back notifying off-duty firefighters to return for duty

calorie amount of heat needed to raise the temperature of 1 gram of water 1 degree centigrade

captain rank used for a company or station officer

carbon dioxide (CO_2) a colorless, odorless, heavier-than-air gas that neither supports combustion nor burns

carbon monoxide (CO) a colorless, odorless, dangerous gas (both toxic and flammable) formed by incomplete combustion

cascade systems several large air cylinders with a capacity of 300 cubic feet or more used to refill smaller self contained breathing apparatus cylinders

centigrade temperature scale at which the boiling point of water is 100 degrees Centigrade and the freezing point is 0 degrees

chafing block blocks placed under hoses or ropes to keep them from abrading or fraying

chain of command the order of rank and authority in an organization

channel locks a pair of pliers slotted so they can be adjusted to fit around different-sized objects, normally used on pipes

charge the fire service uses this term to mean the filling of a hose line with water

check valve a valve that permits flow in only one direction; also known as a clapper valve

Chemical Transportation Emergency Center (CHEMTREC) a United States industry resource that supplies 24-hour information about hazardous materials

chock a tapered wooden, metal, or plastic block to hold open a door, preventing it from closing and locking

circuit breaker a device to automatically interrupt the flow of electricity in a circuit when the circuit becomes overloaded

circumference the distance around the outer edge of a circle

civilian a person other than a uniformed firefighter

class A fire includes ordinary combustibles such as wood, paper, fabric, solid plastics, and rubber

class B fire includes all flammable and combustible liquids, greases, oils, and gases

class C fire involves energized electrical equipment

class D fire involves combustible metals such as magnesium, sodium, aluminum, uranium, and titanium

class K fire fires involving combustible cooking vegetable or animal oils and fats in restaurants and institutional kitchens

combustible capable of burning, generally in air under normal conditions of ambient temperature and pressure, unless otherwise specified

combustion a chemical process in which a substance combines with oxygen to produce heat and light

come-a-Long a system of levers, pulleys, and cables that operates through a ratcheting handle

company the officer and firefighters assigned to work in an engine or ladder truck

conduction transfer of heat through a solid medium

convection transfer of heat through a moving medium, such as a liquid or a gas

corrosion slow deterioration or destruction of metallic materials by chemical or electrochemical processes; contrasted with erosion, which is a mechanical process

coupling can be male or female and is attached to the end of a hose used to couple hoses together

CPR cardiopulmonary resuscitation

cribbing varying lengths of hard wood used for stabilizing vehicles and collapsed buildings

current rate of electrical flow in a conductor measured in amperes

D

damage material injury or loss resulting from fire or other disasters

dead end the end of a street, hallway, or other passageway with only one way in or out

debris unwanted material; refuse left after a fire

decision making the process that occurs prior to a commitment being made to a course of action

decontamination removal of a polluting or harmful substance

deepseated fire a fire that has penetrated deep into bulk materials; a persistent fire that is difficult to extinguish

defensive fire attack exterior fire fight with emphasis on exposures protection

diameter a straight line passing through the center of a figure or body and terminated at the boundaries

direct current electrical current that flows in one direction

dispatcher a person who assigns fire companies to respond to calls for help.

drafting taking water from a static source, such as a pond, river, or swimming pool, as opposed to a hydrant

drill practicing firefighting techniques, including laying hose, raising ladders, and operating pumps

dry chemical extinguisher a fire extinguisher containing a dry chemical powder that is ejected by compressed gas and that extinguishes fire

dwelling any building used exclusively for residential purposes, with no more than two living units, or serving no more than 15 people as a boarding or rooming house

dwelling unit one or more rooms used by one or more people

E

egress a continuous path of travel from any point in a building to the outside at ground level; *see* exit; fire escape

electrical insulation a material possessing a high degree of resistance to the passage of an electric current

elevating platform a basket-like platform attached to mechanical or hydraulic power-operated boom mounted on an apparatus chassis, used to raise firefighters and equipment to upper floors for firefighting and rescue work

emergency a medical condition of recent onset and severity that would lead a prudent layperson, possessing an average knowledge of medicine and health, to believe that urgent or unscheduled medical care is required

emergency exit any of several means of escaping from a building, including doors, windows, hatches, fire escapes, and the like, leading to the outside and not used under normal conditions; also known as secondary means of exit or egress

emergency procedure a plan for action or steps to be taken in case of an emergency

EMSS—Emergency Medical Services System an organization of hospitals, vehicle service providers, and personnel approved in a specific geographic area that coordinates and provides prehospital and interhospital emergency care and nonemergency medical transports at a Basic Life Support (BLS), Intermediate Life Support (ILS), and/or Advanced Life Support (ALS) level pursuant to a System Program Plan submitted and approved and pursuant to the EMS Regional Plan adopted for the EMS Region in which the system is located

Emergency Medical Technician (EMT) a person who has successfully completed a course of instruction in basic life support as prescribed and is currently licensed in accordance with standards prescribed and practices within an EMS System

engine a fire truck that carries hose, water, water pump, and personnel to the fire scene

escape route the egress path that occupants must follow when evacuating a building in the event of fire

exit a way or means for leaving a building and reaching ground level outside; the portion of an evacuation route that is separated structurally from other parts of the building to provide a protected path of travel to the outside

exit marking a prominently displayed sign that identifies access to an exit, or one that identifies a door passage, or a stairway that is not an exit but could be mistaken for an exit

explosive range a mixture of flammable vapors and air, expressed as a percent, above or below which no ignition can occur

exposure the portion or whole of a structure that may be endangered by a fire because of many factors, including proximity to a hazard; the likelihood of property catching fire from neighboring fire hazards

extinguish to put out the flames; to quench a fire

extrication the systematic and safe removal of an individual from pinning or entrapment

F

facepiece the part of a breathing apparatus that fits over the face

Fahrenheit temperature scale on which the boiling point is 212 degrees and the freezing point is 32 degrees

false alarm an alarm for which there is no fire; NOTE: false alarms may be accidental, as in the case of a defective alarm system, or malicious, as in the case of a person calling the fire department to report a fictitious fire

felony a serious criminal offense punishable upon conviction by confinement in a state prison for periods of time in excess of one year; upon conviction of a felony, certain citizen's rights are forfeited

fire rapid combustion of oxygen and fuel in a chemical reaction that liberates large amounts of heat and light that is visible as a flame

fire academy a comprehensive fire department training facility

fire alarm an audible or visible fire emergency signal

fire control fire protection suppression, including efforts to reduce fire losses

fire detector a mechanical or electrical device that senses the presence of a fire from one or more of its signatures (smoke, heat, gas, etc.) and generates a signal or trips another device

fire drill a practice exercise by a fire service unit in firefighting procedures and the use of fire service equipment; the practice of evacuation of a building in the manner to be followed in case of a fire or other emergency

fire escape a means for leaving a building in case of a fire, such as an exterior or interior fire-protected stairway; an emergency fire exit

fire extinguisher portable firefighting device designed to combat small fires

firefighter an active participating member of a fire department, including volunteers and part-time firefighters.

fire ground the area of ground around the fire scene

fire hazard the relative danger of the start and spread of fire; the danger of smoke or gases being generated; the danger of explosion or other occurrence potentially endangering the lives and safety of the occupants of a building or structure

fire prevention precautionary fire protection activities carried out before fires occur, intended to prevent outbreak of fire, facilitate early detection, and minimize life and property loss if fire should occur; activities include public education, inspection, law enforcement, and reduction of hazards

fire point the lowest temperature at which a substance produces ignitable vapors sufficiently enough to flash when exposed to an ignition source and then continues to burn

fireproof the property of a material, such as concrete or iron, that does not burn or decompose when exposed to ordinary fire; NOTE: the term "fire resistive" is recommended by the NFPA in preference to "fireproof" because no material can withstand heat of sufficient intensity and duration

fire resistant having the capability of withstanding fire for a specified period of time (usually in terms of hours) with respect to temperature; possessing the quality of resistance to damage or destruction by fire

fire scene the location of a fire, which must be carefully preserved until a search for evidence is completed

fire science the systematic body of knowledge and principles drawn from physics, chemistry, mathematics, engineering, administration, management, and related branches of arts and sciences, required in the practice of fire protection and prevention

fire service an organization that provides fire prevention and fire protection to a community; the members of such an organization; the firefighting profession as a whole

fire station a building housing firefighters and fire equipment, serving as headquarters for a fire department company

fire tetrahedron this is a chemical reaction and adds a fourth side to the fire triangle; it was discovered that some extinguishing agents actually interfere with the chemical chain reaction that we call fire

fire triangle the components necessary to have a fire: fuel, oxygen, and heat; also *see* fire tetrahedron

fire watch one or more firefighters detailed to be present at a public gathering as a fire safety precaution

first alarm the initial alarm of a fire, or the first signal calling for the first alarm response

first responder a person who has successfully completed a course of instruction in emergency first response as prescribed and who provides first response services before the arrival of an ambulance or specialized emergency medical services vehicle, in accordance with the level of care established in the emergency first response course

flammable subject to easy ignition and rapid flaming combustion

flammable gas any gas that can burn

flashover the ignition of flammable gases that have been heated to their ignition temperature

flash point the minimum temperature at which a liquid vaporizes in order to form an ignitable mixture with air (flash points are determined in the laboratory by cup tests); NOTE: in the fire practice, flammable liquids are sometimes classified as high and low flash point liquids, depending on whether they flash above or below 100 degrees F (37.8 degrees C)

forcible entry tool any of a large assortment of axes, door breakers, pry bars, mauls, chisels, saws, and the like, used to gain entrance through walls and other obstructions to carry out firefighting operations

forensic science the scientific activity related to the development of evidence that is suitable for introduction as evidence in a judicial proceeding

forward lay laying hose from a hydrant to the fire scene

friction the resistance to relative motion between two bodies or surfaces in contact

friction loss the pressure lost while water travels through a pipe or hose

front line apparatus and firefighting units normally responding to alarms, as compared with reserve units

G

gallons per minute (GPM) measurement of the amount of water needed to extinguish a fire or other hazard

general operating guideline (GOG) written orders describing the desired outcome to be achieved under given circumstances; this allows an individual to make their own decisions that are not allowed by a standard operating procedure (SOP)

general order a standing order that remains in effect until specifically amended or canceled; contrasted with a special order that is issued for a limited purpose or temporary situation

gravity the force of mutual attraction between masses; the weight of a body, with g representing the force of gravitational acceleration

gravity tank an elevated water storage tank provided for fire protection or used as a community water supply

grid pattern the process of an aerial search for a small fire by systematically passing over an area along parallel grid lines, also used for water searches

grievance a complaint related to conditions of work, such as unfair or unequal treatment or a situation affecting safety or health

ground a conductor that provides an electrical path for the flow of current into the earth or to a conductor that serves as the earth

H

Halligan or Hooligan bar a prying tool with a claw at one end and a spike at a right angle to a wedge at the other end

halyard a rope that is attached to the fly sections of an extension ladder

handline a small hose line handled manually by a firefighter; a light rope used to hoist fire tools and to secure ladders and equipment

heat exhaustion physical distress characterized by fatigue, nausea, heavy perspiration, pale clammy skin, subnormal temperature, vacant eyes, and general weakness brought on by overexpose to high temperature and deficiency of salt

height distance above a base

helmet protective headgear for a firefighter

hose a flexible conduit used to convey water under pressure; available in various diameters from ¾ inch to 5-inch or more and in standard lengths of 50 feet

hose bed area where hose is kept on a fire apparatus

hose clamp a device used to stop water flow through a damaged hose or to stop water flowing from a source

hose jacket equipment used for emergency repair of a burst or leaking hose or as an emergency adapter for the connection of two hose lines with different threads

hose line two or more lengths of hose connected and ready for use or in use

hose tower an area in the firehouse where hose is hung vertically to dry and drain

housewatch a tour of duty at the fire housewatch desk (*see* watch)

hydrant a cast metal fitting attached to a water main below street or grade level; normally with a control valve and one or more gated or ungated threaded outlet connections for supplying water to fire department hoses and pumpers

hydrant wrench tool used to open and close hydrants and remove the caps from hydrants

I

ignition the initiation of combustion

ignition temperature the lowest temperature at which sustained combustion of a substance can be initiated

incendiary a fire that a trained arson investigator believes has been deliberately set; *see* suspicious

Incident Command System (ICS) or Incident Management System (IMS) defines roles, responsibilities, and standard operating procedures used to manage emergency operations

incinerator a furnace-like apparatus used to burn waste substances

incipient referring to a small fire or a fire in its initial stages

inertia the tendency of a body at rest to remain at rest, or of a body in motion to resist a change in speed or direction

initial alarm the first notification received by a fire department that a fire or other emergency exists

injury physical harm or damage to a person resulting in disfigurement, pain or discomfort, infection, or physical impairment

in service a company or other firefighting unit that is ready and able to respond to assignments

in-service training the continual training given to firefighters to keep up their skill level and to keep them abreast of new laws, procedures, etc.

International Association of Fire Chiefs (IAFC) professional organization that provides leadership to career and volunteer fire chiefs and managers of emergency service organizations

International Association of Fire Fighters (IAFF) professional organization that represents career firefighters and paramedics in labor relationships through local unions

J

jackknife a folding pocketknife; a folding action of something upon itself

Jaws of Life trade name that refers to a rescue tool manufactured by the Hurst Company in widespread use for extrication from autos

joist a structural member, often spanning beams or walls, used to support a floor or ceiling

K

key box or knox box a heavy-gauge steel box mounted on the outside of a business or apartment complex in which keys are stored to provide fire department access to the building

kink to bend hose upon itself to temporarily block the flow of water

knots used for pulling, holding, lifting, and lowering; knots must be fastened to something before they can be used; common knots include the bowline, clove hitch, sheepshank, sheet bend or becket bend, and square knot

K-tool tool used for the removal of door cylinders in dwellings

L

ladder a device of varying length, type, or construction consisting of two rails or beams with steps or rungs spaced at intervals

ladder company a fire company equipped with a ladder truck and trained in ladder work, ventilation, rescue, forcible entry, and salvage work

ladder truck vehicle used to transport ladders, tools, and personnel to the fire scene

lanyard a rope suitable for supporting one person; one end is fastened to a safety belt or harness and the other end is secured to a substantial object or a safety line

large-dimaeter hose (LDH) hose that is usually 4 inches in diameter or larger to move large quantities of water, sometimes referred to as an above-ground water main

latent heat the heat absorbed or liberated when a substance changes from one state to another at a fixed temperature

leeward or lee the direction opposite from which the wind is blowing

length the greatest dimension of a surface or body

life gun a gun that fires a cord attached to a projectile to people trapped in inaccessible places; the cord is used to pull in a lifeline for rescue

life hazard a condition that is dangerous to life

life safety the preservation and protection of life from the hazards of flame, heat, smoke, etc.

line used in the fire service to refer to hose that is used at a fire scene

liquid a substance with a constant volume that assumes the shape of its container

loss prevention a program designed to identify and correct potential accidents before they occur

M

Maltese cross an insignia worn on a fire department uniform or cap

Mayday International distress signal broadcast by voice or blasts of the air horn at a fire scene when impending danger is near

mnemonic a cue for remembering, usually an association made with something familiar

mobile intensive care unit (MICU) another name for an ambulance with advanced life support capabilities (ALS)

molecule the smallest physical unit of a substance, consisting of atoms held together by chemical forces and possessing the properties of the substance

moonlighting work performed by firefighters on their off-duty time for employers other than the fire department

multiple alarm a second or greater alarm

mutual aid mutual assistance among fire departments in the event of a major disaster or event

N

National Electrical Code (NEC) National Fire Protection code 70 is the standard for electrical provisions considered necessary to safeguard people and buildings

National Fire Academy (NFA) a school in Emmitsburg, Maryland, attended by volunteer and career firefighters to gain advanced education

National Fire Codes (NFC) codes and standards pertaining to fire protection

National Fire Incident Reporting System (NIFRS) one of the main sources of reporting about fires in the United States

National Fire Protection Association (NFPA) a nonprofit educational and technical association devoted to protecting life and property by developing fire protection standards and educating the public

National Incident Management System (NIMS) a program standardizing command structure terminology and communications among fire departments and other agencies

National Registry of Emergency Medical Technicians (NREMT) provides registration and certification to first responders, EMT–B's, EMT–I's, and paramedics on a national level

9-1-1 emergency answer and response system in which the caller need only dial 9-1-1 on a telephone to obtain emergency services, including police, fire, medical ambulance, and rescue

night shift a nighttime tour of duty

noncombustible resistant to burning under normal conditions

nozzle a tubular, metallic, constricting attachment fitted to a hose to increase fluid velocity and form a jet; nozzles are often adjustable to provide a solid stream, a spray, or fog

nozzleman a firefighter assigned to handle the nozzle of a fire hose

O

occupancy the purpose for which a building, floor, or other part of a building is used or intended for use

Occupational Safety and Health Administration (OSHA) U.S. federal agency that develops and enforces standards and regulations for occupational safety in the workplace

offensive fire attack interior fire fight with emphasis on rescue and confining the fire to its point of origin. *see* defensive fire attack

officer a member of a fire department with supervisory responsibilities

officer in charge officer at a fire or commanding an on-duty fire department company

off shift off duty

ohm measurement of electrical resistance

ordinary combustibles commodities, packaging, or storage aids that have a heat of combustion similar to wood, cloth, or paper and that produce fires that may be extinguished by the quenching and cooling effect of water

organization the association of people with specified functions and responsibilities for pursuing an agreed purpose

overhauling the terminal phase of firefighting, in which the fire area is carefully examined for embers or for traces of fire; in addition, steps are taken to protect remaining property from further damage

owner the person who holds title to particular land or property

oxygen (O_2) a colorless, odorless, tasteless, nonflammable gas, but combined with other substances makes them flammable

P

Paid-on-call firefighter (POC) a firefighter who receives reimbursement for each call he or she attends

Paramedic a person who has successfully completed a course of instruction in advanced life support care as prescribed, is licensed in accordance with standards prescribed, and practices within an Advanced Life Support EMS System

parapet a wall extending above the roof line that provides a fire barrier

pawl a mechanism or catch that prevents a wheel from turning in a backward direction by engaging a ratchet tooth or by using a cam friction or a smooth wheel

pedestrian a person traveling on foot

perimeter the boundary line of any figure of two dimensions; to measure the perimeter of an object add all of the sides together

permit an official document issued by a fire department or other agency authorizing the use of fire or a hazardous process

personal property a person's possessions that are movable, such as household goods, jewelry, pets, furniture, and other similar objects

pike pole a tool with a hook of steel attached to a wood, metal, fiberglass, or plastic pole of varying length used for pulling, dragging, and probing

platoon an entire shift of a fire department

pneumatic operated by compressed air

pompier a ladder with a large hook on one end that a firefighter can use to ascend from floor to floor on the outside of a building

post indicator valve a valve used in a sprinkler system that indicates open and shut positions

pounds per square inch (PSI) a unit of pressure; the pressure exerted by water at rest or flowing is measured as pounds per square inch

prevention reduction or elimination of hazards, usually as part of a planned program to lessen the probability of harmful or dangerous events

protective clothing firefighting clothing, including coats, boots, turnout pants, gloves, and helmet

pry ax made of metal, the head has a pick on one side and a blade on the opposite side

pumper a fire department pumping engine equipped with 500-gallon-per-minute pump, hose, ladders, and other firefighting equipment

pump operator a firefighter trained and assigned to operate a pumper

pump panel the console of instruments, gauges, and controls used by a pump operator

pump pressure the water pressure produced by a fire department pumper

Q

quint a firefighting apparatus that can perform five functions; carry a hose and a water tank; with a pump; is an aerial device; can perform water tower operations; and contains portable ladders

R

radiation a form of energy that travels through space as an electromagnetic wave; radiant heat travels from a point in all directions equally

radius a straight line from the center of a circle or sphere to its outer edge

rapid intervention team (RIT) also referred to as a rapid intervention crew (RIC); on the scene of an incident, is a specialized crew used strictly for the rescue of firefighters

Rescue Squad or Rescue Company specialized unit dedicated to performing rescue and extrication operations at the scene of an emergency

resistance the opposition to the flow of electrical current

response the act of answering an alarm

reverse lay laying hose from the fire scene to a hydrant, thus keeping the engine at the fire, making it easier to retrieve equipment

roll call the taking of attendance before each tour of duty

rules and regulations an official fire department book of rules specifying the responsibility of officers and subordinates and the proper conduct of fire department operations

S

safety can a container of not more than a five-gallon capacity having a flash-arresting screen, a spring-closing lid, and spout cover, so designed that it will safely relieve internal pressure when exposed to fire

safety shut off a device that shuts off the gas supply to a burner (and sometimes also to the pilot light) if the ignition source fails

salvage procedures or measures for reducing damage from smoke, water, and weather during and following a fire by the use of salvage covers, smoke ejectors, deodorants, etc.

salvage cover a waterproof tarpaulin of standard size made of cotton duck, plastic, or other material, used to protect furniture, goods, and other property from heat, smoke, and water damage during fire fighting operations

SCBA Self Contained Breathing Apparatus; called an *air pack*

search a thorough examination and exploration of a fire scene for life and fire

search warrant a legal writ that authorizes a law enforcement officer to search specified premises for evidence

sector a portion of the fire ground with one person in charge, other than the Incident Commander

siamese a hose fitting that joins two hose lines

size-up the process of observing and evaluating the conditions at the fire scene

smoke detector a device, usually of the ionization or photoelectric type, that triggers an alarm when a sufficient concentration of smoke upsets a balanced electronic circuit or interrupts or otherwise affects a light beam

smoke ejector a power-driven fan used to remove smoke from a burning building or to blow fresh air into a building to expel smoke and heat

specific gravity ratio of the density of a liquid or solid, as compared with the density of equal volume of water, with water having an assigned value of 1

sphygmomanometer the cuff and gauge used to measure blood pressure

spontaneous combustion oxidation of a substance with such rapidity as to have heat sufficient to ignite it, as masses of oiled rags, finely powered ores, sawdust, grain, coal, and certain metals

sprain an injury in which the ligaments are torn, accompanied by pain, discoloration, and swelling

spray nozzle a nozzle that is designed to break up a water stream into fine droplets

sprinkler system a grid system of water pipes and spaced discharge heads installed in a building to control and extinguish fires

standard operating procedures (SOP) methods or rules in which an organization or a fire department operates to carry out a routine function; these policies and procedures are written in a handbook, and all firefighters should be well versed in its contents

star of life symbol used to signify an EMS provider

Storz fitting a fitting that enables a fire department to connect a large-diameter hose quickly to fire hydrants, sprinklers, and standpipe systems

strain an injury to a muscle caused by overexertion

streetbox a fire alarm signal box mounted on a post on a public street

subpoena an order signed by a judicial official commanding a person to appear in court under penalty of law

suction strainer an attachment connected to the pickup end of a hose, either hard or soft suction, to filter out debris during a drafting operation

summons a written notice served to a person, legally obligating that person to answer a charge; a summons is in lieu of an arrest

suspicious a fire that is suspected of being arson but has not been declared as arson by a trained arson investigator; *see* incendiary

T

tarps made of canvas or plastic, tarps are used to cover furniture to protect it from water damage and can be used as chutes to drain water from an upper area

thermal pertaining to heat

thermal imaging camera a camera used to seek out hidden fires and heat; it is used to see through smoke

tone out to dispatch by activating pagers or station-alerting equipment using radio tones

tour firefighters' jargon used to refer to one work day

toxic poisonous; destructive to body tissues and organs or interfering with body functions

triage the systematic sorting of patients at an incident to treat the most critical patients first

trumpets insignia of rank used throughout the fire service that dates back to the time when fire officers gave commands through speaking trumpets

turn out the alert to a fire company to answer a fire alarm

turnout gear personnel protective clothing made of fire-resistant materials, including coat, pants, boots, hoods, gloves, and helmets

U

under control a stage reached in fire fighting in which the fire has been contained and extinguished to the extent that fire authorities are confident of its complete extinguishment

Underwriters Laboratories, Inc. (UL) an independent fire research and testing laboratory that certifies equipment and materials

uniform official dress uniform or work uniform different from protective clothing

uniform fire reports statistical summaries indicating the types and amount of fires occurring in the nation

unsafe act something that is not consistent with normal or correct practice; can lead to death and injury, as well as to waste and destruction

utility gas gas, manufactured gas, liquified petroleum gas, or a mixture of gases

V

vapor density ratio of the density of a vapor, as compared with the density of an equal volume of air, with air having an assigned value of 1

variable a quantity that can assume any number of values

ventilation the act of opening windows and doors or of making holes in the roof of a burning building to allow smoke and heat to escape

visibility the relative clearness with which objects visually stand out from their surroundings under normal conditions

volatility the readiness with which a substance vaporizes

volt a unit of electrical potential; a potential difference of one volt causes a current of one ampere to flow through a resistance of one ohm

volume the amount of space included by the bounding surfaces of a solid

volunteer firefighter a firefighter volunteering his or her time to save lives and conserve property without remuneration

W

warehouse any building, structure, or area within a building used principally for storage purposes

watch the tour of duty at the housewatch desk, including the responsibility for keeping the company journal, receiving visitors, receiving alarms, and turning out the company when required

watch desk the area where the housewatch is assigned; normally near the entrance to quarters

watch line a hose line left at the scene with a detail of firefighters to guard against rekindling of the fire

water curtain a screen of water thrown between a fire and an exposed surface to prevent the surface from igniting

water damage the damage done to goods and materials by the water from fire streams

water hammer a pressure wave traveling along a column of liquid when flow is suddenly halted or the velocity of the fluid is changed abruptly

water motor gong a gong driven by a water motor in a water motor alarm to indicate that water is flowing in a sprinkler system

water tower a firefighting apparatus for lifting hoses to great heights

watt in simple electrical systems, power is equal to voltage times current

welding a process of joining two metallic pieces together by heat

wet barrel hydrant hydrant that has water all the way up to the discharge outlets and has separate valves on each discharge port

width measurement of an object taken from side to side or at right angles to the length

windward the direction the wind is blowing

winch a powered hoisting machine

working fire a fire that requires firefighting efforts from fire personnel assigned to the alarm

Y

yard a distance of 3 feet; an open space usually in the rear of the building

yard hydrant an industrial type of hydrant with independent gates for each outlet